VINCENT ILARDI

GENERAL EDITOR

DISPATCHES WITH RELATED DOCUMENTS OF MILANESE AMBASSADORS IN FRANCE

VOLUME THREE: 1466
11 March–29 June

EDITED BY

Vincent Ilardi

Translated by Frank J. Fata

DEKALB · ILLINOIS · 1981

Library of Congress Cataloging in Publication Data (Revised)
Main entry under title:

Dispatches with related documents of Milanese
  ambassadors in France and Burgundy, 1450–1483.

  Vol. 3–   edited by Vincent Ilardi; translated by
Frank J. Fata. DeKalb, Northern Illinois University
Press.
  Text in English and Italian; prefatory matter and
notes in English.
  "The bulk of the documents published in this edition
are located . . . in the Archivio di stato in Milan."
  Includes bibliographies.
  CONTENTS: v. 1. 1450–1460.—v. 2. 1460–1461.—
v. 3. 1466 (11 March–29 June)
    1. Milan—Foreign relations—France—Sources.
2. France—Foreign relations—Italy—Milan—Sources.
3. Milan—History—To 1535—Sources. 4. France—
History—Charles VII, 1422–1461—Sources. 5. France—
History—Louis XI, 1461–1483—Sources. I. Kendall,
Paul Murray. II. Ilardi, Vincent, 1925–
III. Milan. Archivio di stato. IV. Title.
DG657.8.D57   327.44045'21   68–20933
ISBN 0–8214–0067–3 (v. 1)

THE ITALIAN STATES
AT THE END OF
THE FIFTEENTH CENTURY

1. Principato di Monaco
2. Principato di Oneglia
3. Marchesato di Finale
4. Domino dei Malaspina
5. Contea d'Asti
6. Principato di Masserano
7. Contea di Guastalla
8. Dominio dei Pallavicino
9. Principato di Correggio
10. Contea della Mirandola
11. Marchesato de Mantova
12. Republica de Lucca
13. Contea di S. ta Fiora
14. Principato degli Appiani
15. Republica di San Marino

0   50   100   150
CHILOMETRI

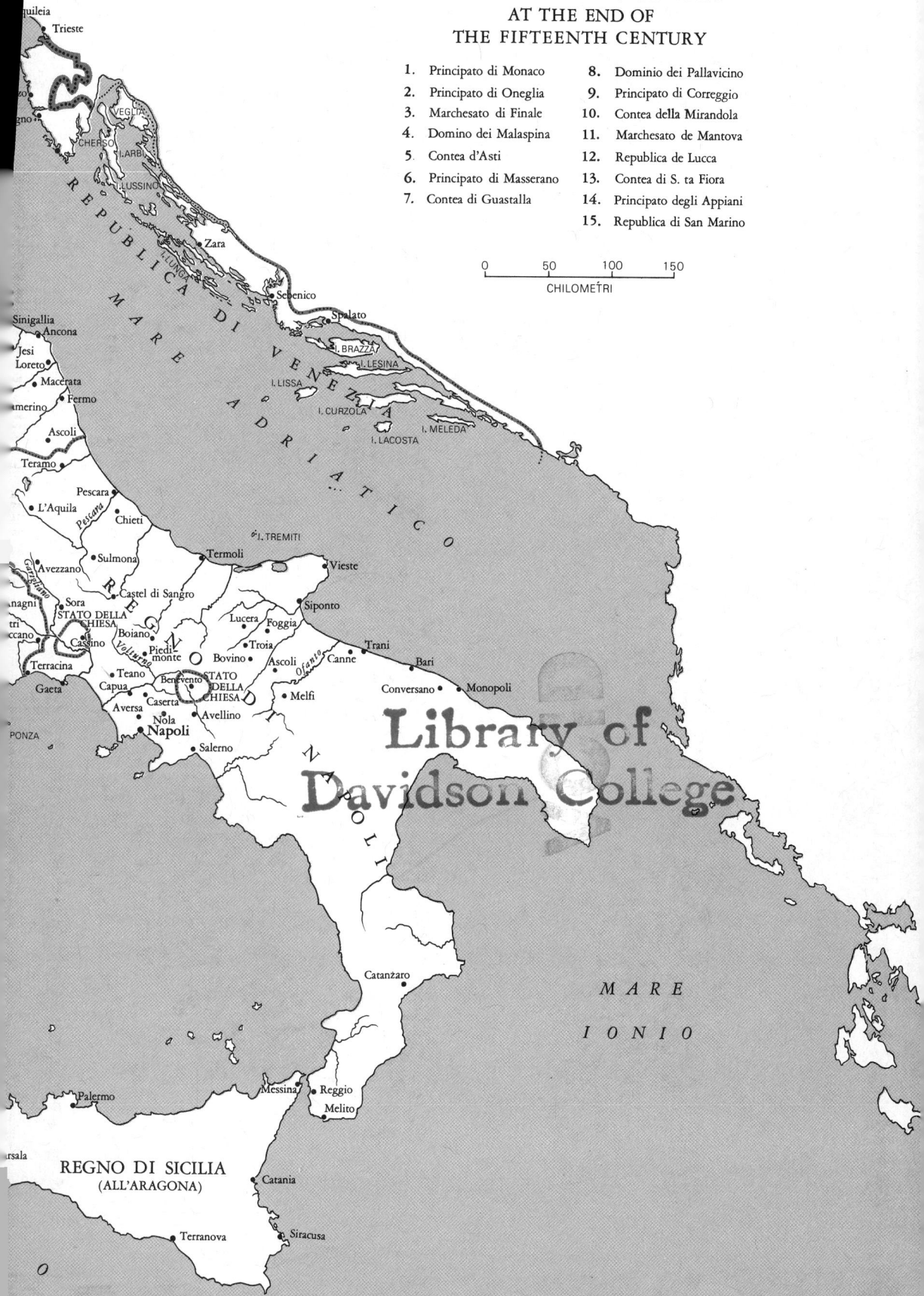

Trieste
quileia
VEGLIA
CHERSO
I. ARBI
LUSSINO
gno
REPUBLICA DI VENEZIA
Zara
MARE ADRIATICO
Sebenico
Spalato
Sinigallia
Ancona
I. BRAZZA
Jesi
Loreto
I. LESINA
Macerata
I. LISSA
amerino
Fermo
I. CURZOLA
I. MELEDA
Ascoli
I. LACOSTA
Teramo
Pescara
I. TREMITI
L'Aquila
Pescara
Chieti
Avezzano
Sulmona
Termoli
Vieste
REGNO
Castel di Sangro
Sora
Lucera
Siponto
nagni
STATO DELLA CHIESA
Boiano
Foggia
tri
Cassino
Piedimonte
Bovino
Troia
Ascoli
Canne
Trani
ccano
Teano
Caserta
STATO DELLA CHIESA
Bari
Terracina
Capua
Benevento
Melfi
Conversano
Monopoli
Gaeta
Aversa
Avellino
Nola
PONZA
Napoli
Salerno
DI NAPOLI
Volturno
Garigliano
Ofanto
Catanzaro
MARE IONIO
Palermo
Messina
Reggio
Melito
arsala
REGNO DI SICILIA
(ALL'ARAGONA)
Catania
Terranova
Siracusa

Dispatches of Milanese Ambassadors, 1450–1483

DISPATCHES

with Related Documents of

Milanese Ambassadors in

FRANCE and BURGUNDY,

1450-1483

NORTHERN ILLINOIS UNIVERSITY PRESS

CONTENTS

Preface   xiii
Acknowledgments   xxxiii
Introduction   xxxv
Note on Paleography and Diplomatics   lxi
Abbreviations   lxvii
Documents
  1.
G. P. Panigarola to the Duke of Milan, 11 March   3
  2.
The Duchess of Milan to Emanuele de Iacopo, 11 March   15
  3.
The Duchess of Milan to G. P. Panigarola, 11 March   19
  4.
G. P. Panigarola to the Duke of Milan, 12 March   23
  5.
G. P. Panigarola to Count Galeazzo Maria Sforza, 18 March   31
  6.
G. P. Panigarola to the Duke of Milan, 20 March   39
  7.
G. P. Panigarola to the Duke of Milan, 21 March   47
  8.
Emanuele de Iacopo and G. P. Panigarola to the Duchess
    of Milan, 23 March   55
  9.
Emanuele de Iacopo and G. P. Panigarola to the Duchess
    of Milan, 24 March   67

10.

Emanuele de Iacopo and G. P. Panigarola to the Duke of
Milan, 24 March   73

11.

Emanuele de Iacopo and G. P. Panigarola to the Duchess
of Milan, 24 March   79

12.

Emanuele de Iacopo and G. P. Panigarola to the Duke of
Milan, 25 March   83

13.

Emanuele de Iacopo and G. P. Panigarola to the Duke of
Milan, 26 March   89

14.

Emanuele de Iacopo and G. P. Panigarola to the Duke of
Milan, 31 March   93

15.

The Duke and Duchess of Milan to G. P. Panigarola, 31
March   101

16.

Emanuele de Iacopo and G. P. Panigarola to the Duke of
Milan, 1 April   111

17.

G. P. Panigarola and Emanuele de Iacopo to the Duchess
of Milan, 1 April   117

18.

The Duke and Duchess of Milan to Emanuele de Iacopo
and G. P. Panigarola, 9 April   119

19.

Emanuele de Iacopo to the Duke of Milan, 10 April   129

20.

G. P. Panigarola and Emanuele de Iacopo to the Duke and
Duchess of Milan, 18 April   133

21.

Emanuele de Iacopo and G. P. Panigarola to the Duke and
    Duchess of Milan, 19 April   139

22.

The Duke and Duchess of Milan to Emanuele de Iacopo and
    G. P. Panigarola, 25 April   151

23.

The Duke and Duchess of Milan to Emanuele de Iacopo and
    G. P. Panigarola, 28 April   153

24.

The Duke and Duchess of Milan to Emanuele de Iacopo and
    G. P. Panigarola, 30 April   157

25.

The Duke and Duchess of Milan to Emanuele de Iacopo and
    G. P. Panigarola, 1 May   163

26.

G. P. Panigarola to the Duke and Duchess of Milan, 1 May   167

27.

G. P. Panigarola to the Duke and Duchess of Milan, 2 May   171

28.

The Duke and Duchess of Milan to G. P. Panigarola, 9 May   177

29.

G. P. Panigarola to the Duke of Milan, 12 May   183

30.

G. P. Panigarola to the Duke and Duchess of Milan, 18 May   187

31.

G. P. Panigarola to the Duke and Duchess of Milan, 19 May   197

32.

G. P. Panigarola to the Duke and Duchess of Milan, 20 May   203

33.

G. P. Panigarola to the Duke and Duchess of Milan, 21 May   211

34.
G. P. Panigarola to the Duke and Duchess of Milan, 22 May   215

35.
The Duke and Duchess of Milan to G. P. Panigarola, 25 May   219

36.
Instructions of the Duke and Duchess of Milan to Pietro da
    Gallarate, 1 June   225

37.
Memorandum of the Duke and Duchess of Milan to Pietro da
    Gallarate, 1 June   253

38.
G. P. Panigarola to the Duke and Duchess of Milan, 1 June   261

39.
G. P. Panigarola to the Duke and Duchess of Milan, 2 June   269

40.
G. P. Panigarola to the Duke and Duchess of Milan, 3 June   279

41.
G. P. Panigarola to the Duke and Duchess of Milan, 4 June   291

42.
G. P. Panigarola to the Duke and Duchess of Milan, 5 June   301

43.
G. P. Panigarola to the Duke and Duchess of Milan, 5 June   313

44.
The Duke and Duchess of Milan to G. P. Panigarola, 11 June   315

45.
G. P. Panigarola to the Duke and Duchess of Milan, 21 June   317

46.
G. P. Panigarola to the Duke and Duchess of Milan, 22 June   325

47.
G. P. Panigarola to the Duke and Duchess of Milan, 23 June   337

48.
Pietro da Gallarate to the Duke and Duchess of Milan, 23
    June   349

49.
G. P. Panigarola to the Duke and Duchess of Milan, 25 June   353
50.
The Duke and Duchess of Milan to Pietro da Gallarate and
     G. P. Panigarola, 27 June   369
51.
G. P. Panigarola to the Duke and Duchess of Milan, 28 June   379
52.
Pietro da Gallarate to the Duke and Duchess of Milan, 29
     June   387

Appendices
     I. The Duchess of Milan to the Duke of Milan, 11 March   391
    II. The Duchess of Milan to the King of France, 15 March   393
   III. The King of France to Count Galeazzo Maria Sforza,
         18 March   395
   IV. The Duke and Duchess of Milan to the King of France,
         20 March   397
     V. The King of France to the Duchess of Milan, 23 March   401
   VI. The King of France to the Duke of Milan, 24 March   402
 VII. Instructions of the King of France to Gaston du Lyon
         and Giovanni Filippo da Trecate, 27 March   404
VIII. The Duke of Milan to the King of France, 13 April   407
  IX. The Duke of Milan to the King of France, 1 May   412
   X. Reply of the Duke and Duchess of Milan to Gaston du
         Lyon and Giovanni Filippo da Trecate, 10 May   414
  XI. Instructions of the King of France to Luigi di Valperga,
         12 May   420

Bibliography   425
Index   433

ILLUSTRATIONS

PORTRAITS

Page 29: Portrait (1471) of Duke Galeazzo Maria Sforza by Piero and Antonio del Pollailo.
Courtesy of the Gabinetto Fotografico Soprintendenza Beni Artistici e Storici di Firenze.

Page 45: Portrait (1465?) of Duchess Bianca Maria Visconti Sforza, attributed to Bonifacio Bembo.
Courtesy of the Pinacoteca di Brera, Milan.

FACSIMILES

Page 299: Document 42. G. P. Panigarola to the Duke and Duchess of Milan. Orléans, 5 June 1466. Partly ciphered.

MAPS

Endsheet: "The Italian States at the End of the Fifteenth Century."
Courtesy of Fondazione Treccani degli Alfieri per la storia di Milano.

Page 65: "France and Burgundian Territories, 1451."
Based on "England and France, 1455–1494" in *Historical Atlas*, William R. Shepherd, © 1964 Barnes & Noble, Inc.

Page 115: "The Duchy of Milan at its Farthest Extension Under the Sforza."
Courtesy of Fondazione Treccani degli Alfieri per la storia di Milano.

PREFACE

A century ago the indefatigable historian of Commynes, Kervyn de Lettenhove, described the correspondence of the Milanese ambassadors in France as the "most precious source" for the reign of Louis XI, and expressed the hope that some day it would be published in its entirety.[1] To date, only two small segments of these documents have appeared, both published outside Italy, approximately a half century apart.[2] Surprisingly, Italian scholars have shown no interest in undertaking the task, even though these sources are equally important for the study of Italian foreign relations, since they reflect France's abiding interest in Italian affairs and Milan's role as the center of diplomatic activity on the peninsula.[3] Likewise, biographers of the King have neglected these

---

[1] *Lettres et négociations de Philippe de Commines,* vol. 3 (Brussels, 1874; repr. Geneva: Slatkine, 1972), Introduction, p. vii.

[2] *Dépêches des ambassadeurs milanais sur les campagnes de Charles-le-Hardi, duc de Bourgogne, de 1474 à 1477,* ed. Frederic de Gingins-La-Sarra, 2 vols. (Paris and Geneva, 1858), and *Dépêches des ambassadeurs milanais en France sous Louis XI et François Sforza,* ed. Bernard de Mandrot and Charles Samaran, 4 vols. (Paris: Renouard, 1916–1923). Only the last volume was edited by Samaran.

[3] There is fresh evidence, however, that this neglect may be ending. This typescript had already been sent to the Press, when the first volume of an Italian edition came to my attention late in 1978: *Carteggi diplomatici fra Milano sforzesca e la Francia,* vol. 1 (*18 agosto 1450—26 dicembre 1456*), ed. Ernesto Pontieri, (Rome: Istituto Storico Italiano per l'Età Moderna e Contemporanea 1978). Pontieri openly announced his intention not to duplicate our edition by including in his first volume a mass of additional documents not directly related to the diplomatic relations of the Duke of Milan with the King of France, many of which were cited in the notes to our first volume. In fact, only 15 percent of the 292 documents published bear directly on these relations,

reports, so rich in biographical data, except for Paul M. Kendall, whose recent one-volume biography,[4] however, precluded extensive use and a systematic analysis of the dispatches. To be sure, a number of monographs and articles, many of which are mentioned in the notes to the texts, have utilized them to a very limited extent, especially the relatively few dispatches deposited at the Bibliothèque Nationale. But these efforts amount to little chips off the huge mountain, comprised of almost two thousand pieces, excluding the correspondence with Burgundy.[5]

As announced earlier (Vol. 1, Preface, p. xii), the present edition intends to make available the totality of these sources, which illuminate not only the reign of Louis XI, but also the entire diplomatic scene in western Europe, since France at this time was the hub of European diplomacy, with its constant involvement in English, Spanish, and German affairs. That it has been undertaken three thousand miles away from the archives is due solely to the advanced technology of microfilming, which has facilitated the assembling of widely scattered sources in one place. The microfilm collection,[6] now consisting of about one million frames, constitutes a giant reference tool that in most cases provides indispensable additional material for a deeper understanding of the documents published, as shown in the notes.

---

but the instructions to Angelo Acciaioli, the joint Florentine-Milanese ambassador at the court of Charles VII, and his dispatches on his second and third missions to France, are excluded without explanation. Actually most of the documents included regard Milan's dealings with the Marquis of Monferrat, an Italian ruler, and with King René of Anjou, many of which have already been published. Nonetheless, at least an equal number of documents bearing on these dealings were omitted. On the other hand, the editor published some documents on private matters that have nothing to do with diplomatic negotiations. It is thus difficult to understand the criteria used for the selection. Judging from the first volume, it appears that the Italian edition intends to publish most if not all Milanese documents containing some reference to French kings and princes. Since such references occur frequently in many archival series deposited at Milan, not considering other Milanese records located elsewhere, one wonders how such an ambitious project will be carried out.

4 Paul M. Kendall, *Louis XI* (New York: Norton, 1971). The best French biography by P. Champion, *Louis XI*, 2 vols. (Paris: Champion, 1927), concentrates on internal developments and is inadequate for foreign relations, making negligible use of the Milanese dispatches already published.

5 The correspondence of the Milanese ambassadors in Burgundy is composed of some three hundred items, only one-fifth of which were published by Gingins-La-Sarra, and most of them in incomplete versions.

6 It includes entire series of documents for the study of diplomacy, and to some extent internal politics, of various European states for the second half of the fifteenth century. A catalogue of the collection is now in preparation.

The series of the Milanese resident ambassadors in France begins with Giovanni Pietro Panigarola, who in the spring of 1465 succeeded the special envoy, Alberico Maletta. As the documents published in our first two volumes and in the Mandrot edition make clear, the first Milanese ambassadors sent to the Delphinal and royal courts were charged with specific tasks, following the completion of which they were instructed to return home. At the end of 1463, the confirmation of the mutual defense alliance of 1460 (Treaty of Genappe) between Louis and Francesco Sforza, and the first signs of the baronial revolt in France, led to closer collaboration between the two princes, out of which the resident embassy gradually evolved. Since this volume deals with the first resident ambassador, it may be useful to trace briefly the evolution of the Milanese resident embassy in France, the chronology of which was given in the preface to the first volume (pp. vii–xi). In doing so, particular attention will be given to the wording of the documents in order to establish more precisely the status of each resident.

In the spring of 1464 the Duke of Milan first raised the question of establishing a resident embassy in France. He informed Maletta that upon the conclusion of his mission he had decided to send as his (Maletta's) replacement Agostino Rossi, "who will reside at the court of His Majesty after you, because we deem it our obligation to continue on keeping a person of ours there by His Majesty as a sign of our reverence and honor."[7] Rossi was to be sent some time before Maletta's departure so that he could be informed of the affairs at hand and of the ways of dealing with the King. Informed of Sforza's decision, the King rejected the idea, saying to Maletta, "Write your lord that the custom of France is not similar to that of Italy, because in these regions to maintain his ambassador here continually would look like an act of suspicion on his part and not at all an expression of amity, whereas in Italy the opposite is true. So write to him that there is no need either for him or me that

---

[7] "Ma perché el ne pare nostro debito de continuare in tenere qualche persona di nostri là appresso Sua M.tà per nostra reverentia et honore, nuy havemo deliberato de mandare là Misser Augustino Rosso, el quale doverà ad dimorare appresso la Corte de Sua M.tà dopo vuy" [F. Sforza to Maletta, Milan, 18 April 1464, *Francia*, cart. 528].

he send others for the time being. Whenever the need arises, he can send Emanuele [de Iacopo] or others as he pleases, who will come and go but not stay here."[8]

Yet, within a year, as his barons were preparing to revolt, Louis came to realize that he needed a Milanese resident to provide a continuous channel of communication with the Duke and make arrangements for his military aid.[9] In addition, scarcely two months earlier the King signified his intention to send his own resident to Milan, Lord Charles de Gaucourt, who was to reside at the Milanese court to cement further the alliance.[10] It is interesting to note that although Sforza was the most consistent user of the resident embassy in Italy and welcomed resident ambassadors from other Italian states, he also rejected the idea, pointing out that such a step would create suspicion among the Pope, the Venetians, and others.[11] Clearly neither party wished to have a resident at his court; but at this time it was the King who needed one.

Panigarola, a young merchant who happened to be in France on private business, was chosen by Maletta to be his successor, a choice that was acceptable to the King and was later ratified by the Duke. Panigarola remained at his post for the next three and a half years, until he was abruptly discharged by Louis in August 1468 for reasons that will be

---

[8] "Voglio scrivati al vostro signore che la consuetudine de Franza non é simile a quella de Italia, perchè in queste parte a tenere continuamente uno suo ambasatore pare una cosa de suspeto e non de tuto amore, et a casa vostra he el contrario. Però scrivetili che non bisogna nè per luy nè per mi ch'el manda altri adeso; ma quando accada cosa alcuna, manda Manuelo o altri como a luy più pare e piace, che vadano et vengano et non stagano fermi" [Maletta to F. Sforza, Chartres, 10 May 1464, *Dépêches des ambassadeurs milanais en France sous Louis XI et François Sforza*, ed. Bernard de Mandrot (Paris: Renouard, 1919), 2:125].

[9] The King proposed that Maletta leave behind his secretary, Christoforo da Bollate, to fill this function: "El Re me manda ad dire che io volesse lassare Christoforo de qua, per lo quale avisaria de quanto accadesse et bisognasse" [Maletta to F. Sforza, Limoges, 2 April 1465, ibid., 3:83].

[10] "[The King] disse anche che, seguito el parentato [Galeazzo Maria Sforza's projected marriage with bona of Savoy], el voleva mandare cum mi Mon.^or de Gaucorto, el quale certamente he uno degno e notabile signore, che venesse a stare a Milano cum la V. S. e cum el conte Galeazo, azochè tuto el mundo intendesse la unione che saria tra la caxa de Franza e la vostra . . ." [Maletta to F. Sforza, Poitiers, 21 February 1465, ibid., 3:52–53].

[11] "Alla parte de Mon^re de Gauocurto, quale dicete la.M.tà del Re dice che, facto el parentato, vole mandare ad stare qui, dicimo che nuy non ne curassemo de questo, perchè serà dare umbreza al Papa, ad Venetiani et ad altri, sichè vedete con quella honestà como da vuy, como ve parerà de fare soprassedere che dicto Mons^re non venga, usando in questo quella piacevoleza et bon modo ve parerà" [F. Sforza to Maletta, Milan, 12 March 1465, ibid., 3:395].

discussed later.[12] Despite Duke Galeazzo Maria Sforza's pleas that Panigarola be allowed to remain in the interest of both parties, since a man of his experience could not be easily replaced,[13] Louis held firm and even refused to accept the Duke's offer to send another ambassador in his place. The King explained that he wished to use one of his secretaries, Alberto Magalotti, to act as a liaison with the Milanese court. Since Magalotti was a Milanese subject and had been sent earlier to the royal court by the Duke himself, Louis maintained that he would be loyal to both parties.[14]

Before receiving the King's letters with respect to Magalotti, the Duke notified him that he was sending another ambassador to "reside" at his court in order to learn daily occurrences and share his happy as well as his unhappy moments.[15] Galeazzo Maria's attempt to promote his new ambassador as a consoler of the King—a rather novel view of ambassadorial functions—was obviously meant to make more palatable his determination to continue the resident embassy with a man of his own choosing. He did not need Panigarola's warning that Magalotti,

---

[12] Panigarola's dismissal is discussed below in the Introduction, pp. lii–liii.

[13] The Duke to Louis XI, Monza, 1 September 1468, *Francia*, cart. 534. The Duke also expressed the view that perhaps false charges against Panigarola had led to the King's action, and gave his word that the ambassador had written nothing but favorable reports about the King. At the same time, Galeazzo Maria instructed Panigarola to remain in France as long as he could, with the King's permission; if not, he should send word, so that another ambassador could be sent in his place [The Duke to Panigarola, Monza, 3 September 1468, ibid., cart. 534].

[14] Louis XI to the Duke, Compiègne, 28 September and Péronne, 13 October 1468, *Lettres de Louis XI*, ed. Joseph Vaesen, 3: (Paris, Renouard, 1887), pp. 283–84, 285–86. Magalotti began his duties immediately, as shown by the great number of letters he directed to the Milanese court, some of which are written in cipher. In one of them [Noyon, 5 September 1468, *Francia*, cart. 534], he reported to the Duke that upon his suggesting that the matter of Panigarola's departure from France be left to the Duke's discretion, the King replied "che non é la usanza de qua de tenere ambassatori fora continui."

[15] "Perché é parso alla M.tà Vostra licentiare Johanne Petro Panigarola, mio fameglio, dal suo Regno, fra tre dì partirà un'altro mio, quale mando ad stare appresso quella per intendere le cose de Soa M.tà [come] alla giornata succederano, per prendere con quella piacere de [le cose] prospere et despiacere de le adverse, et dal quale mio la M.tà [Vostra] più ad pieno intenderà queste cose et ogni occurentia" [The Duke to Louis XI, Abbiate, 18 September 1468, *Francia*, cart. 534]. The document is torn in the lower right-hand corner. The missing words have been supplied within brackets. The Duke also sent word to Magalotti through Cicco Simonetta that he should not handle Milanese affairs at the royal court. Magalotti replied, protesting his devotion to the Sforza and reminding the Duke "ch'io fo taliano et che fo allevo de la Casa como sonno stati li altri mei predecessori, et ultra me cognosce dal capo et pede" [Magalotti to Cicco, Compiègne, 28 September 1468, ibid., cart. 534].

being "inexperienced," "timid," "ignorant of the language," and the "King's man," could not act as a "free person" and as a zealous promoter of Milan's interest as was required of an ambassador[16]—no doubt, the very personal characteristics that had led Louis to choose him. The new envoy, Sforza Bettini, a Florentine long at the service of the Sforza, received his instructions on 22 September. He was directed to "reside" at the royal court as long as the King wished or did not find his stay annoying.[17]

The Duke's prompt action succeeded in prevailing over Louis's aversion to resident embassies. Cordially received after some calculated delays, Bettini reported with evident satisfaction the King's change of mind, quoting him as follows: "We want you to write to the Duke of Milan that we beseech him to keep you here if this is not bothersome or irksome to him, and we ask you to remain if it is not inconvenient for you." This was followed by a tirade against Panigarola, whom the King called "as a big and nefarious scoundrel as a Venetian."[18] This outburst,

[16] Panigarola advised the Duke that if he wanted to keep good relations with the King, he should press Louis to retain him at court or send another ambassador, a "persona che habii ardire di parlare et non habii deppendentia d'altri che la V. Ex.tia, perché Alberto [Magalotti], quamvis abia facto et faza quelo che pò et sa in benefitio vostro, nondimeno per essere timido et novo et havere facto el secretario[?] ad p.ta M.tà, de al quale hé homo, et volendo star di zà, per forza bisogna si acosti et segua alquanto li appetiti de la brigata; oltra che non intende la lingua, non ossa replicare quando gli fu risposto, né parlare se non di cose intenda li sieno grate et gusteno, benché la voluntà sua fosse contraria. Et quanto in questo loco, dove regnono tante passione, bisogni persona libera, lo pò V. Ex.tia iudicare, la quale porà hora provedere como li parirà" [Panigarola to the Duke, Paris, 20 September 1468, ibid., cart. 534].

[17] Bettini was to inform the King that "tu hay in commissione da nuy de dimorare appresso la M.tà Sua quando così sia de suo piacere et non gli sii molesto, per avisarne de le cose occorrentie et de bisogni che occurerano, et così per drizare le cose de qua et avisare de le cose occorerano, perché Sua M.tà ti possi dire et commandare quello che lo vorrà da nuy et tu avisarai" [ibid., cart. 534]. A few days later the Duke wrote to Magalotti [Novara, 7 October 1468, ibid., cart. 535] that henceforth, whenever he had anything of importance to communicate, he should do so through Bettini.

[18] "Noi volemo che tu scriva al Duca di Milano che lo preghiamo, quando non li sia molesto et grave, che te li voglia tenere et te pregamo, quando non ti sia disconcio, che tu li voglia restare." With regard to Panigarola, the King said in part: "ello é magior ribaldo et captivo che s'el fusse vinitiano et per questo lo havemo cacciato di qua . . ." [Bettini to the Duke, Compiègne, 14 November 1468, ibid., cart. 535]. It is interesting to note that in writing to the Duke [Vervins, 6 November 1468, ibid., cart. 535], Magalotti reiterated the King's hostile attitude toward Panigarola, added some charges of his own, and finally reported that he had prevailed on the King to have Bettini stay. The following year, Galeazzo Maria instructed his special envoy, Emanuele de Iacopo [Milan, 31 October 1469, ibid., cart. 536], to inquire of the King whether he was pleased with Bettini or desired another ambassador of his choosing. If Emanuele was pressed to name a substitute, he was to inquire whether Panigarola would be acceptable.

and the reception accorded to Bettini, lead one to suspect that Panigarola's dismissal had more to do with the King's displeasure over his
conduct than with his often stated reluctance to receive resident ambassadors. It is likely that Panigarola's deportment had simply rein-
forced this prejudice, which quickly vanished once the new envoy was
on the scene. In fact, at this time there was no pressing need for a
Milanese resident, as had been the case in 1465, because Louis expressed
his elation to Bettini over the just concluded peace with Charles the Bold
at Péronne, pointing out that now he was able to live in security and
peace and wished the same to Galeazzo Maria.

Bettini remained at the royal court for the next four years in a position of trust and familiarity reminiscent of the earlier period of Panigarola's residency. In July 1472, however, as the King became increasingly
suspicious of the Duke's loyalty, he was suddenly asked to leave the
court, but lingered in France until September under orders from Milan,
working in vain to effect a reconciliation between the two allies.[19]

Bettini's dismissal raised again the question of continuing the resident embassy. Louis reverted to his position that it was not his custom
either to receive or send resident ambassadors.[20] The Duke quickly sent
Marco Trotti with instructions to mollify the King with an offer of
troops and seek to have Bettini remain or obtain his consent for the dispatch of another resident ambassador. In the meantime, he was to remain and report from the court.[21] Trotti was received coldly and was
ruffled by the fact that Louis, feigning ignorance of Italian, ordered
him to deal with his Italian-speaking advisers.[22] In the end, the King

---

[19] Bettini to the Duke, Craon, 26 July, and Laval, 20 August 1472, ibid., cart. 539. In the
second letter Bettini reported that the King had become so irritated at his defense of the Duke
that he feared for his own safety, and felt obliged to leave the court.

[20] "Non era usanza della Corte del Re de Franza tenere niuno ad casa soa d'altri Signori, né delli
suoy ad casa d'altri" [Marco Trotti to the Duke, Villa Simigli, 28 September 1472, ibid., cart.
539]. This was reported to Trotti by the King's councilors.

[21] Instructions to Trotti, Pavia, 22 August and the Duke to Trotti, Pavia, 12 September 1472,
ibid., cart. 539. This mission had been assigned earlier to Emanuele de Iacopo with instructions
dated 11 August 1472 [ibid., cart. 539], but illness prevented his departure [The Duke to
Alessandro Spinola, aboard ship on the Po River, 15 August 1472, ibid., cart. 539].

[22] Unlike Panigarola and Bettini, Trotti had an inadequate command of French [Trotti to the
Duke, Villa Simigle, 28 September and 1 October 1472, ibid., cart. 539]. That Louis knew Italian
well is attested frequently by the Milanese ambassadors, but the following passage from one of

allowed his ally to buy back his goodwill with a gift of fifty thousand gold ducats.[23] On the other hand, he refused at first to reinstate Bettini, alleging that he had written inaccurate and unfriendly reports, but finally relented and expressed his willingness to have him return provided he make truthful reports.[24]

It was obvious that such a conditional acceptance signified that Bettini's usefulness as a resident had come to an end—though not with the same degree of bitterness that had terminated Panigarola's residency —and that a new person was needed to carry on his duties. Galeazzo Maria chose Cristoforo da Bollate, Maletta's former secretary, whom the King himself had proposed as a resident in 1465, and who had discharged other special missions in France.[25] Cristoforo had been sent to the royal court in late October to convey the fifty thousand ducats, and to negotiate together with Trotti the confirmation of the fiefs of Genoa and Savona,[26] originally granted by the King to Francesco Sforza in 1463. Shortly before the conclusion of these negotiations (16 January 1473), the Duke asked Cristoforo to remain as a resident ambassador, a request he deemed flattering but which he obeyed with some reluctance.[27] But there was no reluctance on the part of the King, who not

---

Bettini's dispatches to the Duke [Compiègne, 14 November 1468, ibid., cart. 535] is perhaps the most explicit: "Ascoltomi Sua Mayestà tanto riposata et dolcemente quanto dire si possa, et humanissimamente mi rispose in taliano sì chiaro che non hebbi fatica nessuna ad intenderla." By contrast, Galeazzo Maria had an inadequate knowledge of French despite his earlier stay in France and his continuous involvement with the King. In his reply to the French ambassador, Jacques de Bueil, Lord of Bois [Novara, 21 September 1471, ibid., cart. 538], he stated: "Non intendendo nuy bene la lingua et parlare franzoso. . . .").

[23] Originally the King had asked for a loan of sixty thousand ducats in place of military aid, but the Duke was so eager to win back his favor that he offered fifty thousand ducats as a gift, on condition that it be kept a secret and the money not be used to finance Louis's war in Catalonia against John II of Aragon for fear of offending King Ferrante [The Duke to Trotti, Monza, 17 October 1472, ibid., cart. 539].

[24] Trotti to the Duke, Villa Simigli, 28 September and Fontenay-le-Comte, 21 November 1472, ibid., cart. 539. In the second letter Trotti reported that, with respect to Bettini's return, the King replied as follows: "s'el vene et me dica el vero, l'haverò per amico; se me dirà la bosia, non li vorò puncto bene."

[25] See above, p. xvi, n. 9 and below, p. xxix.

[26] The Duke to Trotti, Monza, 17 October 1472, *Francia*, cart. 539 and Trotti and Cristoforo to the Duke, Lyon, 16 January 1473, ibid., cart. 540. Trotti returned to Milan on 5 February 1473 [*I diari di Cicco Simonetta*, ed. Alfio R. Natale (Milan, Giuffré, 1962), p. 9.

[27] Cristoforo to the Duke, Lyon, 16 January 1473, *Francia*, cart. 540. Actually at the end of October the Duke had already made a tentative decision to choose Cristoforo, for in a firm letter

only received him most graciously, but also gave orders that he always be lodged near him.[28] Encouraged by this response, the ambassador purposely pressed the issue of the resident embassy, mindful of the French view of this matter, and found the King most happy to have a Milanese resident, and particularly pleased to have *him*, saying that he would give orders to have Cristoforo follow him everywhere as one of his own.[29]

Despite this auspicious beginning, Cristoforo's two-year residency never achieved the kind of intimacy that had been established with the King by his predecessors, owing to the mutual suspicions and latent hostility of the two allies, which finally led to the Burgundian-Milanese alliance of Moncalieri (30 January 1475). As the rupture became imminent, in December 1474, the Duke ordered his ambassador to send immediately to Milan all instructions, writings, and copies of his dispatches accumulated since the beginning of his embassy.[30] A month later he was recalled home, and when Louis pressed him to stay at least until the news of the alliance with Burgundy was confirmed, Galeazzo Maria

objecting to Louis's menacing behavior towards Milan, he simply notified the King that Cristoforo was to remain at his court "fin che la M.tà V. sii contenta che gli ritorna Sforza [Bettini]" [Monza, 27 October 1472, ibid., cart. 539].

[28] Cristoforo to the Duke, Tours, 11 February 1473, ibid., cart. 540.

[29] "Et perché la Vostra Sublimità fosse ben chiara como alla Sua M.tà fosse grato el stare qua de continuo de uno de li soy, per le parole dicte che non era così la costuma de qua et che bastava dargli volta doe volte l'anno, etc., me parse dirgli che Vostra Ex.cia per continuare in quella affectione et amore che sempre gli ha portato, fra li altri inditii che Sua M.tà ne havea, gli pariva anche debito demonstrarlo in communicare con quella tutti li soy progressi et dare aviso de le occorrentie de là, maxime de quele pertenghano alla spicialtà de Soa M.tà, adicò che de le cose vostre prospere ne prendesse quella iucundità sperava la Vostra Ex.cia et de le adverse, che Dio non le permetesse, gli potesse dare conforto et adiuto. Et ultra ciò, quando la Sua M.tà connoscesse che per Italia o altroe la Vostra Ex.cia potesse fare cosa ad qualche proposito de le occorrentie sue, ne fosse avisata; che per tute queste rasone pariva bene ad prefata Vostra Ex.cia, quando fosse con bono piacere et volere de Sua M.tà, de tenire de qua continuamente uno de li soy presso di quella, et benché fosse debito tenirli persona de più autorictà et dignità, era facto electione de me. . . . Respose la Sua M.tà . . . che quanto al facto del stare mio qua de continuo, era contentissima; et benché a me non sia licito scrivere, pur adciò che V. Ex.cia intenda et la verità et quello che cede ad honore suo et non mio, Sua M.tà dixe esser più contenta de mi cha d'altri, perché longamente me conosceva et sempre me havea veduto voluntiera; che omne dì omne matina andasse alla messa sua in camera et per tuto unde quella fosse, che così ordinaria, perché non me teniva altramente cha de li soy" [Cristoforo to the Duke, Tours, 18 February 1473, ibid., cart. 540].

[30] The Duke to Cristoforo, Villanova, 1 December and Milan, 24 December 1474, ibid., cart. 541. Cristoforo complied with the request, but fearing for his personal safety, he pleaded: "pregandola et supplicandoli che non mi voglia mettere in periculo . . ." [Cristoforo to the Duke, Paris, 26 December 1474, ibid., cart. 541].

instructed him to return forthwith on pain of perpetual banishment and confiscation of his possessions.[31]

With Cristoforo's departure, the Milanese embassy was interrupted for a period of sixteen months, the first such interruption since 1463. It was resumed in July 1476 with the arrival of Francesco da Pietrasanta, who came to negotiate the renewal of the alliance following several months of secret negotiations by Milanese special envoys. Upon the renewal of the alliance and the confirmation of the fiefs of Genoa and Savona, on 9 August, Francesco was instructed by the Duke to remain at the royal court.[32] This raised the perennial question of the continuation of the resident embassy. At first, the King expressed willingness to receive any Milanese resident other than Antonio de Appiano, the Milanese ambassador in Savoy, or Cristoforo da Bollate, both of whom he deemed unfriendly.[33] Shortly afterward, he changed his mind and asked Francesco to return to Milan, brushing aside his objection that his leaving might lead to talk, since it had always been the custom to have a Milanese resident at court.[34]

Nevertheless, eager to avoid any possible misunderstanding over this question, the King explained to the ambassador directly or through his advisers, Philip de Commynes and Boffilo del Giudice, the reasons for his reluctance to have the resident embassy continued. Aside from the well known French custom, recalled once more on this occasion, Louis felt that Milanese residents had perhaps unwittingly damaged his

---

[31] The Duke to Cristoforo, Milan, 24 January and Vigevano, 14 March 1475, ibid., cart. 542. Cristoforo received the second letter, which contained the threat, on his way home [Cristoforo to the Duke, Susa, 21 March 1475, ibid., cart. 542].

[32] The Duke to Francesco, Pavia, 27 July 1476, ibid., cart. 542.

[33] "Quod autem minimum est, Sua M.tà dici che havendo quamvis de ne a mandare in qua alchuno, non voglia mandare Antonio d'Apiano, il quale veramente é homo da bene quanto dire si possa, ma Sua M.tà l'ha in odio havendo opinione ch'esso habia adiutato a divertire[?] Madama [Duchess Yolande of Savoy] et la S. V. alle confederatione di Borgogna. Item dici che la non gli voglia mandare Christoforo da Bollate, dicendo ch'esso ha seminato zizania et sparlato di Sua M.tà" [Francesco to the Duke, Roanne, 21 July 1476, ibid., cart. 542].

[34] "Et io subgiunssi: 'forse quando questo si facesse, cioé ch'el si restasse tenire qua qualchuno, ne sequirebbe qualche murmuratione tra la brigata, essendo usato tenire sempre altre volte qualchuno appresso a quella.' "Sua M.tà mi rispose: 'forse s'el non mi havesse tenuto colloro appresso, non seriano sequito de le cose sono sequite di mala natura tra mio frate et me, perché tutti quelli ch'el mi ha tenuto appresso non si sono delectati se non di scrivere mille busie et riportare brogliarie, etc.' " [Francesco to the Duke, Tours, 17 August 1476, ibid., cart. 542].

relations with the Duke by reporting preliminary deliberations and plans in the making, not realizing that he often dissimulated his plans by seeming to take decisions contrary to his real intentions. All this led to unfounded speculations on the part of the ambassadors, who with their excellent courier service, immediately reported to Milan every twist and turn of policy in the making without adequate digestion and understanding.[35] As a result, the King came to regard the residents at best as untruthful reporters and at worst as spies, who instead of cementing the good relations with his ally, were actually the cause of much suspicion and dissension. He proposed that this theory be tested by discontinuing the resident embassy and reverting to *ad hoc* missions whenever they proved necessary. He let Francesco know that he preferred him to all others to undertake these missions because he considered him a good and truthful man.[36]

These views, communicated with all possible expressions of cordiality both for the ambassador and his master, did not deceive Francesco as to their real meaning. He came to the conclusion that the King's basic objection to the resident embassy was grounded on his fear that his less

---

[35] For the King's views given directly to Francesco, see preceding notes 33–34. Through Boffilo del Giudice, Francesco received the following message: "Ma che già mo non gli era stato grato che la S. V. havesse miso una brigata de cavallari alle poste, ch'el pare quasi a tutto il mondo che cosa alchuna non si debba fare né accadere nel Reame di Franza che V. S. non lo voglia sapere. . . . Che quanto a tenirme qua me non seria già stato né é ingrato a Sua M.tà, ma non già perhò perché tutte le cose private di casa sua, nec etiam publiche, cioé ogni cosa minuta fosse scritta in Italia, potissimum perché Sua M.tà fa spesso molte cose ad uno fine et tendano ad uno altro, et mostra in evidentia spesso il contrario di quello ch'el vole fare in effetto o ch'el cerca di fare. Et essendo ogni volta scritto tale cose in Italia anze che le siano mature, dariano altra interpretatione che non fosse la veritate, non sanza infamia di Sua M.tà" [Francesco to the Duke, Tours, 23 August 1476, ibid., cart. 542].

[36] Philip de Commynes related to Francesco that the King wanted him to return to Milan to make a report of what had been concluded and assure the Duke of the King's goodwill. Then he added: "che havendo pur Sua M.tà ferma impressione nel animo che Christoforo da Bolla havesse per sue littere riferto de le cose alla S. [*sic*] che havevano generato causa di divertirla da la coniunctione sua, anchora ch'ello l'havesse forse scricto ad qualche altro migliore fine; et item ricordandossi di Panicarola et di Sforza [Bettini], quali similmente havevano seminato et producto più male che bene tra Sua M.tà et V. S. per il loro stare qua continuo, haveva piacere di fare prova, et così si persuadeva di vivere in più amorevoleza con V. S. non tenendo qua alchuno continuo che tenendolo. Ma che se homo al mondo fosse che Sua M.tà vedesse stare qua voluntieri, ch'io era quello, perch'ella mi riputava bono homo et veritevole. . . . Decetero havere questa consuetudine con tutti li Signori del mondo, che may né Sua M.tà appresso a loro né essi appresso a lei tengono ambasciatori continui, ma mandano et rimandano secundo le occurrentie" [Francesco to the Duke, Tours, 22 August 1476, ibid., cart. 542].

honorable acts would be revealed, whereas he was eager to have only his worthy deeds broadcast to the entire world.[37] If the ambassador was right, one can then conclude that Louis's numerous acts of intimacy and familiarity toward the residents were aimed at winning their favor so as to influence the contents of their reports. But this practice placed the envoys in a difficult position, since their loyalty by necessity must be directed to their lord. A divided loyalty was the King's solution of the problem, as shown in 1468 when he proposed to use Magalotti as a liaison agent. A more logical solution would have been to send his own residents to Milan to counteract the reports of the Milanese ambassadors. That he refused to do so in Milan and elsewhere can perhaps be attributed to his reluctance to undergo this expense or to his lack of appreciation of the benefits to be derived out of a reciprocal resident embassy.[38] Moreover, the King himself was largely to blame for the alleged shortcomings of the residents because he used them as advisers and confidants, and often asked them to attend sessions of his Council. The ambassadors, who had orders to report fully and often all that occurred daily, could not refrain from writing all the details, especially to a ruler like Galeazzo Maria who threatened them with death if they failed to do so.[39]

The issue came to be resolved in an unexpected way. Instructed to endeavor to remain at his post,[40] Francesco finally was forced to leave in February 1477 because of illness. Duchess Bona, Regent of Milan after the assassination of Galeazzo Maria (26 December 1476), immediately dispatched Marco Trotti to take up residence.[41] In the mean-

---

[37] "Credo ben che il non curarsi che alchuno de quilli de V. S.ria li stia appresso de continuo sia solum perché li facti suoi, tanto in particulare de casa sua quanto in generale del Stato, non siano intesi, maxime quelli che al iudicio suo medesmo non pareno gli siano honoreveli, che quilli che gli sono honoreveli vorrebbe che tutto il mondo il sapesse" [Francesco to the Duke, Tours, 21 August 1476, ibid., cart. 542].

[38] It is well known that Louis XI did not make use of resident embassies. On this question, see Antoine Degert, "Louis XI et ses ambassadeurs," *Revue historique* 154 (1927): 1–19. For a revealing contrast between Italian and French practice with regard to the use of resident embassies, see doc. 47, p. 336.

[39] Francesco was once so threatened [Francesco to the Duke, Roanne, 21 July 1476, *Francia*, cart. 542]. For an identical threat made to Panigarola, see Introduction, p. lvii.

[40] The Duke to Francesco, Galliate, 29 October 1476, *Francia*, cart. 542.

[41] Trotti was instructed "ad stare presso quella [Louis XI], aciò che per lo mezo tuo li possiamo

time, Milanese affairs were handled by the Florentine ambassador, Angelo Manetti.[42] Trotti, however, was once again coldly received. This time the King was irritated by the fact that he had no mandate to renew the alliance and the fiefs, and by the Duchess's hostile policy toward Galeazzo Maria's brothers. At the end of June, Trotti was summarily dismissed.[43]

Trotti's departure resulted in another interruption of seventeen months in the sequence of resident ambassadors. For much of this interim Milan was represented only by special envoys, including Giovanni Andrea Cagnola.[44] He arrived in October 1478, officially as a member of the embassy that was sent by the allied powers (Milan, Venice, Florence, and Ferrara) to seek the King's aid in their struggle with Sixtus IV and King Ferrante of Naples, arising out of the Pazzi Conspiracy. At the same time, the Regent asked Philip de Commynes to take care of Milanese interests until the arrival, in January 1479, of the new resident, Carlo Visconti.[45]

Although Cagnola remained at the royal court through August 1480, it is clear that Visconti was the resident. The Regent's instructions charged the latter to "take up residence" at the court with the precautionary admonition to "do, say, and write" whatever the King commanded.[46] The long overlap, however, created some confusion and fric-

---

[42] Manetti to Francesco da Pietrasanta, Péronne, 8 February 1477, ibid., cart. 543. On his way home Francesco advised the Duchess to send another resident in his place because he deemed the Florentine ambassador not well suited for the task [Francesco to the Dukes, Bourges, 16 February 1477, ibid., cart. 543].

[43] Trotti to the Dukes: Saint Quentin, 19 June; Paris, 26 June; and Paris [?], 30[?] June 1477, ibid., cart. 543.

[44] Cagnola's instructions are dated 29 and 30 September 1478 [ibid., cart. 543].

[45] The Duchess to Commynes, Milan, 20 November 1478, ibid., cart. 543, in which Commynes was asked to assume this task "fin che manderemo lì el nostro ambaxiatore, quale havarà ad fare firma residentia."

[46] "Te havemo electo ad dovere fare in nome nostro residentia appresso el Christianissimo S.re Re de Franza . . . iudicando noi essere nostro debito retenere uno continuamente appresso Sua M.tà, come credemo ancora che sia de suo bono piacemento, in tal loco havemo deputato te con impositione de fare, dire et scrivere tanto quanto serà la voluntà sua" [Milan, 9 December 1478, ibid., cart. 543]. On the same day, the Regent wrote to the King: "Mandamo lo egregio Karlo Visconte per nostro residente appresso V. M.tà in segno de la fede et observantia nostra verso de quella, come semo obligati . . ." [ibid., cart. 543].

tion between the two envoys, which the Duchess sought to dispel by delineating the special and residential functions in each case.[47] After Cagnola's departure,[48] Visconti continued his residency at least through May 1482.[49] With Visconti, the line of Milanese residents up to the death of the King (30 August 1483) comes to an end, although there were *ad hoc* Milanese embassies during this period. But it should be noted that by the death of Louis XI, the Milanese resident embassy in France was regarded in Milan as a well-established custom or as a post that could not be left vacant. Duke Gian Galeazzo Sforza, or rather his uncle, Lodovico, who governed for him, appealed to this custom in his efforts to continue the resident embassy.[50]

---

[47] In lamenting the fact that on one occasion neither Cagnola nor Visconti had followed the King in his travels, the Duchess clearly distinguished their respective functions in the following passage written to Visconti. "Et però volimo che tu, el quale hay ad fare residentia continua appresso Sua M.tà, et ad che propriamente specta de advisarne delle cose de lì per haverte ad ciò deputato, debii andargli subito drieto et deinceps abandonarla mancho te serà possibile. Et benché se scriva solum ad D. Johanne Andrea [Cagnola], si fa per lo respecto quale tu hay inteso; et essi ambaxiatori della Ill.ma Liga sonno per bisognare le cose comune della Liga et non per advisare et stare attento alle occurrentie de là, como specta a ti" [Milan, 26 May 1479, ibid., cart. 544].

[48] Cagnola had been impatient to leave France. Upon Visconti's arrival, he hoped to return home to take care of his affairs following his wife's recent death [Cagnola to the Dukes, Tours, 15 January 1479, ibid., cart. 544]. Cagnola remained at his post with much reluctance until he was recalled in August 1480 together with the other ambassadors of the allied powers. In the letter of recall, addressed to both ambassadors, the Duchess again confirmed Visconti's residential status: "Et così, havuta grata licentia da la Regia M.tà, pigliarete el camino ad casa et ti, Karlo, restarai ad far residentia presso quella; a la quale, quando pigliarete dicta licentia, farete intendere, ti Karlo, havere commissione di far residentia lì per communicare con Soa M.tà de le cose ce occorrerano di qua importante ad nuy et al Stato nostro . . ." [Milan, 12 August 1480, ibid., cart. 545].

[49] The exact date of Visconti's departure from France cannot be ascertained. His dispatches end in May 1482, but many of them are missing.

[50] On 28 October 1483 the Duke sent Leonardo Sforza and Battista Sfondrati to Charles VIII to offer condolences for the death of his father and congratulations on his succession. Sfondrati was instructed to remain as a resident [*Francia*, cart. 545], but both returned at the beginning of the following year. In January 1484 the Duke intended to send Francesco da Casate "a fare residentia apresso la R. M.tà" [Bartolomeo Calco, ducal secretary, to L. Sforza and B. Sfondrati, Milan, 7 January 1484, ibid., cart. 546], but he refrained from doing so on Commynes's advice, apparently because the King was irritated over the shabby treatment accorded to Duchess Bona at the Milanese court. Instead he asked Bartolomeo Ugolini, the Florentine ambassador in France, to take care of Milanese affairs [The Duke to Ugolini, Milan, 6 April 1484, ibid., cart. 546]. The following year the Duke instructed Bartolomeo Aciani, a Milanese merchant bound for France on private business, to inquire of the Duke of Bourbon and of the Lord and Madam de Beaujeu whether the King was willing to receive a Milanese resident, "per seguire in ciò li costumi de li Ill.mi S.ri nostri, avo et padre, quali nullo tempore lassaveno vacua quella Corte de soi messi . . ." [Instructions to Aciani, Milan, 27 February 1485, ibid., cart. 546]. We do not know the outcome of this mission. There was no Milanese resident in France until Francesco da Casate arrived in 1487. He remained at least until the beginning of 1489, but one cannot be

Doubts have been expressed about the resident status of the Milanese ambassadors at Louis XI's court because the King refused to receive a resident in May of 1464 and never sent an ambassador to reside in Milan.[51] Aside from the fact that consistent reciprocity in resident embassies is a much later development, this view takes no account of subsequent documents which clearly show that Louis later changed his mind and received, often gladly, the Milanese envoys as residents. Furthermore, their instructions contain such phrases as "dimorare," "stare appresso de continuo," and "fare firma residentia" without time limits and subject only to recall or dismissal, all of which clearly denote their resident status. The fact that for almost two decades, but with two brief interruptions, the ambassadors succeeded one another, and often did not depart until they had briefed their successors, suggests the development of the concept of a permanent post or office, which was meant to be filled. This is the first clear evidence of the exportation of the permanent embassy from Italy, an institution that is based on the recognition of the continuous office of the ambassador—a post that can remain vacant for a time, especially in periods of crisis, but with the expectation that it will be filled when normal relations are resumed.[52] Our documents also show the beginning of the modern practice of having envoys of friendly powers stationed in the host country handle the affairs of another state pending the arrival of its resident.

At this initial stage of the institution it would be anachronistic to speak of a fixed abode for the embassy, especially in this case, given the

---

certain of his status because the documents are lacking. Finally, in 1490 Erasmo Brasca was sent to the royal court, and except for two interruptions, he remained until 1493. In 1492 Carlo de Barbiano, Count of Belgioioso, began his stay in France, remaining through August 1494. Whether Brasca and Carlo de Barbiano can be definitely classified as residents remains to be determined.

[51] This view was expressed by F. Ernst, "Über Gesandtschaftswesen und Diplomatie an der Wende vom Mittelalter zur Neuzeit," *Archiv für Kulturgeschichte*, 33 (1951): 77–81, who worked only from published documents and ignored the existence of the sources cited above. On the other hand, Garrett Mattingly, *Renaissance Diplomacy* (London: Jonathan Cape, 1955), pp. 97, 305, concluded also from published documents that the Milanese ambassadors are to be classified as residents.

[52] The continuity of the office of the ambassador, as a means of determining resident status, has been treated recently by Donald E. Queller, *The Office of Ambassador in the Middle Ages* (Princeton: Princeton University Press, 1967), p. 76.

peripatetic habits of Louis XI. The ambassadors moved with the King, carrying with them their small archives for ready reference—copies of Franco-Milanese treaties, copybooks of their dispatches, instructions, and other writings. The Milanese Chancery also kept a separate codex containing treaties and other documents relating to France.[53]

The Milanese permanent embassy in France was the only one operating outside Italy for most of Louis XI's reign, the only exceptions being those of varying duration established by Naples, Venice, and Milan at the court of Charles the Bold in the period 1470–1476.[54] The correspondence of the Neapolitan and Venetian ambassadors, however, has been almost totally lost, and Panigarola's Burgundian dispatches constitute about one-sixth of those generated by himself and his colleagues in France. Therefore, in duration as well as in extant documentation, Milan's embassy in France has no peers outside Italy for the entire second half of the fifteenth century. Its uniqueness lies also in the fact that from 1460 to 1483 Louis was followed almost continuously by Milanese special or resident ambassadors, whose reports allow us to trace every step in the slow evolution of the permanent embassy on the other side of the Alps. This evolution has been documented here for the first time.

It should be mentioned also that special Milanese ambassadors were associated with the residents almost every year. They came to perform specific tasks or negotiate and conclude treaties, at the completion of which they returned to Milan. Some of them lingered in France for several months. Pending a discussion of these special embassies in the appropriate volumes, the following list[55] will provide a general view of the truly pervasive role of Milanese diplomacy in France during the

---

[53] BN, *Fonds Latin*, Cod. 10133.

[54] The best account of these embassies is provided by Richard J. Walsh, "Charles the Bold, Last Valois Duke of Burgundy 1467–1477, and Italy" (Ph.D. diss., University of Hull, 1977), chap. 5. The establishment of the Milanese resident embassy in Burgundy will be discussed in the first volume devoted exclusively to that series.

[55] The list does not include various informants and secret emissaries lacking official status, who often reported to the Dukes. The names enclosed in parentheses comprise one embassy, but they were counted separately in the total number of special envoys.

period of the resident embassy: 1465, Emanuele de Iacopo (two); 1466, Emanuele de Iacopo (two), Pietro de Gallarate, Cristoforo da Bollate; 1467, Emanuele de Iacopo (two), Cristoforo da Bollate; 1468, Tristano Sforza, Emanuele de Iacopo, Zanone Corio; 1469, Emanuele de Iacopo (two); 1470, Emanuele de Iacopo, Alessandro Spinola, (Giovanni Arcimboldi, Sagramoro Visconti, Antonio di Romagnano), Branda de Castiglione; 1471, Emanuele de Iacopo (two), Cristoforo da Bollate; 1472, Emanuele de Iacopo, Marco Trotti, Carlo Visconti; 1473, Antonio da Pietrasanta; 1474–1475, none; 1476, Cardino, Giovanni Bianchi, Alessandro Colletta; 1477, Cristoforo de Castiglione, (Branda de Castiglione, Azzone Visconti, Giovanni Luigi de' Bossi); 1478, Cristoforo de Castiglione, Giovanni Andrea Cagnola; 1479, Branda de Castiglione, Giovanni Pietro da Pietrasanta; 1480, Cristoforo de Castiglione; 1481, none; 1482, Sebastiano de Govenzate.

The above list reveals that there were at least thirty-six special missions in eighteen years, discharged by thirty-five envoys. Several were undertaken by the same person, most frequently Emanuele de Iacopo, whose extended stays at the royal court and his particularly close relations with the King almost qualify him as a resident.[56] The frequency of the same names also suggests the existence of a pool of persons particularly qualified for French assignments. They as well as former residents were often called upon to advise the Duke on French affairs.[57] Most of the envoys in both categories had held diplomatic posts in Italy and elsewhere. Since some of the special ambassadors were charged with ceremonial missions, we find among them members of the high nobility, such as Pietro da Gallarate, Antonio di Romagnano, Alessandro Spinola, and Carlo, Azzone, and Sagramoro Visconti, and also two bishops, Arcimboldi and Branda de Castiglione. Among the residents, only Carlo Visconti was a nobleman, while the others can be classified

---

[56] Bettini reported to the Duke [Tours, 8 December 1469, *Francia*, cart. 536] that the King always welcomed Emanuele with much pleasure, and liked to converse with him in an informal and relaxed manner.

[57] Whenever French affairs were discussed at the ducal court, the names of persons who had discharged missions in France appear most frequently among the advisers [Natale, *I diari, passim*].

as merchants (Panigarola and Bettini) or experienced ducal function-
aries (Cristoforo da Bollate, Francesco da Pietrasanta, and Trotti). The
residents, except for Trotti, were fluent in French and it is likely that
many of the nonresidents had some knowledge of that language.

With the possible exception of the Milanese embassy at the Holy
See, Milan's diplomatic representation in France was the most extensive.
No other European power exerted a comparable effort anywhere. It is
natural, therefore, that Louis XI, seeing himself surrounded by the
ubiquitous Milanese diplomats with their complement of couriers ready
to report every whisper, should feel spied upon. He was faced with a
dilemma. His alliance with Milan carried with it the Duke's insistence
that a resident be kept at his court. Through the residents and the special
envoys the King liked to be kept abreast of all Italian developments,
papal policies, and Turkish movements at the frontiers of Christendom,
gathered through Milan's unequaled network of residents throughout
Italy, although this news was often filtered to promote the Duke's interests. On the other hand, he had to pay the price of having all his
moves and plans reported. Thus he vacillated between happy reception
and angry dismissal of the residents, all the time making efforts to control or influence the contents of their reports. In brief, he was willing and
even eager to accept all the benefits of the resident embassy, but reluctant
to suffer the consequences. Such an attitude was typical of ultramontane
rulers, whose diffidence toward the new institution was an important
factor in their failure to make use of it until the end of the fifteenth
century.[58]

The Dukes of Milan, on the other hand, were in the enviable position of enjoying all the benefits of their resident embassy without suffer-
ing any of the disadvantages because the King did not insist on reciprocity. To be sure, Louis was also kept informed on Milanese and Italian
developments by his own *ad hoc* ambassadors and by a number of in-
formers, whose reports he carefully checked by skillful questioning of
the Milanese envoys. But this was not an adequate substitute for the con-

[58] Cf. Mattingly, *Renaissance Diplomacy*, pp. 145–61.

tinuous flow of reliable information that could be supplied only by residents. Thus the Milanese resident embassy can be likened to a window through which the two most active statesmen in Europe looked into each other's primary sphere of interests, but it was slightly opaque on the French side. For the Dukes it was also a matter of prestige to have permanent representation at the court of the most powerful King in Europe, which allowed them to be the principal purveyors of news relating to all ultramontane powers. In addition, their residents acted as an early warning system should the Orleans or the Angevins plan to prosecute their Italian claims and upset the balance of power on the peninsula.

The kind scholarly reception of the first two volumes suggested only a few minor changes in the edition, some of which had already occurred to the General Editor. The title has been modified to *Dispatches of Milanese Ambassadors in France* and to *Dispatches . . . in Burgundy* in order to separate the two series. Supplementary documents will continue to be placed, untranslated, in the appendix so as not to interrupt the flow of the ambassadorial correspondence. This practice was not strictly adhered to in the first two volumes, owing to the existence of several gaps in the sequence of the dispatches. Documents included in this edition, but previously published elsewhere, will be noted in the Introduction. In order to avoid dealing with cumbersome large numbers, the cumulative numeration has been discontinued; henceforth, documents will be numbered anew in each volume. Bibliographies will contain all archival sources and publications cited in the notes. This volume has a separate index, the cumulative index for all volumes being discontinued. Finally, readers are reminded that, beginning with the second volume, italics are used to indicate passages in cipher.

Some scholars have expressed doubts about the wisdom of providing English translations because they believe that the documents will be used primarily by specialists, who are expected to be familiar with the languages. They have also pointed out that translations cannot always

convey the real meaning of the original, require much time to prepare, and greatly increase the costs of publication by more than doubling the number of volumes. I share these doubts to a considerable degree. American publishing practice, however, requires that translations be provided. The English version, on the other hand, offers certain advantages in view of the fact that the dispatches are replete with information about all western European countries, and thus will be useful to other scholars, whose knowledge of Italian may be inadequate or nonexistent. Furthermore, the intricacy of Italian fifteenth-century prose is such that even specialists may at times find it useful to glance at the translations. In fact, there are a number of passages where an intimate knowledge of the events described is sometimes not sufficient to assess their meaning and properly render it in translation. In these and other cases, different renderings are possible, and we expect others to disagree. At any rate, specialists have the original texts before them, and they may choose to ignore the translations.

Finally, it is my sad duty to note that my former collaborator, Professor Paul Murray Kendall, died in 1973. He had already withdrawn from the edition with the publication of the second volume.

Amherst, Massachusetts   Vincent Ilardi
15 September 1978

ACKNOWLEDGMENTS

The documents published in this volume and in the preceding two were transcribed in Milan by Signora Mariapia Ceruti Gornati and by Dr. Mario Fara, with the former doing the major part. In addition, they carried out many missions to the Archives of Milan—which they know so well—to search out elusive sources and perform many other tasks. I am indeed glad to express publicly my debt to them. Their wish to remain anonymous prevented me from mentioning their names earlier.

I am also grateful to Caterina Santoro, former Professor of Paleography at the University of Milan, who allowed me to intrude in her retirement and in her own publication plans, and graciously consented to help me prepare the Note on Paleography and Diplomatics, and to collate the transcriptions with the original texts, except for the ciphered passages, which were collated by me. I wish to thank also Professor Leonardo Mazzoldi, former Director of the State Archives in Milan and now Director of the State Archives in Brescia, for collating twenty documents. Owing to the pressure of his transferal to Brescia, he was not able to continue the work, but hopefully he will be able to collaborate in the future. Finally, I wish to express my appreciation to Professor Frank Fata of the Department of French and Italian at the University of Massachusetts, who labored hard to transform the documents' intri-

cate prose into free-flowing English and graciously welcomed my frequent interventions. Half of the documents had already been translated by Dr. Mario Fara, which increases my debt to him. Subsequently his translations were reworked by Professor Fata in order to insure a uniform style. My task has been to conduct the archival research, plan the volume, select the documents for publication, draft the Preface, the Introduction, and all the notes, and to encourage and assist the others.

INTRODUCTION

On 15 August 1461 the Dauphin Louis finally realized his long cherished dream of being crowned King of France in the Cathedral of Reims. Among the foreign ambassadors sent to congratulate him, those dispatched by the Italian rulers were most interested to learn the directions of his foreign policy. As Dauphin he had shown himself ready to sacrifice French interests in Italy and frustrate his father's plans there in order to promote his own. This policy had culminated in the Treaty of Genappe (6 October 1460), which bound Louis, as Dauphin and as future King of France, to defend from aggression the principal enemy of French territorial ambitions in Italy—Francesco Sforza, Duke of Milan. Observance of this alliance by the new King meant the repudiation of the Orleans claims over Milan and a setback for those of the Angevins over Naples, since the Duke was bound by the terms of the Italian League to defend King Ferrante of Naples from aggression. This course of action carried with it the danger that these clans might join other discontented nobles in their opposition to the crown.

On the other hand, a repudiation of the Treaty of Genappe and the pursuance of an aggressive Italian policy would have resulted in a certain rupture with Milan and in a probable adverse reaction by other principal members of the Italian League—a compact that was at least partly designed to resist French encroachments on Italy. French claims

to Italian territory, running from Genoa to Naples, added to the ever-present possibility of an election of a French pope, only recently frustrated by Pius II, were simply too extensive to be ignored by the Italian powers, especially if they were pursued concurrently and with energy. Moreover, the Duke of Milan had cleverly cultivated relations with all actual and potential enemies encircling France—Edward IV of England, John II of Aragon, and Duke Philip the Good of Burgundy. In brief, Italian politics had become enmeshed in French internal and foreign affairs, and presented the new King with a dilemma similar to that which had confronted his father.[1]

In an obvious reversal of his father's lethargic behavior, Louis XI attempted to rally support among his barons by taking energetic and bold steps to resolve the dilemma. Ten days before his coronation he informed the startled Milanese ambassador, Prospero da Camogli, that his past actions notwithstanding, he intended to behave as a Frenchman now that he had the burden of ruling France.[2] In September he dispatched his demands to Milan: the Orleans claims were to be settled by a marriage of Galeazzo Maria Sforza and Marie of Orleans or by monetary compensation; Duke John, son of King René, was to become King of Naples and marry Ippolita, Sforza's daughter; the Duke of Milan was to exchange his status of vassal of the Empire for that of peer of France, and aid the King in the reconquest of Genoa.

These demands envisaged French domination of the Italian peninsula, partly through direct control and partly through feudal ties strengthened by marriage alliances. As such, they were politely rejected by Sforza who, together with his ambassadors, was subjected in the following months to a barrage of blandishments and bribes alternating with threats.[3] The Duke resisted this war of nerves, a tactic for which the King was to become famous, and stood firm. In the mean-

---

[1] See the Introductions to vols. 1 and 2, and my article, "The Italian League, Francesco Sforza, and Charles VII (1454–1461)," *Studies in the Renaissance* 6 (1959): 129–66.
[2] Mandrot, *Dépêches*, 1:41.
[3] The King's demands are listed in the Duke's reply of 12 November 1461, ibid., 1:373–84. For the King's determined efforts to secure Sforza's cooperation, see ibid., 1, passim.

time, Angevin defeats in England and Naples, growing enmity with John II of Aragon, and the rebellious mood of his own nobility, including Philip of Bresse's revolt in Savoy and Philip the Good's hostile posture, convinced the King that a change in foreign policy was in order.

In the spring of 1463 he signaled this change by letting Sforza know that he was ready to negotiate another treaty of alliance and was willing to make concessions. The new treaty, signed at Nouvion-en-Ponthieu on 22 December 1463, confirmed the mutual defense alliance of Genappe, as amended in July 1461. A day earlier, the King signed an instrument giving Genoa and Savona in fief to the Duke and Duchess of Milan and their successors. A separate article stipulated that the Duke as vassal of the French crown for Genoa and Savona was not obligated to act in any way contrary to the terms of the Italian League or against any of its members.[4] The settlement of the Orleans's rights over Milan and the County of Asti for a sum of money was left to future negotiations. In the meantime, Sforza was to take possession of his fiefs, by force if necessary. By May of the following year Milanese troops were in full control of Genoa. Milan now had its direct access to the sea, a long-nurtured objective.

The new alliance represents Sforza's greatest triumph in foreign affairs, for he had achieved his two seemingly irreconcilable objectives: the exclusion of the French from Italy (except for Asti), while securing their friendship and protection. For Louis XI it meant the end of his aggressive policy in Italy, pursued even before his ascension to the throne, and the beginning of a new policy aimed at influencing Italian affairs through diplomacy. It seems that this radical change was dictated by superior vision, in the light of past unsuccessful French interventions on the Italian peninsula, and by the threat of a baronial revolt that was about to erupt in the kingdom.[5] It is also clear that the King had become

---

[4] The texts of these agreements were published by Mandrot, *Dépêches*, 1:440–46.

[5] The King himself later confided to the Milanese ambassadors, Alberico Maletta and G. P. Panigarola, that he had contracted the alliance and granted Genoa and Savona in fief in the hope of receiving military aid against his nobles [ibid., 2:148; 3:184]. It should be noted that a few days before the treaty was signed, Cosimo de' Medici, seeking to explain the sudden change of

increasingly convinced that Milan was the key to his Italian policy, and that nothing could be attempted in Italy without the cooperation of the Duke, who controlled such a strategic state, second only to Venice in wealth and first among Italian states in ready military might. Louis never wavered from his new course, and events were to demonstrate the advantages of the alliance for both parties.

The King was the first to invoke the terms of the alliance for his own benefit when, hardly a year later, he was confronted by a coalition of French princes who demanded restoration of their privileges and power in the name of the "public good." Louis himself blamed his father for the revolt, claiming that his exile from the royal court had prevented him from knowing the princes and learning how to control them upon assuming power.[6] Since baronial opposition continued to plague him throughout his reign, this explanation can be regarded as the immediate reaction to the numbing experience of being in danger of losing his throne and even his life. On the other hand, the Milanese ambassador, Alberico Maletta, believed that Louis's abandonment of French territorial claims in Italy had provided the spark for the War of the Public Weal in 1465.[7] The King actually fostered this assessment, for it was in the name of common interests that he requested military aid from Milan as early as the fall of 1464 and welcomed naval assistance against Angevin Provence from Ferrante.[8] Maletta rightly concluded that "this King now seems to be the enemy of our enemies and of those of King Ferrante; nor could there be another King of France who would suit better our purposes and those of King Ferrante."[9]

policy, pointed to the dismal failure of the King's plans in Italy and focused on the overriding factor—Cosimo's prediction that the year 1464 would not pass without serious troubles in the kingdom [Nicodemo Tranchedini to the Duke, Florence, 8 December 1463, published by Albano Sorbelli, *Francesco Sforza a Genova (1458–1466). Saggio sulla politica italiiana di Luigi XI* (Bologna: Zanichelli, 1901), pp. 226–28].

[6] Pietro da Gallarate and Panigarola to the Dukes, Sully, 13 July 1466, BN, *Fonds Italien*, Cod. 1593, fols. 275–77.

[7] Mandrot, *Dépêches*, 2:xxxi, 228–30, 341; 3:92, 121–23.

[8] Ibid., 2:235–36; 3:150–51, 401–2, 425; 4:12, 81, 153–56, 200–201.

[9] "Questo Re me pare adesso inimico de li nostri inimici et de quelli de Re Ferrando, né poria essere altro re de Franza che più se afacesse ad nostro proposto et ad quello del re Ferrando" [Maletta to the Duke, Abbeville, 5 September 1464, ibid., 2:237].

At the end of the summer of 1465, France witnessed an unusual spectacle—the arrival of a Milanese expeditionary force composed of three thousand men. Such an event had not occurred since the Roman legions had left Gaul. Although the small detachment of Milanese troops were far less successful than their Roman predecessors, having arrived more than a month after the Battle of Montlhéry (16 July), they were able to capture several strongholds in the Bourbonnais and in the Lyonnais, and their presence in Dauphiné served to keep the whole of southeastern France loyal to the King. The expedition produced no classical account, such as Julius Caesar's *Gallic Wars*, but it gave rise to a heavy flow of correspondence between its nominal leader, Galeazzo Maria Sforza, its effective commanders (Gaspare da Vimercate, Donato del Conte, Pietro Francesco Visconti, and Giovanni Pallavicino da Scipione) and Francesco Sforza, who almost daily sent directives and advice. Several hundred of these letters have survived, scattered in various series in the state archives of Milan and elsewhere. They are not made part of this edition because they deal primarily with military matters.[10] Those touching on political and diplomatic affairs have been cited in the notes.

Whatever can be said about the effectiveness of the Milanese expeditionary force, whose operations were cut short by the conclusion of the peace treaties of Conflans and St. Maur-des-Fossés (5 and 28 October), the King expressed a high regard for it, and continually pressed Sforza to send more troops as promised. He was intensely interested to learn about Milanese military organization and tactics, and it was believed that he wished to adopt Milanese order of battle and personal armaments for his troops.[11] Louis wanted Galeazzo Maria to winter in

---

[10] The announced plan to publish this correspondence was never carried out by Pietro Ghinzoni, who wrote the only extensive account of the Milanese expedition: "Spedizione sforzesca in Francia (1465–1466)," *Archivo storico lombardo*, ser. 2, 7 (1890): 314–45. The publication of these letters would help military historians assess the efficiency of Italian troops relative to that of their colleagues on the other side of the Alps, a matter of some dispute at the present. On this question, see Piero Pieri, *Il Rinascimento e la crisi militare italiana* (Turin: Einaudi, 1952), pp. 304–19.

[11] Giorgio de Annone to the Duke, Lyon, 12 February 1466, BN, *Fonds Italien*, Cod. 1591, fols. 264–65.

France to help him keep the princes in check and then employ him in a spring campaign in Alsace and Lorraine.[12] All these plans came to a sudden end when Francesco Sforza died on 8 March 1466, and Galeazzo Maria left quickly for Milan to claim his succession. His troops followed him shortly after.

The repercussions of the Duke's death, Louis's continuing troubles with the princes, and his relations with Savoy are the three principal themes running through the documents published in this volume. Each will be discussed briefly in the light of the background given above and on the information supplied in the notes to the documents.

There is no better demonstration of the King's intimate relations with Milan than his prompt and almost frenetic actions taken to insure the peaceful succession of Galeazzo Maria and Bianca Maria, his mother. Letters and ambassadors were immediately sent to Italian rulers, and troops were made ready to cross the Alps to protect the Duchy against aggression from any quarter. In most cases, however, there was no need for concern. Internally, the prompt steps taken by the Duchess to check the traditional separatism of the Lombard cities prevented any serious opposition, including Archbishop Paolo Campofregoso's feeble attempt to return to power in Genoa. Florence and King Ferrante immediately rallied around the new rulers. So did Pope Paul II who, after pointing out that the Italian League was sufficient to protect Milan, remarked somewhat resentfully to the Milanese ambassador that he would rather see the ultramontanes remain at home and not interfere in Italian affairs.[13]

Papal policy at this time aimed at securing more direct control over cities in the Romagna, which conflicted with Milan's support of the Bentivoglio in Bologna and with Venice's territorial ambitions in that region, masked by its defense of Sigismondo Pandolfo Malatesta's

---

[12] Mandrot, *Dépêches*, 3:371–72; 4:104–5, 180–81, 245–47, 259–60.
[13] "Ma che l'haveria anche più piacere che li ultramontani stessено a casa loro et noy altri citramontani stessemo in bona pace senza havere casone de messedarse insieme." [Agostino Rossi to the Dukes, Rome, 19 April 1466, *Roma*, cart. 59].

claims over Rimini.[14] The Milanese rulers wrongly suspected the Pope, member of a leading Venetian family, to be in collusion with the Republic against Milan. Actually Paul II was just as concerned as the other Italian rulers over possible aggressive intentions by Venice and its captain, Bartolomeo Colleoni, who wished to imitate Francesco Sforza by capturing a state for himself. Soon after Sforza's death, which according to the Pope the Venetians "had for so long awaited with more eagerness than the priest awaits Easter," he rejected Venetian overtures for an entente against Milan, and instead menaced the Republic with the forces of the Italian League if it proceeded to attack the Duchy.[15] It should be added that, paradoxically, Paul II's relations with Venice were always cool and often became tense throughout his pontificate.

In reality, aside from Duke Borso d'Este of Modena, whose long-standing anti-Sforza stance was well known, only two other states pursued a hostile policy towards Milan—Venice and Savoy. Venice's antipathy toward the Sforza stemmed from Francesco's rise to power, which had blocked the Republic's expansion into Lombardy after the death of Duke Filippo Maria Visconti. Despite the Duke's repeated efforts to establish amicable relations, the Venetians always remained unreconciled and it is known that the Council of Ten several times considered proposals for his assassination.[16] Venice along with Savoy failed to send an embassy of condolences at Sforza's death, and its contention that it did not feel obligated by the terms of the Italian League because Milan had already violated them with its occupation of Genoa, heightened everyone's apprehensions about its intentions. The Pope,

---

[14] P. J. Jones, *The Malatesta of Rimini and the Papal State* (Cambridge: Cambridge University Press, 1974), pp. 240–44.

[15] In revealing the Venetian overtures to the Milanese ambassador, the Pope expressed his fear about the threat to peace posed by Venice and Colleoni in the following terms: "potissimum perché essendo accaduto el caso del nostro S.re [F. Sforza], quale hanno expectato tanto tempo con più desyderio che non fa il prete la Pasqua, li serà parso forsi potere havere adesso tale opportunità de farse inanti, che lassandola passare, non li poteria poy tornare un'altra volta" [Agostino Rossi to the Dukes, Rome, 27 April 1466, *Roma*, cart. 59].

[16] See Vladimir I. Lamansky, *Secrets d'état de Venise* (St. Pétersbourg, 1884), pp. 9–10, 14–16, 160–62.

citing reports from Venice, believed that population pressure was partly responsible for the widely acknowledged Venetian appetite for territorial expansion in Italy.[17] This is probably the first time that such a theory was recorded in contemporary sources with respect to Venice. At any rate, it seems that the Republic was deterred from taking any aggressive action more by the war it was waging against the Turks and by the lack of support from other Italian states, than by the threats and inducements put forth by Louis XI, whose internal troubles would have prevented him from delivering either.

On the other hand, the King was able to exercise more direct pressure on nearby Savoy. This semi-feudal but strategic state commanding the Alpine passes to Italy was in reality a conglomeration of diverse territories on both sides of the Alps, extending from the Pays de Vaud above Lake Geneva to Turin and Vercelli in the Italian Piedmont, generally and loosely referred to as Savoy-Piedmont. Ruled by weak dukes and strong-willed duchesses, it was racked by persistent factional strife, particularly among Savoyard and Piedmontese nobles representing the two largest sections of the Duchy. It was a region at once difficult and easy to control, depending on circumstances, as Louis had already found out as a Dauphin.[18]

The situation was made to order for the rise of a strong man. The King pinned his hopes on the fifth son of Duke Louis I, Count Philip of Bresse. Philip, however, was an ambitious and able young man (b. 15 November 1443), who longed to control the Duchy without interference from the King. In July 1462 he took control of the government by executing the Chancellor, Giacomo di Valperga, the King's favorite, and by eliminating the Cyprian faction nurtured by the Duchess, Ann of Lusignan, daughter of the King of Cyprus. This coup d'état had been

---

[17] "Adiungendomi Sua S.tà quest'altra parte che l'haveva da Venetia, como gli [the Venetians] erano horamay tanto multiplicati ch'el gli era quodammodo forza alargarse de paese et de dominio per potere dare etiam fora de la terra pastura et aviamento a più de loro, che altramente stavano in periculo de fare qualche scandalo a la zornata" [Agostino Rossi to the Dukes, Rome, 27 April 1466, *Roma*, cart. 59].

[18] See vol. I, Introduction, pp. xxii, xxv, for the Dauphin's policy toward Savoy.

supported by the Swiss and by Francesco Sforza, the latter acting secretly through Antonio di Romagnano, Valperga's rival for the Chancellorship. The King took his revenge two years later by drawing Philip to his court and then having him treacherously arrested.

Duke Louis I's death on 29 January 1465 led to the succession of an even weaker prince, his eldest son, Amédée IX. Subject to epileptic fits, the new Duke had refused to take part in affairs of state before ascending the throne, preferring to reside in his estates, engaging in pious meditation and ascetic practices. As this way of life continued after his succession, it became clear that he was more fitted for the cloister than the throne, a propensity that later earned him beatification from the Church. Effective power was held by the Duchess, Yolande, younger sister of Louis XI—an energetic, ambitious, ingratiating, but not altogether wise woman, whose predilection for intrigue and manipulation matched her brother's.[19] Irritated by her brother's interference in the affairs of the Duchy, widely resented in Savoy,[20] she countered with an anti-Milanese policy aimed at recovering certain border lands ceded to Sforza after the Peace of Lodi [doc. 27].

With this context in mind, it is not surprising that Galeazzo Maria traveled in disguise through Savoyard territory on his return to Milan after his father's death, but was nonetheless detained at the Novalesa by two of the Duchess's highest advisers, Hugonin Aleman and Agostino di Lignana, Abbot of Casanova. It is difficult to believe that this action was taken without her knowledge, as she claimed; but whether

---

[19] A balanced description of the personalities of Amédée IX and Yolande is supplied by Ferdinando Gabotto, *Lo Stato sabaudo da Amedeo VIII ad Emanuele Filiberto, vol.* 1 (*1451–1467*) (Turin, 1892), pp. 91–93. The Milanese ambassador in Savoy explained to the Duke that he was always forced to deal with the Duchess because "questo Ill. Signore quasi mai se parte di camera, né dà udientia, né s'impaza di cosa del Statto, né altra cosa. . . . Madama regie et governa tutto col Consiglio suo, chi é il Cancellero, il Mareschal et Bonivart. . . . Et questa solitudine fa il preditto Signore é per il mal suo, che forte gli dà impazo; é gran peccato, che l'era bel Signore" [Marco Corio to the Duke, Chambéry, 10 February 1466, *Savoia*, cart. 481].

[20] Marco Corio reported to the Duke of Milan [Chambéry, 21 February 1466, ibid., cart. 481] that "la prefata M.tà del Re [Louis XI] qui non é amata da persona e tutti gli voglino male et sonno Brogagnoni; e quando viene qualche bona nova di Sua M.tà, se ne dolle, riservata la Ill.ma Madama, il Canzellero, el Mareschalcho. Credo proceda gran parte per Filippo Monsignore."

it was meant simply to exert pressure for the recovery of the lost territory or to topple the Sforza from power, it is not possible to say.[21] In any case, if there was such a plan, it was frustrated by Antonio di Romagnano, who secured the Duke's release.

Faced by this exasperating situation, the King released the Count of Bresse from prison, and in late spring of 1466 sent him to Savoy with the mission of bringing the Duchess to support royal policies, especially with respect to the projected marriage of Bona of Savoy and Galeazzo Maria. This marriage, which had been first proposed by the King in April 1464, was extremely unpopular at the Savoyard court and became the focus of antiroyal opposition, cleverly fomented by the Duchess and Philip himself. The Savoyards resented the high dowry set by the King (150,000 ducats), and felt an ingrained antipathy for the upstart Sforza, who had taken Piedmontese territory and had deprived the dowager Duchess of Milan, Maria of Savoy (wife of the late Duke Filippo Maria Visconti), of her rightful succession in Milan. Moreover, there was the expectation in Savoy that Galeazzo Maria would not have been able to remain in power for long, owing to the alleged wide popular dissatisfaction against the Sforza. The consequences of this hostile policy toward the Sforza will become more apparent in the documents to be published in subsequent volumes.

If the King's pressure served at best to give pause to Venice and prevent any precipitous aggressive action by the Duchess of Savoy, his efforts to pacify his kingdom failed at this time. Negotiations continued with his younger brother, Duke Charles of Berry, Duke Francis II of Brittany, Duke John of Lorraine, Count Charles of Charolais, the

---

21 The culpability of the Duchess is accepted by most scholars, such as Elia Colombo. *Iolanda, Duchessa di Savoia (1465-1478)*, in *Miscellanea di Storia italiana* 31 (1894): 13-14; Giovanni Filippi, *Il matrimonio di Bona di Savoia con Galeazzo Maria Sforza* (Milan, 1890), p. 13; Lino Marini, *Savoiardi e Piemontesi nello Stato sabaudo (1418-1601)*, vol. 1, 1418-1536 (Rome: Istituto Storico Italiano per l'Età Moderna e Contemporanea, 1962), p. 153; and Franco Catalano, *L'età sforzesca dal 1450 al 1500*, in *Storia di Milano*, vol. 7 (Milan: Fondazione Treccani degli Alfieri, 1956), pp. 229-30. Piero Magistretti, "Galeazzo Maria Sforza prigione nella Novalesa," *Arch. storico lombardo*, ser. 2, 6 (1889): 777-807, argued that Galeazzo Maria was assaulted by brigands without the knowledge of the Savoyard court. Gabotto, *Lo Stato sabaudo*, 1:96-97, withholds judgment.

Armagnacs, among others, as if the peace treaties had not been concluded. The story of these tedious and inconclusive negotiations is related in detail in the documents and need not be treated here. Suffice it to say that Louis was forced to mobilize his army under the guise of fighting the English in order to keep his barons in check. The conclusion of a truce with King Edward (24 May 1466) neutralized that threat for the time being, but his plan to pit the Burgundians and the Angevins against each other so as to control both was not realized. To the Count of Charolais, the King offered his eldest daughter in marriage, the four-year-old Anne, with Champagne as her dowry. The Count, while professing eagerness to conclude the match, was negotiating with Edward for his sister Margaret's hand—a union that Louis wanted to prevent at all costs.

While waiting for the outcome of his negotiations with Charles of Burgundy, the King attempted to lull the powerful Angevin faction, which controlled the Royal Council, through promises of aid to Duke John for his Italian schemes. But, as he confided to the Milanese ambassador, he would refrain from giving them the kind of support that would be sufficient to threaten either Milan or Naples. In the meantime, the King entertained proposals for an alliance with King Ferrante, and fearing for his personal safety, he strengthened his bodyguard [doc. 32].

It is clear that the King wished to honor his alliance with Milan, as he blatantly and repeatedly declared in the presence of the Angevins, and proclaimed to the Italian rulers. While this resolve was taken partly out of self-interest by safeguarding the territorial integrity of a state from which he hoped to receive further support, it can be argued that self-interest alone could perhaps have been better served by forming a coalition with Milan's hostile neighbors—Savoy, Venice, and Modena—for the purpose of installing the Orleans in Milan and the Angevins in Naples. Whether the King rejected such a plan, pressed on him by the Duchess of Savoy and Duke John, because he deemed it unworkable or because it would have strengthened his barons and would not have protected him from Burgundy and the English, it is not possible to de-

termine. In the dispatches Louis is frequently quoted that he felt honor bound to defend the Sforza even at the cost of his life and kingdom.

There is no reason to doubt Louis's profound gratitude and sincere affection for a ruler, who in his hour of need had sent him his heir with a picked body of troops at his own expense, notwithstanding his depleted treasury, and had provided him with valuable advice born out of decades of experience in statecraft and war. In Italy, even Sforza's enemies, such as Venice and Savoy, readily acknowledged that the Duke had played a vital role in saving Louis's throne.[22] Always mindful of this debt, the King named two of his sons Francis, wishing to honor the memory of his late friend.[23] Historians who still regard Louis as the cynical "King Spider," forgetting that he had to deal with other spiders, will be surprised to learn that he was so moved by the news of Sforza's death, that he wept unashamedly in the presence of the Milanese ambassadors [docs. 8 and 10].

With the death of Francesco Sforza, the roles were reversed. Now it was the Duke of Milan who became the tutee. Whereas Louis was a mature man of thirty-eight when he impatiently ascended the throne and had had a good deal of experience in statecraft, war, and diplomacy, the twenty-two-year-old Duke had never governed a province or directed a military campaign, and had no diplomatic experience with the exception of some ceremonial embassies discharged to various Italian states. It was partly to give him some military experience, it seems, that his father made him nominal leader of the expeditionary force sent to

---

[22] Doge Cristoforo Moro remarked to the Milanese ambassador that "lo savio consiglio et ricordo de la Excellentia de quello vostro Signore ha facto ritornare el Re de Franza nel suo primo stato et factoli reacquistare lo honore insiema con lo Stato, per la qual cosa esso Re ha grandissimo obligo con Sua Excellentia." He continued to say that the Duke had done the same for King Ferrante [Gerardo de' Colli to the Duke, Venice, 7 February 1466, *Venezia*, cart. 352]. From Savoy the Milanese ambassador wrote as follows: "Ricordando a Vostra Excellentia che qua non é persona e Madama [the Duchess of Savoy] e tutti che ogniuno crede essa M.tà [Louis XI] non mova i piedi senza consciglio [*sic*] di Vostra Excellentia" [Marco Corio to the Duke, Chambéry, 21 February 1466, *Savoia*, cart. 481].

[23] The first son was born prematurely on 4 December 1466, at the end of the sixth month of pregnancy. Quickly baptized, he died four hours later. The Milanese ambassador pointed out that none in the royal house had ever borne that name [Panigarola to the Dukes, Orléans, 6 December 1466, *Francia*, cart. 532]. In 1472 the King had another son, whom he also named Francis, but he, too, died a few months after birth [Kendall, *Louis XI*, p. 261].

France. The resultant correspondence, however, shows that Francesco Sforza, through his captains, directed the operations and was not infrequently displeased with Galeazzo Maria's behavior. He rebuked him particularly for opening his ambassador's dispatches from the royal court, and for giving leaves to his condottieri and permitting them to sell their horses. Once, with some exasperation, he admonished his son that it was time for him to stop being a child and behave like a man.[24] For Galeazzo Maria's projected trip to the royal court, the Duke sent him detailed instructions on how to act. If the King wished to discuss military matters, he should let his captains speak, and if pressed, he should confine himself to general remarks so that he did not appear to be totally ignorant.[25]

What concerned his parents even more than his inexperience was their son's flawed personality, characterized by irascibility, haughtiness, moodiness, impulsiveness, capriciousness, and intractability.[26] To these weaknesses he added others upon assuming power: indecisiveness, love of luxury and pomp, extreme libido, cruelty, lack of balance and moderation, and, above all, inordinate ambition, shown especially by his chimerical project of becoming king.[27] Except for his amorous escapades, Galeazzo Maria was most unlike his father, the most widely admired and respected prince in Italy, who had raised the Duchy to its

---

[24] The Duke to Galeazzo Maria, Milan, 3 February and 3 March 1466, BN, *Fonds Italien*, Cod. 1591, fols. 260, 278. In the first letter the Duke urged his son to understand "la natura de li soldati, li quali sonno de natura de cercare quello sia el suo utile et non si cura del honore et utile del patrone. Et vogli hormay ussire de le cose de pucti et fae le cose de homo, et provedere a li inconvenienti et a le malitie de li mal composti, et non volere expectare che ogni volta noy siamo quelli che debiamo provedere a li desordini et mancamenti che se commettono per quelli li quali te li havemo dati in cura et governo, perché prima te é in mancamento de reputatione, perché poy se dice che tu non say governarte né attendi a quello devi attendere."

[25] The Duke's instructions to Galeazzo Maria, Milan, 2 March 1466, ibid., Cod. 1591, fols. 274–77.

[26] A good account of Galeazzo Maria's youthful behavior is provided by W. Terni de Gregorj, *Bianca Maria Visconti, Duchessa di Milano* (Bergamo: Istituto Italiano d'Arti Grafiche, 1940), pp. 178–80.

[27] See Bernardino Corio, *Storia di Milano*, ed. E. de Magri, (Milan, 1857; repr. Milan, 1975), 3:313–15, for the best contemporary character portrait of the Duke. A few months before his assassination, Galeazzo Maria asked Charles the Bold to intervene with the Emperor to obtain for him the investiture of the Duchy and the title of king of Lombardy, for each of which he offered to pay 100,000 ducats [The Duke to Panigarola, Pavia, 16 May 1476, *Borgogna*, cart. 519].

apogee of power and prestige. Exhorted by everyone to emulate his father's deeds, he tried to outshine him by his patronage of the arts and letters and his splendid court, but failed in diplomacy and in finding or provoking a war in which he wished to display his generalship. In the end he alienated his father's staunchest allies, including Louis XI. This is not to say that he lacked intelligence and ability, but rather that his few good qualities were submerged by his many faults. The documents to be published in this edition will supply much new material for a deeper understanding of the Duke's personality and policies, which no biographer has yet provided.[28]

Galeazzo Maria's already well-known shortcomings explain why the Duchess attempted to insert herself in the government from the very beginning, basing her rights on the act by the people of Milan recognizing Francesco Sforza and Bianca Maria as Duke and Duchess of Milan (1450).[29] In fact, for the next two years after Francesco's death official acts and correspondence bear the names of both Bianca Maria and her son, with the Duchess given precedence.[30] But almost immediately the first serious dispute between the two arose over the Duchess's wish that her son respect his previous commitment to marry Dorotea Gonzaga, daughter of the Marquis Lodovico Gonzaga of Mantua. While his final decision to marry Bona of Savoy reflected his wish to honor the promise made by his father to Louis XI, his vacillating posture in the matter as well as his arrogant behavior shocked the ducal court[31] [doc.

---

[28] The only biography written by Cesare Violini, *Galeazzo Maria Sforza* (Turin, Società Subalpina, 1943), is a popular uncritical effort far too favorable to the Duke.

[29] Francesco Sforza apparently left no instrument specifically designating his wife and son as co-rulers [Fabio Cusin, "I rapporti tra la Lombardia e l'Impero dalla morte di Francesco Sforza all'avvento di Lodovico il Moro (1466–1480)," *Annali della R. Università degli Studi economici e commerciali di Trieste* 6 (1934): 219].

[30] See below, pp. lxiii–lxiv.

[31] During a visit to the Milanese court, the Marchioness of Mantua wrote to her husband that Galeazzo Maria "conosceva che facendo il parentado de Franza, el seria casone de la morte de la Ill.ma Madonna, sua madre, et ch'el deliberava ad ogni modo farla contenta." Then noting the Duke's indecisiveness, the Marchioness continued: "vedendo tante variatade in lui, me confondo da me istessa, né so quello me ne dica, se non ch'el non habia voglia de tuore né la nostra né quella de Franza. Questo medesimo affirma el Conte Gaspar [da Vimercate] et in mia presentia lo disse a questa Ill.ma Madonna ch'el credeva cusì" [The Marchioness to Lodovico Gonzaga, Milan, 23 April 1466, ASMA, *Lettere Originali dei Gonzaga*, B. 2099].

36, n. 2, and Appendix, doc. VIII, n. 4]. It has not been noted by historians that the Duke's vacillations and dilatory tactics may have been dictated in part by a suspicion that Bona herself may have been afflicted with epilepsy like her brother.[32]

The fundamental problem in the relations between mother and son, however, was that the Duchess, used to wielding a great deal of influence in her husband's court, and being an admirer of his prudent and cautious approach to statecraft, attempted to restrain her son's rash and impulsive behavior and wished to be treated as a co-ruler in name as well as in fact.[33] The irreconcilable conflict at this critical moment dismayed the friends of Milan,[34] and finally led to permanent

---

[32] Two years earlier Francesco Sforza had investigated this matter, and had been informed that only three first-born males of the House of Savoy had been epileptic [Mandrot, *Dépêches*, 2:194–98]. The Duke had also warned his son not to believe rumors about Bona's health, deeming them lies spread by those who were opposed to the marriage [The Duke to Galeazzo Maria, Milan, 28 December 1465, *Potenze Sovrane*, cart. 1458]. These rumors were most likely spread by the Angevins, for in a letter to Panigarola [Milan, 10 October 1466, *Francia*, cart. 532], Galeazzo Maria accused Duke John of Lorraine of deliberately spreading these lies because he wished to marry Bona himself. For his part, Galeazzo Maria affirmed that he was certain about Bona's condition, and that in any case he would marry her whether she was epileptic or not. It should be noted that the Duke had never met his prospective bride, but had seen her portrait while he was in France, and had remained satisfied. The portrait was then forwarded to the Duchess of Milan [Zanone Corio to the Duchess, Lyon, 24 January 1466, BN, *Fonds Italien*, Cod. 1591, fol. 254].

[33] For his part, Galeazzo Maria accused his mother of wanting to govern alone. Among the numerous letters dealing with this feud, the following quotations from two of them written by the Duke to his mother reveal the divisive issues and the depth of feeling generated within eight months after Francesco's death. "Prego quella voglia essere contenta che io faza lo officio mio como faceva al tempo de la felice memoria del Signore, mio patre; cioé de pregare et domandare delle gratie per li mei amici et servitori, et non havere altra superiorità de commandare como haveva alhora, se non in tanto quanto fosse per commandamento de V. S. in tollergli le fatiche, como el debito mio rechiede" [Vigevano, 15 July 1466, BN, *Fonds Italien*, Cod. 1591, fol. 357]. Three months later his tone changed to one of bitter sarcasm: "Respondendo anche ad una vostra per la quale me scrive che voglia venire a Milano, perché essendo lì se spazaria qualche cossa, respondo che prego la S.ria Vostra non me calefi, perché ella sa ben ch'io non sono quello che facia facende a Milano, ma é lei solla. Et cognoscendo io esser stato fiolo de la bona memoria del Duca Francesco, non voglio venire lì per essere auditore de V. S. et senza salario. Et hora cognosco essere vero quello che la S. V. più volte ha dicto, cioé io essere zovene et pocho savio; et questo é perché credeva el Stato esser comune de la S.ria V. et de mi, ma comprehendo solo de la S. V., la quale Meser Dominodio la conservi in esso Stato" [Vigevano, 5 November 1466, *Carteggio Interno—Milano*, cart. 878]. On Galeazzo Maria's conflict with his mother, see Terni de Gregorj, *Bianca Maria Visconti*, pp. 193–209.

[34] King Ferrante was particularly solicitous in his attempts to prevent and heal the feud. Shortly after Francesco's death, he wrote to Galeazzo Maria urging him not to degenerate from his father's manners and above all obey and respect his mother, whom he called, "honore, corona et gloria de nostri seculi, et ferma columna de questo Stato" [Naples, 22 March 1466, BN, *Fonds Italien*, Cod. 1591, fol. 307–307v]. Later, when rumors about the conflict began to circulate in

estrangement and to Bianca Maria's enforced retirement to her dower city of Cremona two years later, where she died shortly thereafter.

Galeazzo Maria, however, had the good sense of retaining at his service most of his father's officials and advisers, including the chief secretary and principal executor of his foreign policy, Cicco Simonetta. He also wisely confirmed the resident ambassadors to their posts. It was a group of able and experienced diplomats—probably the best that Milan was able to muster at any given time—consisting of Marco Corio in Savoy, Gerardo de' Colli in Venice, Nicodemo Tranchedini in Florence, Agostino Rossi at the papal court, Antonio da Trezzo in Naples, and Giovan Pietro Panigarola in France.

Panigarola's initial diplomatic assignment was entirely fortuitous. At least since April 1464 he was in France on private business, in the course of which he came in contact with the King and with the Milanese ambassador, Alberico Maletta.[35] In April of the following year he was still in France when Maletta was about to end his mission. When the King suggested that the ambassador leave his secretary, Cristoforo da Bollate, in his place, Maletta proposed Panigarola instead, describing him as an "intelligent young man and apt for the task," whereas he deemed Cristoforo "little informed and not well suited for the affairs at hand." Furthermore, he pointed out that Panigarola had spoken with the King several times and had previously served the Duke of Milan.[36]

Panigarola, who was about to return to Milan with Maletta after the conclusion of his business, readily agreed to stay, exclaiming with youthful enthusiasm, "I will stay, even if I should lose my life."[37] This dra-

---

Rome, Florence, and Venice, the King wrote to the Duchess, exhorting her to make peace for the good of her state and peace in Italy [Naples, 21 June 1466, ibid., Cod. 1591, fol. 353].

[35] Mandrot, *Dépêches*, 2:108–9, 361.

[36] "Et che lassaria volentera Christoforo con la M.tà soa, se non fosse de poca complexione, et non bene habile alle presente fatiche; ma piacendo alla M.tà soa, io faria restare de qua Johanne Petro Panigarola, el quale più volte gli haveva parlato, giovane intendente et habile ala faticha, e adoperato per la V. S. in altre vostre facende" [Maletta to the Duke, Limoges, 2 April 1465, ibid., 3:83].

[37] "Se gli dovesse lassare la vita, io gli starò" [ibid., 3:93]. In his first dispatch to the Duke of

matic and nearly prophetic acceptance undoubtedly alluded to the dangers arising out of the increasingly threatening posture of the princes, which had prompted Louis to grant leave to the ambassador in order to solicit aid from the Duke. Maletta's surprising action in choosing his successor without consulting his master can only be explained by the King's urgent need for a reliable person capable of reporting accurately the momentous events that were about to take place.

At that time Panigarola must have been in his early twenties, probably of the same age as Galeazzo Maria, because ten years later he was still described as a "young man."[38] Although Maletta mentioned his previous service for the Duke, no trace has been found of his having held an important post either in the internal administration or in the diplomatic service.[39] He was a member of a prominent and numerous Milanese family of notaries, merchants, bankers, and industrialists, who had originated either in Genoa or in Gallarate, in Lombardy.[40] Around the middle of the fourteenth century, the Panigarola were granted by the Visconti the right to direct in perpetuity the *Ufficio degli Statuti*, which registered the statutes and official acts of the Dukes and

12 April 1465 [ibid., 3:102], Panigarola stressed the fact that, although he was not inclined toward diplomacy, he had obeyed Maletta's "command" given in the Duke's name, and had undergone the perils of his assignment, in order to serve Sforza, who in the past had extended favors both to him and his family.

[38] Marco Antonio Morosini to the Doge of Venice, in the camp against Neuss, 18 March 1475, *Borgogna*, cart. 516. In general, it seems that at this time a man in his thirties was still considered young [Creighton Gilbert, "When Did a Man in the Renaissance Grow Old?," *Studies in the Renaissance* 14 (1967): 13–18]. Neither the year of birth or death of Panigarola is known.

[39] For brief biographical sketches of Panigarola, see Mandrot, *Dépêches*, 2:108–9, n. 1; 3:111–12, n. 1; Frederic de Gingins-La-Sarra, ed., *Dépêches des ambassadeurs milanais sur les campagnes de Charles-Le-Hardi, duc de Bourgogne de 1474 à 1477*, vol. 1 (Paris-Geneva, 1858), pp. xi–xii, which is not entirely accurate; and Lydia Cerioni, *La diplomazia sforzesca nella seconda metà del Quattrocento e i suoi cifrari segreti*, vol. 1 (Rome: Centro di Ricerca, 1970), pp. 205–6.

[40] The Genoese origin is advanced by Gino Barbieri, "Onori e profitti alla corte sforzesca: l'attività industriale di Gottardo Panigarola e compagni," in his *Origini del capitalismo lombardo. Studi e documenti sull'economia milanese del periodo ducale* (Milan: Giuffré, 1961), p. 383. Nevertheless, Antonio Cappellini, *Dizionario biografico di Genovesi illustri e notabili* (Genoa: Tipografia Olcese, 1941), mentions only one member of the family, Agostino, who lived in the fifteenth century. Nicola Ferorelli, *Inventari e regesti del R. Archivio di Stato in Milano*, vol. 3, *Registri dell'Ufficio del Governatore degli Statuti di Milano* (Milan: Archivio di Sato 1920; repr. Milan: Cisalpino-Goliardica, 1971), p. v, believes that the Panigarola emigrated from Gallarate to Milan around 1236.

of the Commune of Milan, and in time became known as the *Ufficio dei Panigarola*.[41]

Giovan Pietro was the first son of Arrigo or Enrico Panigarola, who together with his brothers, Antonio and Cristoforo, formed a commercial and banking firm with branches at Venice, Geneva, and Genoa, and was also associated with the Borromei Bank of London. Several members of the family held important posts within the internal administration of the Duchy, including Giovan Pietro's brother, Luigi, who in 1466 became *Coadiutore* in the Chancery of the ducal Secret Council.[42] Except for a brief diplomatic mission discharged by his father in Venice (1449) on behalf of the Ambrosian Republic, Giovan Pietro was the only member of the family to hold a leading diplomatic post in the fifteenth century.[43] This may partly explain his readiness to accept Maletta's request.

Panigarola remained at his post for the next three and a half years, becoming the first Milanese resident ambassador at the royal court. In August 1468 the King abruptly terminated his mission and ordered him to return to Milan. In notifying the Duke, Louis alluded to reasons of state that had forced him to take this action, but praised the ambassador for his diligence and loyalty in discharging his mission, declaring himself well satisfied with him. He also pointed out that there was no need to send a replacement since his own secretary, Alberto Magalotti, was apt to fulfill Panigarola's functions with loyalty to both parties.[44]

It is difficult at the present to ascertain the real reasons for the King's action. Panigarola himself blamed the Angevins, who resented the presence of any Milanese ambassador at the royal court, and also Maga-

---

[41] Part of the house where this *Ufficio* was located is still standing in the Piazza dei Mercanti in Milan.

[42] Santoro, *Gli Uffici*, p. 36 and passim. Antonio Panigarola, Giovan Pietro's uncle, once reported to Francesco Sforza from France in 1455 [Vol. I, pp. 176–80], but this was the kind of report that merchants traveling on private business often made to their lords.

[43] Cf. Cerioni, *La diplomazia sforzesca*, 1:71.

[44] The King to the Duke, Senlis, 17 August, Compiègne, 28 September, and Péronne, 13 October 1468, Vaesen, *Lettres*, 3:264–65, 283–84, 285–86.

lotti, who had put himself forth as being well connected with the
Sforza and had poisoned his relations with the King in order to take
his place.[45] Whatever the reason, it is clear that Louis had become dis-
enchanted with him, and he persisted in this feeling in later years.[46]
Forced to leave the court, Panigarola retired to Paris to await further
instructions from the Duke and the arrival of his replacement, Sforza
Bettini. He then lingered in France almost till the end of 1468.[47]

This incident did not shake the Duke's confidence in his ambassador, because in the following year he entertained hopes of sending him
back to the royal court[48] and he continued to use him for other diplomatic missions. In July 1469 he was sent to Genoa to settle some matters
connected with a truce concluded between John II of Aragon and
Genoa.[49] In October of the same year, in September 1471, and in December 1473, he was in Savoy.[50] He was back in France in 1472 for a
brief mission to King René.[51] But his most important and prestigious
assignment after his return from France was his embassy to Charles
the Bold on the heels of the latter's alliance with Milan (Treaty of

---

[45] Panigarola to the Duke, Senlis, 18 August and Paris, 4 October 1468, *Francia,* cartelle 534 and
535, respectively. The second letter is full of accusations against Magalotti. Magalotti himself informed the Duke [Compiègne, 10 August 1468, ibid., cart. 534] that although the King had for
some time complained to him about the ambassador's deportment, he did not know the truth of the
matter, and believed that his discharge was more the result of others' instigation than of any
personal failing. Mandrot, *Dépêches,* 3:122, maintains that Alberto Magalotti was a former Sforza
courier, who since April 1464 had been making frequent trips into France. This is hardly possible,
for the ambassadors always referred to this courier as "Alberto cavallaro," never noting his last
name, and Magalotti's letters, written in a beautiful humanist hand, display a degree of education far above what could be expected of any courier. Magalotti continued in the King's service
up to the latter's death, and was used for several important diplomatic missions in Italy [Cerioni,
La diplomazia sforzesca, 1:189].

[46] See Preface, p. xviii, and Cristoforo da Bollate to the Duke, Senlis, 26 February 1474, *Francia,*
cart. 541.

[47] His last dispatch, written from Lyon, is dated 14 December 1468 [*Francia,* cart. 535]. Bettini
arrived in early October.

[48] See Preface, p. xviii, n. 18.

[49] See the Duke's instructions to Panigarola, Abbiate, 12 July 1469, *Genova,* cart. 1514.

[50] *Savoia,* cartelle 483, 486, and 490 respectively. Cf. also letter of credence for Panigarola, addressed to Duchess Yolande [Milan, 20 December 1473], *Registri Missive,* Reg. 117, fol. 8.

[51] The Duke to King René, Pavia, 6 September 1472, *Registri Missive,* Reg. 111, fol. 48v, accrediting Panigarola. Cf. the Duke to King René and to Giovanni Cossa, Galliate, 13 November 1472,
Francia, cart. 539.

Moncalieri, 30 January 1475). For the next seventeen months he followed the Duke's footsteps, reporting on every detail of his duel with Louis XI and on his dogged determination to teach the Swiss peasants a lesson, the latter being a futile enterprise from which Panigarola tried his best to dissuade him. His dispatches constitute the only extensive eyewitness account of this struggle, the outcome of which changed the history of Europe.[52]

Panigarola was the only ambassador of the age who had the opportunity to work closely and at some length with the two most powerful princes in Christendom. During his Burgundian embassy he came closest to fulfilling his brash prophesy made at the beginning of his diplomatic career: at the battles of Grandson and Morat (2 March and 22 June 1476), he narrowly escaped capture or death, but lost one servant in the former and two servants and all his baggage in the latter.[53] Considering that earlier in France he was frequently in danger of losing his life at the hands of the Angevins, it can be said that few of his colleagues had undertaken so dangerous and at the same time crucial missions.

The mission to Burgundy seems to have been Panigarola's last important diplomatic assignment. Within the Duchy he held various posts, but he never attained membership in the prestigious Secret Council, unlike some of his colleagues. In 1474 he was appointed Vice-Governor of Genoa.[54] Three years later he was appointed secretary in the Secret Chancery,[55] and in this capacity he was sent on various internal missions from 1477 to 1479, including one to the Milanese army fighting

---

52 A full account of Panigarola's mission to Charles the Bold will be given in subsequent volumes dealing with Burgundy. Richard J. Walsh, "Charles the Bold, Last Valois Duke of Burgundy 1467–1477, and Italy," (Ph.D. diss., University of Hull, 1977), has made ample use of Panigarola's Burgundian dispatches. See especially chap. 5, passim, for his excellent, detailed account of the ambassador's role at the Burgundian court.

53 Ibid., pp. 474–75.

54 In July 1474, Panigarola was sent on an unspecified mission to Genoa [The Duke to Panigarola, Milan, 24 July 1474, Biblioteca della Società Storica Lombarda, *Carte Morbio*, N. 110], in the course of which he was apparently made Vice-Governor of the city, for the Duke addressed him with that title in October and November of that year [*Registri Missive-Frammenti*, cart. 7, fasc. XCVII]. His dispatches are in Genova, cartelle 453–56.

55 The date of his appointment was 1 April 1477 [Santoro, *Gli Uffici*, 50].

the Swiss.[56] Finally, in 1482, Panigarola received probably the only territorial concession granted to him for his services when Duke Gian Galeazzo Sforza invested him with the fief of Castano near Milan. But he died in 1485, for in the course of this year the fief was given to another for lack of suitable male heirs.[57]

Panigarola's dispatches exhibit a high degree of intelligence and insight, as already noted by Mandrot.[58] By 1466 he had gained a great deal of experience in dealing with the King, who treated him as a confidant with whom he shared some of his secret plans. Louis's confidence in him is also demonstrated by the fact that he invited him to attend sessions of his Council, and requested him to draft some of his letters to Italian rulers and even instructions to his ambassadors on missions to Italy [docs. 20 and 30]. Later described by one of his colleagues as a "good and discreet person and well liked by everyone,"[59] Panigarola used these gifts to cultivate the friendship of influential people at court, such as the Duke of Bourbon, Gaston du Lyon, Giovanni Filippo da Trecate, and Franceschino Nori, among others. As a result, his dispatches are packed with confidential and generally accurate information, for he took pains to investigate rumors and search out the truth of the matter. His zeal and efficiency naturally posed a threat to all

---

[56] For his missions to Genoa in 1477–1478, see *Genova*, cart. 996, *Trattati*, cart. 1542, and *Famiglie*, cart. 136. Memorandum for Panigarola on mission to the Governors of the ducal camp against the Swiss, Milan, 31 December 1478, *Svizzera*, cart. 596; Alfio R. Natale, ed., *Acta in Consilio Secreto in Castello Portae Jovis Mediolani*, 3 vols. (Milan, 1963–1969), passim.

[57] Giovan Pietro died sometime after 26 March 1485, which is the date of the last known letter addressed to him by the Duke of Milan [*Registri Missive-Frammenti*, cart. 7–8–9, fasc. 130, fol. 229]. He had been invested with the fief on 20 September 1482 [*Registri Panigarola*, Ref. 10, fols. 264v–267; cf. Enrico Casanova, *Dizionario feudale delle province componenti l'antico Stato di Milano*, 2nd ed. (Milan: Biblioteca Ambrosiana, 1930; repr. Bologna: Forni 1970), p. 30, who dates it 10 October]. In the next entry Casanova cites another charter, which is simply dated 1485, granting the fief to Luigi Terzaghi. Giovan Pietro, however, was survived by a son, Giovanni Enrico, a minor, who toward the end of the century petitioned Duke Ludovico Sforza to be allowed to inherit the land near his father's houses, located in Milan between Porta Vercellina and Porta Ticinese. The petition is undated [*Famiglie*, cart. 136].

[58] Vol. 2, p. 109, n. 1.

[59] "Lo dicto oratore cognosco, chiamasi Johanni Petro Panigarola, et parmi una che bene et discreta persona, vene pratico, et sa ben fare honore al suo principe, et é homo da farse voler bene da omni persona" [Francesco Bertini, Neapolitan ambassador at the Burgundian court, to Antonio Cicinello, Neapolitan ambassador in Milan, Ex castris, etc., 18 March 1475, *Borgogna*, cart. 516].

anti-Milanese elements at court and even to the King himself, whose suspicions of resident ambassadors reporting all his moves have been discussed in the Preface.

Panigarola followed the discursive style of writing common in ambassadorial reports at this time. Although he is generally clear, his long strings of interlocking sentences present problems of interpretation at times. Like his colleagues, he frequently reported the exact words spoken. He excelled in vividly describing dramatic moments, such as when the King taunted the Angevins [doc. 41], or when Louis, jubilant over the Venetian-Turkish conflict, remarked, "if the Turk were to pour a spoonful of water over his head professing, 'I am a Christian,' he would help him and go to his aid against the Venetians" [doc. 40]. Panigarola's language is vigorous, and reflects the high level of education that was often possessed by Italian Renaissance merchants engaged in international commerce. He was fluent in French and proud of his knowledge of Latin,[60] but he cannot be considered an intellectual at the level of some of his predecessors, such as Tommaso Moroni da Rieti, Tommaso Tebaldi da Bologna, or even Prospero da Camogli.[61] Unlike many members of his family, he was not a notary.[62] In social standing, he was not equal to his frequent partner during his residency, Emanuele de Iacopo, who is called "nobile" and in almost every case signed first their joint dispatches.

Galeazzo Maria seems to have had a high regard for Panigarola's abilities, having employed him for the two most sensitive embassies outside Italy. But the Duke was a difficult and suspicious prince. At the end of 1467 he warned Panigarola to report straightforwardly and

---

[60] His fluency in French is attested by his colleagues at the Burgundian court [Ibid., and Marco Antonio Morosini to the Doge of Venice, In the Camp against Neuss, 18 March 1475, ibid., cart. 516]. As for his command of Latin, Panigarola informed the Duke with evident satisfaction that he had dictated the letters sent by the King to all Italian rulers because the royal secretaries were unable to draft them properly in Latin [doc. 20].

[61] See vol. 1, pp. xliii–xlvii, and vol. 2, p. xxi.

[62] Writing to Cicco Simonetta [Orléans, 27 October 1466, *Francia*, cart. 532], Panigarola asked him to intercede with the Dukes so that he be charged with drafting the marriage contract between Galeazzo Maria and Bona of Savoy, in place of Alberico Maletta, even though he was not a notary.

truthfully and avoid behaving like some of his colleagues, who in seeking to please their host princes, neglected their duty.[63] Thus the ambassador was being suspected of being too favorable to the King only a few months before he was dismissed partly for being overzealous in the service of his master! Ten years later, during Panigarola's mission to Burgundy, the Duke ordered him "on pain of his head" to write and send his dispatches every day, and not let them accumulate, for the couriers were at their posts and were costing him four hundred ducats a month.[64] This was frequently an impossible request. Couriers were not always available, and the peripatetic habits of the host rulers made the task of putting quill to paper difficult, especially when contending with a cipher consisting of some two hundred signs and numbers. It will be noted in this volume that Panigarola did not write every day. In addition there are gaps in his correspondence in April, May, and June, all of which are explained in his dispatches.

If the career of a Renaissance diplomat was often dangerous and thankless, as that of Panigarola and of some others amply demonstrates, it was also not adequately compensated. Unlike his father, Galeazzo Maria was quick with his rude orders and cruel threats, but followed his example in being laggard in the payments sent to his ambassadors. Panigarola was paid at the daily rate of twenty-six *soldi imperiali* for each person and horse assigned to his embassy, eight *soldi* more than had been paid to his predecessors.[65] This rate was established in 1465 for Milanese ambassadors serving outside Italy where expenses were expected to be higher. The new rate also took into account the decreased value of the Milanese ducat in that the old rate of eighteen *soldi* constituted one-third of the value of the ducat, but by 1465 it amounted to less

---

[63] The Duke to Panigarola, Milan, 27 December 1467, postscript, ibid., cart. 533. In an undated postscript to a letter yet to be found [ibid., cart. 561], Panigarola replied in dignified terms, pointing to his work and the attendant dangers of his mission as ample evidence of his loyalty.
[64] The Duke to Panigarola, Vigevano, 21 March and 5 April 1476, *Borgogna*, cart. 518, and an undated postscript, evidently originally attached to one of the two letters, found misfiled in *Napoli*, cart. 1249.
[65] For a fuller treatment of the compensation given to Milanese ambassadors at the time of Francesco Sforza, see vol. 1, Preface, pp. xx–xxi.

than one-quarter.[66] Since Panigarola at this time held no office in the ducal administration, unlike some of his colleagues, the *per diem* allowance was his only compensation. Furthermore, his salary was always in arrears, forcing him to use his personal funds and borrow heavily from friendly merchants. In June 1466 he complained that he had not been paid for three months [doc. 42], and in the following October he again pleaded for his salary.[67] There is no doubt that his long and devoted service deserved more recognition and compensation.

The documents published in this volume date from 11 March to 29 June 1466. All dispatches were written by Panigarola, except those of March and April, which were drafted jointly with the special envoy, Emanuele de Iacopo.[68] In late June there were three dispatches by Pietro da Gallarate, dealing with his arrival in France to discuss the projected marriage of Galeazzo Maria with Bona of Savoy. The documents arising out of his mission, which effectively began when he reached the royal court in July, will be published in the next volume together with his biographical sketch. Seven of the documents included in the present volume have been previously published.[69] It has been thought advisable

---

[66] The reasons that led to the establishment of the new rate are noted in an undated document instructing Benedetto Caimi [Francia, cart. 555] to meet with the Secret Council and the *Maestri delle Entrate*, and deliberate whether the new rate should be reduced in view of the fact that the cost of living in ultramontane states had declined. The instructions were issued at Pavia, but the date is torn off. From the context it appears that the document may have been drafted in Galeazzo Maria's Chancery. The composition of Panigarola's retinue cannot be determined at the present, but it is likely, in view of his lower rank, that he was assigned the minimum complement of three horses. The summary account of his total expenses and payments for his missions to France and Piedmont, dated 13 February 1470 [*Francia*, cart. 537], is not enlightening on this subject.

[67] Panigarola to Cicco Simonetta, Orléans, 27 October 1466, ibid., cart. 532. Panigarola later lodged similar complaints from the Burgundian court, where he reported that the cost of living was much higher than it had been in France, primarily because of the shortages caused by the war. He pointed out that the rate of twenty-six *soldi* for each of his assigned five-member retinue, amounting to fifty écus per month, was simply not sufficient to cover his expenses, especially since he found it necessary to employ six servants and eight horses. In addition there were extraordinary expenses [Panigarola to the Duke, In the Camp against Nancy, 31 October and 20 December 1475, *Borgogna*, cart. 517; cf. Walsh, "Charles the Bold," pp. 572–77].

[68] For biographical information on Emanuele, see vol. 1, Introduction, p. xlvii.

[69] Docs. 1, 4–5 were published by Mandrot, *Dépêches*, 4:313–21, 321–26, 326–31; docs. 3, 5–6 by Vaesen, *Lettres*, 3:25–26, 37–38, 40–41; doc. 10 by Magistretti, "Galeazzo Maria Sforza," pp. 802–4. No absolute claim can be made, of course, that some other documents have not ap-

to include three dispatches already printed in the Mandrot edition in order to place in the chronological sequence other documents not published in that edition. Thus this volume begins with documents dated immediately after the death of Francesco Sforza.

The present collection forms part of various series of documents deposited in the Archivio di Stato in Milan and in the Bibliothèque Nationale of Paris, all of which have been described in the Introduction to the first volume (pp. xlvii–xlix).

---

peared elsewhere. Readers may note that the transcription of the three documents published in the Mandrot edition differs at times from ours. This is explained chiefly by the fact that Samaran, the editor of the fourth volume, relied on Chancery's copies for ciphered passages, whereas our transcription is always the result of our own deciphering. See especially doc. 1, n. 2.

NOTE ON PALEOGRAPHY

AND DIPLOMATICS

Panigarola's dispatches are written in a minuscule cursive chancery script, affected by the roundness and openness of the new humanist script. It is a graceful and clear hand, which reflects at times the hurried pace demanded by the waiting couriers. Abbreviations are relatively few: by suspension, especially used for appellatives applied to persons; by contraction, sometimes limited to one letter; and syllabic, which appear quite often. Punctuation is generally limited to colons used in the place of commas, and to a single point normally indicating a longer pause. A line slanting upwards to the right and placed between two points usually ends the paragraphs, which are also separated from one another by double spacing. The use of capitals is not consistent, as one would expect at this time. On the other hand, the scribes who drafted the ducal minutes wrote in more cursive Gothic and semi-humanistic scripts, reflecting their personal styles and education.

Ciphered dispatches were written continuously without punctuation or paragraphs. Panigarola at times used meaningless signs or one or more words in clear to signal the beginning of a new topic or paragraph. His cipher,[1] consisting of some two hundred signs and numbers,

---

[1] The matter of the cipher used by Panigarola is somewhat confusing. He adopted Maletta's cipher, the key to which was reconstructed by Mandrot, the original having been lost [BN, *Fonds Italien*, Cod. 1593, fol. A]. From Milan, he was subsequently supplied with another cipher, bear-

used the typical substitution system current at the Milanese Chancery, which has already been described [vol. 1, Preface, p. xviii].

In drafting their dispatches, Milanese ambassadors nearly always used the same opening and ending formulas of address and salutation. The last line of the text contains the city and date, the latter written in Roman or Arabic numerals, followed on a separate line by the ending formula and the signature. The address is written on the back of the dispatches, but it is sometimes included on separate lines after the signature. Because of their repetitious nature, these formulas have been omitted from the transcriptions for the sake of brevity. Since they may be of interest to students of diplomatics, they will be listed below for each ambassador and for the letters exchanged by rulers. Only significant variants will be registered in subsequent volumes.

Giovan Pietro Panigarola

Signature: Johannespetrus Panicharolla; rarely, Panigarola

Invocation: Yesus,[2] written on top center of all dispatches

Writing to (1) Count Galeazzo Maria Sforza, (2) Duke Francesco Sforza, (3) Duke Galeazzo Maria Sforza, (4) Duchess Bianca Maria Visconti Sforza and Duke Galeazzo Maria Sforza.

1. Beginning: Illustris ac Excelse Domine et Domine mi Colendissime

    Ending: Illustrissime et Excellentissime Dominationis Vestre servitor fidelis

      Address: Illustri ac Excelso Domino et Domino meo Colendissimo,

---

ing the date of 8 January 1466, which apparently was the same one forwarded to him from Lyon by Giovanni Bianchi [Bianchi to the Duke, 1 April 1466, *Francia*, cart. 532]. But Panigarola continued to use the Maletta cipher with few additional signs, the meaning of which we have discovered with the aid of the Chancery copies. Basically it is this cipher that was reissued to him on 2 February 1475 for his mission to Burgundy. The keys to both ciphers were published in facsimile by Cerioni, *La diplomazia sforzesca*, vol. 2, and in Francesco Tranchedino, *Diplomatische Geheimschriften. Codex Vindobonensis 2398 der österreichischen Nationalbibliothek. Faksimileausgabe*, W. Höflechner, ed. (Graz: Akademische Druck- u. Verlagsanstalt, 1970).

[2] Panigarola used the Greek-Latin abbreviated form, "Yhus," which is extended into "Yesus," rather than "Yhesus," by the majority of paleographers. For a recent discussion of this question, see Catello Salvati, "I 'nomina sacra' nella normative dell'edizione delle fonti documentarie," *Rassegna degli Archivi di Stato* 31 (1971), pp. 104–12.

    Domino Galeaz Marie Sfortie Vicecomiti Comiti, etc., Du-
    cali Primogenito ac Regio Locumtenenti, etc.

2. Beginning: Illustrissimo et Excellentissimo Signor mio
   Ending: Excellentie Vestre servus
   Address: Illustrissimo Principi ac Excellentissimo Domino et Domi-
        no Singularissimo, Domino Francisco Sfortie Vicecomiti,
        Duci Mediolani, etc., Papie Anglerieque Comiti, Ianue ac
        Cremone Domino, etc.

3. Beginning: Illustrissimo et Excellentissimo Signor mio
   Ending: Excellentie Vestre fidelissimus servitor
   Address: Illustrissimo ac Excellentissimo Domino et Domino meo
        Singularissimo, Domino Galeaz Marie Sfortie Vicecomiti,
        Duci Mediolani, etc., Papie Anglerieque Comiti, Ianue ac
        Cremone Domino, etc.

4. Beginning: Illustrissima Madona et Excellentissimo Signor mio
   Ending: Illustrissimarum Dominationum Vestrarum servitor
       or Excellentiarum Vestrarum fidelissimus servitor
   Address: Illustrissimis ac Excellentissimis Domine Ducisse Medio-
        lani Cremoneque Domine nec non Domino Duci Medio-
        lani, Papie Anglerieque Comitibus ac Ianue Dominis,
        Dominis meis Singularissimis

Emanuele de Iacopo

Signature: Emanuel de Jacoppo
Writing to Duke Galeazzo Maria Sforza.
Beginning: Illustrissime Princeps et Excellentissime Domine Domine
        mi Singularissime
Ending: Eiusdem Illustrissime Dominationis Vestre fidelissimus servi-
        tor
Address: Illustrissimo Principi et Excellentissimo Domino Galeaz Ma-
        rie Sfortie Vicecomiti, Duci Mediolani, etc., Papie Anglerie-
        que Comiti, Ianue Domino, Domino suo Singularissimo

Emanuele de Iacopo and G. P. Panigarola

Joint dispatches to (1) Duchess Bianca Maria Visconti Sforza, (2) Duke Galeazzo Maria Sforza, (3) Duchess Bianca Maria Visconti Sforza and Duke Galeazzo Maria Sforza.

Invocation: Yesus, when the dispatches are written by Panigarola

1. Beginning: Illustrissima et Excellentissima Domina et Domina nostra Singularissima

   Ending: Excellentie Vestre fidelissimi servitores

   Address: Excellentissime Domine et Singularissime Domine Blanche Vicecomiti, Ducisse Mediolani, etc., Papie Anglerieque Comitisse, Ianue ac Cremone Domine, etc.

2. Beginning: Illustrissimo et Excellentissimo Signor nostro

   Ending: Excellentie Vestre servitores or Excellentie Vestre fidelissimi servitores

   Address: Illustrissimo Principi ac Excellentissimo Domino et Domino nostro Singularissimo, Domino Galeaz Marie Sfortie Vicecomiti, Duci Mediolani, etc., Papie Anglerieque Comiti, Ianue ac Cremone Domino, etc.

3. Beginning: Illustrissima Madona et Excellentissimo Signor nostro

   Ending: Illustrissimarum Dominationum Vestrarum fidelissimi servitores

   Address: Illustrissimis ac Excellentissimis Domine Domine Ducisse Mediolani Cremoneque Domine nec non Domino Galeaz Marie Sfortie Vicecomiti, Duci Mediolani, etc., Papie Anglerieque Comitibus ac Ianue Dominis Singularissimis, etc.

The ducal minutes are headed by the name or names of the ambassadors with the city and date noted in the top left-hand corner. All ducal missives to ambassadors were composed by Cicco Simonetta or his brother, Giovanni, the only secretaries who had the authority to countersign the originals.[3]

---

[3] This practice, already followed by Francesco Sforza, was confirmed by Galeazzo Maria [The Duke to the Reformatori delle Entrate, Vigevano, 13 July 1466, *Carteggio Interno-Milano*, cart. 878].

For the letters exchanged by the rulers, we have the complete formulas only for those sent by the King, the originals of the Dukes not being available.

Louis XI writing to (1) Count Galeazzo Maria Sforza, (2) Duke Galeazzo Maria Sforza, (3) Duchess Bianca Maria Visconti Sforza.

1. Beginning: Illustris Princeps, consaguinee et frater noster carissime or
   Trés cher et trés amé frère et cousin

   Ending: No special formula. The last line of the text contains the city, the day and month, and rarely the year. Louis's signature [Loys] appears on the bottom center of the letter and that of his secretary on the lower right-hand side.

   Address: Illustri Principi consaguineo et fratri nostro carissimo Comiti Galeaz Vicecomiti, Armorum Capitaneo ac Locumtenenti nostro in Delphinatu et Lugdunensi, or A nostre trés cher et trés amé frère et cousin le Conte Galeaz

2. Beginning: Trés chier et trés amé frère et cousin

   Ending: same as no. 1

   Address: A nostre trés chier et trés amé frère et cousin le Duc de Millan

3. Beginning: Trés chière et trés amée tante

   Ending: same as no. 1.

   Address: A ma trés chière et trés amée tante la Duchesse de Millan

Ducal minutes addressed to the King by (1) Duke Galeazzo Maria Sforza, (2) Duchess Bianca Maria Visconti Sforza.

1. Heading: Serenissimo Domino Regi Francorum

   Beginning: Serenissime et Christianissime Rex Domine mi Singularissime

2. Heading: Domino Regi Francorum

   Beginning: Serenissime et Christianissime Princeps et Excellentissime Domine Pater Honorandissime

ABBREVIATIONS

B.	Busta
Cart.	Cartella
C. C.	Chancery Copy or Copies
D.	Domino
F.	Filza
Ill.mo	Illustrissimo
Mag.tia, Mag.co	Magnificentia, Magnifico
Mons., Mons.re	Monsignore
N. S.	Nostro Signore
Orig.	Original
P.to	Prefato
Reg.	Register
R.mo	Reverendissimo
Ser.mo	Serenissimo
S., Sig.re, S.re	Signore
Sig.ria, S.ria	Signoria
S. M., S. M.tà	Sua Maestà
S. Sig.ria, S. S.ria	Sua Signoria
S. S.tà	Sua Santità
V. Cel.	Vostra Celsitudine
V. E., V. Ex.tia	Vostra Excellentia
V. P.	Vostra Paternità
V. S., V. Sig.ria, V. S.ria	Vostra Signoria

DISPATCHES

Recently, Madame de Orléans caused supplication and request to
be made to the King in public Council, that His Majesty deign to commend to Your Excellency her affairs in Asti and all her possessions
there at all times and in every situation that might occur. Since this request seemed very just it was ordered to be executed by His Majesty
and his Council, and suitable letters were ordered to be written. Although [the request] was made in general terms, from what I am told,
I understand that Madame made it with the intention of being able to
gain help and support from Your Excellency because it seems that between her and the Marquis of Monferrat there are certain differences
about their borders. It is said that not long ago the Marquis took from
her certain castles and possessions by force, which she does not intend
to permit. From two notable individuals I have learned that *the King
is not at all pleased with the Marquis of Monferrat,*[2] *and in this connection I will extend every effort to learn the truth. Having ascertained it,
I will notify Your Lordship.*

It is also confirmed that the people of Dinant and Liége have brok-
en their agreement with My Lord of Charolais, being willing to die
rather than become subjects of the Burgundians.[3]

King Don Pedro was sending certain ambassadors to the Count of
Armagnac [Jean V] and to My Lord of Charolais in order to request

1·GIOVAN PIETRO PANIGAROLA *to the*

DUKE OF MILAN[1]

BN, Fonds Italien, Cod. 1593, fols. 227–30. Orig.

Questi dì Madama de Orliens in publico Consiglio, dove era questo S. Re, fece supplicare et requirire, che ad la M.tà Soa piacesse di ricommandare le soe cose di Ast, et che ha delà ad la V. Ex.tia in ogni tempo et in ogni caso che li potesse occorere; la quale domanda parendoli assay iusta, fu per la prefata M.tà et suo Consiglio ordinata di exequire, et furono imposte le lettere. Et quamvis fosse facta in generalità, intendo per quanto sono avisato, che essa Madama lo fa ad questo fine, che possa conseguire adiuto et favore da la V. Ex.tia, perchè pare fra quella et lo S. Marchese di Monferato siano alchune differentie in le loro confine, et dicono che esso Marchese da pocho tempo in qua li ha tolti certi castelli et beni per forza, el che non intende però di sofrire. Et per quanto da doe notabile persone mi hé referto, *questo Signor Re non essere ben contento del prelibato Marchese de Monferato,[a] de la quale cosa mi studio de intendere più oltra la verità, et intesa darone aviso a la S. V.*[2]

Si confirma etiam che quelli de Dinant et di Legia hanno romputo l'acordo cum Monsignor Chyaroloes, non intendendo a modo alchuno essere subgietti ad Berghognoni, ma prima morire.[3] El Re Don Pietro mandava certi ambassatori al Conte d'Armignac et ad Mon.re Chyaroloes per domandarli socorso, li quali sono stati spiati et presi in le con-

---

a. C. C. incorrectly reads: del parentato del prelibato Marchese de Monferato.

their aid. They were discovered and taken on the borders of Languedoc by the King's men. Among other things, it was found mentioned in their instructions that should they not be able to obtain help from the Counts of Armagnac and of Charolais, they should go to His Majesty to ask for assistance, telling him that the County of Rousillon was rightfully part of his kingdom. If His Majesty were willing to send him [Don Pedro] six hundred lances, paid up for half a year, the latter would grant him such letters of cession that neither he nor his successors could ever raise any question regarding their former rights. The County would then belong freely and truly to His Majesty. The King ordered that these ambassadors be sent to Usson in Auvergne, an extremely well-fortified castle, where they were to be examined and closely interrogated regarding all the business they had come to transact.[4]

My Lord of Candale[5] remains as governor of Rousillon, with his usual provision. Whereas His Majesty wanted to take from him seventy lances in order to give them to the Duke of Brittany, he has now decided to leave him fifty and give him three thousand francs a year, in order to pay so many foot soldiers for guarding the country, in place of the twenty lances which he took away. He then made other provisions for the Duke. The Count of Dunois[6] is here and the King almost every day goes to consult with him in his residence, demonstrating just how dearly he holds his counsel. As I believe Your Lordship knows, the Count of Dunois held as security certain territory of Savoy from the Most Illustrious Duke of Savoy [Amédée IX], and, from what I hear, for the sum of twenty-five thousand ducats; during the recent wars, upon insistence of His Majesty to whom he was an enemy, these lands were taken from him by the Duke of Savoy. In an attempt to have them restituted to him, His Majesty now has decided to send the Bailli of Lyon[7] to Savoy for this reason, saying that he wishes to give him every help and support so that all might be restituted to him as before; presently they are drafting the instructions for his mission there to deal with this affair.

4

fine di Lengua d'Ocha per queli de questo S. Re. Tra le altre cose in le loro instructione trovate si conteneva, che non potendo obtenire adiuto da essi Conti de Armignac et de Chyaroloes, venisseno da la M.tà Soa pregandoli adiuto, et dirli che el Contato de Rosiglione li aparteneva et era del suo regno, se quela li voleva dare lanze sex cento pagate per mezo anno, che li faria tale littere et cessione che per luy o soy successori may non poria essere domandata cosa alchuna per el drito che loro specta, ma dicto Contato restaria libero et proprio de la M.tà Soa; la quale ha mandato a menare essi ambassatori ad Usson in Alvergna, castello fortissimo et lì ordina che siano examinati et inquisiti subtilmente di tute practiche che vegnivano per fare.[4] Monsignor di Candela[5] rimane governatore di Rossiglione cum la solita soa provisione, et sicondo che la M.tà Soa li voleva tore le lanze LXX.ta per darle al Duca di Bertagna, hora hé concluso di lasargline L.ta et darli franchi tremillia per anno per asoldare tanti fanti a piede ad la guardia dil payse, in loco de le lanze XX li tolle, et così altrove ha provisto al prefato Duca.

El Conte di Dunoes[6] hé in questa terra. El S. Re quasi ogni giorno va a tenere Consiglio in casa soa, dimonstrando havere caro el consiglio suo. Como credo V. S. sapia esso Conte de Dunoes tegniva certe terre in Savoya in pegno da quello Ill.mo Duca di Savoya, sicondo intendo per ducati XXV.M., et durando queste guerre ad instantia di la M.tà Soa di la quale era inimico, esse terre li furono tolte per el prefato Duca di Savoya. Cerchando hora che li siano restituite, la M.tà Soa ha ordinato mandare el Baylì de Lione[7] in Savoya per questa casone, et dice volerli dare ogni adiuto et favore, adciò che el sia restituito come prima, et al presente si ordinano le instructione per mandarlo delà ad operare circha questa materia.

Ulterius *Madama de Savoia cerca et fa instare di comprare el Contato de Ast,*[8] *dicendo che venderà collane, argento et tuto per pagare el pretio di che sarano d'acordo.* Sicondo sono informato, el Conte de Dunoes gli é renitente et contrario ad tutta brida et ultimamente *rispose che quando pure el Contato de Ast si dovesse vendere et alienare, più*

Madame of Savoy, moreover, *seeks and strives to buy the County of Asti,*[8] *saying that she would sell necklaces, silver, and everything else in order to pay the price to be agreed upon.* From what I am told, the Count of Dunois is completely contrary and recalcitrant in the matter; most recently *he responded that if the County of Asti* must *be sold and alienated, he would rather that Your Lordships have it for the sum of two thousand ducats than Madame of Savoy for any price whatsoever, regretting that he might never have this satisfaction. He says that if in the past he was no friend of yours,* this proceeded out of respect for the late Duke of Orléans [Charles], his brother, who wanted it so; nevertheless, at present he is your friend. Considering the merit of all the things you have done, [he feels] it fitting that Your Highnesses be loved and in possession of the Duchy of Milan, thus speaking very much in your praise and commendation.

The Bailli of Asti [Regnault du Dresnay] *returned into His Majesty's good grace through the influence of his daughter, who is staying here with Her Serene Highness the Queen.* The Bailli has offered his services to me out of respect for Your Lordship, showing himself to be a servant of yours. He made a fine report about you, telling His Majesty all that you had offered to do for him in Asti, and how ready you are to help them in every need. He says in a short while he will return to Asti.

My Lord Filippo and companions are still in prison. Although His Majesty is being greatly pressed to set them free, and has said that he will do so once the Most Illustrious Count Galeazzo has arrived here;[9] at the present, I understand that *he is much inclined to release them* owing to the assiduous prayers of the Queen and others. He sent to the Grand Chancellor [Guillaume Jouvenel des Ursins] a document signed in his own hand (I have seen it and read it), *which asks Lord Luigi di Valperga, brother of the late Lord Iacopo di Valperga, and three other councillors here, all of them together, to inspect the trial record and accusations made and ventilated against Filippo and his companions. They are to report immediately to His Majesty on what they find in*

tosto voria la S. V. lo havesse per ducati dominlia[b] *cha Madama de Savoia per pretio alcuno, né mai si vedesse questa consolatione; et dice che se per el passato non vi era amico,* procedeva per rispecto dil quondam Duca de Orliens suo fratello, che così voleva, ma che al presente hé vostro amico; et merito ad le cose haveti facto apartiene la Cel. V. essere amata et havere quello Ducato di Millano, parlandone molto in Vostra laude et commendatione. *El Bailì de Ast ritorna in la gratia de la prefata Maiestà per mezo de una soa fiola quale sta qui con la Serenissima Regina.* Esso Baylì me si hé offerto assay per rispecto de la V. S. monstrandosi suo servitore, de la quale ha facto digna rellatione, et dicto ad essa M.tà de le offerte li mandò a fare in Ast la V. Ex.tia et como sempre hé presta ad ogni loro bisogno, et in breve spazato dice ritornarà in Ast.

Filippo Mon.re e compagni sono ancora prisonieri, et quamvis la M.tà Soa sia molto infestata de lassarli et habia dicto volerlo fare venuto che sia lo Ill.mo Conte Galiazo,[9] al presente intendo per le assidue pregere de la prefata Regina et de li altri *essere molto condescenduta ad la liberatione loro.* Ha mandato al Gran Cangellero per uno scrito sotoscripto di soa propria mano, lo quale io ho visto et lecto, *che domandi Miser Loise di Valperga, fratelo del* quondam *Misere Iacomo de Valperga, et qua tri altri consiglieri,*[c] *et tuti insieme visiteno el processo et examinatione facte et agitate contra esso Filippo Mon.re et compagni, facendo statim rellatione ad la Soa M.tà de quelo trovarano in essi processi et de chi serà stato casone de la morte del prefato quondam Misere Iacomo da Valperga.*[10]

Ceterum, essendo stato pure referto ad questo S. Re de alchune resistentie facte a Viena et altrove al prefato Conte Galiazo, carestia missa in le victualie et la pocha obedientia facta in Delphinato, la M.tà Soa, turbata molto de tale cose, ha ordinato mandare Mons.re de Chiastionovo di delà, el quale hé partesano de la V. S., cum commissione che quelli che ad Viena li fano resistentia siano messi in uno fondo di tore

---

b. C. C. incorrectly reads: ducati XX.M.
c. C. C. incorrectly reads: che questi altri consiglieri.

*these records and especially discover who was responsible for the death
of the aforementioned Lord Iacopo di Valperga.*[10]

Further, a report was also made to the King of the resistance put
up at Vienne and elsewhere in the Dauphiné against Count Galeazzo,
in reference to the withholding of victuals and to the scarce obedience
given him. His Majesty, very much disturbed by these things, ordered
My Lord of Châteauneuf [Soffrey Allemand] to go there (he is a partisan of Your Lordship), with instructions that those who oppose him in
Vienne be placed in a deep dungeon and punished, etc.; that he see to
it that the Count be obeyed as if he were His Majesty himself, placing
the Dauphiné in his hands; that he order provisions for the [Milanese]
troops, to be supplied at the proper price, and in a similar manner provide all that will be necessary regarding the obedience of the country.
These instructions are being drafted by Gaston [du Lyon][11] and by My
Lord of Châteauneuf, who have said to me that they were commanded
by His Majesty to show them to me; when I have seen them, I will
make every effort to notify Your Excellency of their tenor, or if I can, I
will send you a copy.[12] Verbally, His Majesty says in a heated manner
that he expects the Count to be more feared, revered, and obeyed in
the Dauphiné than he himself; he adds that whoever is recalcitrant will
receive such a punishment that he will be a perpetual example to others.

During the recent war His Majesty, upon great insistence from
King René [King of Sicily], gave him Gap in the Dauphiné, a fortified
pass through the mountains, because he could not do otherwise. Presently, he has commissioned My Lord of Châteauneuf to insure that Gap
remain in His Majesty's possession as it was before; he does not wish to
observe the written agreement made with King René, because he says
it was made under duress, and to ingratiate him while he was in their
hands.[13] It has seemed proper to me to indicate all these things to Your
Most Illustrious Lordship, to whom I constantly commend myself.

Postscript. Just this hour the King once again requested and greatly
pressed me, if ever I desired to do him a favor, that I have sent to him

puniti etc.; che faza obedire el prefato Conte come la persona propria de Soa M.tà dandoli el Delfinato in mano, et facendo provedere per el vivere de le gente d'arme che le victualie siano a debito presio, e così a provedere di quanto sarà necessario circha la obedientia del payse. L'instructione si fano per mano di Gastoneto[11] e di esso Mon.re de Chiastionovo, li quali mi hanno dicto havere commandamento da la prefata M.tà di monstrarmi dicta instructione, la quale vista che l'habia, sforzaromi avisare V. Ex.tia dil tenore, o mandarogline si potrò la copia;[12] et a le parole dice la M.tà Soa molto caldamente, intende ch'el prefato Conte sia più temuto, reverito et obedito in Delfinato cha quella propria, et chi li serà renitente dice li farà tal punitione, che sarà perpetua memoria et exemplo ad altri. Postremo in queste guere la prefata M.tà, instando molto el Re Reynero, li donò Gap in Delfinato, passo in le montagne forte, perché non poteva fare di manco; al presente ha commisso ad Monsignor de Chiastionovo provederli talmente che Gap rimagna de la M.tà Soa come era usato et non volere observare le littere fece al prefato Re Reynero, perché dice sono facte per forza, et per compiacerli in el tempo che era in le loro mane.[13] Siché de tute queste cose mi hé parso avisarne la V. Ill.ma Signoria, a la quale continue me ricomando.

Post scripta. In questa hora di novo questo S. Re mi ha pregato et instato grandissimamente, se may desyderay farli cosa grata, che li faza portare la sargia negra et morella per fare doe o tre payra di calze per questo caldo, de la quale tante volte mi ha parlato, et che dovesse mandare un homo proprio ad torla, afinché qui fosse presto, che pagaria ogni spessa, et più me la pagaria come veluto; carichandomi stretissimamente ad così fare. Donde ne aviso le S. V. ricordandoli et pregandole che per honore suo et per satisfare al desiderio et appetito de la M.tà Soa subito li piacia mandare dicta sargia per uno cavalaro, quando bene lo dovesseno mandare aposta volando, et per tre o IIII.to para di calze tantum, perché non porano fare ad la prefata M.tà cosa più grata, et la haverà più cara cha se gli ne mandasseno mille pezze. Ben li ricordo essere

9

some black and brown cloth sufficient for two or three pairs of warm weather hose. He has spoken of it to me so many times, even saying that I should send a man especially to get it, in order that it be here soon; he would pay every expense even at the price of velvet, and he charged me most vigorously to do so. Wherefore, I notify Your Excellencies, reminding and begging you that for your honor and in order to satisfy the desire and appetite of His Majesty, it might please you to send immediately the aforementioned cloth by a speedy courier, even if it were necessary to send him especially for this purpose: a sufficient amount for three or four pairs of hose. For you could not do a greater favor for His Majesty, and he will consider it more dear than if you were to send him a thousand pieces of cloth. Once again I remind you that it is necessary to make every haste, because I have promised His Majesty to send a man expressly for this alone.

HISTORICAL NOTES

1. Francesco Sforza, Duke of Milan since 1450, had died on 8 March 1466, but definite news of his death did not reach the French court until 20 March [see doc. 6]. The dispatch of 12 March, doc. 4, is also addressed to him.

2. The King's displeasure over this border dispute between the Duchess of Orleans, Marie de Clèves, and the Marquis Guglielmo VII of Monferrat, has nothing to do with the latter's marriage with Marie de Foix, daughter of Count Gaston IV, which had been arranged a year earlier by the King himself [Henri Courteault, *Gaston IV, Comte de Foix, Vicomte souverain de Béam, Prince de Navarre, 1423-1472* (Toulouse: Privat, 1895), pp. 290-91]. This erroneous interpretation is based on a faulty Chancery's deciphering of this passage [see above, n.a.], reproduced in Mandrot, 4:315, and n. 1. Samaran, who edited the last volume of the Mandrot edition, depended on Chancery deciphering, at least for the dispatches republished here, thus differing at times from our transcription, which is always based on our own deciphering.

3. The peace treaty of St. Trond (22 December 1465) between Liège and Burgundy, from which the town of Dinant had been excluded, had just put

necessario usare cellerità, perché ho promisso ad la M.tà Soa di mandare uno homo expresso per questo solamente.

a temporary end to the armed struggle over the appointment (1456) of Louis de Bourbon, nephew of Duke Philip the Good, as Bishop of Liège, and over Burgundy's attempts to dominate the two towns, pursued with vigor by Philip's son, Charles, Count of Charolais [Richard Vaughan, *Philip the Good. The Apogee of Burgundy* (London: Longmans, Green, 1970), pp. 391–96].

4. Cf. the instructions to the two ambassadors, Jaume d'Aragó and Joan Benages, dated 16 December 1465, published by Jésus E. Martinez Ferrando, *Pere de Portugal, "Rei dels Catalans"* (Barcelona: La Renaixenca, 1936), pp. 227–28. The Catalans, in revolt since 1462 against King John II of Aragon, had recognized, late in 1463, Don Pedro, Constable of Portugal, as the legitimate King of Aragon. In the following months, Don Pedro, a man of thought rather than a diplomat, sought aid everywhere for his struggle against his rival. In this instance he hoped to entice Louis XI by offering the County of Roussillon, which along with the County of Cerdagne, was temporarily in Louis's control, according to the terms of the Treaty of Bayonne (9 May 1462) concluded with John II. Louis's attitude toward Don Pedro, however, was always semi-hostile, as shown here [Joseph Calmette, *Louis XI, Jean II et la*

révolution catalane (1461–1473) (Toulouse: Privat, 1903), pp. 65 ff., 236–49].

5. Jean de Foix, son of Gaston de Foix, and Count of Candale.

6. Jean, son of Duke Louis of Orleans and Mariette d'Enghien, Count of Dunois since 1439, known as the Bastard of Orleans and famous for his support of Joan of Arc [Léon Lecestre, "Essai biographique sur Jean, Batard d'Orléans, Comte de Dunois (1400–1468)," École des Chartes, *Positions des Thèses* (1882), pp. 29–35].

7. François Royer, originally from Asti, whose Italian name was Roeri or de Rottariis [1:83; Mandrot, *Dépêches* 1:91].

8. Duchess Yolande of Savoy, sister of Louis XI, is here renewing the centuries-old struggle with Milan for the control of the border County of Asti, which had come into the possession of the House of Orleans in 1387 as part of the dowry of Valentina Visconti, daughter of Duke Gian Galeazzo Visconti of Milan and stepmother of the Count of Dunois.

9. Count Galeazzo Maria Sforza, who was in Dauphiné with the Milanese troops sent by Francesco Sforza to help the King subdue the baronial revolt in 1465. His projected visit to the royal court never took place, owing to the death of his father.

10. In July 1462 Philip of Savoy, the ambitious fifth son of Duke Louis I of Savoy, virtually took control of the Duchy by expelling the Cyprian faction surrounding his mother, Anne of Cyprus, and executing the powerful Chancellor, Giacomo di Valperga, a favorite of Louis XI, through whom the King sought to control the Duchy [Introduction, p. xlii]. In April 1464 Philip accepted a royal safe-conduct to seek a reconciliation with the King.

On the way to the royal court at Orléans, he was treacherously arrested with few of his closest supporters and confined in the Castle of Loches, where he was still being held. This breach of faith shocked the chilvaric world and soon appeals for his freedom reached the King from Philip's many friends and supporters, including his sister, Queen Charlotte of France [M. C. Daviso di Charvensod, "Filippo Senza Terra: la sua ribellione nel 1462 e le sue relazioni con Francesco Sforza e Luigi XI," *Rivista storica italiana*, ser. 4, 6 (1935); 127–200, and *Filippo II, il Senzaterra* (Turin: Paravia, 1941), pp. 37–48].

11. Gaston du Lyon, Seneschal of Saintonge, Chamberlain and confidant of Louis XI, utilized for many missions to Italy before and after Louis ascended the throne [vols. 1–2, passim; Anne-Marie Lardy, "Gaston du Lyon, serviteur de Louis XI et de Charles VIII," Ecole des Chartes, *Positions des Thèses* (1936), pp. 87–93].

12. These instructions, undated, are in *Francia*, cart. 532. They were probably written on or before 18 March, on which date the King wrote from Orléans to Count Galeazzo Maria accrediting the Lord of Chateauneuf [ibid., cart. 532, Italian translation; BN, *Fonds Italien*, Cod. 1591, fol. 295, orig., published by Vaesen, *Lettres*, 3:27–28

13. Panigarola may have been misinformed on this question. In 1463 Louis XI had negotiated with King René the exchange of Gap for other lands, but the actual transfer never took place owing to the opposition of the Parlement and Chamber of Accounts of Dauphiné [Mandrot, *Dépêches*, 4:320, n. 1].

Emanuele.[1] Our son Galeazzo is on his way to come here, owing to the sad event of the passing of the late Illustrious Lord our husband, of which we did not inform you, being certain you would have heard it from Galeazzo himself. We are sure, therefore, that you will have directed your journey toward the King of France in order to inform him of the lamentable death, of Galeazzo's departure to come here, and also to fulfill the instructions you received from our late consort.[2] If you have not done so, as soon as you receive this letter, we wish you to go immediately to His Majesty to execute what has been said above; that is, to inform him of the sad event and of Galeazzo's departure; to fulfill what is assigned in the aforementioned instructions, and also what is written in our own instructions, herewith enclosed.[3]

Commend us to His Majesty as fervidly as you possibly can, letting him know that all our comfort and hope are placed in him. Thank God, after the sad event, our affairs here are improving every day and our people are peaceful and quiet; they bear us and demonstrate that love, trust, and obedience which they had for our late husband.

HISTORICAL NOTES

1. Emanuele was frequently sent on missions to France before and after the present one. For a brief sketch of his career, see vol. 1, Introduction, p. xlvi.

2 · *The* DUCHESS OF MILAN *to*

EMANUELE DE IACOPO

Francia, cart. 532. Minute

Emanuel.[1] Venendo in qua Galeazo nostro figliolo, como vene, per el doloroso caso seguto del Ill.mo quondam Signore nostro consorte, del quale non te havemo avisato altramente rendendone certa l'haveray inteso da esso Galeazo, siamo certissime haveray agrezato[a] el tuo camino verso la M.tà del Ser.mo S. Re de Franza per notificarli dicto lacrimabile caso, et la partita d'esso Galeazo per venire in qua et exequire quanto havevi in instructione del prelibato quondam nostro consorte.[2] El che, quando non l'havesti facto, volimo che subito, havuta questa, debii andare via dala prefata M.tà per fare quanto et dicto et cioé avisarla del caso dela venuta de Galeazo, et exequire quanto in dicta instructione se contene, et etiam quanto se contene in questa altra nostra instructione inclusa,[3] et ne recomanda alla prefata M.tà tanto strictamente quanto may più saperay, et potray, certificandola ogni nostro conforto et speranza l'havemo collocate in Soa M.tà. Queste nostre cose de qua Dio gratia depoy el caso passano ogni dì meglio et tutti li nostri popoli stano pacifici et quieti, et ne portano et demonstrano quello amore, fede, et obedientia che facevano al prefato quandam nostro consorte.

---

a. Read: adrezato.

2. Emanuele must have left Milan immediately after he received his letter of credence [The Duke to the King, Milan, 3 March 1466, BN, *Fonds Italien*, Cod. 1593, fol. 146], because by 11 March he had met Galeazzo Maria as the latter was leaving for Milan [Appendix, doc. IV and doc. 36, n. 1]. On the same day he received brief written instructions [BN, *Fonds Italien*, Cod. 1593, fol. 147], charging him to carry long and detailed instructions to Galeazzo Maria [Milan, 2 March 1466, BN, *Fonds Italien*, Cod. 1591, fols. 274–77] for the Count's forthcoming trip to the royal court. Galeazzo Maria was to assure the King that both Milan and Naples were ready to support him in every way. If the King asked for advice on war strategy, the Count should let his captains provide it, but if pressed, he should say something in general, "adcioché non para che ne sii in tucto ignorante." With regard to his projected marriage with Bona of Savoy, Galeazzo Maria was to say that Alberico Maletta was coming to the royal court with full powers to negotiate it. However, if the King insisted on negotiating it with him directly and on celebrating it in France, he

should obey the King, although such celebrations were customarily held at the house of the groom. He was also to urge the King to remain on friendly terms with the Count of Charolais, to whom the Duke and King Ferrante of Naples were about to send ambassadors for this purpose. Finally the Count was to notify Louis that additional Milanese troops were being made ready to be dispatched to France. Emanuele, who was to accompany Galeazzo Maria to the royal court, was also instructed to urge the King to postpone his pledge of obedience to Pope Paul II until affairs in France were settled so as to induce him to be more favorably disposed. Next Emanuele was to discuss with the King another proposed marriage between Galeazzo Maria and Marie of Burgundy, for which the ambassador received oral instructions.

3. The Duchess's instructions were never received by Emanuele [doc. 11]. They may have been intercepted along with other letters sent by the Duchess to the Milanese captains in France soon after the Duke's death [Zanone Corio to the Duchess, Lyon, 18 March 1466, *Francia*, cart. 532].

Giovan Pietro. As we are certain that Galeazzo will have informed you and sent the letters[1] which we wrote to him about the sad and lamentable passing of the late lord our consort, we have not written to you anything more; but instead, with this letter, we inform you that after the sad event nothing new has occurred here: the population of this city and all our other peoples maintain obedience, reverence, and faith toward us and our state, just as before—not the slightest disturbance of any kind has followed. Thus, we hope to God that every day things will improve in quiet and peace. From Genoa, we have received a letter of which we send you a copy, herewith enclosed, so that you may show it to the king.[2] We are taking all those measures which seem to us necessary for the safety of our peoples and state, and we have already attended to many things, although we hope that we shall not be molested nor hindered by anybody.

Emanuele de Iacopo[3] is coming to the most Christian King to communicate to him what he was instructed by our late illustrious consort, together with some other matters that we wrote to him after in letters which we sent our son Galeazzo, requesting that he forward them to Emanuele. Therefore, if it should happen that the said letters arrive there before Emanuele, we want you to open them and execute what is

3 · *The* DUCHESS OF MILAN *to*

GIOVAN PIETRO PANIGAROLA

Francia, cart. 532. Minute

Iohannepetro. Rendendone certa che Galeazo te haverà avisato et mandate le littere[1] gli havemo scripto del dolente et lacrimabile caso successo del Ill.mo quondam Signore nostro consorte, non te ne havemo scripto altro, ma per questa te avisamo che poy dicto caso, de qua non é seguito altro de novo. El populo de questa nostra cità et tutti l'altri nostri popoli sonno in quella obedientia, reverentia et fede verso nuy et Stato nostro che erano prima, et non gli é seguita più una minima novità de alcuna maynera, et cossì speramo in Dio ogni dì passarano meglio et più quiete et pacifice; da Zenoa havemo havuto littere de le quale te mandamo la copia inclusa perché la monstri ad quello S. Re.[2] Nuy attendiamo a fare tutte quelle provisione ne pareno necessarie per salveza de li populi et Stato nostro, et già havemo proveduto ad molte cose, benché però speramo non ne sarà dato né molestia, né impazo da alcuno. Emanuel de Iacopo[3] vene da la M.tà de quello Christianissimo S. Re per referirle quanto haveva in instructione dal Ill.mo quondam nostro consorte, et alcune altre cose li havemo poy nuy scripto dreto per nostre littere quale havemo mandate ad Galeazo nostro figliolo, che gli le mandi; siché se l'accadesse che dicte littere fossero presente lì, che Emanuel non li fosse, volimo le apra ti et exequischi quanto in quelle se contene. Et sopra tutto ne recomandaray ad quello Ser.mo Signore nuy,

written in them. Above all commend us, our sons, and state to that very Serene Lord as fervently as you can, making him understand that all our trust and hope are placed and rest in His Majesty, who is the only remaining comfort in midst of our great anguish.

HISTORICAL NOTES

1. The Duchess of Milan had written and sent messengers to apprise Galeazzo Maria of the death of his father, but these early letters have not been found [cf. Appendix, doc. I].

2. The disorders and revolts that often followed the death of the Dukes of Milan, partly due to the autonomist aspirations of the subject cities, as well as the relative insecurity of the recently established Sforza dynasty, led to fears of revolt, particularly in the always restive city of Genoa.

3. See doc. 2.

nostri figlioli et Stato tanto strectamente quanto possible te sarà, facendoli intendere che ogni nostra fede et speranza é posta et colocata in la M.tà Soa, la quale é quanto conforto ne sia remasto in tanto nostro affano.

Your Lordship will have learned from my last letters of the sixth and seventh of this month[1] how things stood in this kingdom. Moreover, every day I endeavor to learn if something new occurs, in which connection I inform Your Lordship that yesterday letters arrived from My Lord of Craon, who is the King's ambassador with My Lord of Charolais.[2] They say in effect that My Lord of Charolais will not give refuge or extend any assistance to the Duke of Berry, and also he will not give him his daughter in marriage, as had been discussed and negotiated.[3] Furthermore, as he promised at other times, he offers to marry His Majesty's daughter[4] and is quite willing to serve His Majesty everywhere and at any time with all means and powers at his command. My Lord of Craon assures His Majesty of all this, as he will more fully relate to him.

Today, by a special messenger, the King sent these very letters to his ambassadors in Brittany,[5] so that in light of them, they might better know how to act and obtain what the King wishes—that is, that the Duke of Brittany should not keep the Duke of Berry in his country, if the latter refuses the offer the King makes him. So the Duke of Berry, seeing that My Lord of Charolais will not give him refuge, should have even more reason to accept the agreement. I inform Your Excellency that in addition the said ambassadors have also been charged by the

4 · GIOVAN PIETRO PANIGAROLA *to the*

DUKE OF MILAN

Francia, cart. 532. Orig.

Haverà la V. Ex-tia per le ultime mie de dì VI et VII dil presente[1] inteso in che termino stavano le cose di questo Reame. Io autem quottidie mi sforzo intendere se altro de novo sopravene, donde aviso la Vostra Signoria che heri sono gionte littere di Monsignor de Crean, ambassatore di questo S. Re ad Mons. Chyaroloes,[2] continente in effecto como esso Mons.re Chyarolloes non acceptarà né darà favore a modo alchuno al Duca di Berri, et così anche non li darà soa fiola per mogliere, di che si era ragionato et si practichava.[3] Item si offere ad torre la fiola de la M.tà Soa per mogliere, como una volta ha promisso,[4] et si offere dispositissimo ad servire la prefata M.tà in ogni loco et tempo con ogni soa possanza et facultà; et di questo conclude Monsignor de Crean certifica la prefata Soa M.tà, como più a pieno luy refferirà; le quale littere questo dì la M.tà Soa per meso proprio ha mandato in Bertagna ad li soy ambassatori,[5] aciò che vedendo et intendendo queste cose, possano meglio operare et condure lo effecto che quella desydera, cioé che el Duca di Bertagna non tegna el Duca di Berri in el suo payse, quando refudi la parte che li manda ad offerire. Et hora, vedendo che Monsignor Chyaroloes non lo acceptarà, più tosto habii casone di condescendere a l'acordo. Avisando la Vostra Ex.tia che li dicti ambassatori oltra questo hanno etiam commissione da questo S. Re, et sono andati per reconfirmare la liga che fu facta fra dicto Duca di Bertagna et la M.tà

King to reconfirm the league which had been made in Normandy between the Duke of Brittany and His Majesty (as I wrote to Your Lordship),[6] [so that it will be considered] as spontaneously made without constraint in his own country, in order that no one may ever take exception to it. Furthermore, since the Duke of Brittany has no children, except an illegitimate son[7] he had from Madame de Villequier, mistress of the late King, *and the Duke wants to legitimate him and make him his heir, in this case the King offered through the said ambassadors to give one of his daughters to the Duke of Brittany's son.* His Majesty is doing this in order to continue the nascent friendship and so that the Duke of Brittany may better serve and more strictly obey, and be unchanging toward His Majesty who thus may better avail himself of him. His Majesty has also been informed that as soon as the Duke of Brittany reached his country, he immediately let his subjects know of the league he had concluded with the King and upon what terms he had settled with the latter; it seems the Duke of Brittany's subjects have greatly rejoiced and are quite pleased with such an agreement. The Duke had His Majesty informed of this consent and of the dismissal of Tanneguy du Chastel, Grand Master in Brittany, whom the King very much disliked and considered an enemy. The Duke also assured His Majesty that he intends to serve as best he can and in every way against all those whom the King at his discretion may designate.

The ambassador who went to King René and to Duke John[8] is returning and has written he is on his way back, but has informed His Majesty that Duke John is doing all he can to be in the King's favor: he has sent a sealed document written and signed personally by the Duke and with his own seal, wherein he promises with an oath to serve His Majesty against all those it may please the King to command; and promises not to attempt, favor, give his consent to or negotiate anything that may be contrary to His Majesty. Even if King René, his father, or Charles of Anjou,[9] his uncle, should turn against His Majesty, he will be contrary to them and within his powers will not let them do anything, nor consent to it, but will defend the King and guard against such situa-

Soa in Normandia, di che scrissi ad la Vostra Signoria,[6] como liga facta in el payse suo, in libero arbitrio di soa spontanea volontà et non coacto, ad ciò che may non se li possa opponere exceptione. Ulterius, essendo el Duca di Bertagna senza fioli, si non uno bastardo[7] auto da Madama de Vilchier che fo femina dil quondam Re passato, *et volendo alegiptimarlo et farlo suo herede como demostra, la prefata Maiestà per li dicti ambassatori li manda ad oferire una de soe fiole in quelo caso per darla ad esso suo fiolo; et questo fa per* meglio intertenere l'amicitia commenzata, et a fine ch'el prelibato Duca di Bertagna possi meglio et più sicuramente servire, obedire et essere stabile per la M.tà Soa, et di luy si possi meglio aydare. Insuper la M.tà Soa hé avisatta che, zonto che fo el Duca di Bertagna in el payse suo, subito fece notificare al populo la liga che haveva presa con quella, et in che termino si era assetato con la prefata M.tà Soa; di che pare el populo facesse grande allegreza et demonstratione di essere contentissimi di tale acordo. La quale contenteza etiam esso Duca ha mandato ad nottificare ad questo S. Re et avisarlo como haveva facto dare licentia ad Tanachin du Chiatel, Gran Metre di Bertagna, lo quale la M.tà Soa haveva exosissimo et lo teneva inimico; et che intende servirla a tuto suo potere in ogni cosa et contra tuti che ad quella parirà et piacerà commandare.

Ulterius, lo ambassatore andato dal Re Renato et Duca Iohanne[8] se ne ritorna, et ha scritto essere in camino per vegnire; ma avisa la M.tà Soa como el Duca Iohanne non cercha cha essere in la soa bona gratia, et ha mandato el sigillato scripto et sotoscripto di mano propria del Duca Iohanne et sigillato del suo sigiello, per lo quale el promette con sacramento servire la M.tà Soa contra tutti che quella vorà et comandarà, et non atemptare, favorire, consentire né tractare cosa alchuna contra quella; ma se el Re Renato suo patre o Carlo d'Angiò[9] suo barba facesseno contra la prefata M.tà, che luy li sarà contra et a soa possanza non li lassarà fare né li consentirà, ma defenderà et guardarà da tal caso, concludendo che la vole servire et desydera vegnire da quella. Ma più a pieno scrive esso ambassatore rafferirà a bocha, el quale fra tre o quatro giorni si aspecta, et gionto ch'el sarà, mi sforzarò avisare la Vostra Ex.tia

tions, concluding that he wants to serve His Majesty and go to him. The ambassador, who is expected in three or four days, writes that he will verbally relate more amply. As soon as the ambassador arrives, I will make every effort to inform Your Excellency of the report he will make. *I inform Your Lordship, however, that in the Court these Angevins are effecting many secret negotiations which for the moment I have not been able to discover fully; above all it is Duke John who by all means is trying to install himself in the Court.* I am doing my best to come to understand these dealings, and as your faithful servant, *I will try as much as I can to obviate them if they concern Your Lordship's interest and I will keep you informed.*

Finally concerning the provisions that are to be included in the league with the Swiss,[10] and also concerning the other things Your Highness writes to me, His Majesty has been so very busy reforming the Estates and governing this kingdom, that he has not, and does not occupy himself of other matters, but presently he says he will think things over and will give me response to everything. About the coming of the Illustrious Count Galeazzo, nothing else has been arranged and I thought it was not the case to make further insistance, but only await His Majesty's pleasure and for him to speak to me about the matter. Therefore, concerning what will be settled regarding the aforementioned things, I will inform Your Illustrious Lordship, to whom I always commend myself.

HISTORICAL NOTES

1. These dispatches have not been found [cf. Mandrot, *Dépêches*, 4:322, n. 1].

2. Georges de la Trémoille, Lord of Craon, had been sent on this mission in December 1465. He was subsequently instructed to remain at his post to promote a permanent reconciliation between the King and the Count of Charolais [ibid., 4:178, 225].

3. The marriage between Marie, daughter of the Count of Charolais, and Charles of France, Duke of Berry and younger brother of Louis XI, had

del reporto ch'el farà. *Ben aviso la S.ria Vostra che questi Angiovini fanno de molte secrete practiche in questa Corte, che per anche non ho ben potuto intendere, maxime el Duca Iohanne, el quale con ogni via cercha di vegnire a stare in Corte.* Io mi studio quanto più posso de intendere esse practiche, ad le quale sicondo el potere mio et como vostro fidele servitore, *me sforzarò obviare se concernerano l'interesse dela S.ria Vostra et del tuto l'avisarò. Ceterum, circha li capituli che se deno mettere in la ligha de Suiceri*[10] et così de le altre cose che Vostra Cel. mi scrive, la prefata M.tà hé stata tanto ocupatissima circha far reformare li Stati et provisione dà in questo Regno, che non ha atteso né attende ad altro, ma al presente dice li farà pensiero et a tuto mi farà risposta. De la venuta de lo Ill. Conte Galiazo non hé poi ordinato altro, né a me hé parso farne altra instantia, ma solo atendere el bon piacere de la prefata Soa M.tà, et che quella me ne parli. Siché di quanto sopra le predicte cose si ordinarà, ne darò aviso ad la Vostra Ill.ma Signoria, ala quale sempre me ricommando.

been discussed since 1463. The King strenuously opposed such an alliance between two leaders of the League of the Public Weal [Henri Stein, *Charles de France, frère de Louis XI* (Paris: Picard, 1921), pp. 399–403.

4. Louis XI had agreed to marry his eldest four-year-old daughter, Anne, to the Count of Charolais in a document signed on 3 November 1465. The Count's second wife, Isabelle of Bourbon, had died on 25 September 1464 [Mandrot, *Dépêches*, 4:88].

5. Jean Balue, Bishop of Évreux, and Jean de Montauban, Admiral of

France, sent in preceding month to Duke Francis II of Brittany, with whom the Duke of Berry had taken refuge a year earlier [Henri Forgeot, *Jean Balue, Cardinal d'Angers (1421?–1491)* (Paris, Bouillon, 1895), pp. 36–37].

6. In his dispatch of 11 December 1465 [Mandrot, *Dépêches*, 4:157–58], in which he had announced the agreement between the King and the Duke of Brittany, signed on 23 December 1465 [Forgeot, *Jean Balue*, p. 36].

7. Francis, Count of Vertus and of Goello, illegitimate son of the Duke of Brittany and of Antoinette de Maignelais, wife of Baron André de Villequier and former mistress of Charles VII [Mandrot, *Dépêches*, 3:139, n. 2].

8. John of Anjou, Duke of Lorraine, titular Duke of Calabria and son of René, Duke of Anjou and of Bar, Count of Provence, and titular King of Sicily. Duke John had been one of the leaders of the League of the Public Weal.

9. Charles of Anjou, Count of Maine, brother of King René and of Marie of Anjou, mother of Louis XI.

10. The projected alliance among Milan, Louis XI, and the Swiss League that Francesco Sforza had been in the process of negotiating [The Duke's instructions to Antonio de Besana, sent on this mission, 1 March 1466, BN, *Fonds Italien*, Cod. 1591, fol. 272].

PORTRAIT (1471) OF DUKE GALEAZZO MARIA SFORZA BY PIERO AND ANTONIO DEL POLLAILO. COURTESY OF THE GABINETTO FOTOGRAFICO SOPRINTENDENZA BENI ARTISTICI E STORICI DI FIRENZE.

The seventeenth of the present month at six o'clock I received Your Lordship's letter notifying me of the grave illness of the Most Illustrious Lord your father, of your departure, and of the reason for it. Having comprehended what Your Lordship wrote me, I immediately went to His Most Serene Highness the King, presented him your letter and had him understand all that was necessary; while we were speaking about this, a letter was brought to His Majesty addressed to me from Emanuele de Iacopo. It related that a Milanese citizen had arrived at Lyons, and reported that on the eighth day of this month the aforementioned Lord had left this life—this was being said publicly throughout the land. At this news His Majesty became so disturbed, unhappy, and sorrowful that he dismissed all those in the chamber. He attempted to speak to me, but he was not able to formulate what he wanted to say because of the great grief he was undergoing. He requested that I defer until this morning, for at that moment he did not know how to reply—and from what I was told last night, he did not wish to speak with anyone. Then this morning His Majesty took me aside and said to me that he could not believe that our Lord had passed from this life, for he was most certain that either the Most Illustrious Lady your mother, or Your Lordship, if it were so, would have immediately written. Nevertheless, he ordered and commissioned me to write what follows below.

5·GIOVAN PIETRO PANIGAROLA *to*

COUNT GALEAZZO MARIA SFORZA

Francia, cart. 532. Orig.

A dì XVII dil presente ad hore XXIIII ho receputo le littere de la V. S. per le quale mi avisate dil accidente ocorso alo Ill.mo S. vostro padre, de la partita vostra, et de la cagione di quella. Et inteso quanto la S. V. mi scrive, statim anday ad trovare questo Ser.mo S. Re, li presentay la vostra littera et così li feci intendere quanto fu neccessario. Et stando ad questo ragionamento fu portata ad la M.tà Soa una littera directiva a me che Emanuel de Iacop scriveva, in la quale si conteneva che a Lione era gionto uno milanese che diceva como a dì VIII dil presente el prefato S. nostro era passato di questa vita e che questo per la tera publicamente si diceva. De la qual novella la M.tà Soa monstrò essere tanta turbata, mesta et dolente che dete licentia ad tuti queli de la camera; et volendomi parlare non posse compire quello che voleva dire per el grande dolore ne haveva, pregandomi che volesse differire fino a questa matina, che alhora non mi sapeva rispondere, et per quanto mi hé stato riferto non volse heri sera parlare ad persona. Dapoy questa matina la prefata M.tà mi ha dicto a parte che non poteva credere el prefato S. nostro fosse trapassato, rendendossi certissima che la Ill.ma Madona Vostra o V. S., se così fosse, subito haveriano scritto; tuta volta mi ha dicto et commisso scrivere le infrascripte cose. Et primo li piace che la S. V. sii andata a Milanno, et lassato la gente d'arme, sì per obedire Madona vostra matre, sì etiam per obviare a molti inconvenienti che poriano

First, it pleases [the King] that Your Lordship has gone to Milan, leaving the troops behind, both in order to obey My Lady your mother, and also to obviate any difficulties that might occur. When Your Lord father's health improves, he says that he will be most happy if Your Excellency returns with the troops, and he so requests, since he greatly desires to see you. In the case, however, where it has pleased God to dispose otherwise of His Highness, he grieves and will grieve until death for such a great loss, and he reminds Your Excellency to conduct yourself with great prudence in these new circumstances, as he is most certain you will do. Since His Majesty fears that the Venetians if not publicly at least secretly are most inimical to you and might take advantage of this misfortune to make trouble and declare war against you, he would not want you in this case to safeguard and take such great care of his affairs that yours should become undone. So that if you should have any need of your troops that are in the Dauphiné, [His Majesty] is very happy and it seems correct to him that you send for them for the purpose of defending and preserving your state; this, in order to be prepared against the Venetians or whomever else might decide to make a move.[1] If you have need of troops, His Majesty offers to send you some of his, as many as you might wish and in the number requested, giving every help and favor he can, because for many reasons he is highly obligated to you. He says he intends to do so and not fail you in anything whatsoever. He affirms that he can do this because, as is manifest, he is in tranquil control of his kingdom, and in the presence of the Duke of Bourbon [Jean II], the Grand Chancellor [Guillaume Jouvenel des Ursins], the Bastard of Bourbon [Louis], and certain others, he demonstrated with efficacious phrases that he was willing to do everything for Your Lordships as he was obliged. Then he expressed his fears to me that through physicians or otherwise by means of money the Venetians may have been involved in administering some poisonous drink or food to your father. He cautioned that it would be wise to look into this.[2]

The King said, moreover, that he feared the Genoese might make trouble and cause a change in government, especially with the aid of

achadere; et megliorando el S. vostro padre, dice sarà bene contenta la Ex.tia V. ritorni con le gente d'arme et così prega, desyderando sumamente di vedervi. Quando autem̄ sia piaciuto a Dio disponere altramente de Soa Cel., il che fino ala morte li dole et dolerà di tanta perdita, dice ricorda ad la V. S. in questi principii governarsi con bona prudentia como hé certissima fareti. Et perché dubita che Venetiani, si non publice tamen secrete vostri inimicissimi, per questo caso farano qualche novità, et vi romperano guera, dice la M.tà Soa non voria però guardare et curare tanto li facti soy che se disconzasseno li vostri. Si che, se haveti bisogno de le gente d'arme vostre sono in Delfinato, hé contenta et li pare le mandiati a tore per conservatione et deffensione dil Stato vostro, et questo per essere provisto contra Venetiani o qualonche altro si movesse.[1] E se vi bisogna gente d'arme, si offere la M.tà Soa mandarvene de le soe tante quante vorete, et in quelo numero richiedereti, et così darvi ogni adiuto et favore che quela saperà et porà, perché per più rispecti hé obligatissima. Et così dice intende fare, et non manchare in cosa alchuna; et questo dice porà fare, perché come si vede hé signor pacifico dil suo regno. Et qui presente el Duca di Borbon, el gran Canzellero, Bastardo de Borbon et alcuni altri dimonstrò con efficace parole volere fare ogni cosa per la V. S. che così era obligata. Poy mi disse dubitare che per via di medici o altramente per dinari, ad instantia et opera de Venetiani, sii stato dato bevere o mangiare qualche cosa sinistra al prefato vostro padre, che in questo voliati havere aviso.[2] Ulterius dice dubitare che Ienovesi farano novitate et vorano cambiare stato, maxime havendo Venetiani sempre sostenuto quelo Arcivescovo da Campofregoso,[3] che ancora li pare V. S. habii advertenzia ad provederli in tal modo che non possono recalcitrare. Poy mi domandò che gente d'arme havevati a Milano, como vi potevati adiutare di Fiorentini et del S. Re Ferando, et in che numero. Ale quale cose rispose quelo che mi hocorse in favore dela V. S., et como mi pare comprendere con la ragione in mano, tenendo continue le cose de la V. Ex.tia propitie et favorevele, et così mi sforzarò fare per l'avenire Questo dico perché alchuni già cerchano di prevaricare la M.tà Soa, dicendo che haveriti tanto a fare che non saperiti

the Venetians who have always supported the Archbishop [Paolo] da Campofregoso.[3] So it seems wise to him that Your Lordship be careful in making provisions in such a way that they cannot be recalcitrant. Then he asked me what troops you have in Milan and what you can expect from the Florentines and from King Ferrante, and in what number. To all of this I responded what occurred to me as being favorable to Your Lordship and as seemed best to me given the situation at hand, always keeping in mind the affairs of Your Excellencies, just as I will make every attempt to maintain them auspicious and favorable for the future. I say this because already certain individuals are trying to shift His Majesty's position, by saying that you would have so much to do that you would not know where to turn next. They, especially the Angevins, are already making very sinister statements in my presence, so that I have faithfully wanted to notify Your Lordship.

In addition, today I have learned from a good source that on the evening of the fifteenth of this month seven Venetian horsemen dressed in green passed through Bourges, riding in haste toward Anjou to Duke John. I notified the King of this, and from what he tells me, he will try as best he can to find out and ascertain what they have come to do; as soon as he knows, he will notify me.

Regarding my remaining here, as Your Excellency writes me to continue as in the past, etc., [I reply that] for my part I have decided to live and die as an obedient subject and servant of Your Lordship; if not as well as you deserve, then at least with as much faith and devotion as I am capable of, I will execute your orders and do as in the past and even better if I am able.

There are many things to be written about news here and by way of answer to that which our Most Illustrious Lord [Francesco Sforza] wrote, but in order to send this courier quickly on his way, and also impeded by the great grief caused me by the unforeseen event, I do not have time to write. So I ask Your Excellency to pardon me, for I will send further word with another courier.

Lastly, just this hour the King has shown and given to me the en-

onde tornare el capo; et già dicono di sinistre parole, et in mia presentia, maxime Angiovini; si che fidelmente ne ho voluto avisare V. S. Insuper hogie mi hé stato riferto da bon loco che adì XV da sera dil presente passono a Borges VII cavali di Venetiani vestiti di verde, quali se ne vanno batando in Angiò dal Duca Iohanne. Il che ho notificato ad questo S. Re, el quale farà con bon modo, sicondo mi ha dicto, per scrutare et cercare di intendere quello che sarano venuti a fare, et subito di quelo intenderà me ne avisarà. Circha el mio romagnire di qua, como la Ex.tia V. mi scrive, et che faza como per el passato etc., quanto a me ho deliberato vivere et morire subdito et servitore de la V. S. et obedirla; et se non così bene como ad quela apartegneria, cum fede tamen et devotione mi sforzarò sicondo el mio picol ingegno exequire li soy comandammenti, et fare como per el passato et meglio si saperò. Molte cose haveria a scrivere de le novele ocorono di qua, et risposta di quelo mi ha scripto lo Ill.mo S. nostro, ma per mandare questo cavalaro batando, et impedito dal grande dolore ho di questo inopinato caso, non ho tempo ad scrivere; perdonemi adonche la V. Ex.tia che per uno altro el farò. Postremo questa hora el S. Re mi ha monstrata et data la alligata littera,[4] quale scrive ad la V. Cel. et mi ha commisso la mandi volando, aspectando cum extremo desyderio sentire ch'el prefato S. vostro padre sii megliorato, o se pure altramente sii successo, che fine prenderano quele cose di là, perché dice non intende manchare di quanto saperà et porà in conservatione et bene de la V. S. Qui si dice de molte novele, maxime che Bartolamio da Bergamo[5] ha de molte gente et de novo fa gente, et più che el Marchese di Monferato fa el simile, et che sono vostri inimicissimi et che vi voleno fare guera. Et queste cose sono state referte ad la prefata M.tà, ad la quale, domandandomene, ho dicto quelo che mi hé parso, et factola chiara che quando el S. vostro padre manchi, sareti pacifico signore, et non tantum bastante ad batere questi, ma etiam de li altri con lo adiuto deli vostri parenti et maxime de la M.tà Soa. Starò atento di quanto intenderò segua, et sicondo che Dio me inspirarà mi governarò, dando dil tuto notizia ad la prefata V. Ex.tia; né a me hé parso richiedere altra cosa né dimonstratione ad questo S. Re in favore

closed letter[4] which he writes to Your Highness, ordering me to send it as quickly as possible. With great desire, he expects to hear that the Lord, your father, has improved or (if indeed it is otherwise) what shape matters will take there, because he says in so far as humanly possible he has no intention of sparing anything for Your Lordship's welfare and preservation. Here, there are many rumors, especially that Bartolomeo da Bergamo[5] has many troops and is enlisting more; also that the Marquis of Monferrat is doing the same; and that they are most inimical to you and wish to wage war against you. These things have been related to His Majesty, who asked me about them. I responded what seemed best to me and made clear to him that even if your father were no longer with you, you would succeed peacefully and be capable not only of beating back these but also others with the help of your relatives and especially with that of His Majesty. I will be alert to learn what follows in this regard and I will conduct myself as God inspires me, always giving full notification to Your Excellency. It has not seemed correct to me to ask anything else of the King in your favor, until Your Lordship writes to me about it, even though under the appearance of goodwill and of love for you, many have advised me to do so. However, not knowing otherwise nor having other instructions, as I said, I did not want to reveal any need on the part of Your Excellency, to whom I always commend myself as a good subject and faithful servant eagerly awaiting some good news.

HISTORICAL NOTES

1. It was widely feared that the death of Francesco Sforza would have provoked a resumption of another struggle among various claimants for the succession in the Duchy, among whom the Venetians were considered to be the most likely to attack because of their well-known dislike of the Sforza. Of these claims, see Fabio Cusin, "L'Impero e la successione degli Sforza ai Visconti," *Arch. storico lombardo*, new ser., 1 (1936): 6–10, 54–57.

2. This was no idle speculation. The Venetian Council of Ten had discussed several times and accepted some proposals to have Francesco Sforza

vostro, se prima V. S. non m'el scrive, benché molti soto spetie di bene et di amarve me habiano voluto consigliare el contrario; ma io, como ho dicto, non ho voluto monstrare habiati bisogno, non sapendolo né havendo altra commissione da la prelibata V. Ex.tia, a la quale suo vero subdito et servitore fidele sempre me ricomando, expectando cum desyderio qualche bona novella.

assassinated both before and after he became Duke of Milan [Introduction, p. xli].

3. Archbishop Paolo Campofregoso, former Doge of Genoa, who had been expelled by Francesco Sforza soon after the latter was granted the city in fief by Louis XI at the end of 1463 [Sorbelli, *Francesco Sforza a Genoa,* pp. 95–100].

4. See Appendix, doc. III.

5. Bartolomeo Colleoni, leading mercenary captain in the service of Venice.

By means of the courier Boffa, who left at a gallop on the eighteenth of the present month, I advised Your Excellency of what was taking place here. On the twentieth of this month the noble Giovanni Andrea Tizzoni arrived here, and he told me the reason for his coming and showed me Your Excellency's instructions,[2] fully explaining all to me. While in the midst of doing this, we received letters from Lyons written by Zanone Corio and Giovanni Bianchi,[3] which told of the bitter and sorrowful event of the death of the late Most Illustrious Lord your father. They say it took place on the eighth of this month at about midday. They further notified me that a servant of Franceschino Nori[4] had met Your Highness at Borghetto,[5] and two leagues ahead of you [had met] *the Abbot of Casanova and another Savoyard lord*[6] *who were going to close the passes to Your Excellency. Having arrived at Chambéry,*[7] *he found that this was true, and was told by the Illustrious Madame of Savoy,* among other things, *that she wanted to possess the state of Milan.* Wherefore, out of fear *for the life of Your Lordship,* I immediately notified His Most Serene Highness of these things, entreating His Majesty to take good and mature counsel in the whole matter, and apply those remedies that seemed best to him. I urged him with the best and most courteous language at my command to hold Your Excellency

6·GIOVAN PIETRO PANIGAROLA *to the*

DUKE OF MILAN[1]

Francia, cart. 532. Orig.

Per el Boffa cavalaro, quale partì a li XVIII dil presente et se **ne** viene volando, avisay la V. Ex.tia di quanto achadeva. A li XX dil presente sopragionse qui el nobile Iohanne Andrea Tizone, el quale narrandomi la casone de la venuta soa, et monstrandomi le soe instructione de la V. Ex-tia[2] ad plenum mi explicò el tuto. Essendo in questo tale acto, in quello instanti zonseno littere da Lione da Zanone Coyro et Iohanne Blanco,[3] continente l'acerbo et doloroso caso del obito dil quondam Ill.mo S. vostro padre, che dicono essere stato ad li octo dil presente, circha mezo giorno; et più mi avisano che uno servitore di Franceschino Nori[4] haveva scontrato la V. Cel. al Borgetto,[5] et davanti da quela circha doe lege *l'Abbate de Casanova et uno altro Signor Savoino,*[6] *che andavano per serrare li passi ad la S.ria Vostra. Et venuto ad Chiamberit*[7] *trovò così essere vero, et che la illustre Madama de Savoia li disse che voleva havere quelo Stato de Millano et* alchune altre parole. Donde statim per el dubio poteva *ocorere de la persona de la S.ria Vostra*, statim nottificay queste cose ad questo Ser.mo S. Re, pregando Soa M.tà volesse avere sopra tuto bono et maturo aviso, facendoli quelle provisione li parerà. Et li supplicay si dignasse havere per riccomandata la V. Ex.tia et el suo Stato como di vero, fidele et affectionato suo servitore, aducendoli quelle bone et humane parole che **mi furono**

and your state in his good graces, since you are his true, faithful, and most affectionate servant.

First His Majesty was as extremely upset as one might possibly imagine when he heard of the death of your father, for which he grieves greatly and each day continues to do so bitterly, saying that he has lost the best friend that he ever had or could wish to have in the world. It seems to him that fortune was running very much against him, having deprived him of so great a lord with whom, had he lived yet another two years, he would have been able and was about to do many great things. *His Majesty showed great anger and indignation toward Madame of Savoy and the Abbot of Casanova, etc., saying that it seemed to him a very foolhardy and grave blunder, done thoughtlessly. He in no way intended to suffer it* because it would be the greatest dishonor that ever had befallen a King of France, if one who in time of great need had come to the aid of His Majesty were recompensed in such a way for his services, receiving for them damage, opprobrium, and detriment. His Majesty added that Your Lordship can be certain that he wishes to help, defend, and preserve you and your state with his troops, his state, his powers, and every faculty, no less than he would his own kingdom. *He would first intervene himself in person in order to* prevent this; he said so many good things in your favor and to the effect of maintaining you *in the state of Milan, that in truth be made a very great show of his mind in the presence of the Duke of Bourbon and the Bastard of Bourbon.*[8] These two, in my presence, said that His Majesty was obliged to do much more if this were possible, and he should seek every way *of supporting Your Lordship. For their part they offered their own persons and their every means in order to facilitate the passage of your troops, make war against the Duke of Savoy,* and every other effort within their power. It seems to them that His Majesty must and can serve you in this difficulty, sending ambassadors throughout Italy to make known to all the world that he wishes to preserve Your Lordship, giving in this manner great aid and support to your state. Having spoken in this fashion for a long time, I reminded His Majesty that it might please

possibile. La M.tà Soa primo fo tanto turbata quanto dire si potesse de la morte dil prefato S. vostro padre, de la quale grandemente si ne hé condoluta, et ogni dì si condole amaramente, dicendo havere perduto el miglior amico che may essa Soa M.tà ha auto né crede haverà ad questo modo;[a] et parerli che la fortuna li adversi molto, havendola privata de uno tanto Signore, con lo mezo dil quale se doy anni ancora fosse vivuto, intendeva et era per fare di molte cose grande. *De Madama de Savoia et del Abate de Casanova etc., la M.tà Soa se mostrò molto turbata et indignata contra de queli, dicendo parerli ben cose legiere et enorme et facte senza consiglio; el che ad modo alcuno non intendeva sofrire,* perché saria la magiore vergogna che may havesse Re di Franza, che essendo venuto ad li servitii de la M.tà Soa et in lo suo extremo bisogno, dil suo servitio fosse talmente recompensato, ricevendone danno, obprobio et detrimento; subiongendo la M.tà Soa che sii certa la S. V. et così vole adiutare, defendere et conservare quella et el suo Stato con le soe gente d'arme, Stato, facultate et ogni soa potentia, non mancho cha questo proprio Regno. Et *ananti vegniria con la propria persona che* così non fusse. Et qui disse tante bone parole in vostro favore et per volervi mantenire *in quelo Stato de Millano, che invero fece grande dimonstratione del animo suo al Duca di Barbone et Bastardo de Borbon*[8] *che lì erano presenti*; li quali, me audiente, dissero la M.tà Soa essere tenuta fare molto più anche se fusse possibile, et dovere cerchare con ogni via *de mantegnire la S.ria Vostra. Et dal canto loro si oferivano con la loro persona et facultate ad fare passare le vostre gente, fare guerra ad Duca di Savoia et ogni* altra cosa a loro possibile. Et parerli che la M.tà Soa vi debbia et possa servire ad questo tracto, *et mandare ambassatori per tuta Italia, facendo noto ad tuto'l mondo che vole mantegnire la S.ria Vostra, et con questa via darà grande favore et adiuto ad Stato vostro.* Et havendo in questa forma gran pezo ventilato, io ricorday ad la M.tà Soa *che li piacesse fare bene guardare Filippo Mons., quale intendeva voleva rellassare, ad fine che se la S.ria Vostra havesse auti disturbo* alcuno, con questa via si potesseno batere. Essa M.tà statim *mandò ad*

---

a. Read: mondo.

him to have My Lord Filippo, whom he had intended to release, well guarded, so that if Your Lordship had been in any way molested in this manner it could be countered. His Majesty immediately ordered My Lord Filippo, who was nearby, to be fetched; last night he was brought here and he is being well guarded. He also ordered that the son of the Duke of Savoy[9] be brought here from Amboise. The King said he will never release them until Your Lordship is in a safe place, and he made many minatory and injurious statements against the Savoyards. Finally he told me to make a memorandum of what was to be done, and ordered me to appear the next day before the Council, where he wished to make provisions for everything and not be lacking in any way. My Lord, I have worked toward a good end in the above matters and I said what seemed to be necessary as faithfully as possible for Your Excellency's welfare; I will continue to do so in the future, giving notification of all that transpires to Your Most Illustrious Lordship, to whom I always commend myself.

HISTORICAL NOTES

1. Galeazzo Maria Sforza. Henceforth all dispatches are addressed to him or jointly to him and the Duchess.

2. Actually these instructions were drafted by the Marquis Giovanni Pallavicino da Scipione, left in command of the Milanese troops in Dauphiné, and by Pietro Francesco Visconti, another leading Milanese condottiere, a few days after Galeazzo Maria's departure. [Two dispatches by Giovanni Pallavicino to the Dukes, Beaurepaire, 21 March 1466, *Francia*, cart. 532]. These instructions have not been found, and Tizzoni's two surviving dispatches from the royal court [Orléans 21 and 25 March 1466, ibid., cart. 532] give no details about his mission. The purpose of his mission, however, can be gathered from doc. 7.

3. Corio and Bianchi were attached to the Milanese expeditionary force in Dauphiné as paymasters and provisioners. The news of Francesco Sforza's death reached Lyon by 18 March [Zanone Corio to the Duchess, Lyon, 18 March 1466, ibid., cart. 532].

tore Filippo Mons., quale era qui apresso. Heri sera fu qui menato et lo fa ben guardare. Così etiam ha mandato ad pigliare ad Ambosa el fiolo del Duca de Savoia,[9] *li quali dice non lassarà mai fino che la S.ria Vostra sia in loco sicuro, et più disse molte parole minatorie et execretive contra essi Savoini. Infine me disse che* facesse un pocho di memoria de le cose sariano ad fare, et domane mi trovasse con quela in Consiglio dove vole ad tuto dar provisione, né li voleva mancare in cosa alchuna. Io, Signor mio, ad bon fine mi sono operato in le sopradicte cose et ho dicto quele parole mi sono parse necessarie, fidelmente, per bene dela V. Ex.tia; così mi sforzarò fare per l'avenire, dando dil tuto notizia ad la V. Ill.ma S., ad la quale sempre me ricommando.

4. Franceschino di Francesco Nori was on the staff of the Medici Bank in Lyon [Raymond de Roover, *The Rise and Decline of the Medici Bank, 1397–1494* (New York: Norton, 1966), p. 310].

5. I am unable to identify this small locality, evidently situated between Susa and the Mont Cenis pass.

6. Agostino Corradi di Lignana, Abbot of Casanova, was an experienced diplomat frequently used by the Savoyard dukes. He was also a persistent enemy of the Sforza, as this episode demonstrates. The other Savoyard lord was Hugonin Aleman, Lord of Arbent [Ferdinando Gabotto, *Lo Stato sabaudo da Amedeo VIII ad Emanuele Filiberto*, vol. 1 (1461–1467) (Turin, 1892), p. 96].

7. Chambéry in Savoy was at this time the habitual residence of the Savoyard court.

8. Louis de Bourbon, son of Duke Charles de Bourbon and of Jeanne de Bournan, and thus half brother of the present Duke of Bourbon, Jean II. A

month earlier he had married Louis XI's illegitimate daughter, Jeanne [*Lettres*, 2:233–34, n. 2].

9. Charles, Prince of Piedmont, ten-year-old first son of Duke Amédée IX of Savoy, who was being raised under the tutelage of Louis XI.

PORTRAIT (1465?) OF DUCHESS BIANCA MARIA VISCONTI SFORZA, ATTRIBUTED TO
BONIFACIO BEMBO. COURTESY OF THE PINACOTECA DI BRERA, MILAN.

This morning His Most Serene Highness the King held council in the house of My Lord of Dunois, going there personally. After much discussion, the Duke of Bourbon, My Lord of Dunois, and all the others said that His Majesty ought to give all help and succor to Your Lordship for the preservation of your state, being obligated to you in many respects. [He ought] to make every demonstration before both God and the world that this is his intention, and that he does not wish to suffer that violence, ignominy, or wrong be done to you. They therefore immediately decided to dispatch the Quartermaster of Cavalry,[1] who is a good friend of Your Lordship, to the Illustrious Madame of Savoy; and he leaves this very hour with letters and with instructions from His Majesty. [He is to say] *that if they had detained Your Lordship,[2] as is feared, then they must immediately release you without fail,* for it is incredible that they presume so much and that they dare to do things that are so infamous; he is to notify them that for the preservation and welfare of Your Excellency, His Majesty intends at this time to engage his realm, state, possessions, and even his own person, being determined not to suffer such a wrong or dishonor. In like manner the King writes to the Illustrious Duke of Savoy and to his Council, requesting that they give help, favor, and aid to all supporters of Your Lordship, and that they not do anything at all which might give cause for war to His Majesty.

7·GIOVAN PIETRO PANIGAROLA *to the*

DUKE OF MILAN

Francia, cart. 532. Orig.

Questa matina el Ser.mo S. Re ha tenuto Consiglio in caxa di Mons.re de Donoes et la M.tà Soa in persona li hé venuta. Drieto ad molti ragionamenti el Duca di Borbon, Mons.re de Dunoes et tuti hanno dicto che la M.tà Soa debbe dare ogni adiuto et favore, et per più rispecti essere obligata ad la V. S. et conservatione dil Stato vostro, et fare ogni dimonstratione a Dio e al mondo che così sia soa intentione, né volere patire che violentia, ignominia o torto li sia facto. Et per questo statim hé stato spazato el Marescalco de Logis,[1] che hé bono amico de la V. S., per andare da la Ill. Madama de Savoya. Et questa hora parte con littere e commissione de la prefata M.tà, *che se ha arestato la S.ria Vostra,*[2] *come se dubita, subito ve rellasse senza exceptione* alcuna; maravigliandosi forte di tale presomptione et che ardiscano fare cose così enorme, nottificandoli che per conservatione et bene de la V. Ex.tia la prefata Soa M.tà intende ad questo poncto meterli el Reame, Stato, beni et la propria persona, et non volere patire tanto torto né dishonore. Et così scrive ad lo Ill. Duca di Savoya et al suo Consiglio, pregandoli che ad tuti queli de la V. S. vogliano dare adiuto, favore et subsidio, et non fare cosa per la quale Soa M.tà habii casone di farli guera. E così di bocha etiam esso Marescalco ha ad dire di molte altre parole, sicondo che vederà la materia richieda.[3] Ritornato che sia esso Marescalco et habiamo altre novelle, hé ordinato che el Senescalco de Poitò, quale hé

The Quartermaster is also to add verbally whatever seems fit as the situation develops.[3]

As soon as the Marshall returns, bringing additional news, it has been decided that the Seneschal of Poitou [Louis de Crussol], who is a man of authority and reputation *in Savoy, go there as an ambassador and give the Savoyards to understand that His Majesty intends to preserve Your Lordship in the state of Milan. To that end they should give you every help and support possible. If any changes or preparations of troops are made in Savoy, this ambassador is to see on behalf of the King that they withdraw and not do anything against Your Lordship, as* I will more particularly notify you *when the ambassador is about to leave.*

Regarding the requests I made of His Majesty *to send* [envoys] *and write to the rulers of Italy, as outlined in the instructions*[4] of Giovanni Andrea [Tizzoni], they seem quite correct to the King; as does *the sending of three hundred lances in support of Your Lordship. He is also willing to let your troops return to Milan and provide them with an escort to lead them across the mountains.* Just now he has ordered a morning meeting of the Council *to decide which road will be best for the passage of the troops and who will be a proper escort*; and also to *choose persons of rank to send as ambassadors to the Venetians, the Duke of Modena [Borso* d'Este], the Marquis *of Mantua* [Ludovico Gonzaga], *the Marquis of Monferrat, the Florentines, the Pope* [Paul II], *and to other rulers of* Italy. *I think there will be great difficulty at Court in finding* such individuals because there are few of them *who are not dependent upon Brittany, the Angevins, or their allies*; nevertheless I will bend every effort to keep my eyes open so that *no one comes there who has inclinations other than toward the welfare of Your Lordship and of My Lord the King of France. I will advise Your Lordship of the decisions taken and will try to have the troops in the Dauphiné cross over as soon as possible as you ordered and mandated* Giovanni Andrea; I will keep Your Excellency advised of everything.

I mention further *that His Majesty the King of France has* also *written to My Lord of Charolais regarding the death of your father and*

homo di auctorità et di reputatione *in Savoia, vada delà per ambassatore ad fare intendere ali Savoini che la M.tà Soa intende conservare la S.ria Vostra in el Stato de Millano, che vi vogliano dare favore et farve ogni spala possibile. Et questo ambassatore haverà per parte del Re di Franza ad operare, che se in Savoia sarà facto mutatione o aparechiato gente, che se retirano adrieto et non fazano contra la S.ria Vostra,* come più distinctamente avisarò quela *quando esso ambassatore sarà per partire.*

Insuper le domande ho facto ad la M.tà Soa *che mandi et scriva ale potentie de Italia, come in la instructione* de Iohanne Andrea si contiene,[4] gli sono parse honestissime e così *de mandare trecento lanze in favore de la S.ria Vostra, et essere contenta che la gente de quela retorneno ad Millano provedendo de persone che le conducha oltra li monti.* Siché questa hora hé ordinato di trovarsi da matina al Consiglio *per disponere qual camino sarà miglior per el passare dele gente, et chi sarà bono per condurle, et* così a dar forma *de mandare ambassatori ad Venetiani, Duca de Modena, de Mantoa, Marchese de Monferrato, Fiorentini, Papa et altri Signori de* Italia, et avisare *de persone digne; in el quale caso cognosco grande dificultà in questa Corte perché* poche sono persone degne, *che non habiano dependentia da Bertagna, Angiovini o da loro alligati.* Tutavolta mi sforzarò aprire gli ochii ad ciò *che delà non vegna persona che penda altrove cha al bene dela S.ria Vostra et de questo Signor Re de Franza; et de che si concluderà ne avisarò la S.ria Vostra, operando più presto che serà possibile che le gente che haveti in Delfinato passeno da delà, secondo che haveti ordinato et comisso ad esso* Iohanne Andrea, dando dil tuto adviso ad la prelibata V. Ex.tia. Ulterius aviso quela etiam *che questo Signor Re de Franza ha scrito ad Mons. Chiaroloes dela morte del Signor vostro padre, et intendere che li Savoini cercano di farvi molestia che lo prega se loro o altri cercassero con lui liga, che non li voglia consentire* né darli favore, adiuto né socorso per amore de la M.tà Soa, la quale intende mantenere et conservare quello Stato come se fusse suo proprio Regno. Et in pari forma ha *mandato a dire al Duca de Bertagna, et* scrito ad li ambassatori de la M.tà Soa che di là ritornavano, se bene fosseno in camino che torneno indrieto per fare questa ambassata. Et

telling him that the Savoyards are trying to cause you trouble; he entreats him that if they or others were to seek an alliance with him, that he not consent to it nor give them help or aid of any kind out of love for His Majesty, who intends to maintain and preserve the state [of Milan] as if it were his own kingdom. He has similarly *sent word to the Duke of Brittany*, ordering his ambassadors who were returning [from that Court] to turn back in order to perform this mission. He says he does this because, if in the meantime the aforementioned lords were approached *by the Venetians, the Duke of Savoy or by others regarding some alliance, they would have reason to avoid it*, having been previously advised.

Further, *regarding the request Your Lordship wished to make of the King on the subject of a loan of fifty thousand écus (as* mentioned in Giovanni Andrea's instructions), *up until now we have not said anything about this, since we feared making too many requests at one time and not being able to obtain them; so we have postponed that request to a good end and in order to bring about the effect desired by* Your Excellency if possible. Once the aforementioned matters have taken shape, we will speak [about the loan] *in the best manner we know and can find, giving immediate notification of the answer we receive to* Your Most Illustrious Lordship, to whom I always commend myself.

HISTORICAL NOTES

1. Josselin du Bois, Bailli des Montagnes d'Auvergne and Quartermaster of Cavalry, usually called Rosolino by the Italians [Vaesen, *Lettres*, 2:91–92, n. 2].

2. On his return home from Dauphiné, Galeazzo Maria, traveling in disguise, with a few companions, including Count Gaspare da Vimercate, had been assaulted (14 March) by a mob of peasants on the road to Susa, and had taken refuge in the nearby Abbey of Saint Peter in the locality of Novalesa in Piedmont. Although two leading Savoyard nobles—Agostino Corradi di Lignana, Abbot of Casanova, and Hugonin Aleman—had been involved in

questo dice fa, che se in questo mezo dicti Signori fusseno practichati *da Venetiani, Duca di Savoia o altri de fare liga alcuna, non habiano casone de farla* essendone prima advisati.

Ceterum, circa la requesta che la S.ria Vostra voria si facesse al Re de Franza che li prestasse scuti cinquantamillia, come ad Iohanne Andrea ha commisso, *fino qui non ne habiamo anche facto parola, dubitando de non domandare tropo cose ad uno tracto et non poterle obtenere. Et per questo si hé sopraseduto ad bon fine et per tirare la domanda ad l'efecto de* la prelibata V. Ex.tia se possibile serà; ma dato forma ad le sopradicte cose, ne parlaremo *con quelo migliore modo saperemo et poremo, dando statim noticia dela risposta che haveremo ad la* prelibata Ill.ma V. S., a la quale sempre me ricomando.

this incident, it was and still is not known with certainty whether they had acted independently or at the orders of the Duchess of Savoy [Introduction, pp. xliii–xliv, and next doc. 8].

3. The envoy arrived at Chambéry on 28 March. In addition to the instructions outlined here, he was charged to request the following: safe passage through Savoyard territory for the Milanese troops returning to Milan and for a force of two thousand horse, which the King wished to send to Milan in case of need; a Savoyard envoy to accompany Josselin du Bois to Milan to express regrets for the incident; the surrender of the Duke's assailants, to be

escorted to Milan for suitable punishment [Ziliolo Oldoini, Milanese ambassador in Savoy, to the Duke, Chambéry, 28 March 1466, Francia, cart. 532, published by P. Magistretti, "Galeazzo Maria Sforza prigione nella Novalesa," *Arch. storico lombardo*, ser. 2, 6 (1889): 805-7].

4. See preceding doc. 6, n. 2.

From my last letters of the twentieth, twenty-first, and twenty-second[1] of this month, Your Excellency will have heard how deeply the King was upset and each day grieved even more for the loss of the Most Illustrious Lord, your husband, thinking that he will never be able to find such a singular friend. From the same letters you will also have learned of the preparations made to send the Quartermaster of Cavalry to Savoy, and of other actions contemplated if the Most Illustrious Lord, your son and new Duke, had been molested or detained on his journey. On the twenty-second of this month I, Emanuele,[2] arrived here, and just then we received the sad and sorrowful news from Chambéry and Lyon[3] which heaped grief upon grief; that is, that at Novalesa your son had been arrested by the Abbot of Casanova and by My Lord of Arbent [Hugonin Aleman], and that later Magnificent Count Gaspare [da Vimercate] had also been arrested together with his retinue, by the above mentioned lords.

We immediately communicated the event to the King, begging him to make appropriate provisions and not allow that such an affront be made to you. The King, hardly being able to speak and weeping, answered that that was the bitterest and worst piece of news he had ever had, and so afflicted was he that not even when he was in Paris in danger for his own life and for his kingdom,[4] was he so oppressed with grief

8 · EMANUELE DE IACOPO *and*

GIOVAN PIETRO PANIGAROLA *to the*

DUCHESS OF MILAN

BN, Fonds Italien, Cod. 1593, fols. 231–32v. Orig.

Per le ultime mie de dì XX, XXI et XXII[1] dil presente haverà la V. Ex.tia inteso quanto questo S. Re era turbato et ogni dì più si condoleva de la perdita di lo Ill.mo S. vostro consorte, parendoli che may non recuperarà un tale singulare amico; per quelle etiam haverà inteso le preparatione si erano facte ad mandare in Savoya el Marescalcho de Logis et così le altre si facevano, se lo Ill.mo S. vostro fiolo, novo Duca, in l'andare suo havesse auto disturbo o fosse arestato. Ad li XXII di questo zonsi in questa tera, io Emanuel,[2] et in quella hora hebbemo la trista et dolente novela da Chiamberì et da Lione,[3] che multiplicò dolore a dolore, cioé che ala Novaresa esso S. vostro fiolo era stato arestato per l'Abbate di Casanova et Mons.re Darban et deinde el Mag.co Conte Gasparo con li soy similiter era preso per li sopranominati. La qual cosa statim nontiata ad la M.tà dil prelibato S. Re, suplicandoli de provisione oportuna et non volere sofrire esserve facto tale et tanta iniuria, la M.tà Soa non potendo quasi parlare et piangendo rispose questa essere la più trista et più cativa novela che may havesse né de la quale più si dolesse, adeo che quando era a Parise in periculo de la persona et del Regno[4] non si trovasse pegio contenta che sia al presente, et volerli ley medexima andare in persona et meterli Stato, Reame et ogni soa possanza per la liberatione del p. to S. vostro fiolo. Et post multa fece congregare el Consiglio in el quale stetemo fino ad nocte scura, et essendo

as he was now. He said he meant to go personally and stake his state, realm, and all his power for the liberation of your son. After much discussion, the King assembled the [Royal] Council, where we remained till late at night.

Following especially the opinion of My Lord of Dunois (who showed himself very much a partisan of Your Ladyship) and also that of the Duke of Bourbon, the unanimous conclusion was as follows: for the honor, welfare, and advantage of the Crown of France and so that perpetual infamy should not taint the kingdom for the fact that such a lord, having come in aid of the Crown in time of dire need should be treated and rewarded in such a manner, it seemed to them that the King ought in this case to employ all his powers and make such a show of strength against the Savoyards that memory of this event might remain as an exemplum for all time. The Duke of Bourbon and the Bastard of Bourbon offered to go personally with their subjects and with all their forces anywhere it might be necessary without sparing themselves in any way, with as much enthusiasm and love as if it were for their blood brother or father.

Your Excellency would not believe to what extent the other lords of the Council were supportive, and how day and night they are attentive to arrangements that are being made. We would never have imagined such dismay and demonstration of grief in this court.

In fact, the King began to speak with as much dignity as he could, recollecting the help he had received from the late Most Illustrious Lord your husband, from Your Ladyship, and from the Most Illustrious new Duke: the obligation he had toward them, their kinship, his duty, and the many other compelling reasons which called for His Majesty to lay down his life for your son's defense and liberation. With all this, he confirmed what these lords had done and said; he would postpone all other state affairs and pursue this undertaking, since we had already reminded him that this emergency required celerity and men of high reputation. That very instant, the Seneschal of Poitou was ordered to mount a horse and ride to the Illustrious Madame of Savoy bearing a

per ogniuno generalmente concluso, maxime per Mons.re de Dunoes, che si hé monstrato molto partesano de la V.S., e così per el Duca di Borbon che per honore, bene et utile de la Corona di Franza et aciò che questa perpetuale infamia non rimanesse ad questo Regno che uno tanto Signore venuto in socorso de la Corona et in lo suo extremo bisogno fosse talmente tractato et remunerato, gli pareva la p.ta M.tà havesse in questo caso ad exponere ogni soa potentia et fare tal dimonstratione contra Savoyni che in ogni tempo rimanesse memoria et exemplo di tal caso; offerendo essi Duca di Borbon et Bastardo di Borbon loro proprie persone, loro subditi et possanza ad andare in qualonche loco sia neccessario et non sparmirse in cosa alcuna cum tanta affectione et amore che se fusse stato per loro fratelo carnale o padre. Così etiam non poria la V. Ex.tia credere quanto li altri Signori di Consiglio siano stati propitii e dì et nocte siano vigilanti a le expeditione si fanno, et comunamente in questa corte non haveriamo may existimato ogniuno stesse così smarito como fanno et facesseno tanta dimonstratione di dolore. In effecto la p.ta M.tà commenzò a parlare tanto dignamente quanto fu possibille, ricordando li servitii facti ad quella per el quondam Ill.mo S. vostro consorte, V.S. et lo Ill.mo S. Duca novo, l'obligo haveva ad quelle, el parentato, el debito suo et molte altre rasone, che constrenzevano la M.tà Soa dovere morire in la defensione et rellassatione del p.to vostro fiolo, confirmando quanto essi Signori hanno facto et dicto; et volere postposto ogni altra cosa di questo Regno seguitare la impresa, essendo ricordato per noy questo inopinato caso richiedere celerità et homeni di reputazione. Ipso instanti fu ordinato et montò a cavalo el Senescalco di Poytò per andare da la Ill. Madama di Savoya con littera di mano de la p.ta M.tà, et cum commissione che prega quela subito fazi rellassare esso Duca vostro fiolo et non li volia fare tanta vergogna; se lo relassa, farali piacere et el debito suo quanto che non, li notifica meterà in mano et possanza de la V. Ex.tia el Principo di Piemonte, suo primogenito, et Filipo Monsignor; et ulterius li desfida la guera, procedendoli fino a la totale desfatione di essi Savoyni, se ben li dovesse consumare la mità del suo Regno, et di questo ne sii certa. Siché consyderi bene et guardi

letter in the King's own hand, requesting her to have the Duke, your son, released at once and thus avoid causing him such an insult. If she does free him, the King will be very grateful to her and she will have done her duty; otherwise, he is to notify her that His Majesty will deliver her first born, the Prince of Piedmont, and My Lord Filippo to Your Excellency. In addition, he will declare war against her and will continue it until the complete defeat of the Savoyards, even if this should mean the loss of half his realm—of this she may be sure. Therefore, she had better reconsider and see that things do not go too far, as she might repent when it is too late. At this point, His Majesty, very angry, repeatedly swore he would rather have his arm broken in a thousand pieces, or that Madame of Savoy take the Dauphiné from him rather than such an outrage be done to the Duke, your son. If his two daughters[5] and Her Serene Highness the Queen were dead, he would not be in more evil humor than he is now. The King prayed God never to give him consolation if he should not at once personally go to war in Savoy, engaging all his power and dying in the enterprise until he rescued his brother-in-law, in case Madame of Savoy should impede his release. The King extends heartfelt condolences for the sorrow Your Ladyship must feel in this matter, as you will be able to see from his letter herewith enclosed.[6] He says he can well go personally to Savoy because he feels secure with regard to My Lord of Charolais, the Duke of Brittany, and even the English. In fact, an envoy of the Earl of Warwick [Richard Neville] was here to negotiate a truce,[7] so that this week the King hopes to be secure from this quarter and will be better able to provide what is needed. Thus the Seneshal of Poitou is going at full speed; we spoke to him and offered him what we thought necessary, as he is the best person the King might send, for whom Madame [of Savoy] will do even more than for the King himself—he has many friends and is very well thought of in Savoy, and thus we hope he may have success. Furthermore, His Majesty has written to My Lord of Comminges,[8] Marshal of France, in Bordeaux for him to go without losing a moment to the Dauphiné with three or four thousand crossbowmen of Gascony. Besides this, we

bene ad non lassare procedere la cosa tanto inanzi, che poy se ne repentischa, perchè poy li valerà pocho. Et qui la M.tà Soa turbatissima giurò et sacramentò che amaria più tosto et voria havere uno brazo in mille pezi o che la p.ta Madama di Savoya li havesse tolto el Delfinato, che havere facto questo oltragio ad esso Duca vostro fiolo; e se doy fiole[5] che quella ha et la Ser.ma Regina fusseno morte, non saria di tanto malla voglia, ma pregava Dio che may non li desse consolatione, se, facendo difficultà di liberarlo, la M.tà Soa statim in propria persona non andasse a fare guera in Savoya con ogni suo per forza, et morire in la impresa fino che haverà suo bel fratelo, condolendosi grandemente del despiacere che V. S. dovea havere di questo caso, como per le alligate scrive ad quella.[6] Et dice che ben porà andarli in persona, perché da Mons.re de Chyaroloes hé sicura, et dal Duca di Bertagna etiam con Englexi, che qui era uno di quelli dil Conte di Vervic per tractare certe tregue,[7] et questa septimana sperava asicurarsi da quel canto et porà meglio scrivere al bisogno. Siché esso Senescalco de Poitò se ne va batando. A luy habiamo parlato et offerto quanto ne hé parso neccessario, essendo el migliore che questo S. Re li potesse mandare et per chi la p.ta Madama farà più cha per la propria persona de la M.tà Soa, et in Savoya ha de molti amici et hé molto reputato; che pure speramo debia fare bon fructo.

Ulterius la M.tà Soa ha scrito ad Mons.re de Comingia,[8] Marescalcho di Franza, a Bordeos che subito descenda in Delfinato, menando con si III o IIII. M. balestrieri di Guascogna, et in questo non perda tempo un'hora. Et più ne hé parso che saria bene le gente d'arme che sono di qua in Delfinato vegnisseno da la V. Ex.tia per ogni caso che li potesse ocorere, donde havendo la M.tà Soa offerto di mandarle et parerli che si mandasseno, più tosto l'abiamo aceptato ad la riquesta et consiglio di quela cha richiederlo nuy; et per questo ha ordinato che passeno per el Marchisato di Saluces et de qui li manda el fiolo dil Marchese di Saluces,[9] quale sta con la prelibata Soa M.tà, per provedere al passo et a le victualie. Insuper che passate le gente d'arme rimagna in Ast governatore in nome de la M.tà Soa con le gente d'arme che quela li mandarà da qui per dare socorso ad la V. Ex.tia, et li ordina che in ogni cosa obe-

thought it a good thing that the troops who are here in the Dauphiné should return to Your Excellency for any eventuality that might occur. Since His Majesty, considering it a good move, offered to send them [of his own accord], we thought it better to accept his offer and advice, rather than make this request ourselves. The King ordered the troops to pass through the Marquisate of Saluzzo, and from here he will send the Marquis of Saluzzo's son,[9] who is with the King, so that he may see to the passage and provisioning of the troops. Furthermore, the King ordered that when the soldiers had passed, he should remain at Asti as governor in His Majesty's name, together with the soldiers the King will send him from here in aid of Your Excellency, ordering him to obey Your Excellency in everything and do all you will command. Besides this, the Bastard of Bourbon, his son-in-law, is to go immediately to the Bourbonnais and Dauphiné. He has elected him his lieutenant, charging him to lead there his troops (composed of one hundred lances), to assume command of the soldiers, of the lords, and of the francs archers of the Bourbonnais, Forez, Vivarais, Lyonnais, and of the Dauphiné, to amass them at once, so as to have from five to six thousand troops ready for war against Savoy. The King will send three hundred lances from his companies [d'ordonnance] with the Bastard, who will form the escort and will lead our men across the pass as far as Asti, where they will remain if Your Excellency needs them. The King has chosen the Bastard because he is hostile to the Savoyards; he is a person of great value, competent in military matters, and is His Majesty's son-in-law, which gives him greater reputation. Then, so that everyone should know that the King wants to defend the Duchy of Milan and your son, the Duke, with all his means and his own person, just as he would his own kingdom, His Majesty has chosen Gaston, My Lord of Gaucourt,[10] My Lord of Roppolo,[11] and Master Giovanni Filippo da Trecate, the President of Grenoble, to go immediately as ambassadors to visit and comfort Your Excellency. Gaston will return soon, but the others will remain as long as Your Excellency wishes, in order to give you more support and comfort.

60

dissa et faza quanto la S. V. li comandarà. Et più ha ordinato che el Bastardo di Borbon, suo zenero, di presente vada in Borbonese et in Delfinato; halo facto suo locotenente et così commisso che meni là le soe gente d'arme, che sono lanze C, che comandi le gente d'arme et commandi le gentilhomeni et franchi arcieri di Borbones, di Fores, di Vivares, de Lionese et di Delfinato et li metta statim suxo in modo habii da cinque in VI.M. persone per far guerra in Savoya. Et de le soe ordenanze mandarà trecento lanze con esso Bastardo, el quale farà compagnia et condurà li nostri per el passo fino in Ast et lì rimagnerano, se la Ex.tia V. ne haverà bisogno. La p.ta M.tà ha ellecto esso Bastardo, perché hé inimico di Savoyni, hé valente homo de la persona, savio in el facto de le arme et zenero di quela, che farà magiore reputatione. Poy afine che ogni uno intenda la M.tà Soa volere deffendere el Ducato di Milano et el Duca vostro fiolo come questo Regno, exponendoli le facultate et la propria persona, ha ordinato di presente di mandare ad visitare et confortare la V. Ex.tia et ha ellecto Guastoneto, Mons.re di Gocurt,[10] Mons.re di Ropol,[11] et Maystro Iohanne Filipo da Trechà, Presidente di Granoble, li quali vegnirano per ambassatori. Guastoneto tornarà presto, ma li altri gli starano tanto che ad la S. V. parirà per darli più favore et conforto. Così etiam ha ordinato la p.ta M.tà di scrivere a tute le potentie de Italia, facendoli intendere che soa intentione hé di defendere quelo Stato come si fosse de la propria soa Corona. Noy sollicitamo queste cose dì et nocte ad fine che si exequissano et non li perderemo ponto di tempo. Cinque secretarii giorno et nocte ordenano le instructione, commissione et littere neccessarie per la expeditione de li sopradicti; non atendendo né pure volendo odire parlare la p.ta M.tà et suo Consiglio de altra cosa dil mondo, se non di questa expeditione, et may non haveriamo creduto che con tanta fede havesseno servito. Avisando la V. Ex.tia che chi vede questo S. Re al viso iudica bene la M.tà Soa essere mesta et havere cative novelle. Tuta volta sollicitaremo queste cose cum fede et sollicitudine, certificando essa V. S. che como fidelissimi soy servitori deliberamo non may cessare da questa faticha fino che esso nostro Ill.mo S. sia liberato o morire in questo travaglio. Et così suplicamo

Furthermore, His Majesty has also ordered that letters be written to all states of Italy to inform them that he means to defend Milan as if it belonged to his crown. Day and night we seek to expedite all of the above, seeing to their accomplishment without the slightest waste of time.

Five secretaries labor day and night to draft the instructions, the charges, and the letters necessary for the dispatch of the aforementioned, as neither the King nor his Council want to attend to anything other than this matter; never would we have believed they would have served us with such faith. Your Excellency must know that whoever sees the King's face can realize how sad he is, and what bad news he has had. Nevertheless, we shall expedite things with fidelity and solicitude; we assure Your Ladyship that, being your faithful servants, we have decided never to give up these efforts until our most Illustrious Lord is liberated or die in the attempt. Therefore, we beg Your Excellency for your own sake, and for the sake of your people, to put up patiently with this event, wise as you are, the more so seeing that His Majesty is so much engaged in and desirous of this liberation. Owing to the actions that are being taken, we hope we shall soon see the Savoyards repenting of their errors and restoring to us Our Most Illustrious Lord. We remind Your Ladyship that, as the King has deprived himself of his dearest, closest, and most faithful men, engaging them in this matter, we must trust that he will do better and better everyday, even as he says he will intervene in person. As we come to know what is happening daily, we shall inform Your Excellency, to whom we humbly commend ourselves. Written in great haste.

HISTORICAL NOTES

1. This dispatch of 22 March has not been found.
2. See doc. 2, n. 1.
3. The news of Galeazzo Maria's detention reached Lyon on 18 March, and was quickly relayed to Panigarola and Emanuele de Iacopo [Zanone Corio to the Duchess, Lyon, 18 March 1466, *Francia*, cart. 532]. Two days

quela, per conservatione soa et de li soy populi, tollerare questo caso cum patiente animo como prudentissima ch'el hé, ben che vedendo questa Ser.ma M.tà tanto abrasata et desyderosa di questa liberatione et le preparatione si fanno, speramo vedere presto presto Savoyni pentiti de li loro errori et restituirne el p.to nostro Ill.mo S.; ricordando ad la p.ta V. S., che privandosi questo S. Re de li più fidati et più cari habia a l'intorno de la persona de la Soa M.tà, como fa per operarli in questo bisogno, habiamo a sperare farà ogni giorno di bene in meglio et dice non li mancarà fino a meterli la persona. In le quale cose di quanto ad la giornata seguiremo ne daremo notizia ad la p.ta V. Ex.tia, a la quale humilmente si riccomandiamo.

earlier the Milanese envoys at the Savoyard court had received the news directly from Galeazzo Maria [Two dispatches by Cristoforo da Bollate and Ziliolo Oldoini to the Duke, Chambéry, 16 March 1466, BN, *Fonds Italien*, Cod. 1591, fols. 288–89]. On 15 March the Duchess of Milan had written to the King asking him to intervene at the Savoyard court for the release of her son [Appendix, doc. II].

4. That is, in late summer of 1465 when the King was besieged in Paris by the forces of the League of the Public Weal after the battle of Montlhéry.

5. Anne, born in 1461, and Jeanne, born in 1464.

6. See Appendix, doc. V.

7. The truce was not actually signed until 24 May 1466 [Joseph Calmette and Georges Périnelle, *Louis XI et l'Angleterre (1461–1483)* (Paris: Picard, 1930), p. 73].

8. Jean de Lescun, Bastard of Armagnac, son of Arnaud-Guillaume de Lescun and of Annette d'Armagnac, Marshal of France (1461) and Count of Comminges (1462) [Jean de Jaurgain, "Deux Comtes de Comminges Béarnais au XVe siècle. Jean de Lescun, dit le bâtard d'Armagnac," Societé Archéologique du Gers, *Bulletin* (1914), pp. 20–25, 201].

9. Ludovico, eldest son of Marquis Ludovico I of Saluzzo and of Isabella, daughter of Marquis Giangiacomo of Monferrat, who since 1461 had been in the King's service [Mandrot, *Dépêches*, 2:214, n. 1].

10. Charles, Lord of Gaucourt, son of Raoul and of Jeanne de Preuilly, and the King's Chamberlain.

11. Lodovico di Valperga, Lord of Roppolo in Piedmont, and brother of Giacomo, the slain Chancellor of Savoy.

FRANCE AND BURGUNDIAN TERRITORIES, 1451

French territories ▢ Burgundian territories ▢ Other ▢

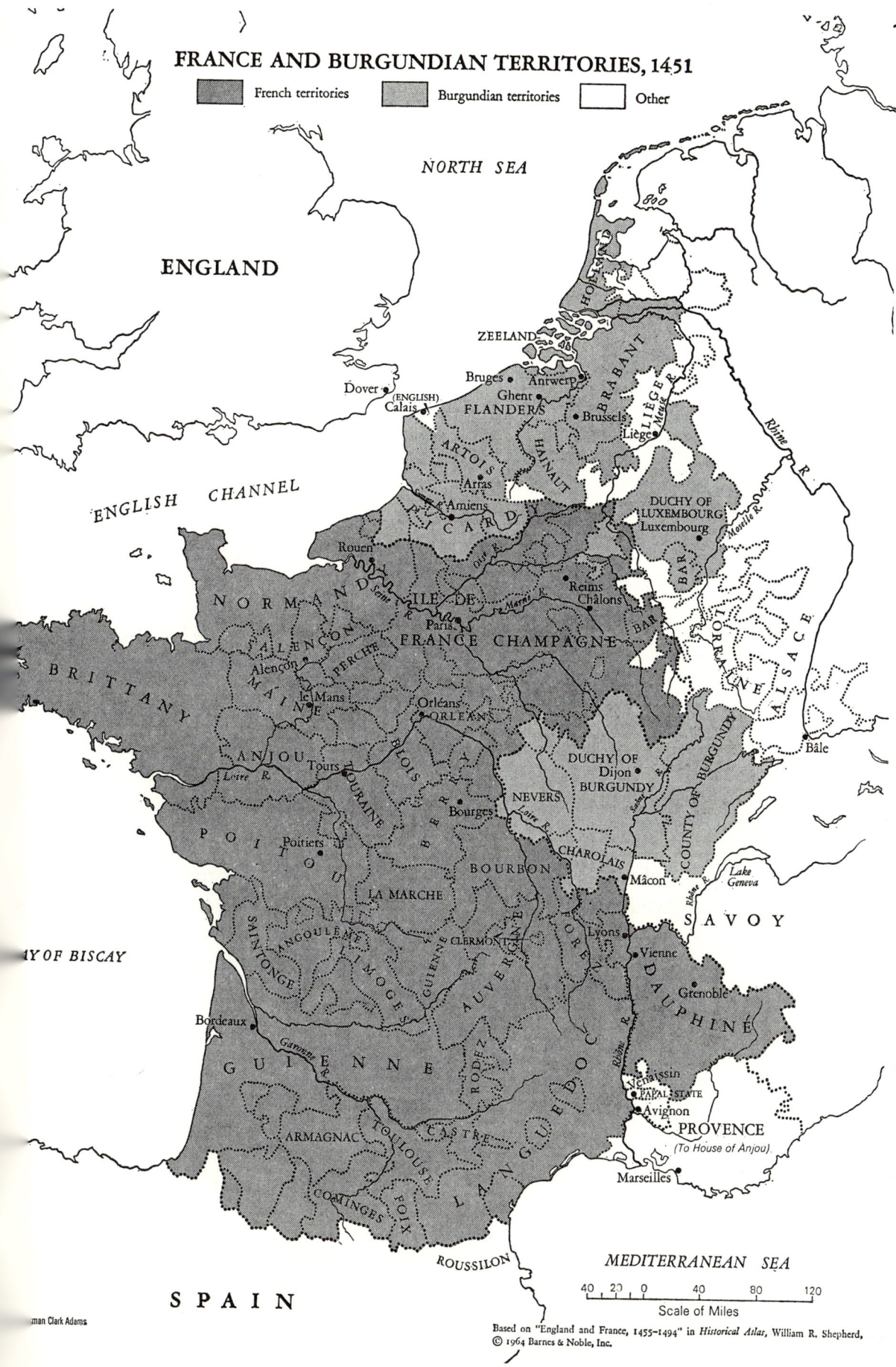

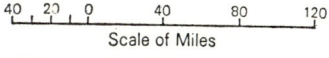

NORTH SEA

ENGLAND

ENGLISH CHANNEL

Dover

Calais (ENGLISH)

ZEELAND

Bruges · Antwerp

Ghent · Brussels

FLANDERS · Liège

LIÈGE

HOLLAND

BRABANT

ARTOIS

Arras

Amiens

PICARD

HAINAUT

DUCHY OF LUXEMBOURG

Luxembourg

Rouen

NORMANDY

ILE DE FRANCE

Reims
Châlons

CHAMPAGNE

Paris

BAR

LORRAINE

ALSACE

ALENÇON

Alençon

PERCHE

MAINE

le Mans

Orléans

ORLEANS

BLOIS

BERRY

ANJOU

Tours

TOURAINE

Loire R.

BRITTANY

POITOU

Poitiers

LA MARCHE

BOURBON

NEVERS

DUCHY OF
BURGUNDY

Dijon

CHAROLAIS

COUNTY OF BURGUNDY

Mâcon

Bâle

Lake Geneva

SAVOY

BAY OF BISCAY

SAINTONGE

ANGOULÊME

LIMOGES

GUIENNE

AUVERGNE

FOREZ

Clermont

Lyons

Vienne

Grenoble

DAUPHINÉ

Bordeaux

GUIENNE

RODEZ

LANGUEDOC

Rhône R.

Garonne R.

ARMAGNAC

TOULOUSE

CASTRE

COMINGES

FOIX

ROUSSILLON

Venaissin
PAPAL STATE
Avignon

PROVENCE
(To House of Anjou)

Marseilles

MEDITERRANEAN SEA

SPAIN

Scale of Miles
40 20 0   40   80   120

Based on "England and France, 1455-1494" in *Historical Atlas*, William R. Shepherd,
© 1964 Barnes & Noble, Inc.

man Clark Adams

This morning at dawn we appeared before the [Royal] Council with the Bastard of Bourbon with regard to his departure; we worked all night and the matter has been settled. We have arranged with him what has to be done, and today after dinner he is setting out. He has already collected his soldiers which, being an esteemed and authoritative man, he was able to do in a single day—not a small achievement. We find that he is leaving willingly and eagerly, knowing what the King's will is, which makes us hope for a happy result. The Bastard will place himself in the field with a great number of troops wherever your son, the Duke, is imprisoned, at Susa in Piedmont, or in any other place, and will use force to have your son set free—and he is just the man to do the deed, especially since the King has told him not to have any regard for expenses or anything else.

Likewise, today or tomorrow morning the Marquis of Saluzzo's son will surely leave. As My Lord of Gaucourt was coming here, the King sent him a letter telling him to go back and start for Lyons, where in two or three days Gaston and the other ambassadors would arrive with the instructions and charges which are being prepared, and from there they will at once set out to come to Your Excellency. The King has also offered to send his Captain, [Jean de] Village, with galleys flying the French flag to Genoa and Savona, so that if Genoa were to revolt or

9 · EMANUELE DE IACOPO *and*

GIOVAN PIETRO PANIGAROLA *to the*

DUCHESS OF MILAN

BN, Fonds Italien, Cod. 1593, fols. 233–33v. Orig.

Questa matina a l'alba dil giorno siamo stati in Consiglio con el Bastardo di Borbon per la expeditione soa; tuta notte si hé lavorato et hé expedita. Con luy habiamo ordinato quanto ci hé a fare et hogie apreso disnare parte, havendo già mandato ad levare le gente d'arme soe, che essendo esso Bastardo homo di reputazione et di auctorità come hé, in uno giorno se sii spachiato. Non hé stato pocho, ma trovamo li va cum tanto amore et desyderio, cognoscendo anche la volontà di questo S.Re, che speramo in Dio farà bono fructo; et essendo el S. Duca vostro fiolo a Susa o in Piemonte arestato in che terra se sia, esso Bastardo metterà gente assay insieme andando a campo ad quela terra, che si vederà di haverlo per forza et hé ben homo per fare un gran facto, et così la M.tà Soa li ha commisso non guardi a dinari né cosa alchuna. Similiter hogie o domatina partirà el fiolo dil Marchese di Saluces infallanter. A Mons.re de Gocurt ha facto scrivere che se ritorni, perché vegniva qui aviandose a Lione, e lì fra II o III giorni spazati vidariano Gastoneto et li altri ambassatori con le instructione e commissione che si fanno, et de lì statin vegnirano da la V. Ex.tia. Ulterius la prelibata M.tà si hé offerta di volere mandare Villagio, suo capitanio, con le galee et bandere franzese ad Zenoa et Savona, aciò che se Zenoa havesse qualche mutazione o Vostra S. altramente ne havesse bisogno, se ne possa valere. Et così ha mandato per Villagio, quale hé in questa terra, per farli dare dinari et mandarlo

if Your Ladyship were in need, you might avail yourself of them. Therefore, he has sent for Jean de Village, who is here, in order to give him
money and send him off.

During the night the King sent a messenger to My Lord of Charolais to inform him of the capture of our Lord. He wrote very warmly
and affectionately, requesting him to be hostile toward the Savoyards
and lend every assistance for the liberation of the aforementioned Lord,
because he means to free the Duke and preserve his state, acting with
no less vigor than he would for the preservation of this kingdom. Further, His Majesty has ordered ambassadors sent to Venice, Ferrara,
Mantua, to the Marquis of Monferrat, to Florence, Bologna, and Rome,
to inform those lordships and states of his intention to protect the state
of Milan with all his power. He has ordered that some notable persons
be picked for these missions. We have already had some letters[1] drafted,
addressed to those lords, and we are sending them to Your Excellency
herewith enclosed, so that while awaiting the arrival of the ambassadors,
they may be of use to you. The King himself ordered and dictated the
general contents of these letters, and we are also sending you the copies
for your consolation. His Majesty thought wise to write some letters to
the people and to the Council of Milan,[2] as Your Ladyship will see from
the copies. These letters can then be forwarded by Your Ladyship, depending upon your judgment of their usefulness, especially those addressed to the Venetians which seem to us to be well written. Moreover,
the King is of the opinion, and so are we, that I, Emanuele, should go
to the Dauphiné to encourage our soldiers and then to Chambéry to meet
the Seneschal of Poitou in order to solicit from there what will have to
be done. Since Giovan Pietro's presence here is sufficient, I, Emanuele,
will leave in two or three hours,[3] and I will bend every effort to keep you
informed of both what follows and of my actions.

Master Giovanni Filippo da Trecate, President of Grenoble, has
been and is a great help to Your Excellency in this case. Since we received the news up to this hour, day and night, he has done nothing but

via. Questa nocte ad Mons.re Chyaroloes ha mandato uno cavalaro, notificandoli la presa dil p.to nostro S. et di novo pregarlo che con Savoyni volia essere inimico e sporgere ogni adiuto per la liberatione dil p.to S., perché la M.tà Soa intende liberarlo et mantenire el suo Stato non mancho che faria per la recuperatione di questo Reame, scrivendoli molto caldamente et affectionatamente. Ulterius la p.ta M.tà ha ordinato di mandare ambassatori a Venesia, Ferara, Mantoa, Marchese di Monferato, Fiorenza, Bologna et Roma, a loro signorie et potentie ad notificarli l'intentione de la prelibata Soa M.tà che hé di mantenire el Stato di Millano con ogni soa possanza, et ha commisso che si avisa qualche notabile homeni per mandare in esse ambassade. Tamen zà habiamo facto spazare alcune littere[1] directive ad essi Signori, quale alligate ad questa mandiamo ad la V. Ex.tia, aciò che in questo mezo che li ambassatori vegnirano in questo tempo se possi adiutare de queste littere, le quale essa M.tà di bocha propria ha commisso et dictato el tenore de quelle, siché anche vi ne mandiamo le copie a vostra consolatione. Et hé parso ad essa M.tà di scrivere alcune littere a la Comunità et Consiglio di Milano,[2] como per le copie porà la S.V. vedere, le quale littere, sicondo che a quela parirà habiano a fare fructo porà mandare, maxime quelle de Venetiani, perché ne pare sieno in bona forma. Ceterum hé parso a la p.ta M.tà et anche a noy che io, Emanuel, vada in Delfinato a confortare le nostre gente d'arme et poy a Chyamberì a trovare el Senescaco di Poytò e sollicitare di là quanto sarà da fare, essendo assay al presente di me Iohanepiero qui; et cosi io, Emanuel, fra II o III hore mi partirò[3] et, sicondo seguirà et operarò, mi sforzarò advisare la V.S. El Presidente di Granoble, cioé Metre Iohan Filipe da Trechà, ha servito et serve molto bene la V. Ex.tia in questo caso et, dopoy havemo le nove fino questa hora, dì et nocte non ha facto altro cha essere in Consiglio et ordinare lettere et instructione, le quale facte speramo vegnirà da la p.ta V. Ex.tia. El Duca Iohane ha mandato da questo S. Re alchuni de li soy. Soa M.tà statim li dete audientia, la quale ne ha dicto che non gli hanno parlato niente de la morte dil Ill.mo S. vostro consorte né del S. Duca vostro

participate in the Council in order to secure letters and instructions. After this we hope he will come to Your Ladyship.

Duke John has sent envoys, and they were immediately granted audience by the King. His Majesty told us that they said nothing about the death of the Most Illustrious Lord, your husband, or about your son, the Duke. He was quite astonished at this, and fears they may have done so designedly and with some plot in mind, which he will try to discover. He asked that we also should stay alert in case we should hear anything, which we will do.

We have no news of Your Ladyship, which makes us fear that the [Alpine] passes are closed; and not knowing how to send safely the enclosed letters, we decided to send the present bearer, Cristoforo, Giovan Pietro's servant, though he is very much needed by me. He knows all the roads and shortcuts and he will also be able to inform you orally of several matters we charged him with. We beg Your Ladyship to send him back at once, and if you wish to entrust him with anything or send a message, you can do so because he is a discrete and faithful man. Cristoforo is setting out with great urgency and has orders not to worry about expenses concerning horses or anything else, so long as he is as speedy as possible. I, Giovan Pietro, for my part, will expedite things with my usual faith and diligence, and will do my best so that all these provisions may have a successful result, as I hope, and will bend every effort to inform Your Excellency to whom we humbly commend ourselves.

HISTORICAL NOTES

1. Originals and copies of these letters, dated 24 March, are in *Francia*, cartelle 532 and 559, and in BN, Fonds Italien, Cod. 1591, fols. 326–27, published by Vaesen, *Lettres*, 3:28–34; 10:233. On the same day the King also wrote to the *Anziani*, etc., of Genoa [*Francia*, cart. 532; *Lettres*, 3:38–40].

2. Both are dated 23 March [*Francia*, cart. 532; BN, *Fonds Italien*, Cod.

fiolo; di che dice si maraviglia dubitando fazano questo con arte et meneno qualche practiche, le quale si sforzarà intendere, che anche noy voliamo stare avisati se nulla intendemo et così faremo. Non havendo novelle da la V.S. ne fa dubitare li passi siano serrati et non sapendo como mandare salvamente le alligate litterre, ne hé parso mandare Cristoforo presente exhibitore, servitore di me Iohannepiero, quamvis qui me sia necessariissimo, perché sa tuti li camini et traversi, et ulterius a bocha informarà la V.S. de più cose che li habiamo commisso. Pregamola subito lo fazi spazare et, parendo ad quella de dirli cosa alchuna o mandarlo, lo pò fare perché hé persona secreta et fidata. Dicto Christophoro parte volando, al quale cometemo non guardi a spesa de cavali né altra cosa per andare presto. Io autem Iohanepiero sollicitarò queste cose con la solita mia fede et diligentia, operando a tuto mio potere che queste provisione tute sortissano effecto, como ho speranza, et dil tuto mi sforzarò avisare la V. Ill.ma S., ala quale humilmente si ricomandamo.

1591, fol. 308; *Lettres*, 3:34-37]. The date of 19 April, given to the letter addressed to the Council of the Duke of Milan [*Lettres*, 3:34, n. 1], on the basis of a copy found in the State Archives of Florence, is incorrect.

3. Emanuele, however, was still at Orléans as of 19 April [doc. 21].

While we were attending a session of the Council with the King in order to settle the measures to be taken for the liberation of Your Lordship, and while [Jean] de Village was about to be sent to Genoa with his galleys in the service and at the orders of both the Most Illustrious Lady, your mother, as well as Your Excellency, at about 1 P.M. the news of Your Lordship's release,[1] written by Messer Giovanni di Scipione [Pallavicino] and Zanone Corio, reached us. Enclosed with their letter was a copy of the one Your Excellency wrote to them. We immediately read these letters, word by word, to His Majesty who was grieving and very sad because of the unexpected event.

It would take a long time to repeat what His Majesty said in your honor and how much pleasure and relief he felt on hearing this great and happy news. In fact, it was recognized by all the lords present that His Majesty had never shown more satisfaction or joy for the recovery of his kingdom or for any other thing that had occurred to him, than he did and does for this good news. His Majesty was standing in the midst of many lords being conjubilant over your liberation; he spoke about the measures he wanted to adopt on your behalf, mindful of the honor of his kingdom and crown as well as of the enormous benefits received by him from Your Most Illustrious father and from Your Highness. For all these reasons he would have engaged his kingdom and would have

10 · EMANUELE DE IACOPO *and*

GIOVAN PIETRO PANIGAROLA *to the*

DUKE OF MILAN

Francia, cart. 532. Orig.; BN, Fonds Italien, Cod. 1593, fol. 235. Copy

Ritrovandosi essere con questo S. Re al Consiglio suo per la expeditione de le provisione si facevano per la liberatione de la V.S. et essendo per spazare Villagio, quale doveva presentarsi ad Zenoa con le soe galee ad li servitii et commandi de la Ill.ma Madona vostra madre et così de V.ra Ex.tia, circha ad hore XVIIII° zonseno le novele de la rellaxatione de la V.S.[1] che misser Zohanne de Scipione et Zannone Coyro ne scriveno insieme con la copia de la littera che quella gli ha scritto. Le quale littere et copia eo instanti legemo de verbum ad verbum ad la M.tà Soa, quale stava dolente et mestissima per tal inopinato caso. Et dovendo narrare le parole che essa M.tà disse in grandissimo vostro honore et il singularissimo piacere et consolatione che quella ha auto di questa bona et rellevata novella, ne bisognaria grande spatio di tempo, peroché per comune dicto de tuti li astanti Signori fu concluso non havere may essa M.tà monstrato maiore contentamento né allegreza de la recuperatione del suo Regno né de altra cosa che li sia acaduta quanto fece et fa di questa bona nova. Stava essa M.tà in piede in mezo di molti Signori congratulandosi de la liberatione vostra, aducendo le provisione che anche li voleva fare ricordando lo honore del Reame, de la Corona et li immensi benefitii collati per lo Ill.mo vostro genitore ac Vostra Cel. ad quella, per li quali rispecti intendeva meterli el Reame et prima volere morire cha patire questa infamia né che V. Cel. fosse in periculo. Et dicendo queste

died rather than bear this disgrace or permit that Your Highness be in peril. While saying this, there were tears in his eyes. As can be seen from his letter[2] to Your Excellency, herewith enclosed, he says he will send you troops and any other help necessary for the maintenance of your state, which he wants to defend no less than his kingdom, because he is very much obliged to you.

After saying this, he immediately returned to the church of Our Lady of Good Tidings,[3] where this morning he had attended mass, in order to give thanks for the good news, and then donated two hundred écus, which with his own hands he had carried there from his residence. Then he had the Queen, his sisters-in-law, and the ladies in waiting come to dine at his table, and there was great entertainment and joy— something he was not in the habit of doing. Having dined, he mounted his horse and went hunting. If one had not seen it with his own eyes, one would not believe how great was the satisfaction of the Duke of Bourbon who wept with joy, the Bastard of Bourbon, My Lord Filippo, who was also present, the Marshal of Lohéac [André de Laval, Lord of Lohéac and Marshal of France], Marshal Joachim [Rouault, Marshal of France], and many other lords. The Queen sent for us just now to extend congratulations on Your Excellency's liberation, and God only knows all she did and said in commending herself to Your Highness. Furthermore, His Majesty immediately sent express messengers to inform My Lord of Charolais and the Duke of Brittany of your release and of the felicitous condition of your state, which is as tranquil and peaceful as it was in Your Most Illustrious father's time, maintaining the same devotion, faithfulness, and respect. Each day brings better hopes for the future, as can be seen from your mother's letter of the twelfth of this month,[4] which we gave him to read. The King sent word to the Seneschal of Poitou not to return, but to go to the Most Illustrious Madame of Savoy to thank her for the liberation of Your Highness and tell her that even if she had freed His Majesty himself, he would not be more pleased or thankful. He begs her, as well, to give every aid, favor, and subsidy to Your Lordship for the preservation of your state,

parole tuta via descendevano le lachryme da gli ochii de la p.ta Soa
M.tà, la quale, como per le alligate littere[2] che scrive ad V.Ex.tia, porà
vedere, dice vi mandarà gente d'arme mandandove etiam ogni altro
socorso che vi serà necessario per conservatione dil Stato vostro, volendolo
deffenderlo non mancho cha questo Regno, così cognoscendosi essere obligatissima. His dictis statim andò ad la chiesia de la gloriosa nostra
Dona di Bone Novelle,[3] dove questa matina haveva odito messa, rin-
gratiola di questa nova et donoli scudi ducento, quale essa M.tà con proprie mane haveva portato dal Jogiamento suo fino lì. Poy al disnare suo
fece venire la Ser.ma Regina, le Ill. soe cognate et le damisele stando in
festa et alegreza, el che non ha may acostumato fare. Et disnata, montò
a cavalo et andò a cazare. Quanta alegreza habii auto el Duca di Borbon
che di consolatione piangeva, el Bastardo di Borbon, Filipo Mons.re lì
presente, el Marescalcho de Loyac, Marescalco Ioachin et tuti quelli Signori, et le dimonstratione ne fano hé cosa incredibile et tale che chi non
vedesse, non lo crederia. La p.ta Regina questa hora ne ha mandato a
domandare congratulandosi de la liberatione de la V. Ex.tia, che Dio sa
le feste ne fa et le parole dice, riccomandandosi ad la V. Cel. Insuper per
mesi [*sic*] volando la prelibata M.tà ha mandato ad notificare ad Mons.re
Chyaroloes et al Duca di Bertagna la rellaxatione vostra et li propitii et
felici successi dil Stato vostro, pacifico et quieto, con quelli amore, fede,
observantia et tranquilitate che era al tempo del quondam Ill.mo vostro
padre et ogni giorno sperare meglio, como per littere de la Ill.ma V.
madre de dì XII dil presente[4] monstramo ad quella. Al senescalco de
Poitò ha mandato che non ritorni per modo alcuno, ma vadi da la Ill.
Madama di Savoya, ringratiandola de la rellaxatione de V.ra Cel. et
dicendoli se havesse liberato la propria persona di Soa M.tà non li haria
facto magiore contentamento né cosa più grata. Ulterius la prega volia
dare ogni adiuto, favore et subsidio ad la V.S. et conservatione dil Stato
suo, governandosi in bono amore et amicitia con quella como si conviene,
intendendendo [*sic*] la M.tà Soa fare non manco per quello cha per el
suo proprio Regno.[5] Postremo quanto ogniuno universalmente si relegri
di questa vostra liberatione et l'amore che monstrano in questa corte

keeping proper, friendly, and cordial relations with you, for the King means to do no less for your state than he would for his own kingdom.[5] Finally, we would never have thought or imagined how much everybody rejoiced in this court over Your Excellency's release and to what a degree they are attached to you and esteem you. You have greatly gained in stature here, and if formerly they were astonished and dismayed, now they are merry and in good spirits. Having pondered these things, we wanted to inform Your Highness for your satisfaction. We realize how this indicates that all your labors have not been performed in vain, for which we congratulate you and pray Almighty God to preserve and increase your prosperity and felicitude, and may He always keep these lords favorably disposed.

Regarding further occurrences, we will in other letters more fully inform Your Excellency, to whose good grace as true subjects and servants we always commend ourselves.

HISTORICAL NOTES

1. Galeazzo Maria had been detained on Friday, 14 March, and was freed about twenty-four hours later [The Duke to Pietro Francesco Visconti and Giovanni Pallavicino, Milan, 21 March 1466, BN *Fonds Italien*, Cod. 1591, fols. 305–6v]. For a chronology of the Duke's return trip, see Appendix, doc. IV, n. 1].

2. See Appendix, doc. VI.

3. Presumably the Church of St. Paul in Orléans, which contains the Chapel of Notre-Dame des Miracles, with an ancient statue of the Black Virgin. Joan of Arc prayed in this chapel during the siege of Orléans in 1429.

4. This letter has not been found, but cf. Appendix, doc. 1.

5. The Seneschal arrived at Chambéry on the evening of 31 March, having received, on the way, this message from the King. The Duke and Duchess of Savoy agreed to support the new Duke of Milan, and reaffirmed their intention to grant free passage to the Milanese troops returning to Lombardy [Ziliolo Oldoini to the Duke, Chambéry, 1 April 1466, BN, *Fonds Italien*, Cod. 1591, fol. 330].

portare ad la V. Ex.tia may non lo haveriamo creduto né pensato, nottificandoli che qui ha acquistato uno grande credito, et dove ogniuno
stava stupefacto et di dolore smarrito, ora stano alegri et di bona voglia.
Le quale cose consyderate ne habiamo voluto ad vostra consolatione
avisare V. Cel. et cognoscendo maxime per le dimonstratione fano la
Et.tia V. non frustra laborasse, con quella se ne congratulamo, pregando
l'Omnipotente Idio l'augumenti et conservi in el suo prospero et felici
Stato, et questi longamenti conservi in la loro bona dispositione. De le
cose che achadeno per altre più amplamente scriveremo ad la prelibata
V.Ex.tia, a la cui bona gratia come soy veri subditi et servitori sempre si
ricommandano.

What great pleasure, satisfaction, and joy the King derived from the release of the Most Illustrious Duke, your son, and the way in which he made show of it, even to the point of weeping with joy, Your Excellency will clearly see from the letter[1] we wrote to His Lordship; so we will dwell no longer on the subject. The letter dated the twelfth of this month[2] that Your Excellency wrote to me, Giovan Pietro, arrived today and I immediately communicated its contents to the King; I also read to him the copy of the letter sent to you by the city of Genoa which you forwarded to me. His Majesty was extremely well satisfied to know that Your Excellency's subjects continue to be faithful, devoted, and obedient as before, and that no troubles have ensued so far, and hopes none will, for which he prays God. As regards the letter of the Genoese, he recommends caution because under cover of such nice expressions, the Genoese, who are inconstant and volatile, may actually prefer to revolt; nevertheless it is a good sign they have not done so up to now.

We commended Your Excellency and your children as warmly as possible to His Majesty who, almost weeping, answered that you may rest assured that he will never abandon you, owing to the benefits he has received [from you], and that to every request of yours he will not only offer his troops but also his every means, no less that he would do for his own kingdom—of this Your Ladyship may be quite sure. Concern-

11·EMANUELE DE IACOPO *and*

GIOVAN PIETRO PANIGAROLA *to the*

DUCHESS OF MILAN

BN, Fonds Italien, Cod. 1593, fol. 234. Orig.

Quanto piacere, contentamento et alegreza habia auto questo S. Re de la liberatione de lo Ill.mo S. Duca vostro fiolo et le dimonstratione ne ha facto, la Ex.tia Vostra porà vedere per le littere[1] che scrivemo ad la Soa. Sig. ria, la quale hé tale et tanta che la M.tà Soa di alegreza pianzeva. Si che ad questo non si extenderemo più oltra. Ad le littere de dì XII dil presente,[2] che essa V. Ex.tia scrive a me Iohanepetro, recepute questo dì, dico che statim nottificay quanto in quelle si conteneva a la p.ta M.tà, lezendoli la copia de la littera che la Comunità di Zenoa scrive, che mi haveti mandata. Essa M.tà hé stata tanto di bona voglia quanto dire si possa, intendendo li populi de la V. Ex.tia perseverare in la fede, devotione et obedientia como prima et fino in quela hora non essere seguita novitate alcuna, et dice sperare che anche non seguirà, dil che così prega Dio. De la littera di Zenovesi dice ricorda ponerli mente, perché sotto spetie di tal parole, Zenoesi varii et volubili più tosto fariano novitate cha altramente; tuta volta hé bono signo poyché infino quel hora non la havevano facta. Ricomandamo etiam tanto stretamente quanto fo possibile la V. Ex.tia et soy fioli ad la prelibata M.tà, la quale quasi pianzendo ne rispose fosse certa la V.S. che may non li abando- narà, perché li benefitii ricevuti così richiedeno, et non solum ad ogni vostra riquesta exponerà le soe gente d'arme, ma ogni soa facultate, non mancho che faria per el suo Regno, et di questo ne sii certa essa V.S.

ing the instructions that Your Highness writes of having sent to me, Emanuele, I reply that I did not receive them and that the letter[3] was sent to me open from Lyons in a packet of letters for Giovan Pietro, without the instructions, and of this I inform you.

I shall wait to see if Your Excellency writes more to me, and then as soon as possible, I shall return informed of everything.

Finally, the King advises and begs Your Excellency to bear patiently what has happened, however difficult it may be, and to provide for the maintenance of the state with your usual prudence, offering on his part his readiness to do everything possible. Of what is happening here we will write more fully in other letters; we always commend ourselves to Your Most Illustrious Ladyship.

HISTORICAL NOTES

1. See preceding doc. 10.
2. The ambassadors are in error. This letter is dated 11 March [doc. 3].
3. Letter of 11 March, doc. 2.

De la instructione che V. Cel. scrive havere mandata ad me Emanuel, rispondo che non la ho auta et la littera[3] mi hé stata mandata aperta da Lione in uno mazo di Iohanepietro senza instructione, si che vi ne aviso. Aspectarò vedere se altro me scriverà V. Ex.tia et al più presto mi sarà possibile ritornarò informato dil tuto. Postremo ricorda la p.ta M.tà et prega V. Ex.tia ad tollerare patientemente el caso seguito, quamvis sia difficile, et provedere ala conservatione di quello Stato con la solita vostra prudentia, offerendosi dal canto suo aparechiata ad fare quanto sarà possibile. De le cose di qua per altre scriveremo a compimento, ricommandandosi sempre ad la V. Ill.ma S.

Yesterday, when the King heard from us of Your Lordship's liberation, at that very moment, he drew us aside in a corner and said that he thought that I, Emanuele, without returning to Milan, *should immediately go to My Lord of Charolais to probe whether he would give his daughter in marriage to Your Lordship, as this had already been spoken about when the Lord, your father, was alive.*[1] He added that he wanted to give me a letter of credence worded in such a way that *My Lord of Charolais* would trust me and freely reveal his intentions and wishes in this matter. I, Giovan Pietro, should go to Savoy to further and bolster the marriage negotiations already in progress with the House of Savoy,[2] and then I should return immediately.

The King thinks that such a *family tie with My Lord of Charolais* would be a very good thing for Your Lordship, and he would be truly satisfied if it were to come about; *but if it were not, he advises* and would always advise the tie with the House of Savoy in order to strengthen and maintain your state. He advances many reasons for this, above all because My Lord Filippo has a great following among the Bernese, the Swiss, and within the League. He is a very able individual who could help you and lead a great number of troops in support of Your Excellency.

The King told me [Emanuele] to go and sound out *My Lord of Charolais* on the subject of this marriage, as if it were of my own initia-

12 · EMANUELE DE IACOPO *and*

GIOVAN PIETRO PANIGAROLA *to the*

DUKE OF MILAN

BN, Fonds Italien, Cod. 1593, fol. 236–36v. Orig.

Havendo heri questo S. Re intesa per noy la liberatione de la V.S., in quelo instante ne tirò a parte in uno cantone, dicendone che gli pareva che io, Emanuel, di presente senza ritornare ad Milano *andasse da Mon.re de Chiarlois ad temptare se voleva dare soa fiola ad la S.V., come altre volte vivendo el signore vostro padre fu ragionato,*[1] dicendo volermi dare tale littera di credenza *che esso Mon.re de Chiarlois* me poria credere et dire liberamente l'intentione et volere suo circha questo; et che io, Iohannepetro, andasse in Savoya a dare speranza et intertenere el parentato di Savoya[2] comenzato et statim ritornasse, parendoli *che el parentato de Mon.re de Chiarlois* saria optimo per la V. S.; et in verità li saria piaciuto quando havesse potuto havere loco; *quando che non, dice sempre* consigliaria et consigliava quelo di Savoya per stabilimento et conservatione dil Stato vostro, aducendo molte ragione, maxime che Filipo Monsignor ha grande seguito dil payse di Bernesi, de Suyceri et de la Liga, hé apto de la persona et poria secorere et menare gente assay in favore de la V. Ex.tia. Et che di questo parentato *con Mon.re de Chiarlois* io l'andasse a temptare como da me et non in nome de la M.tà Soa né de V.S., domandando *essa fiola nuda, perché el prefato Mon.re de Chiarlois é scarso, benché dubita la cosa non haveria* effecto, havendo *Mon.re de Chiarlois tenuto tante practiche di quela soa fiola, come ha et calefato* [*sic*] *ogniuno.* Ad le qual cose li rispondemo non ne parere

tive, without mentioning either His Majesty's name or Your Lordship's. I should make proposal for the *daughter without dowry, because My Lord of Charolais is short of money. Nevertheless,* [His Majesty] *doubts it will succeed because Charolais has in the past entertained many proposals for his daughter, but has mocked everyone.*

We answered that we did not believe it wise to try such tactics before receiving further instructions from Your Excellency and before knowing your intention after your accession to the dukedom. Without being charged by Your Lordship, we said we would not dare undertake such a thing, and that anyway we were waiting hourly for news which would certainly not be long in reaching us. Since it seemed to us that His Majesty had spoken those words fearing perhaps that Your Lordship would change his mind [about the Savoyard marriage] after becoming Duke, I, Emanuele, repeated the words that Your Lordship said to me just recently at Moirans[3] when I was taking leave, begging His Majesty to take thought in the matter because I was sure that you would always do what would please His Majesty.

The King answered that he would be pleased to remain Your Lordship's friend—as he had been your Most Illustrious late father's; he would always be of service to Your Lordship, even if you were to do otherwise, and he would never do anything that would be contrary or unpleasant to you, in memory of the immense benefits he had received in the past, etc.

Nothing else was concluded or mandated then, save that My Lord Filippo, who has been released,[4] summoned us to tell us that His Majesty had charged him to treat us well and kindly, and so he made us many offers of troops and of other help he might contribute to the service of Your Lordship. Furthermore, he said he will send someone to take possession of his castles [in Savoy] and order his friends to stay at the ready, offering to send you if necessary five hundred of his noble followers and the same number of Burgundians, and finally to go the scene himself.

He thinks that when he becomes an ally of Your Excellency, whom

di temptare queste vie fino che da la V. Ex.tia non havessimo altro aviso et da quella intendessemo, da poy l'asomptione di questo Stato novo, la dispositione soa, non ossando senza comissione di essa V.S. temptare tal cosa, et che di hora in hora aspectavamo aviso che non poteva però tardare ad venire. Et perché ne parse la M.tà Soa dire queste parole, dubitando forsi che la Ex.tia V. essendo facta Duca non cambiasse proposito, io, Emanuel, gli repplicay le parole che quella mi disse ad Moyran[3] ultimamente quando presi licentia da essa V. S., pregandola gli piacesse fare sopra ciò bono pensiero, perché era certissimo quela sempre faria tuto quelo fusse piacere et contentamento de la prelibata Soa M.tà. La quale ne rispose che haria piacere et consolatione che V. S. gli fosse amica, como ha facto el quondam Ill.mo vostro genitore, perché sempre la serviria, quando anche facesse altramente, chey may però non faria cosa contra quella né che li havesse a despiacere, richiedendo così l'immensi benefitii receputi per il passato, etc. Et per alhora non fu concluso né ordinato altro salvo che dapoy Filipo Mons.re, quale hé rillassato in soa libertà,[4] ne ha mandato a domandare et dicto che essa M.tà gli ha commisso ne debba festezare et acarezare. Et così ne ha facto infinite proferte di gente d'arme et d'ogni altra cosa ch'el possa fare in servitio de la V. Ex.tia, dicendo ch'el manda di de là a pigliare la possesione de le soe castelle et ordinare che li soy amici stiano a poncto, offerendosi quando achada el bisogno, mandarvi cinquecento gentilhomeni de li soy seguaci et altratanti Bergognoni et venirli luy proprio in persona, parendoli che quando sia alligato ad la V. Ex.tia, quale desydera molto di servire, che siati per fare di gran facti. Et ulterius dice manda uno in Piemonte per intendere secretamente si qualche practicha si facesse contra la V. S. et como le cose vostre passano, perché più presto sii advisato di preparare li amici soy ad l'adiuto et conservatione vostra, bisognando; et etiam dice vi vole scrivere prima littera dil parentato di soa mano. Così etiam la Ser.ma Regina ne ha mandato a domandare, congratulandosi dil augumento de la V. S. et che bisogna exequire el parentato comenzato. Dicto Filipo Mons.re tuto 'l giorno sta con questo S. Re, el quale lo vede volentiere et fali festa como de prima,

he eagerly wishes to serve, you will do great things together. Further, he says that he will send someone to Piedmont to investigate secretly if there is any plot against Your Lordship and [ascertain] how the situation stands in your respect, so as to be informed in time to prepare his friends, in order that they may help you to maintain your state in case of need. He also says he means to write the first letter concerning the matrimony in his own hand.

Even Her Most Serene Majesty summoned us to express her congratulations for Your Lordship's aggrandizement and to say that it is necessary to conclude the negotiations for the marriage. My Lord Filippo spends the whole day with the King, who sees him willingly and welcomes him as he did before, both showing to have forgotten the past.

We urgently inform Your Excellency of these things so that you may give thought to them as you wish and send us a swift reply so that we know how we are to proceed. We always commend ourselves to Your Most Illustrious Lordship.

HISTORICAL NOTES

1. The possibility of a marriage between the Count of Charolais's only daughter, Marie, and Galeazzo Maria had been advanced to the King unofficially by Emanuele toward the end of 1465, evidently with Francesco Sforza's knowledge. The King, who had just agreed to marry his daughter, Anne, to the Count, liked the idea, hoping to protect himself further from Burgundy by way of this three-power alliance [Mandrot, *Dépêches*, 4:88, 299–305].

2. In April 1464 the King had proposed to the Milanese ambassador, Alberico Maletta, a double marriage between his two sisters-in-law, Maria and Bona, daughters of Duke Louis I of Savoy, and King Edward IV of England

monstrando tute doe parte non havere memoria alcuna dil passato. Si ché de queste cose, volando, ne avisamo V. Ex.tia, aciò che li facia el pensiero che li parerà et subito ne faci risposta, adciò che sapiamo como governarsi. Si riccomandamo sempre ad la V. Ill.ma S.

and Galeazzo Maria. At that time, Galeazzo Maria was betrothed to Dorotea Gonzaga, daughter of the Marquis of Mantua, but rumors had reached the royal court that the betrothal had been dissolved [ibid., 2:71–77]. While the Savoyard-English marriage never took place, that of Galeazzo Maria with Bona of Savoy, constantly urged by Louis XI, was finally celebrated in 1468.

3. Moirans, 21 kilometers northwest of Grenoble.

4. He was released from prison on 23 March [Daviso di Charvensod, *Filippo II*, p. 48].

On behalf of Your Lordship we have thanked all those who seem to us to have spoken vigorously in favor of your release, above all My Lord of Dunois who behaved honorably and truly showed great relief over it; though brother of the late Duke of Orléans, he offered to do whatever might be useful to Your Lordship, to whom he commends himself. We did the same with the Duke of Bourbon, who was your partisan, and with the Bastard of Bourbon, who showed great friendship on this occasion, being willing to risk himself and his possessions so that this kingdom would not suffer such shame. After your liberation, he offered, with all his heart, to put himself at your disposal and at your command—and if the occasion should arise, he will prove it.

Furthermore, the King has ordained that Gaston and Master Giovanni Filippo da Trecate[1] be sent to visit Your Excellency and Your Most Illustrious mother; they will leave tomorrow or the day after. Then the Archbishop of Vienne[2] and My Lord of Gaucourt will leave for the Italian states; but first of all they will come to Milan in order to show greater favor for your interests and demonstrate that His Majesty is greatly concerned in this matter, asserting that he wants to defend your state as if it were his own kingdom. [Should Your Excellency think that so many embassies to the Italian states are not necessary, you may

13 · EMANUELE DE IACOPO *and*

GIOVAN PIETRO PANIGAROLA *to the*

DUKE OF MILAN

Francia, cart. 532. Orig.; BN, Fonds Italien, Cod. 1593, fol. 235v. Copy

Habiamo per parte de la V.S. ringratiato quelli che ne hé parso habiano parlato per la liberatione de la V.S. caldamente, maxime Mons.re de Donoes quale se gli hé dignamente portato; et in vero ne ha dimonstrato havere grande consolatione, et in ogni cosa che achada, quamvis fusse fratello dil condam Duca de Orliens, si offere fare per la V.S. ala quale si ricomanda. El simile habiamo facto al Duca di Borbon, che hé stato vostro partesano, et al Bastardo di Borbon che in questo bisogno si hé monstrato affectionatissimo, et volerli exponere la persona et quanto haveva per non patire tanta infamia a questo Reame. Di poy la liberatione vostra ne ha dicto offerendosi ad la V. Ex.tia sempre volere essere ad li comandi vostri, di bono et perfecto core, et quando achada dice lo trovarà con effecto. Ulterius la M.tà di questo S. Re ha ordinato di mandare Gastoneto et Maystro Iohan Filipo da Trechà[1] ad visitare la V. Ex.tia et la Ill.ma vostra Madre et domane o l'altro partirano. Poy apresso vegnirano l'Arcivescovo di Viena[2] et Mons.re di Gocurt et si ordinarano andare per le potentie di Italia, ma questi prima partirano et subito vegniranno a Milano per dare più favore a le cose vostre, et monstare che questa cosa tocha ad la M.tà Soa, quale dice volere deffendere quelo Stato como el suo proprio Regno. [Et[a] se ad la V. Ex.tia paresse non

---

a. The original text shows three pairs of bracket-like signs enclosing three passages, which were

inform us of your intention, and we accordingly will make every effort to follow and adjust to your orders].

Regarding the troops that are in the Dauphiné, His Majesty wants them to proceed to the defense of your state; at the moment he is settling things so they may leave the Dauphiné with dignity and return in a readied condition, so that Your Excellency may dispose of them if there is need. [From what we have heard, it is said that they will be given about six thousand écus, but His Majesty has not mentioned any sum, merely repeating that he will see to their leaving with honor. Therefore, we will inform Your Lordship of the manner in which this is settled.]

An English embassy[3] is here in order to ask the King for a four-year truce, avowing their desire for peace. It has been arranged that the English ambassadors should meet in the next few days with His Majesty in order to reach a conclusion, if possible.

[As regards Your Excellency's request for fifty thousand écus, nothing further has been done. In view of the provisions that had to be made for your release, we did not think it prudent to advance too many requests all at once, especially since every day His Majesty complains of being short of money. Similarly, we also thought it wise to put off the matter for certain other reasons, which Your Excellency will hear from Giovanni Andrea Tizzone, who is leaving shortly. Therefore we shall do nothing more concerning this matter until we receive orders from Your Excellency, to whom we humbly commend ourselves.]

HISTORICAL NOTES

1. The King's instructions to Gaston and Giovanni Filippo are in Appendix, doc. VII.

2. Antoine de Poisieu. On 11 February 1466 he, together with Charles de Gaucourt, Pierre Salat, and Giovanni Filippo da Trecate, had been in Milan, sent by Louis XI to thank Francesco Sforza for the Milanese troops already in France, expedite the dispatch of additional troops, and request that the Duke send an envoy to the royal court with full powers to conclude the marriage of Galeazzo Maria and Bona of Savoy [The Duke to Gerardo de' Colli,

havere bisogno di tante ambassate ad le potentie de Italia, ne porà advisare de la intentione soa, che sicondo quela si sforzaremo adaptare et seguire li comandamenti soy.] Circha la gente d'arme che sono in Delfinato, intende la p.ta M.tà che passeno per conservatione dil Stato vostro et al presente hé in questa impresa per darli forma, intendendo che passeno honorevolmente et che si posseno levare et ritornare in poncto, aciò che essendo bisogno V. Ex.tia se ne possi valere. [Et per quanto ne hé stato riferto, hé stato ventillato di darli circha scudi sey millia; pure essa M.tà peranche non ne ha dicto somma alcuna, salvo che proverderà in modo se levarano con honore; siché como in questa facenda si concluda ne avisaremo V.S.] Qui si ritrova una ambassata di Englexi[3] quale cerchano tregua con questo S. Re per anni quatro, monstrando volere pace, et fra pochi dì hé ordinato si troveno insieme le ambassate de Englexi et di Soa M.tà per concludere in questa facenda se si porà. [Circha la riquesta che V. Ex.tia faceva de scudi L.ta M. non si hé facto altro, perchè dovendo havere le provisione che si facevano per la rellaxatione vostra non ne parse di metere tante domande ad uno tracto, et maxime condolendosi la p.ta M.ta ogni dì di essere senza dinari como fa. Siché ne hé etiam parso de differire di parlarne per certi altri rispecti, como da Iohanne Andrea Tizone porà V.S. intendere, quale in breve si partirà; donde non faremo altro in questa materia fino che da quela habiamo aviso, ala quale humilmente si riccomandiamo.]

Milanese ambassador in Venice, Milan, 11 February 1466, BN, *Fonds Italien*, Cod. 1591, fol. 262]. About a week later, they were on their way back to France [The Duke to Giovanni de' Attendoli and Gandolfo de Bologna, Milan, 17 February 1466, *Registri Missive*, Reg. 72, fol. 95].

3. The English ambassadors, empowered by Edward IV on 22 March 1466 to negotiate the truce, were the Earl of Warwick, Lord William Hastings, John Wenlock, Peter Taster, Thomas Montgomery, Thomas Kent, Thomas Colt, and Richard Whetehill [Calmette-Perinelle, *Louis XI*, p. 72].

---

omitted from the copy in Cod. 1593. This copy was apparently sent by the chancery to other rulers and Milanese ambassadors, as it was often done by the Dukes of Milan. In this case, the omitted passages were probably deemed too sensitive to be shared with others.

While conversing on various matters with the King, who very much wishes that Your Lordship have and maintain your state in a condition of peace and tranquility and even augment it, if possible, *he told us that here Your Lordship has two adversaries; that is, the House of Orléans which is not* to be feared, because it is much reduced in power and in men. *At the Count of Dunois' death*[1] (*which* by law of nature must be quite near), the House of Orléans would be still more weakened. *Then there is the House of Anjou, which is much more powerful both in members and allies, not to mention its claims over the Kingdom of Naples. Although His Majesty will always keep this House so subdued and under control that it will not be able to cause trouble or harm to Your Lordship, it would greatly please him and he would approve of it, if there were found by way of money a means to reach an agreement between King Ferrante and Duke John;*[2] *or indeed some compensation might be established, as for instance, King Ferrante could give some territory there* [in the Kingdom of Naples] *to the Pope in exchange for Avignon*[3] *which could be given to Duke John. This would be an apt exchange because it* [Avignon] *is on the borders of Provence. The King says that should such an accomodation be found, he would support it vigorously in order to avoid any trouble in the future, and in this way Duke John would no longer have any reason to go over there* [to Italy].

14 · EMANUELE DE IACOPO *and*

GIOVAN PIETRO PANIGAROLA *to the*

DUKE OF MILAN

BN, Fonds Italien, Cod. 1593, fol. 237–37v. Orig.

Ritrovandone ad varii ragionamenti con questo S. Re, la M.tà Soa quale grandemente desydera che V.S. habia et tegna el Stato suo pacifico et quieto et etiam, si possibile est, lo augmenti, *ne disse che de qua la S.ria V. haveva doi adversari, cioé la Casa de Orliens, dela quale non* bisognava dubitare per essere quela molto abassata et di potentia et de homeni *et morto el Conte de Dunos,*[1] *quale sicondo* legie di natura hé assay proximo, ancor più seria nichillata. *Deinde la Casa de Angiò, quale hé molto più potente et de persone et de alligati, et non hé che non pretenda drito suso el Reame de Napoli, et quanvis la M.tà Soa la tegnirà sempre così bassa et curta che non porà offendere né dare impazo ad la S.ria V., li piaceria molto et collodaria se si potesse trovare mezo de acordo per via de dinari tra el Signor Re Ferrando et el Duca Iohanne,*[2] *overo fare qualche recompensatione come saria se delà esso Re Ferdinando potesse dare cambio al Papa de Avignone*[3] *et darlo al prefato Duca Iohanne et seriali assai conforme, perché confina con Provenza. Et quando questa via se li potesse trovare, dice la collodaria grandemente per rimovere ogni inconveniente che ad tempo avegnire potesse adcadere, dicendo che anche in questa forma se li rimoverà la casone de vegnire delà, cioé ad esso Duca Iohanne,* subgiogendo etiam che la p.ta Soa M.tà poria molto *servire in questo caso che andando quela ad conquistare questa estate Mes*[4] *in le* confine de *Lorena, come spera, el quale confina con el*

His Majesty also pointed out that he might *contribute greatly to this solution if this summer he were to go, as he hopes, to the conquest of Metz,*[4] *on the borders of Lorraine. Duke John might then fear that after the conquest of Metz the King might have the intention of taking away from him the Duchy of Lorraine, which has extensive borders with Metz. Therefore, Duke John, in order to safeguard this side and to relieve himself of that other burden [Naples], also knowing that he cannot conquer the Kingdom of Naples without His Majesty's help (who is not willing to offer any), would resign himself to the above mentioned agreement through the King's efforts.* His Majesty, who wishes your welfare, *informs Your Lordship of all this so you may give it some thought, assuring you that he will always do his best so that the accord may effectively turn out to your advantage and benefit.*

Three days ago Gaston left here and will come to Milan without wasting time. On his way he will see Madame of Savoy and the Marquis of Monferrat, with whom he will speak at length on His Majesty's behalf, urging them to remain on friendly terms and give every aid and support to Your Lordship in the maintenance of your state, since His Majesty intends to use his every power in defending and preserving it. The Archbishop of Vienne and My Lord of Gaucourt have arrived here. Tomorrow they will have an audience concerning their diplomatic mission,[5] and we hope that they will soon be able to depart.

Master Giovanni Filippo da Trecate left today; he will go to the Dauphiné, then will join Gaston on the journey to Milan.[6] Giovanni Filippo has been charged by the King to meet the Treasurer of the Dauphiné [Claude Cot], who was to give Your Lordship's troops *four thousand écus so that they could depart. The King will then charge the money against his own income* from the Dauphiné. The King has also sent the President of the Parlement of Grenoble [Pierre Gruel] with orders to intervene where the soldiers have accumulated debts, so that they may leave without having to pay them.[7] Although we regarded this provision to be rather unseemly for Your Lordship, and one that might provoke trouble and confusion in that region, we thought better not to

Ducato de Lorena gran parte, el Duca Iohanne se dubitarà che, conquistato quelo, non li toglia poi el paise de Lorena. Donde per havere questo sicuro et uscire di quelo altro afano, cognoscendo etiam che non pò guadagnare esso Reame de Napoli senza spala de la M.tà Soa, la quale non li vole fare, spera per suo mezo se reduria ad questo acordo. Siché dice la prefata M.tà, desyderosa dil bene vostro, *che volentieri ne avisa la S.ria V. aciò che li possi fare pensiero che lei sempre li meterà ogni studio, perché la cosa reinscia ad efecto, utile et bene dela prelibata S.ria V.*

Insuper Guastoneto hogie III giorni partite de qui et se ne vegnirà senza perdere tempo a Millanno, facendo el camino di Madama di Savoya et dil Marchese di Monferrato, a li quali dirà per parte di la p.ta M.tà molte parole, confortandoli ad stare et perseverare in amore et dare ogni adiuto et favore ad la V. Ex.tia et conservatione dil Stato suo, intendendo essa M.tà con ogni soa potentia mantenerlo et deffenderlo. L'Arcivescovo de Viena et Mons.re de Gocurt sono arivati in questa terra; domane debeno havere audientia ad exponere la loro ambassata[5] et in breve, speramo, sarano spazati. Metre Iohanne Filippo da Trechà, Presidente, hogie hé partito; vasene in Delfinato et poy si trovarà cum Gastoneto a vegnire a Millanno.[6] El dicto Iohannefilipo ha auto commissione da questo S. Re di trovarsi cum el Tesorero di Delfinato, che proveda ale gente d'arme de la S.V. *de scudi quatro millia per levarsi, che poi la M.tà Soa gli li farà boni in le intrate soe del* Delfinato. Et ulterius ha mandato el Presidente dil Parlamento di Granoble cum commissione che proveda dove le gente d'arme hanno debito, che si leveno senza pagare loro cosa alchuna.[7] Et perché ne hé parso questo essere un pocho di caricho al honore de la V. Ex.tia et apto ad mettere scandalo et confusione in el payse, *monstrandose etiam essa Maiestà essere al presente molto streta de dinari per le guerre* ocorsse [*sic*] et havendo io, Emanuel, sicondo che mi commisse V. Ex.tia statim che foi zonto, *riquesto ad quela che li facesse provissione de scudi sei millia o octo millia*[8] *et non vedendo al efecto facta altra provisione, se non come de sopra hé dicto, per* questi rispecti non ne hé parso di cazare la

discuss it further, *such a small sum being involved and considering the great expenses and* important services that your late father and Your Lordship had undertaken for the King. We also had in mind the fact that *the King evidenced a great scarcity of funds owing to past wars* and that I, Emanuele, upon my arrival here, had been charged by Your Excellency *to request the King to make provisions for the payment of six or eight thousand écus,*[8] *but saw that in effect no other provision was being made other than the one mentioned above.* For all these reasons we decided to reserve our efforts for some greater need, particularly because we feared that the four thousand écus to be paid by the Treasurer might be disbursed with some delay, so that the troops would be kept in suspense and with further expenses. We felt that perhaps Your Lordship might have a need for these troops unknown to us. It has been our wish to inform Your Lordship quickly of all this so that you may make suitable provisions for the troops' departure, since the King is willing, as he is, to have not only our own troops return, but add some of his own if needed. They will be escorted as far as Your Lordship's territory by My Lord of Châteaneuf,[9] sent there as Lieutenant General.

Today His Majesty is going to Jargeau,[10] four leagues distant from here, in order to spend a peaceful and quiet Easter; he is anxious to receive news from Your Lordship. If anything else should arise, we will do our best to inform immediately Your Lordship, to whom we humbly commend ourselves.

HISTORICAL NOTES

1. Jean d'Orléans, Count of Dunois, was born between 1400 and 1402. The allusion here refers to the well-known rights over the Duchy of Milan claimed by the House of Orléans.

2. By 1464, Duke John of Lorraine had lost his four-year war to dethrone King Ferrante of Naples, illegitimate son of Alfonso V, King of Aragon, Naples, and Sicily. The House of Anjou, however, continued to pursue its claims over Naples, dating back to 1265, when Pope Clement IV invested

cosa più avanti *per così picola somma né farne altra instantia, considerato la grande spesa et el* rellevato servitio ch'el quondam Ill.mo S. vostro padre et la V.S. hanno facto ad la p.ta Soa M.tà, *ma reservarvella ad magiore bisogno. Et perché dubitiamo che li scudi quatro millia del Tesorero non* vadano un pocho a la longa, et per questo le gente d'arme stiano in pendente et con spessa, dele quali forsi V. S. poria havere bisogno che non sapiamo, habiamo voluto dil tuto, volando, avisare V. Ex.tia, adcioché essendo questo S. Re contento (como hé) che le gente d'arme se ne ritorneno et non solum li nostri, ma de quelli de Soa M.tà, bisognando, possi fare quela provisione gli parerà al levare di quelle. Et quando se partirano, con loro sarà Mons.re de Chiastronovo,[9] mandato di delà Locotenente Generale, che le condurà fino in le terre de la prelibata V.S. Questo dì la M.tà Soa va ad Gargeos,[10] longhi da qui leghe IIII.to, per fare lì Pasqua pacifica et senza strepito, atendendo con desyderio novelle de la V. S. Se altro sopravenerà, si sforzaremo avisarla subito, ala quale humilmente si reccomandiamo.

Charles, Count of Anjou and Provence, with the Kingdom of Sicily, which at that time included Naples.

3. The city of Avigon was sold in 1348 to the papacy by Countess Joanna of Provence.

4. Metz, imperial city situated on the Moselle River between the two largest portions of the Duchy of Lorraine, was claimed by the French kings in their self-proclaimed role as true descendants of Charlemagne [Mandrot, *Dépêches*, 4:244, n. 1].

5. Presumably this refers to their February mission in Milan [doc. 13, n. 2].

6. On 27 March 1466 Emanuele and Panigarola had written briefly from Orléans to the Duke, announcing this mission by Gaston du Lyon and Giovanni Filippo de Trecate [*Francia*, cart. 532].

7. The Milanese troops in Dauphiné had not been paid for some time, and it was feared that some of them, discouraged over Galeazzo Maria's sudden departure, would disband and return to Milan in disorder. Milanese officials were forced to pawn with the Medici Bank in Lyon the silver and clothes left behind by Galeazzo Maria in order to cover their more immediate expenses [Giovanni Pallavicino to the Dukes, Beaurepaire, 14, 21, 30 March 1466, *Francia*, cart. 532; Giovanni Bianchi to G. Pallavicino, Lyon, 14, 15 March 1466, BN, *Fonds Italien*, Cod. 1591, fol. 283, and *Genoa*, cart. 425, respectively; G. Bianchi to the Duke, Beaurepaire, 20 March 1466, BN, *Fonds Italien*, Cod. 1591, fols. 286, 302–3].

8. See doc. 21, n. 8.

9. Soffrey Alleman, Lord of Châteauneuf, had already arrived in Lyon on 26 March on his way to the Dauphiné [Giovanni Pallavicino to the Duke, Beaurepaire, 30 March 1466, *Francia*, cart. 532].

10. Jargeau, 19 kilometers southeast of Orléans.

From the letters of His Most Serene Majesty and Most Christian King,[1] and also from yours, dated at Orléans the eighteenth of this month,[2] we have come to know how much worry, sorrow, and grief His Most Serene Majesty felt about the passing of the Most Illustrious late Lord, our husband and father; we have also His Majesty's wise and kind exhortation to behave with wisdom and caution, and his generous and gracious consent not only to the fact that we, Galeazzo, have followed the will and orders of the Most Illustrious Lady, our mother, to return here and call back our troops that are there [in France], but also if necessary to send us some of his troops, as many as we might need and ask for, etc.

In answer, we say that as soon as you receive this letter, we want you to go to His Majesty to whom we reply briefly with the enclosed letters,[3] committing ourselves under your letters of credence. First of all, you will thank His Majesty, with all the cordiality and reverence you are able to express, for all the love, charity, and generosity he has deigned to show us in our time of need, in grieving over the death of the late Lord, our husband and father. He really deserved [such deep sorrow] because His Lordship during his life was most affectionate toward His Majesty and was the most faithful friend and servant he ever had. You will thank the King for the offers and good advice he

15 · *The* DUKE *and* DUCHESS OF MILAN *to*

GIOVAN PIETRO PANIGAROLA

BN, Fonds Italien, Cod. 1593, fols. 240–42. Minute[a]

Per littere de la Ser.ma M.tà de quello Christianissimo S. Re,[1] et
cossì per le toe de dì XVIII del presente,[2] date in Orliens, havemo inteso
quanto affano, dispiacere, et dolore ha presso [*sic*] Soa Ser.ma M.tà del
caso del Ill.mo quondam S. nostro consorte et patre; el bon et amorevelle
recordo ne dà in governarne con consiglio et prudentia; et cossì la soa
tanto magnanima et liberale offerta ne fa, non tanto de contentarse che
nuy, Galeazo, habiamo seguite la voluntà et commandamento de la
Ill.ma Madona nostra madre in venire de qua et le nostre gente sono
delà retornano ad casa, ma bisognando, gli ne mandarà de le soe tante
quante se serà bisogno, et domandaremo etc. Respondendo dicimo che
volimo quam primum haveray recevuta questa nostra te ne vadi alla
M.tà prefata, alla quale per l'aligate brevamente respondiamo,[3] remettendone in toa credenza. Et primo quanto humanamente et reverente-
mente saperay et poray regratiaray Soa M.tà de tanto cordiale amore,
carita et magnanimità se é dignata monstrarne in questo nostro caso, in
dolerse dela morte del prefato quondam S. nostro consorte et patre; et me-
ritò veramente, perché Soa Signoria finché vixe li fo tanto amorevele et fi-
do amico et servitore, quanto may havesse Soa Ser.ma M.tà, et de le offerte
ne fa et bon recordo ne dà. Per la quale cosa, et per molti benefici rece-

---

a. The numerous erasures and corrections in this document have presented difficulties in
transcription.

gives us; in view of which and because of many benefits received from
him by our consort and father, we, following in the footsteps and faithful to the memory of our late Lord, our husband and father, will always
be His Majesty's true and devoted sons and servants. In this most bitter,
sad, and sudden event, all our remaining hope and comfort lie with His
Majesty who, we are quite sure, will never fail in every possible way to
advise and help us in whatever necessity might occur for the preservation
of this state of ours, upon which His Majesty may always rely for help
as if it were his own.

Commend us to His Majesty as warmly as you can; then, since he
wishes that our troops there come home, beg him to deign to dispatch
a commissary to the Dauphiné, with orders to break camp and accompany the troops across the mountains, so that we may dispose of them
for any occurrence that might arise. In order that His Majesty know
how things stand with us, tell him that after the passing of our late
husband and father, our people remained and are tranquil and peaceful,
nor did they show any signs of restlessness, but on the contrary have
exhibited most faithfulness and obedience.

His Holiness the Pope is sending us an ambassador to comfort us
and let us know he is always disposed to help and support us in the maintenance of our state; by means of apostolic briefs he has written to all
the rulers of Italy to let them know that he has the firm intention of
maintaining peace in Italy, and urging each one not to molest us in any
way.[4]

His Majesty King Ferrante, with great liberality, does everything
to give us help and support. First, he has sent twelve galleys with sufficient infantry to Genoa for the maintenance of that state, and we, for
our part, have dispatched there some infantry; furthermore, the Genoese
are well disposed toward us. The Archbishop of Genoa had left Padua
where he was staying, and with the money he received from the Venetians, he had engaged some soldiers with whom he reached the Lunigiana
in order to establish himself on the eastern Riviera. Having learned of

vuti da quella per el prefato nostro consorte et patre, sempre imitando li vestigii et recordi del prefato quondam S. nostro consorte et patre, li saremo veri et cordialissimi figlioli et servitori. Et quanta speranza et conforto ne sia restato in questo nostro acerbissimo, repentino et doloroso caso consiste in la Soa M.tà quale siamo certissimi, in alcuna cosa ad essa possibile, non ne mancarà may de consiglio et aiuto in qualunche necessità ne potesse accadere per conservatione de questo nostro Stato, del quale sempre se porà valere et aiutare como de le soe cose proprie; et ne recomandaray alla M.tà Soa tanto strectamente quanto possibile te serà. Deinde^b la pregaray che se digni, poy che é de suo piacere, che quelle nostre gente sono dellà retornano ad casa, ordinare et mandare qualche suo commissario^c in Delphinato per farle levare et acompagnare de qua dali monti, perché de quelle ne possiamo valere ad ogni caso potesse occorerne. Et perché Soa M.tà intende in che termine sono le cose nostre, l'avisaray che dapoy seguitò el caso del prefato quondam nostro consorte et patre, questi nostri populi sonno stati et stano in pace et quiete, né alcuna novità hanno facta, ma se sonno monstrati fidelissimi et obedientissimi. La S.tà de Nostro Sig.re manda qui da nuy uno suo ambassatore ad confortarne et offerirne de essere sempre in nostro aiuto et favore per conservatione de questo nostro Stato, et per brevi apostolici ha scripto ad tutti li potentati de Italia essere soa ferma intentione de conservare la pace italica, confortando caduno ad non farne novità alcuna.[4] La M.tà del Re Ferrando molto liberamente fa tutto per nostro aiuto et favore. Et primo ha ma[n]date ad Zenoa XII galee con una bona fantaria per conservatione de quello Stato, et nuy li havimo proveduto certi fanti et anche quilli citadini sonno ben disposti verso nuy. L'Arcevescovo de Zenoa era partito da Padua dove stava, et con certi dinari haveva havuti da Venetiani, haveva facti alcuni fanti con li quali é venuto in Lunesana, poy per intrare in la rivera de Levanto; ma intese le provisione facte, se é retirato in quello del Ill.mo S. Duca de Modena dove sta, non

---

b. Crossed out: l'avisaray che da poy seguitò tale caso, questi nostri populi non hanno facto novità alcuna.

c. Crossed out: ad Lione.

the measures taken, however, he retired to the Duke of Modena's territory where he still is—we have no idea what he means to do.[5]

His Majesty King Ferrante has also written and sent envoys to all the lords and states in Italy to urge and persuade them to maintain peace in Italy; to favor and help us in the defense of our state, making them understand that His Majesty considers the destiny of our state to be the same as his own. In particular, he has sent envoys and written a letter to the Venetians, whose contents you will learn from the enclosed copy. The King has given money to our troops who were in Abruzzo and to those of our brother-in-law and uncle,[6] Lord Allesandro, Grand Constable of the Kingdom, in order that they may prepare themselves for the return journey. His Majesty has also allocated funds for his own troops and wants to gather them in Abruzzo so that they may be more handy to help us defend the state if needed.[7]

As soon as the Marquis of Monferrat heard about the passing of our husband and father, he came to us and offered himself with great generosity: now he has left for home and is well disposed toward us and our state.[8]

The Count of Urbino,[9] the Grand Constable, and the Florentine ambassadors[10] are here. The ambassadors have offered to do all that is necessary for the maintenance of our state. From Venice, we have some word of assurance that that government wants to live in peace and be a good neighbor. Nevertheless, Bartolomeo da Bergamo is mustering and collecting troops, cavalry and infantry, even new recruits, and paying them; but we do not know to what purpose. We think it unwise to trust what the Venetians say, but it is not an easy task to equip our troops who are in Lombardy, given that all of them lack mounts because our late husband and father left all the revenue pledged and heavily in debt, while we face many immediate expenses. Yet, we are doing our utmost to prepare as many of our troops as we can so that we may be ready to defend ourselves if there should be any need, whether it is a question of Bartolomeo or others. In this case we shall resort to the King's offers because, as we have already said, all our hope and comfort are placed in

sapemo quello farà.[5] Ha ancora la prefata M.tà del Re Ferrando scripto et mandati suoy oratori ad tutti li Sig.ri et Signorie de Italia ad confortarli et persuaderli alla conservatione dela pace italica, et esserne in favore et aiuto nostro per defensione de questo Stato, facendol intendere che Soa M.tà intende che quello sarà de questo nostro Stato sia del suo. Et precipue ha scripto et mandato ad Venetiani quanto per la copia inclusa intenderay. Ale nostre gente d'arme erano in Apruzo et ad quelle del S. Alexandro, nostro cognato et barba,[6] Gran Connestabile del Reame, ha dati dinari per meterse in ordine et ne le remanda de qua; cossì fa dare dinari ale gente de Soa M.tà, et vole unirle in Apruzo per essere più vicino alli nostri favori et defensione del Stato[7] quando bisognasse.[d]

El S. Marchese de Monferrato, como hebbe inteso el caso del prefato nostro consorte et patre vene qui da nuy, se ne oferse molto liberamente; mo se é partito[e] per retornare a casa et é ben disposto verso nuy et Stato nostro.[8] Qui se trovano el S. Conte de Urbino,[9] et cossì el prefato Gran Connestabile, et li ambassatori firentini,[10] qual ambassatori se sono offerti largamente ad fare quanto bisognare per conservatione del Stato nostro. Da Venetia havemo bone parole che quella Signoria dice volere vivere in pace et ben vicinare con nuy. Pur Bartolomeo da Bergamo fa gran movimenti de gente con dare dinari ale soe gente, et toltone dele nove, con dire volere fare gran conducta de gente de cavallo et da pede, non sapiamo ad che effecto. Et parendone poterne male fidare dele parole de Venetiani, licet mal habiamo el modo de remettere queste nostre gente d'arme che sono in Lumbardia, quale sonno tutte a pedi, per haverne lassate el prefato quondam S. nostro consorte et patre l'intrate tutte impignate et de grandi debiti, et molte spese ne occoreno alla iornata; tamen ne sforzamo metterne in ordine più che possiamo, aciò che se altro occoresse ne possiamo defendere: volesse fare dicto Bartolomeo o altri, nel quale caso bisognando usaremo dele offerete de quello S. Re, perchè havimo dicto ogni nostra speranza et conforto consiste in quello S. Re

---

d. Crossed out: et con quelle venire lí in Apruzo Soa M.tà con lo Ill.mo S. Duca de Calabria, suo figliolo, con fermo proposto, bisognando, de venire ley qui in persona alli nostri favori.

e. Crossed out: per certa novità pare li voglia essere facta in alcuno suo loco in Pedemonte; non sapemo però che se sia.

him, to whom you must continue to commend us, the state, our sons and brothers.

For the above reasons we have written that our troops in Abruzzo be sent back to us immediately; and similarly you will entreat the King that he deign to send back those who are there, so that we may be ready for any danger or occurrence.

The Illustrious Lord Ercole, brother of the Illustrious Duke of Modena, has returned home, too, after coming to visit us.

Addition: regarding those Venetians[11] who are going to Duke John, etc., we wish you to thank His Majesty for what he has deigned to communicate to you about this matter, and make every effort to ascertain who they are and what they are trying to do. Let us know at once what you hear.

Postscript. From a trustworthy source we have been informed that the Illustrious Duke of Savoy has sent to Venice the Abbot of Casanova to prompt that government to declare war against us,[12] and he is similarly urging the Marquis of Monferrat. Consequently, as soon as you receive this letter, we want you to inform the King about what is being said and tell him on our behalf that it would be a good thing for His Majesty to send one of his capable and authoritative men to the Duke of Savoy to dissuade him from such maneuvers—one that might remain with that Lord with the purpose of persuading him and making him favorable to His Majesty's will and welfare, as well as the welfare of his friends and servants, so that he should not undertake any activity that may displease His Majesty and his friends and servants. Let us know at once the King's answer and the measures he means to take.

HISTORICAL NOTES

1. Appendix, doc. III.
2. Doc. 5.
3. On the day this letter was written, the Dukes wrote to the King [*Fran-*

ala quale vogliamo che nuy, Stato, figlioli et fratelli nostri debii continue recommandarne. Per le quale casone, come é dicto, havemo scripto che con celerità ne sian mandate le gente nostre sono in Apruzo, et cossì pregaray quello S. Re se digni remandarne quelle che sono dellà, aciò possiamo prevenire ad ogni pericolo et via.

Lo Ill. D. Hercules, fratello del Ill. S. Duca de Modena, quale é stato qui ad visitarne, anche luy é ritornato a casa.

Poliza.

De quelli Venetiani[11] vano dal Duca Iohanne, etc., volemo ne regratii la M.tà Soa de quello s'é dignata comunicare con ti in queste cose, et vedi de sforzarte intendere chi sonno et quello vanno facendo, et cossì de quanto intenderay alla iornata avisane.

Post scripta.[f] Nuy havemo aviso da loco digno de fede che lo Ill. S. Duca de Savoya ha mandato l'Abbate de Casanova ad Venetia ad instigare quella Signoria ad moverne guerra,[12] et similiter fa instigare el Marchese de Monferrato. Però volimo che subito havuta questa, notifichi ad quello S. Re quanto é dicto, et li dighi da nostra parte che saria bene che Soa M.tà mandasse uno deli suoy, che fosse persona intelligente et de auctoritate, dal prefato del [sic] Duca de Savoya per torlo da tale pratiche, et che stesse presso esso S. per persuaderlo et drizarlo ad quello che é la voluntà et bene de Soa M.tà et deli amici et servitori suoy, aciò non habia casone intrare in praticha che possa essere molesta ad essa M.tà et amici et servitori suoy. Et de quello che circa questo te responderà et la provisione li farà Soa M.tà, avisane subito.

---

f. Next to the date of this postscript there is the Chancery's notation, "in zifra," signifying that the postscript was to be written wholly or partly in cipher. Since the original has not been found, we have preferred to omit italics in this case because it cannot be determined what portions were written in cipher.

cia, cart. 532], again expressing deep appreciation for his offers of support and requesting the immediate return of their troops from France. They also notified him that they had decided to send a special envoy to inform him more fully on the situation in Milan.

4. Upon hearing the news of Francesco Sforza's death, Pope Paul II called a Consistory of the cardinals, during which the common view was expressed "essere extinta la luce et gloria de Italia." It was decided that the Church take Milan under its protection to ensure the peaceful succession of the Dukes and preserve the peace of Italy, felt to be necessary for a common front against the Turks. In his capacity as the leader of the Italian League, the Pope sent briefs to all Italian rulers urging them to keep it intact. He also decided to send to Milan the Bishop of Leon (Spain), Antonio Giacomo de Veneris, to offer condolences and support [Agostino Rossi, Milanese ambassador at the papal court, to the Duchess, Rome, 18 March 1466, BN, *Fonds Italien*, Cod. 1591, fols. 293–94]. The Bishop left Rome on 20 March with instructions to pass through Siena and Florence where he was to urge support for Milan [Rossi to the Duke, Rome, 20 March 1466, *Roma*, cart. 59].

5. The Archbishop and former Doge of Genoa, Paolo Campofregoso, had never reconciled himself to Sforza's seizure of the city, and was constantly plotting his return to power. On this same date, the Duke of Milan wrote to Borso d'Este, Duke of Modena, requesting that he not give aid or refuge to the Archbishop [BN, *Fonds Italien*, Cod. 1591, fol. 319]. Borso denied that he had given such aid or that he had any intention of doing so [Ferrara, 4 April 1466, ibid., Cod. 1591, fol. 331].

6. Alessandro Sforza, Lord of Pesaro in the Marches, Grand Constable of Naples and brother of Francesco Sforza.

7. King Ferrante's feverish activity in support of Milan, even before he had received confirmation of Francesco's death, is attested by many documents. See particularly the following: Antonio da Trezzo, Milanese ambassador in Naples, to the Duchess, Naples, 18, 20 March 1466, BN, *Fonds Italien*, Cod. 1591, fols. 296–96v, 300–300v; Ferrante to the Duchess and to the *Dodici di Provvisione* of Milan, Naples, 19 March 1466, ibid., Cod. 1591, fols. 298–99v and 297 respectively; Ferrante to Louis XI, Castronovo in Naples, 22 March 1466, *Registri Missive*, Reg. 77, fols. 66–67v.

8. Marquis Guglielmo of Monferrat arrived in Milan on 11 March [Maria Damarco, "Guglielmo I Paleologo (Marchese di Monferrato, 1420–1483)," *Rivista di storia, arte e archeologia per le province di Alessandria e Asti*, 42 (1933): 563, n. 1]. He escorted Galeazzo Maria's entry into Milan on 19 March [Appendix, doc. IV].

9. Federico III di Montefeltro.

10. The Florentine ambassadors were Bernardo di Filippo Giugni and Luigi di Piero Guicciardini. Their instructions, dated 12 March 1466, are in the ASF, *Signori, Carteggi, Missive. Legazioni e Commissarie. Elezioni e Istruzioni a Oratori*, Reg. 16, fols. 20v–21v.

11. See doc. 5.

12. In Milan it was believed that the mission of the Abbot of Casanova had the purpose of promoting a coordinated attack by Venice and Savoy [The Dukes of Gerardo de' Colli, Milan, 1 April 1466, *Venezia*, cart. 353].

After the departure of Cristoforo,[1] Giovan Pietro's servant, whom we urgently sent to Your Excellency with suitable letters telling in full what was happening, we were and still are in great apprehension and quite sorrowful, considering that it is fifteen days since Your Lordship was to arrive in Milan; but up to this very hour you have neither written nor given orders as to what we must do. Feeling the apprehension and sorrow that Your Highness can well imagine, given what occurred to you, we certainly are very astonished and amazed that you did not take pity and at least write to give us a little consolation and comfort, telling of your return to Milan and to that prosperity and felicitude we wish you.

We inform you that a hundred times a day His Majesty asks us if we have any news, if Your Lordship had arrived, and how things stand over there; he is astonished at such a long delay, because, as he says publicly, he is no less eagerly waiting for that news as if it concerned the recovery of his kingdom. Knowing how eager His Majesty is to hear about your accession and prosperity, we faithfully remind Your Lordship to write often, especially since from various quarters Your Excellency's adversaries are spreading news and rumors that are contrary to your welfare and honor, such that reflect what they wish would come true, though we are certain that through divine grace and owing to Your Lordship's good government and wisdom, their words and wishes will

16 · EMANUELE DE IACOPO *and*

GIOVAN PIETRO PANIGAROLA *to the*

DUKE OF MILAN

Francia, cart. 532. Orig.

Dapoy la partita di Christoforo,[1] servitore di me Iohannepetro, quale mandamo batando da la V. Ex.tia con littere opportune et ample di quanto achadeva, continue siamo stati et stiamo in grandissimo affanno et despiacere, consyderando che hogie siano quindeci giorni che la S.V. doveva arivare ad Millanno et fino in questa hora non ne habii scritto né ordinato quello che di qua habiamo a fare et operare. Et per certo ne restiamo molto stupefacti et cum grandissima admiratione, che stando noy in quello dolore et affano che pò V. Cel. pensare per el caso intervenuto ad quella, non ne sia auto compassione et scrittone almanco per darne questa consolatione et refrigerio, che essa V.S. sia reducta ad Millanno in quella prosperità et felicitate quale desyderamo. Nottificandoli che questo S. Re cento volte el giorno ne domanda se altro habiamo di novo, che la S.V. sia gionta et como passano le cose di là, maravigliandosi molto di tanta tardatione, parendoli et così publice dice, non cum magiore desyderio aspectare questa novella, como si havesse recuperato el suo Regno. Donde fidelmente recordiamo ad la p.ta V. S. per el grande desyderio che monstra havere la M.tà Soa di sentire de la successione et prosperità vostra, fare scrivere di qua spesso, maxime che qui da molti canti per li adversarii de la V. Ex.tia sono spanse [*sic*] varie voce et murmuratione contrarie al bene et honore di quella, et tale le dicono como voriano che succedesseno, benché si rendiamo certi mediante la

come to nothing. Your Highness will understand, therefore, how relieved we will be when we hear that you have arrived in Milan safely and in good health. Do not be astonished at our insisting, for we are so constrained by our affection and fidelity.

Further, King René's son-in-law, the Count of Vaudemont,[2] and the Bishop of Marseilles,[3] who are King René's and Duke John's ambassadors to the King, have arrived here to see His Majesty. According to our information, they have come to beg His Majesty to help Duke John in conquering the Kingdom of Naples instead of favoring and helping Your Lordship after the passing of Your Illustrious father. They say they have the Venetians and other Italian powers on their side, and if His Majesty condescends to do so, they would offer to put the House of Anjou and its kinsmen at his service and his orders, in such a manner that he might make greater use of them than any French king had been able to.

The matter is very important. Although up to now the ambassadors have not been granted audience, and we hope that their arrival will be thwarted by the great affection His Majesty bears Your Excellency, nevertheless we will stay alert and, according to events, do our best to watch faithfully over Your Lordship's welfare, honor, and preservation. This week the Bastard of Bourbon and My Lord Bishop of Langres,[4] a member of the [Royal] Council, will go to England as ambassadors in order to negotiate peace between the King of England and His Majesty. The Earl of Warwick and the English ambassadors have already arrived at Calais. We shall give news of what follows to Your Most Illustrious Lordship, to whom we always commend ourselves.

HISTORICAL NOTES

1. Cristoforo left Orléans for Milan on 24 March [Doc. 9].

2. Ferry II of Lorraine, Count of Vaudemont, married to Yolande of Anjou, eldest daughter of King René [Albert Lecoy de la Marche, *Le roi René. Sa vie, son administration, se travaux artistiques et littéraries*, vol. 1 (Paris, 1875), p. 238].

divina gratia et el bon governo et prudentia dela p.ta V. S. le loro voce et pensieri sarano falliti. Iudichi adonche essa V. Cel. di quanto affanno ne tirarà ogni hora che sentiamo quella essere sana et salva gionta ad Millanno et non si maravigliì di tale instantia, perché amor et fede ne constrenze ad questo. Ceterum qui sono arivati el Conte de Vaudemont,[2] zenero dil Re Renato, et el Vescovo di Marsiglia,[3] ambassatori dil p.to Re Renato et Duca Iohanne ad questo R. Re Per quanto ne hé stato refferto veneno per supplicare la M.tà Soa che, essendo manchato el quondam Ill.mo S. vostro padre, non voglii dare favore né adiuto ad la V. S., ma voglii adiutare esso Duca Iohanne ad la conquista dil Reame di Napoli, dicendo hanno Venetiani et altre potentie de Italia dal canto loro; et quando Soa M.tà lo vogly fare, offerono la Casa d'Angiò et li Signori dil sangue alligati ad quella a li servitii et commandi di essa Soa M.tà talmente che se ne potrà aydare tanto che may facesse Re di Franza. Il che hé una gran cosa; et quamvis peranche dicti ambassatori non habiano auto audienzia, et che speramo la venuta loro sarà stata frustratoria per lo grande amore che monstra portare la M.tà Soa ad la V. Ex.tia, nondimancho staremo attenti et sicondo che vederemo le cose disposite, si sforzaremo fidelmente provedere al bene, honore et conservatione de la p.ta V. S. El Bastardo di Borbon et Mons.re de Langres,[4] Vescovo et dil Consiglio, debeno partire questa septimana ambassatori in Inglitera per tractare la pace tra el Re de Inglitera et questo S. Re. Et de già el Conte de Vervic et li ambassatori englessi sono venuti a Cales. Di quello che più oltra seguirà, ne daremo notizia ad la V.ra Ill.ma S., ad la quale sempre si riccomandamo.

3. Nicolas de Brancas, who died on 21 April 1466 [Conradum Eubel, *Hierarchia catholica Medii Aevi*, vol. 2 (1431–1503) (Münster: Typis Librariae Regensbergianae 1914; repr. Padua, Il Messaggero di S. Antonio, 1960), p. 187]. In October 1458 the Bishop and other ambassadors had been sent by King René to Francesco Sforza in a fruitless effort to secure his support for a projected Angevin invasion of Naples [vol. 1, p. 292, n. 3].

4. Guy Bernard, Bishop of Langres, and Louis de Bourbon, together with other envoys, were to go to Calais, not to England, to negotiate the truce with the English ambassadors [Calmette-Perinelle, *Louis XI*, p. 73].

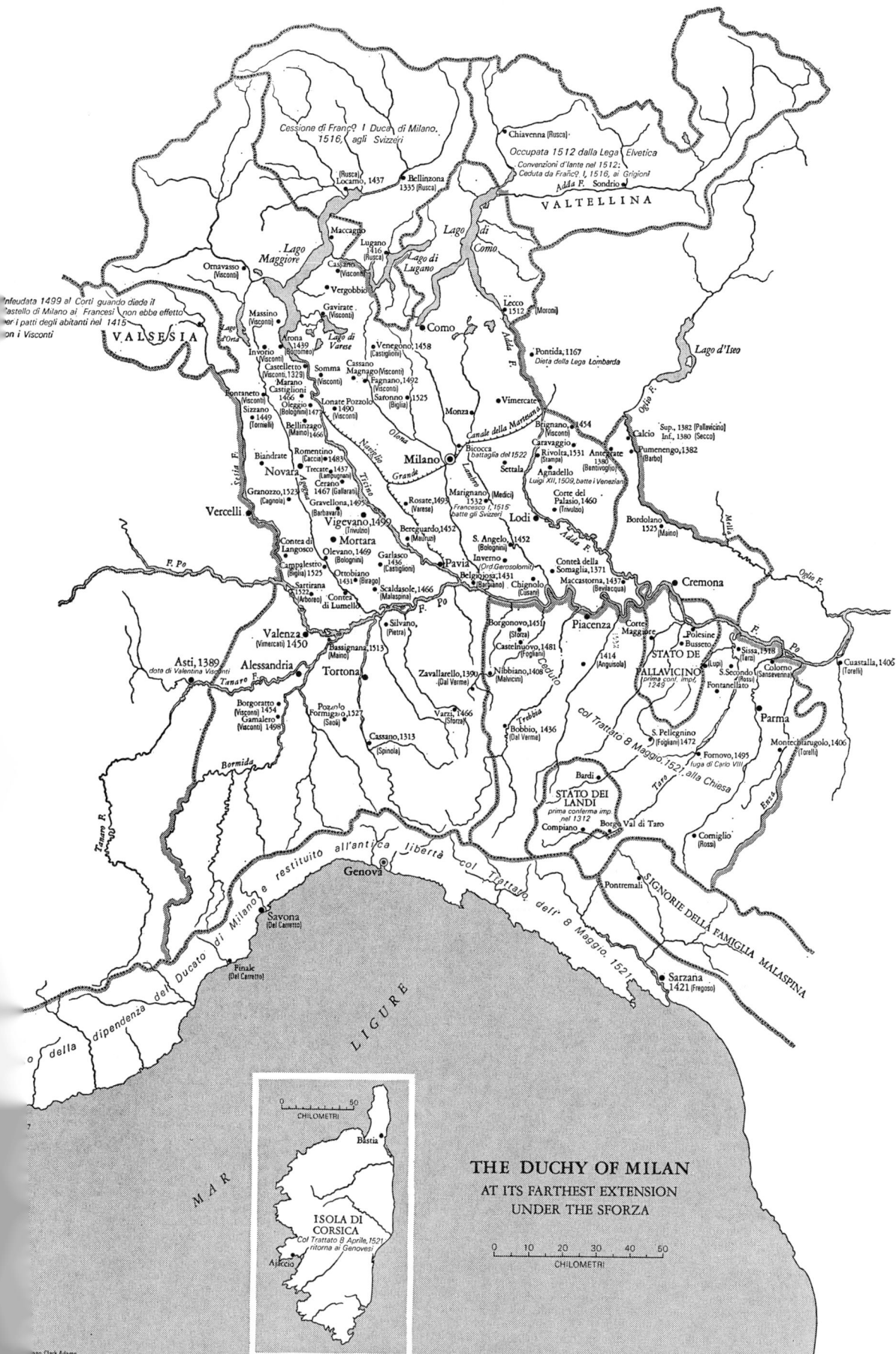

Cessione di Franc° I Duca di Milano, 1516, agli Svizzeri

Chiavenna (Rusca)

Occupata 1512 dalla Lega Elvetica
Convenzioni d'Iante nel 1512;
Ceduta da Franc° I, 1516, ai Grigioni

Adda F. Sondrio

VALTELLINA

(Rusca), 1437
Locarno, 1437

Bellinzona
1335 (Rusca)

Lago di Como

Maccaggio

Lago Maggiore

Lugano
1416
(Rusca)

Lago di Lugano

Ornavasso
(Visconti)

Cassano
(Visconti)

Vergobbio

Lecco
1512
(Moroni)

Lago d'Iseo

Infeudata 1499 al Corti quando diede il
Castello di Milano ai Francesi non ebbe effetto
er i patti degli abitanti nel 1415
on i Visconti

VALSESIA

Massino
(Visconti)

Gavirate
(Visconti)

Lago di Varese

Como

Pontida, 1167
Dieta della Lega Lombarda

Arona
1439
(Borromeo)

Invorio
(Visconti)

Castelletto
(Visconti), 1329)

Marano
Castiglioni
1466

Oleggio
(Bolognini)1477

Venegono, 1458
(Castiglioni)

Cassano
Magnago (Visconti)

Somma
(Visconti)

Fagnano, 1492

Saronno
(Biglia)1525

Lonate Pozzolo
1490
(Visconti)

Vimercate

Monza

Brignano, 1454
(Visconti)

Caravaggio

Rivolta, 1551
(Stampa)

Calcio
(Secco)

Sup., 1382 (Pallavicino)
Inf., 1380 (Secco)

Pumenengo, 1382
(Barbo)

Fontaneto
(Visconti)
Sizzano
1449
(Tornielli)

Bellinzago
(Maino)1466

Biandrate

Romentino
(Caccia) 1483

Novara

Trecate 1437
(Lampugnani)

Cerano
1467 (Gallarate)

Narviglio

Milano

Bicocca
battaglia del 1522

Settala

Antegrate
1380
(Bentivoglio)

Agnadello
Luigi XII, 1509, batte i Veneziani

Granozzo, 1523
(Cagnola)

Gravellona, 1452
(Barbavara)

Vigevano, 1499
(Trivulzio)

Rosate, 1493
(Varese)

Bereguardo, 1452
(Malruni)

Marignano, 1532
(Medici)

Francesco I, 1515
batte gli Svizzeri

Lodi

Corte del
Palasio, 1460
(Trivulzio)

Bordolano
1525
(Maino)

Vercelli

Contea di
Langosco

Mortara

Olevano, 1469
(Bolognini)

Garlasco
1436
(Castiglioni)

Pavia

S. Angelo, 1452
(Bolognini)

Inverno
(Ord.Gerosolimit.)

Contea della
Somaglia, 1371

Cremona

Campalestro
(Biglia) 1525

Ottobiano
1431 (Birago)

Belgioioso,1431
(Barbiano)

Chignolo
(Cusani)

Maccastorna, 1437
(Bevilacqua)

Sartirana
1522
(Arborio)

Contea
di Lumello

Scaldasole, 1466
(Malaspina)

F. Po

Silvano,
(Pietra)

Borgonovo,1451
(Sforza)

Piacenza

Cortemaggiore

Polesine
Busseto

Sissa, 1518
(Terzi)

Cuastalla, 1406
(Torelli)

Valenza
(Vimercati) 1450

Bassignana, 1513
(Maino)

Castelnuovo, 1481
(Fogliani)

1414
(Anguisola)

STATO DE
PALLAVICINO
prima conf. imp.
1249

(Lupi)

S. Secondo
(Rossi)

Colorno
Sansevernia

Asti, 1389
dota di Valentina Visconti

Alessandria

Tortona

Zavallarello, 1350
(Dal Verme)

Nibbiano, 1408
(Malvicini)

col Trattato 8 Maggio, 1521, alla Chiesa

Fontanellato

Parma

Borgoratto
(Visconti) 1454

Gamalero
(Visconti) 1498

Pozzolo
Formigaro, 1527
(Saoli)

Varzi, 1466
(Sforza)

S. Pellegrino
(Fogliani) 1472

Fornovo, 1495
fuga di Carlo VIII

Montechiarugolo, 1406
(Torelli)

Tanaro R.

Cassano, 1313
(Spinola)

Bobbio, 1436
(Dal Verme)

Trebbia

Bardi

Fornovo, 1495

Corniglio
(Rossi)

Bormida

STATO DEI
LANDI
prima conferma imp
nel 1312

Compiano

Borgo Val di Taro

o della dipendenza del Ducato di Milano e restituito all'antica libertà col Trattato dell' 8 Maggio, 1521

Genova

Pontremoli

SIGNORIE DELLA FAMIGLIA MALASPINA

Savona
(Del Carretto)

Finale
(Del Carretto)

Sarzana
1421 (Fregoso)

LIGURE

MAR

0   50
CHILOMETRI

Bastia

ISOLA DI
CORSICA
Col Trattato 8 Aprile, 1521,
ritorna ai Genovesi

Ajaccio

THE DUCHY OF MILAN

AT ITS FARTHEST EXTENSION
UNDER THE SFORZA

0   10   20   30   40   50
CHILOMETRI

man Clark Adams

With due reverence, we cannot but be astonished and greatly grieved in thinking that fifteen days have already elapsed since our new Illustrious Lord ought to have reached that city, and we have had no news concerning His Excellency's situation, either by letter or in any other way. As conflicting reports contrary to the honor and welfare of Your Lordships are referred to us every day by people hostile to you who wish they were true, Your Excellency can well imagine how vexed and grieved we are, above all because the Most Christian King asks us ten times a day whether there is any news. Hours seem interminable to him while awaiting to hear and be assured that our Most Illustrious Lord has arrived safely. His Majesty is quite astonished and sorry about such a long delay. Therefore, we do not know what else to say other than we continually pray to Almighty God in His mercy to soon release us from this worry.

As we are sure that our Most Illustrious Lord will convey to Your Excellency all we wrote to him, we shall not write further. For our part, we shall be mindful according to our usual fidelity and diligence. We devoutly commend ourselves to Your Ladyship, whom we will always keep informed of what is happening.

17·GIOVAN PIETRO PANIGAROLA *and*

EMANUELE DE IACOPO *to the*

DUCHESS OF MILAN

Francia, cart. 532. Orig.

Non possiamo cum debita reverentia non maravegliarse et grandissi-mamente condolerse, che dovendo già quindece giorni passati essere gionto il nostro novo Ill.mo Segniore in quella città, mai in sino qui né per littere né altramente non habiamo havuto notitia alcuna de li successi de Sua Ex.tia; et essendone ogni dì refferto [*sic*] diversamente cose con-trarie al honore et bene de Vostre Segniorie per gente forse che cussì voriano, pò ben pensare Vostra Ex.tia in quanto continuo dolore et affano nuy siamo, maxime che quisto Christianissimo Re dece volte el giorno ne domanda et fa sapere se havemo altro di novo, como quello a chi pare una hora mille, ad intendere et essere certificato ch'el prefato nostro Ill.mo Segniore sia gionto a salvamento. Et nel vero sua Maiestà si maraveglia et ha despiacere assai de tale et tanta tardità. Si ché non sapemo che altro dire nomà[a] che pregiamo [*sic*] continuamente l'Omni-potente Dio che per sua pietà presto ne cave di questo affano. Altro non se estendiamo a scrivere a Vostra Seg., però se rendiamo certi ch'el prelibato nostro Illu.mo Segniore communicherà cum Vostra Ex.tia quanto havemo scripto a quello. Nui dal canto di qua staremo attenti cum la nostra solita fede et ogni diligentia a nuy possibile, et de quanto accaderà, faremo semper avisata Vostra Segnioria, ala quale devotamenti se riccomandiamo.

---

a. "Nomà" or "domà" are Lombard dialectical words meaning "soltanto, salvo che."

We have received many letters from you, individually and in common; we herein reply to your last ones dated March twenty-fourth, twenty-fifth, and twenty sixth,[1] in which we learned how bitterly the Most Serene and Most Christian King grieved over the sudden death of the late Illustrious Lord, our husband and father. And well he might, because it can be said that His Majesty has lost as faithful a friend and dedicated and affectionate a servant as he might ever hope to have—one who spent day and night in thought and in deep concentration regarding how he might do some act favoring and honoring His Majesty. The greatest desire he had in this world was to be once personally by His Majesty's side to help extricate him from the difficulties in which the King found himself and to perform those acts that would be useful to the increase of his Kingdom, reputation, and perpetual glory. Of this, true testimony can be rendered by us, Bianca Maria, with whom each day he discussed and shared this desire, which, if God had granted him longer life, he would in some way have fulfilled.

In those letters we have also learned of the very great dismay and displeasure that the King felt at our, Galeazzo's, capture at Novalesa; just as we gathered what great pleasure, joy, and contentment he took in our release—not only His Majesty but also the entire Court. Similarly, we learned of the preparations and provisions taken by His Majesty for

18 · *The* DUKE *and* DUCHESS OF MILAN *to*

EMANUELE DE IACOPO *and*

GIOVAN PIETRO PANIGAROLA

Francia, cart. 532. Minute

Havemo recevute molte vostre littere separate et commune, ale quale responderemo per questa nostra, alle ultime, che sonno de XXIIII, XXV, et XXVI[1] del passato, per le quale havemo inteso, quanto amaramente, quello Ser. mo et Christianissimo S. Re, se dolse primo dela morte repentina del quondam Ill. S. nostro consorte et patre; como veramente posseva, perchè pò dire Soa M.tà havere perduto uno sì fidelissimo amico, et dedicato et affectionato servitore, quanto Soa M.tà may potesse havere, quale dì et nocte stava in pensero et continua cogitatione, como potere fare cosa grata et honorevelle ad essa M.tà; et el maiore desyderio havesse in questo mondo era de essere una volta potuto trovarse personalmente appresso Soa M.tà, per aiutarla ad cavare deli travagli dove se trovano, et operare cosa che li fosse stata grata, et augmento del suo Regno, reputatione, et perpetua gloria; et de questo ne possamo rendere bon testimonio nuy, Bianca Maria, con la quale ogni dì rasonava et comunicava de questo suo desyderio, quale se Dio li havesse prestata vita, haveria per qualche modo exequito. Deinde havimo inteso l'affano grandissimo et despiacere ha preso el prefato S. Re dela presa de nuy, Galiazo, alla Novalese et cossì quanto piacere, alegreza, et contentamento ha recevuto della nostra liberatione, et non tanto Soa M.ta, ma etiam tutta quella Corte; et similiter le preparatione et provisione facte per Soa M.tà per la liberatione nostra, per la quale voleva mettere la gente, Regno, facultate, et propria per-

our release, for which he was willing to make use of his troops, his Kingdom, his every means, and even his very person, determined not to abandon the enterprise until we were set free. In addition, we also learned of
the measures taken by the King in writing to the rulers of Italy, sending
ambassadors, and making great and generous offers for the preservation
of ourselves and of our state, as it also has been amply related to us by
the Magnificent Lord, Quartermaster of Cavalry, whom His Majesty
sent here as his ambassador.[2]

When you have received this letter you are to go to His Majesty and
give him the following response on our behalf. If we could or knew how
to render sufficient thanks for so great, so loving, and so heartfelt a
demonstration [of support] and for the generous offers he has deigned
to make, and continues even more so each day to make toward us in our
time of need, we would try mightily to properly express them; but considering that our abilities and our powers are not sufficient for this task,
we abandoned the effort and pray God, who rewards all good actions,
through His grace to repay His Majesty for us, both for these benefits and
for other innumerable ones conferred by him upon the late Lord, our
husband and father, and upon us.

We instruct you to confirm the coming of those envoys whom His
Majesty intends to send here to us and to the rulers of Italy, because they
can only help and will be a great aid to us when all are given to understand that that King is disposed to our preservation and that of our state.

We are glad that you did not make any requests of His Majesty for
the fifty thousand écus, as Giovanni Andrea was instructed to do; you
have done well, and we do not wish you to do otherwise than to let the
King pay what he wishes, because we are certain that he will do more
and better than we ourselves would know how to request.

You gave a proper response regarding the [proposed] kinship with
My Lord of Charolais because there is no point in wasting effort over
this; we will soon send to the King an envoy who will fully make our
answer regarding the kinship with the [house] of Savoy, in such a man-

sona, et non abandonare may l'impresa sinchè non fossemo restituiti in nostra libertà. Cossì ancora havimo inteso le preparatione facte per el prefato S. Re in scrivere ale potentie italiche et mandare ambassatori, et le grande et liberale offerte ne fa per conservatione nostra et de questo nostro Stato, como ancora largamente ne ha dicto ad boca el Mag.co Mons.re el Marescalco de Logis, oratore de Soa M.tà per quella mandato qui da nuy.[2] Al che rispondendo, dicimo, che havuta questa ve retrovati da la prefata M.tà ala quale direte da nostra parte, che se sapessemo o potessemo renderli digne gratie de tante et sì amorevelle et cordiale demonstratione, libere offerte s'è dignata fare, et fa ogni dì più verso nuy in questo nostro caso, ne faticaressemo in renderli gratie; ma consyderato che non siamo habili, nè possenti ad questo, lassaremo questa provincia et pregaremo Dio remuneratore de ogni bene, che per soa gratia renda merito per nuy alla M.tà Soa, et de questi beneficii et de l'altri innumerabili per quella conferiti nel prefato quondam S. nostro consorte et patre, et nuy.

Li oratori che Soa M.tà dice de mandare qui ad nuy et ale potentie de Italia, dicimo gli lassate venire perchè non pò altro che zovare et ne sarà gran favore, che se intenda per tutto quello S. Re essere disposto alla conservacione nostra et del Stato nostro.

Che non habiate facta domanda alcuna ad quello S. Re del L.M. scudi secondo l'instrucione de Iohanne Andrea, dicimo ne piace, et haveti facto bene, nè volimo ne faciati altro ma lassati spendere a luy secondo li parerà, perchè siamo certi farà più et meglio non saperessimo nuy domandare.

+[a] Circa el parentato de Mon.re de Chiarlois haveti resposto bene, perchè non bisogna darse fatica de questo, et presto mandaremo uno nostro oratore da quello Ser.mo S. Re, per lo quale ad pieno risponderemo del parentato de Savoya in modo siamo certi Soa M.tà resterà ben contenta et satisfacta de nuy.

---

a. This sign, placed on the left margin of this paragraph, may signify that it was to be written in cipher.

ner that we are sure that His Majesty will be most content and satisfied with us.

Regarding [Jean de] Village, whom you wrote us His Majesty was sending to Genoa in order to help and give support to affairs there, we inform you that he has arrived and is robbing both the Genoese and everyone else he can get his hands on: we do not understand whose side he is on, His Majesty's or someone else's. Bring this to the attention of His Majesty.

As we wrote in other letters, our affairs here go quite well; our people in Lombardy are all quiet and remain obedient, without causing any disturbance anywhere. The Genoese still persevere in proper devotion and fidelity toward us; the Archbishop of Genoa who, with certain funds raised in Venice had mustered some troops, and had proceeded into Lunigiana in order to establish a foothold on the eastern riviera, once he heard of the presence of King Ferrante's galleys at Genoa together with the other provisions made by us, and given that the city was united, he drew back into the territory of the Duke of Modena—we do not know what he will do. The Marquis of Monferrat came to us immediately after the death of the late Lord, our husband and father, making broad offers of his own person, his troops, and state; he stayed here a few days and then returned home. The Illustrious Messer Ercole d'Este, brother of the Most Illustrious Duke of Modena, likewise returned home after being here to visit with us. As you have learned from the other letter, His Majesty King Ferrante generously does all that he can for us and for the preservation of our state. The Florentine ambassadors are still here offering to help us in any way they can. A Papal ambassador is here to visit and comfort us, and to make every show of His Holiness' support for us and for the preservation of the League and peace of Italy. In addition, there are Sienese ambassadors[3] who came to visit us, offer their condolences, and to help in any way they can. Bolognese ambassadors[4] have also been here. In addition, Lord Alessandro, the Count of Urbino, and Lord Roberto da Sanseverino[5] are here to help us deal with daily occurences.

Villagio, quale ne scriveti Soa M.tà mandava verso Zenoa per aiuto et favore de quelle cose dellà, dicimo che esso Viglagio [*sic*] è venuto, et robba et Zenoesi et tutti l'altri ch'el pò havere,[b] non intendemo se l'è con la M.tà o con chi; el che ve notificate alla prefata M.tà.

Le cose nostre de qua, como per altre nostre havimo scripto, passano bene. Tutti quisti nostri populi de Lumbardia vivano in quiete, nè altre novità hanno facte in alcuno loco, mat stano tutti obediente. Zenoesi ancora perseverano in bona devotione et fidelità verso nuy et l'Arcivescovo de Zenoa, quale con certi dinari recevuti da Venetia haveva facti alcuni fanti, et era venuto in Lunesana per intrare in la rivera de Levante, havendo inteso la provisione facta ad Zenoa con le galee del S. Re Ferrando, che sonno ad Zenoa, et l'altre provisione facte per nuy, et la città stare unita, s'è tirato in dreto in quello del Duca di Modena. Non sapemo quello farà. Qui da nuy vene el Marchese de Monferrato immediate seguito el caso del prefato quondam S. nostro consorte et patre, et se ne offerse laragamente [*sic*] la persona, gente, et Stato molto liberalmente, et stato qui alcuni dì se ne retornò a casa. Similiter se ne tornò a casa lo Ill. Messer Hercules da Est, fratello del Ill.mo Duca de Modena, quale fo qui da nuy ad visitarne. La M.tà del Re Ferrando, per nuy et conservatione del Stato nostro, como per l'altra havereti inteso, fa liberamente tutto quello che pò. Qui ancora sono ambassatori firentini, quali se offereno fare per nuy ciò che possano. Qualli [*sic*] gli è uno ambassatore del Papa, quale è venuto per visitarce et confortarne, et fare ogni demonstratione in nome de Soa S.tà per nostro favore et conservatione della liga et pace italica. Gli sonno etiam ambassatori senesi[3] quali ne sonno venuti ad visitare, ad condolerse del caso, et offerirse per quello possano. Similiter gli sonno stati ambassatori bolognesi.[4] Qui etiam se trovano el S. Alexandro, Conte de Urbino, et D. Roberto da Sancto Severino,[5] quali ne aiutare ad consultare quello ne occore alla giornata.

Dali nostri ambassatori mandati ad Venetia[6] havemo sempre havute littere che quella Sig.a dice bene de volere ben vicinare; et cossì in ultimo

---

b. Crossed out: et questo é el favore et subsidio ne dà, el che volimo con quello destro et bon modo [and this is the support and aid he gives us, of which we want you tactfully and appropriately].

From our ambassadors sent to Venice[6] we constantly have letters reporting the Signoria's assurances that it wants to be a friendly neighbor. Most recently the Signoria has written us that it wants to live in peace and persevere with us as it did with the late Lord, our husband and father. Nevertheless, deeds do not match words, because they are badly disposed and badly inclined toward us, as can be seen from Bartolomeo Colleoni's giving money to his troops, and amassing new soldiers every day, while giving other indications of wanting to attack our state. Just recently he has written to our Councillor, Pietro da Pusterla,[7] as you will see from the enclosed copy. This is not a good or propitious sign, nor is it to be thought that Bartolomeo does this of his own initiative, but rather with the consent and knowledge of the [Venetian] Signoria. We want you to read the enclosed copy to the King and make him understand that the intentions of the Venetians toward us are not good, and that we must put our troops at the ready, arming ourselves according to our own possibilities and also with the help of friends, to defend ourselves against them in case they wish to cause us some harm, as seems clear to everyone from the moves Bartolomeo Colleoni is making.

We want you to commend us as fervently as you can to the King, in whom we place our every comfort and hope, entreating His Most Serene Majesty that he deign to take mature and wise thought as he is wont to do in all his affairs, [so that he may suggest] those provisions that seem opportune to him for our preservation, that of our children, brothers, and of our state. [We ask him] to give us his counsel and help in so great a difficulty, since we consider it most certain that he will know how to provide and will provide better than we ourselves could ever conceive or remind him of. For all he does for us he does for himself, because His Majesty will always be able to count upon and avail himself of us, our troops, our state, and our very person in whatever need he may have, not otherwise than he can of his own possessions.

essa Sig.a ne ha scripto per soe littere de volere vivere in pace, et persevere-rare con nuy come facevano con lo prefato quondam S. nostro consorte et patre. Tamen li effecti son contrari perchè hanno male dispositione et mala voluntate, como se vede perchè Bartolomeo Colione ha dato dinari ad sue gente, et toltone dele altre de novo et ogni dì ne tole, et fa altre dem-onstratione de volere insultare questo nostro Stato; et de presente ha scrip-to ad Petro da Pusterla,[7] nostro Consigliere, quanto vedereti per l'inclu-sa copia. El che non è bono nè bello signo, nè anche è da pensare che esso Bartolomeo se mova ad tale cose da luy, ma con consentimento et saputa de la Sig.a; quale copia volimo legati ad quello S. Re et li faciati intendere l'animo de Venetiani non bono verso nuy, et che a nuy è necessario pon-erse in ordine con la nostra gente, et armarse con quello possiamo da nuy, et con l'aiuto de l'amici per defenderne da loro, quando ne vogliano dare molestia, como pare assay chiaro agnuno [*sic*] per li movimenti fa dicto Bartolomeo Colione. Et ne recomandareti ad quello Ser.mo S. Re, tanto strectamente quanto possibile ve sarà, pregando Soa Ser.ma M.tà in la quale consiste ogni nostro conforto et speranza, se degni fare quelli matu-ri et savii pensieri che sole fare in tutte le cose soe, de quelle provisone li pareno opportune alla conservatione de nuy, figlioli, fratelli, et Stato nos-tro, et drizarne, consigliarne, et aiutarne in tale et tanto nostro caso, como tegniamo per constantissimo saperà meglio fare, et farà, che nuy non saperessemo pensare nè recordare, perchè tutto quello farà per nuy el farà per Soa propria M.tà, perchè de nuy, gente Stato, et propria persona se potrà sempre vallere et aiutare in ogni soa occurrentia, non altra-mente con le cose soe proprie.

HISTORICAL NOTES

1. Docs. 9–13.

2. The Quartermaster of Cavalry arrived in Milan on 3 April [The Dukes to Gerardo de' Colli, Milan, 4 April 1466, *Venezia*, cart. 353], after he had discharged his mission at the Savoyard court [Ziliolo Oldoini to the Duke, Chambéry, 28 March 1466, *Savoia*, cart. 482]. He was still in Milan on 7 April when the Dukes wrote to the King, thanking him for the embassy and recommending the Marquis Antonio di Romagnano and his clan, who had taken a leading role in the Duke's release in the Novalesa [*Francia*, cart. 532].

3. The letter of credence for the Sienese ambassador, Luigi di Piero de' Compari, is dated 25 March 1466 [*Siena*, cart. 264]. He left Siena the next day [ASS, *Concistoro, Legazioni e Commissarie*, Reg. 2608, fol. 176].

4. Bologna sent the poet Cola da Ascoli [Giovanni Bentivoglio and the City of Bologna to the Dukes, Bologna, 18 March 1466, *Romagna*, cart. 165].

5. Leading Italian condottiere and nephew of Francesco Sforza. The other dignitaries and ambassadors mentioned in this paragraph have been identified in the notes to doc. 15.

6. Francesco de Arezzo and Scipione de Casate [ASV, *Senato Secreta*, Reg. 22, fols. 146v–47].

7. Pietro da Pusterla had been Milanese ambassador to Louis XI in 1461–1462. At this time he functioned as an intermediary between the Dukes and Colleoni [Bortolo Belotti, *La vita di Bartolomeo Colleoni* (Bergamo: Istituto Italiano d'Arti Grafiche, 1923), p. 367, n. 1.]. Colleoni's letter to him has not been found.

Your Excellency will have heard from Giovan Pietro's letters and mine of the great anguish and extreme grief that this Most Christian King felt about what happened to Your Lordship at Novalesa, and how surprised His Sacred Majesty was that up to the date of our letters—that is, on the first day of this month[1]—no news had been received of Your Excellency since your release. For this reason His Majesty was afraid that, with malice and false maneuvers, Your Lordship might have been removed from the sanctuary of the Abbey and taken elsewhere, so that the Savoyards might have more liberty, and Your Lordship's enemies could better dispose of you. This suspicion was more than natural in such tension, because as they say, "when one is in trouble, confidence always turns to fear, and active anxiety always inclines one to fear the worst." But as His Majesty and we are still very preoccupied and worried, I can only say that I pray Almighty God to forgive the person responsible for such a great error. For in my opinion it was the duty of every faithful servant of yours, as soon as Your Lordship arrived in Milan, to remind you to send a courier at full speed to tell the Most Christian King the news of your safe arrival.

Only God and we ourselves know how much [this news] would have encouraged and strengthened the Most Christian King against various reports and unfavorable pressures that certain individuals are making

19 · EMANUELE DE IACOPO *to the*

DUKE OF MILAN

BN, Fonds Italien, Cod. 1593, fol. 243. Orig.

Debe havere inteso Vostra Ex.tia per più littere de Iohannepetro et mie l'immenso affano et extremo despiacere ha havuto questo Christianissimo Re per la novità occorsa ala Vostra Segnioria ala Novalesa, et quanto Sua Sacratissima M.tà se maravegliava che per insino al datum d'esse nostre littere, che fu al primo del presente,[1] non se havesse notitia alcuna de li successi de quella, poi che fu liberata; per che Sua Sacratissima M.tà dubitava più che malitiosamente et cum falsa demonstratione Vostra Segnioria fusse cavata fora de la franchisia del Priorato et menata altrove, unde Savoyni havesseno più libertà et potesseno li inimici de Vostra Segnioria meglio disponere di quella. Il quale suspecto era assai secundo le naturale passione, però como se dice prona est timori semper in penis fides et ad deteriorem partem strenua semper tendit suspitio; ma vedendo che ancora al dì presente Sua Sacratissima M.tà et nuy siamo in le medesime passione et pene, non so que dire altro, salvo ch'io prego l'Omnipotente Dio chi perdone a chi é stato cagione de tale et tanto errore; però che debito era al iudicio mio de ogni vostro fidele servitore, immediate che Vostra Illu.ma Segnioria fu gionta a Milano, recordare a quella che subito metesse uno a cavalo, il quale volando portasse novella a questo Christianissimo Re como Vostra Ex.tia era gioncta a salvamento. Il che Dio sa et nuy quanto havesse confortato et ingagliardito questo Christianissimo Re contra diverse relatione et disfavorevole in-

against Your Lordship; but in all this may Almighty God as well as His Majesty's constancy be praised, because up to now he has not given due audience to your enemies, and I am most certain he will not in the future. Your Lordship will soon be more clearly informed of everything from Giovan Pietro's letters and my own. However, Your Excellency may be sure that so long as I live, I will never feel so much consolation and happiness to equal the anguish and worry Giovan Pietro and I felt because of this delay in writing after what had happened to Your Lordship, to whom I devoutly commend myself.

HISTORICAL NOTE

1. It appears that in the interval, 2–9 April, the ambassadors wrote no dispatches.

stantie se fano per alcuni presso di quello contra Vostra Segnioria; ma de tuto sia laudato lo eterno Dio et la constantia de Sua M.tà, la quale per insino a qui non ha dato, et sono certissimo non darà più audientia, como bisognia, a tali inimici de Vostra Ex.tia, la quale per littere de Iohannepetro et mie del tuto presto faremo più chiara. Ma sia certa Vostra Ex.tia che, vivame quanto se voglia, mai non haverò tanta consolatione né piacere quanto affano et pena havemo havuto Iohannepetro et mi per lo suprascripto tardo scrivere dopo la novità occorsa ala Vostra Illu.ma Segnioria, ala quale devotamente me reccomando.

We beg Your Excellencies to forgive us for not having written sooner, after Franceschino Nori's arrival[1] seven days ago. This is due to our riding together with the King in the vicinity and also to our waiting for the conclusion of certain affairs as you will gather from this letter.[2] When Franceschino Nori arrived, he immediately presented himself to His Most Christian Majesty who greatly welcomed him in order to have news from Italy, since he had heard various and unfavorable reports about Your Lordships. The next day, Franceschino explained the reason for his coming here, and found His Majesty very well disposed toward doing everything possible for the preservation of Your Lordships. Although most of the necessary measures had been taken, the King said that he wanted to do what both he and we thought would be useful. He told us this too, adding that he would pray God to grant him the grace of being able to help Your Lordships, because the benefits received [from you] deserved engagement of his every means and his very Kingdom. In effect, His Majesty was quite pleased, but he ordered that additional letters be written to all the rulers of Italy; these letters will be forwarded by means of a herald in two or three days. Even though the first set of letters seemed sufficient to us, the ones sent with my, Giovan Pietro's, servant Cristoforo, who could be considered French in both speech and writing, not to mention his experience, nevertheless, to

20·GIOVAN PIETRO PANIGAROLA *and*

EMANUELE DE IACOPO *to the*

DUKE *and* DUCHESS OF MILAN

Francia, cart. 532. Orig.

Ne perdoneno Vostre Ex.tie se dapoi el giongere de Franceschino Nori,[1] che hogie sono VII giorni, più presto non li habiamo scripto; il che é proceduto per essere cavalcati cum questo Segniore Re qui al intorno, et anche aspectando conclusione de le cosse che per queste nostre littere intenderano.[2] Franceschino Nori, gioncto che fu qui, statim se presentò ala M.tà de questo Christianissimo Re, quale lo vide molto voluntieri per intendere de le cosse de Italia, de le quale diversamente gli era reportato et in desfavore de le Vostre Segniorie. El dì sequente expose la casione de la venuta sua, et trovò essa M.tà benissimo disposta a volere fare tuto per conservatione de le Vostre Seg. et, quamvis già fusseno facte le maior parte de le necessarie provisione, dixe ancora volere fare quanto per lui et nuy dinnovo serà avisato. Et cussì poi dixe anche a nuy, subiungendo che pregava Dio li prestasse gratia di potere servirve, perché li beneficii rechiediano exponesse ogni sua facultà et proprio Reame. In effectu la prefata M.tà fu contenta; et cussì se sono fate di novo littere a tute le potencie d'Italia, le quale fra dui o tre dì se manderano per uno ayraldo. Et ben ché a nuy paresse che bastasse per havere mandato le prime et Christoforo, servitore de mi Iohannepiero, che se pò dire essere franzoso di lengua et littere et assai pratico, nondimeno per satisfare ala voluntà de le Vostre Ex.tie, di novo se sono refacte, secundo Franceschino ha dimandato, in latino, le copie de le quale mandiamo qui alligate;

satisfy Your Excellencies' wish, these letters have been written again in Latin according to Franceschino's request, of which we enclose the copies. We inform you that since the French are not able to write the letters accurately [in Latin], it was necessary for me, Giovan Pietro, to compose and dictate them.

In addition, we are at the moment, by His Majesty's order, preparing instructions for the ambassadors whom the King has decided to send to the states of Italy, above all to Venice. His Majesty told us that as soon as these instructions are ready he would immediately dispatch the ambassadors, among whom he has chosen My Lord of Vienne and My Lord de Gaucourt. We will urge that this is done quickly. His Majesty then concluded by saying that he would never abandon Your Excellencies, for whom he is willing to exert himself as he would for his own Kingdom; you can be sure of this, as he has no greater regard for anything else. Franceschino came in time, because Duke John's ambassadors were here and were trying with new artifices and fabrications—which afterward we clearly understood to be lies—to have the King renounce his affection for and his alliance with Your Lordships. However, when His Majesty heard from Franceschino that your affairs were settled and in good order, contrary to what was said, he called the ambassadors to his table and asked Franceschino to relate details about the conditions of the Duchy. He answered point by point in favor and praise of Your Lordships. Although we had made clear twice to the king that what those ambassadors were saying was dictated by passion and was contrary to the truth, as probably they would have wished it to happen, His Majesty interpellated us once more in their presence, declaring that, whatever they might sustain, he would rather die first than do anything that might cause any harm to Your Lordships. On the contrary, he will defend you with all his power against those who might wish to offend you, and of this you could be quite sure. Therefore, the ambassadors were able to obtain nothing, and returned to King René and Duke John without accomplishing anything. This is what has happened up to now, and being so occupied, we have not been able to write. Now, however, we will

notificandoli che, per non saperne questi Franzosi cavare constructo, é stato necessario che io Iohannepetro le habia dictate et composte.

Ulterius al presente per commandato de la prelibata M.tà metemo a ponto la instructione de li ambassiatori, che quella ha deliberato mandare ale potentie de Italia, maxime a Venesia et, ordinate siano, ne ha dicto che spacerà essi ambassiatori statim, fra li quali ha deputato Monseg. de Viena et Monsegniore de Gaucurt et cussì sollicitaremo che se facia; concludendo poi essa M.tà che mai non abandonerà Vostre Ex.tie, et per quelle exponerà como per lo Reame suo et di questo siano certe, non havendo respecto di cossa alchuna. Dicto Franceschino vene in tempo, perchè li ambassiatori del Duca Iohanne erano qui, li quali cum nove arte et inventione, le quale habiamo poi manifestamente compreso essere busie, cercavano de removere questo Segniore Re da l'amore et ligha de le Vostre Segniorie. Et intendando la M.tà Sua per dicto Franceschino le cosse vostre essere in bona dispositione et asesto et altramente che non diciano, fece venire essi ambassiatori ala tavola, domandando particularmenti a Franceschino de le cosse di là; el quale a parte per parte respose in grande favore et laude de Vostre Segniorie. Et quamvis già doe volte per nuy fusse chiarito che quanto diciano essi ambassiatori erano cosse dicte per passione et senza verità et como forsi voriano che succedesseno, tamen Sua M.tà dinnovo ne domanda in loro presentia, dicendo che dirano quello vorano, che prima moriria cha fare cossa che potesse generare uno minimo preiudicio ale Vostre Seg., ma quelle defenderà contra chi li vorà offendere a tuta sua possanza et de questo fussene sicuri. Si che nulla hanno potuto obtenire, et senza conclusione sono retornati dal Re Rayneri et Duca Iohanne. Questo é quanto è seguito fino qui; circha el che occupati, non havemo potuto scrivere, ma horamai sollicitaremo cum più instantia la expeditione d'essi ambassiatori, et de quanto seguirà daremo aviso a Vostre I.S., ale quale devotamente se raccomandemo.

urge with more insistence for His Majesty's ambassadors to be dispatched, and of what follows we will inform Your Illustrious Lordships, to whom we devoutly commend ourselves.

HISTORICAL NOTES

1. Nori left Milan around 13 March with letters of credence addressed to Louis XI and to the Duchess of Savoy [The Duchess of Milan to the King, Milan, 13 March 1466, *Registri Missive*, Reg. 74, fol. 49]. Earlier he had been requested to come from Florence to Milan by Francesco Sforza because the French ambassadors coming to Milan [doc. 13, n. 2] wished to have him take part in the discussion of their mission, which included the Savoyard-Milanese marriage [The Duke to Nicodemo Tranchedini, Milanese ambassador in Florence, Milan, 3 February 1466, *Firenze*, cart. 272]. Nori, who at this time was a Councillor and Chamberlain of the King, as well as agent of the Medici Bank in Lyon, was frequently employed by the King in state affairs, and seems to have been influential at the Savoyard court. He was present when the King first mentioned the marriage to the Milanese ambassador in April 1464, and he played a leading role in arranging it [Mandrot, *Dépêches*, 1-4, passim, and particularly 2:33, n. 1, and 66-69].

2. This explains the second interval, 11-17 April, during which no dispatches were written.

With incredible pleasure and consolation we have received Your Lordships' letters dated the twenty-third and thirty-first of last month,[1] addressed to me, Giovan Pietro. They relieved us greatly from our pre-occupation at not receiving letters from you. After having examined to-gether the contents of these letters, we immediately went to the King to deliver the letter Your Excellencies had written him and to inform him of your successful entrance in Milan, and also to offer him the apologies contained in Your Lordships' letter.[2] As soon as His Majesty was in possession of the letter, he with great joy and relief, took off his bonnet and hat, and thanked God, the Holy Virgin, and Your Highnesses, and inquired solicitously about your health. Then he led us into his chamber, wanting to know exactly how things were going with you, and whether you needed his help or whether he could do anything for you, saying he was quite ready and felt obligated to do so. For you, My Lord, his fine brother, who have served him so faithfully and devotedly, he said he would have come personally and would have been willing to lose two-thirds of his Kingdom rather than suffer that the Savoyards should com-mit such an outrage against you as they had undertaken. He added many kind words, saying above all that he hoped to count on Your Lord-ship even more than he would have counted on your late father. Then having whispered to the King some assurances about Your Lordship's

21·EMANUELE DE IACOPO *and*

GIOVAN PIETRO PANIGAROLA *to the*

DUKE *and* DUCHESS OF MILAN

Francia, cart. 532. Orig.

Con incredibile piacere et consolatione havemo recepute le littere de le V.S. de dì XXIII et ultimo dil passato,[1] directive ad me Zohannepetro, le quale ne hanno cavato di extremo affanno, in el quale eramo per non havere littere da quelle. Et comunicato fra noy el tenore di esse littere, subito si trovamo con questo S. Re dandoli la littera che V. Ex.tie li scrivevano, facendoli notizia de la felice vostra intrata in Millanno, et facendo etiam la scusa che in le littere de le V.S. si contene.[2] Statim che la M.tà Soa ebbe le littere in mano, con infinita alegreza et consolatione si cavò el boneto et el capello ringratiando Dio, Nostra Donna et le V. Cel., dil essere di le quale molto stretamente ne domandò. Dapoy ne menò in la soa camera, dove molto distinctamente volse intendere in che dispositione erano le cose vostre, et se bisognava la M.tà Soa adiutasse o fesse cossa alchuna, offerendosi promptissima et essere obligata a farlo. Et per voy Signor, suo bel fratello, quale con tanta fede et devotione havevati servito la Soa M.tà, disse saria venuto in propria persona et perduto le doe parte del suo Reame cha havere patito Savoyni farvi tale oltragio, como commenzono; cum molte amorevele parole, maxime che anche sperava più valersi de la V. Ex.tia che non haveria facto dil quondam S. vostro padre. Et essendo per noy a la orechia di quella dicto alchune parole de l'amore et devotione de V. S. verso la Soa M.tà, quella essendo lì alchuni Signori particulari, disse: "Sapia chi

affection and devotion to him, he, in the presence of some important lords, declared: "Let whoever is interested know that I mean my brother to remain Duke of Milan, and if I am ever able to do anything, I will maintain him a peaceful Lord in his own state; I serve notice to those who attempt to offend him that they will thereby offend me." Therefore, owing to these letters and to what we have continued to tell him verbally, His Majesty was greatly comforted and stopped worrying about Your Excellencies; it is wonderful to see how much happiness not only His Majesty but all this court demonstrated that night, and even after. These letters were awaited with no less eagerness than that of the souls in Purgatory in expectance of the Messiah. Your Lordships could not do better than to write often, because His Majesty is anxious to hear how things are going, and asks us constantly whether we have other news.

The next day, both of us were in a room alone with the King, and we told him that though from many quarters Your Excellencies have received ample offers [of aid], and a number of lords and embassies have come to Milan to show support, nevertheless, all your hope was placed in His Majesty, and we commended you to him as warmly and cordially as we could. We informed him of the preparations Bartolomeo da Bergamo is making, and that if it is necessary, you will avail yourselves of his offers. We mentioned King Ferrante's demonstrations [of support], and we also let him know that the Abbot of Casanova had gone to Venice and to the Marquis of Monferrat; that is, we informed him on every subject contained in your last letter and thanked him as you specified. Then His Majesty, recollecting the sad passing of your late husband and father (whom he seems to remember so often), replied that he has so many obligations toward Your Excellencies because of benefits received from you, that he does not know when he will be able to reciprocate. Nevertheless, as far as he is able, he will not fail to give you every possible aid and support. Your Lordships may be quite sure of this, and you need not thank the King for his offers because he has merely done his duty. Although his Kingdom is not completely in hand, (but he hopes it will be this year), if the Venetians went to war against you—which never-

voglia, che io delibero mantegnire mio fratello Duca di Millano, et se
may potrò cossa alchuna lo conservarò Signor pacifico in el Stato suo, et
farò intendere ad chi cercharà di offenderlo, che offendano a me proprio."
In modo che per esse littere, et per quanto continue di bocha li havemo
dicto, essa M.tà si hé molto riconfortata et stabilita la mente soa per le
Vostre Ex.tie; et l'alegreza che quella sera et dapoy ha monstrata hé
una maraveglia, et non solum essa M.tà, ma tuta questa Corte. Essendo
queste littere cum desyderio non mancho expectate che fo el Mesya dale
anime dil purgatorio, non possendo Vostre S. meglio fare come spesso
scrivere, perché continue essa M.tà desyderosa di sentire como passano
le cose, ne domanda se altro habiamo di novo. El dì sequente si trovamo
la prelibata M.tà et noy doy soli in una camera, et dicendoli quamvis da
più loci siano facte grande proferte ad le V. Ex.tie et più Signori et ambassate siano venute a Millano in favore di quelle, tamen ogni vostra
speranza hé in la M.tà Soa, riccomandandovi ad quella tanto stretta-
mente et cordialmente quanto ne fo possibille; nottificandoli le preparatione che fa Bartolameo da Bergamo et che bisognando usareti dele proferte soe; le dimonstrazione ha facto el S. Re Ferando, et così etiam
avisandola de l'andata de lo Abbate di Casanova a Vinesia, et al Marchise
di Monferato; et così di parte in parte quanto quelle scriveno per l'ultima
littera, ringratiandola como in quelle si contiene. Alhora la p.ta M.tà
Soa ricordando el doloroso caso dil quondam S. vostro consorte et patre,
dil quale pare continue ne habii memoria, rispose che tanti sono li oblighi
et benefitii receputi da le V. Ex.tie che non sa quando poterli satisfare;
tuta volta che fino dove poterà, non li mancharà a dare ogni adiuto et
favore possibile ad le V.Ex.tie, et de questo ne siano certe et non bisognare
ringratiarla de le offerte facte, perché ha facto el debito suo. Et quamvis
non habia peranche dil tuto assicurato el suo Regno, sperando questo anno
bene stabilirlo, non dimancho quando Venetiani vi fesseno guerra, che
non pò però credere per molti respecti, maxime si consigliarano bene
el facto loro, dice dil Delfinato sempre vi manderà circha lanze trecento,
et di queste soe ordinanze quando bisognarà da CCC in CCCC° lanze per
conservatione et defensione dil Stato vostro, riputando si conservasse ad

theless he does not believe for many reasons, above all if they well consider their own situation—he says that he will send you about three hundred lances from the Dauphiné together with another three hundred to four hundred lances from his companies [d'ordonnance], if needed, for the preservation and defense of your state, as if he were maintaining it for himself. God only knows how willingly he would destroy the Venetians and join in pushing them back as far as the sea, owing to their pride and their haughtiness, for which he holds them his enemies.

Moreover, His Majesty meant to send to Asti his Lieutenant, the Duke of Bourbon's brother, My Lord of Beaujeu, who from there would be able to give aid to Your Lordships. Since the King is negotiating the purchase of Asti, or the granting of compensation for it in France to the seller, either to Madame of Orléans or to My Lord of Beaujeu (who makes claim to it as dowry for the late Duke of Orleans's daughter, his wife),[3] His Majesty says he will now try to settle the matter. Already the King promises that were he to buy it, he would appoint Lord Roberto da Sanseverino his governor and Lieutenant in Asti. He added that he will always keep two thousand cavalry in Asti, for the country is rich and they will be easily maintained there, so that it will be easier for Your Excellencies to make use of them.

Furthermore, he mentioned he had heard that Your Lordships have appointed the Marquis of Monferrat Lieutenant General of your troops; he was greatly grieved and sorry about this, saying you were not well advised. Several days ago I, Giovan Pietro, wrote that the King did not like the above mentioned Marquis and that there were hidden rancors between them which I could not well understand. Now His Majesty has shown his dislike for him and his displeasure if the appointment had been made. We answered by saying that we neither knew nor believed this to be true, and that His Majesty could be certain that Your Highnesses would not conceive of or do anything that in some way might disturb or upset him; if by any chance such a thing had unknowingly been done, you would want to revoke it. So [it is clear that] by no means would the King like the Marquis to hold such a high office.

la M.tà Soa propria. Et Dio sa quanto volontieri dice distrueria essi
Venetiani, et li adiutaria cazare ala marina per la superbia et ellatione
loro, dimonstrando haverli per soy inimici. Ulterius che la M.tà Soa
intendeva mandare in Ast Monsignor de Biogiu, fratello dil Duca di
Borbon, suo Locotenente, quale daria de là favore a le cose de le V.S.;
et perché hé in practicha di comprare Ast o dare di qua recompensatione
ad chi la vegnirà[a] o ad Madama d'Orliens o al dicto Mons.re de Biogiu,
quale lo pretende per dotta dela fiola dil quondam Duca de Orliens, soa
mugliere,[3] dice cercharà di exequirla. Et fino di questa hora promette di
fare Governatore et suo Locotenenti in Ast, comprandolo, el S. Roberto
da Sanseverino; et lì, dice, tegnirà sempre cavali II.m. ch'el payse hé
grasso et li starano bene, et più facilmente V. Ex.tie se ne potrano valere.

Ulterius disse havere inteso che V. S. havevanno facto el Marchise di
Monferrato suo Locotenenti Generale di gente d'arme di là; di che se ne
doleva grandemente et li despiaceva, dicendo non eravati ben consigliati.
Più dì fa io, Zohannepiero, scrissi che questo S. Re non amava dicto
Marchese, et che fra loro eranno certi ruzeni secreti che non poteva bene
intendere. Hora essa M.tà ne ha monstrato non lo amare, et condolersene
quando così fusse. Noy risposemo a la M.tà Soa non lo sapere né credere,
et fusse certa quella che non solum V. Cel. non voriano pensare né fare
cosa che aliqualiter havesse a turbare o alterare la mente soa, et se a casu
fusse facta inscienter la vorebbono revocare; si ché nullo modo li piacer-
ebbe esso Marchese a dicta dignitate.

De le demonstratione fa el Re Ferando piacque molto ad la M.tà
Soa, dicendo che faceva el debito suo a ricognoscere li servitii auti da la
Casa Sforzescha, et facendolo, faceva como digno et gratto [sic] Re,
così etiam voleva fare la M.tà Soa fino dove si poranno extendere le facultate soe. Del abbate de Casanova rispose essere alchuni cativi al lato di
Madama di Savoya che la governano, ali quali hé necessario provedere,
et teneno Filippo Monsignor, quali sono queli che la inducono a fare
queste legiereze et instigatione. Et primo, la M.tà Soa ha scritto ad quella
Ill. Madama una littera di tal tenore, quale per la copia qui inclusa poreti

---

a. Read: vendirà.

His Majesty was very pleased with King Ferrante's show of support for you, pointing out that he was discharging his obligations for the favors he had received from the Sforzas, and was thus acting as a worthy and grateful King. His Majesty meant to do the same to the limit of his capacity. Concerning the Abbot of Casanova, he replied that there were some bad people surrounding and influencing Madame of Savoy, who induce her to do these foolish and provocative things. They should be attended to because they also influenced My Lord Filippo.

First of all, His Majesty wrote that Most Illustrious Madame a letter whose tenor you can gather from the copy herewith enclosed, which we have sent by this courier to Lord Ziliolo,[4] so that he may deliver it, send us back the reply, and let Your Excellencies know what the response is.

Secondly, the King has induced My Lord Filippo, who seems to want to do everything in favor of Your Lordships, to send instructions to his Majordomo, Trofarello[5] (who is already there with letters of credence to those who are influencing Madame), charging him to get together with them and make them understand that if they consent to or deal with anything against Your Lordships, they will be most unhappy. [He should] warn them that from now on they ought to stay clear of such activities, since His Majesty and My Lord Filippo have decided to support and help Your Lordships against all and any. Thus they should have their eyes open. Trofarello was also instructed to add whatever seems useful to Lord Ziliolo, with whom he must confer on the entire matter, as we wrote him.

Thirdly, His Majesty has sent for one of his lawyers in Paris, whom he says he means to send to Madame so that he can keep her properly disposed and dissuade her from further intrigues, and work together with Lord Ziliolo in Your Lordships' favor. Fourthly, His Majesty has written to Venice about the Abbot of Casanova, as you can see from the copy herewith enclosed.[6] He concludes by assuring Your Excellencies that, regarding Savoy, he will see to it that they do not wage war against you, nor harm you in any way. Nevertheless, for many reasons

vedere, la quale habiamo mandata per el presente cavalaro a D. Ziliolo,[4] che la presenti, mandandone qui la risposta et avisando V. Ex.tie de la risposta che ne harà. Secundo, ha facto che Filipo Mons.re, quale si monstra volere fare ogni cosa per le V. S., ha mandato a Trufarello,[5] suo Maystro di Casa, quale di presente si trova di là con littere di credenza ad quelli che governano essa Madama, commetendoli si trovi con costoro, et farli intendere se consentirano né tractarano cosa alchuna contra le p.te V. S., ne sarano malcontenti et da hora inanzi se ne vogliono guardare, perché la prelibata M.tà et luy deliberano mantegnire et adiutare quele contra tutti. Si ché aprano gli occhi, et dirà esso Trufarello quanto etiam a Domino Ziliolo predicto parirà, con el quale debbe conferire dil tuto, et così gli ne habiamo scritto. Tertio, ha mandato la p.ta M.tà a domandare uno doctore de li soy che hé a Paris, quale dice volere mandare ad stare apresso la prelibata Madama per tenerla bene hedificata, rimoverla da ogni altra practicha, et operare cum D. Ziliolo quanto serà neccessario in favore de le V. S. Quarto, la prelibata M.tà scrive di esso Abbate de Casanova ad Venesia, quanto per l'aligata[6] poreti etiam vedere, la quale conclude et assicura V. Ex.tie che dal canto di Savoya proverderà bene non li farano guerre né danno. Ben dice, consiglia ad la V. S. el parentato di Savoya per più rispecti, et che li pare lo habiati ad fare, che non vi pò cha grandemente giovare, persuadendolo molto. E così anche Filipo predicto ne disse, che acceptando V. Ex.tia el parentato, havereti tuta Savoya propitia et in mano ali bisogni vostri. Et perché ne pare sopra questo fazano grande fondamento, et essa M.tà alquanto dubia che quella non accepti el parentato, se siamo sforzati cum parole generale tenere le cose ben disposite fino che da la V. S. habiamo altra risposta, la quale cerchano di havere et chiara.

Insuper essa M.tà dice non farà la obedientia al Papa fino che intenda chiaro como favorisse V. S., et li scrive in la forma che per l'aligata copia[7] porrano vedere. Avendo il Tesorero dil Delfinato[8] mandato a richiedere certe segureze, questa matina gli le habiamo mandate per uno cavalaro nostro, tale quale le domandava per pagare li scudi sex millia ale gente d'arme vostre, aciò che si possano levare como hé l'intenzione

he advises and urges Your Lordship to contract the marriage with the House of Savoy, for he believes that it cannot but turn to your advantage. My Lord Filippo also spoke to us in this vein, pointing out that by agreeing to the marriage, Your Excellency would have Savoy on your side and ready for any need you might have. Since it was obvious that they place much stock in all this, and as His Majesty seemed rather doubtful that Your Lordship will accept the match, we tried our best with a general approach to keep matters well disposed, until such time as we receive a definite and clear statement from Your Lordship.

Besides this, His Majesty declared he will not pledge obedience to the Pope until he knows for certain how the Pope will support Your Lordships, and he wrote to him in the tone that Your Excellencies will be able to gather from the enclosed copy of the letter.[7] Since the Treasurer of the Dauphiné[8] requested some guarantees, this morning, with one of our couriers, we sent them to him exactly as he had asked, in order to pay the six thousand écus to your troops so that they may set out as His Majesty wants them to do. To this purpose Franceschino has similarly written to his people in Lyons, so that hopefully there will be no difficulty this time. My Lord of Miolans,[9] the Chancellor of Cyprus, and two others had come here as ambassadors from Savoy bringing documents with seals which contained guarantees on the part of that state and of the Swiss League regarding My Lord Filippo whom the King had already freed many days ago. But the King sent them back, declaring that he would not accept them and that he definitely trusted Filippo without such guarantees. The Bastard of Bourbon and the Bishop of Langres have gone to England as ambassadors to conclude the truce the English have asked for.[10] There is some other special and secret news which for several reasons we shall delay communicating to you until my, Emanuele's, return, which will be soon because I shall not waste time in coming. If our letter is too prolix, we beg that Your Excellencies deign to forgive us, because we were not able to say many and various things in just a few words. We always commend ourselves to Your Most Illustrious Lordships.

146

dela prelibata M.tà. Et così Franceschino à scritto ali soy ad Lione oportunamente, in modo che speramo non li sarà al presente exceptione alchuna. Monsig.or de Miolan,[9] el Cancellero de Cipri, et doy altri eranno venuti qui ambassatori di Savoya; et havendo portati li sigillati et promesse dil payse et de la Ligha per Filippo Mons.re, el S. Re li ha rimandati, dicendo non li volere acceptare, et fidarsi assay di esso Filippo senza altra loro promissione, el quale già più dì ha lassato. El Bastardo di Borbon et Vescovo di Langres sono andati ambassatori in Inglitera per concludere la tregua, quale essi Inglexi hanno domandato.[10] Alchune altre novelle particulare et secrete occoreno, le quale per più rispecti aspectaremo dirle ala venuta di me, Emanuel, di bocha, quale serà presto et al venire mio non perderò tempo alchuno. Se in scrivere siamo tropo longhi, supplicamo V. Ex.tie si degneno haverne per excusati, che cose assay et diverse non sapiamo dire in poche parolle. Ricomandandose sempre ad le prefate Vostre Ill.me S.

HISTORICAL NOTES

1. Doc. 15. The letter of 23 March has not been found.

2. Appendix, doc. IV.

3. In 1461 Duke Charles of Orléans had signed a contract for the marriage of his four-year-old daughter, Marie, with Pierre de Bourbon, Lord of Beaujeu and brother of Duke Jean II de Bourbon. This union of two powerful families displeased Louis XI, who was finally constrained by his perilous position to give his consent in November 1465. In the contract, Duke Charles gave in dowry to his daughter all his territories, except those held in appanage from the French crown, and his claims over the Duchy of Milan and the County of Pavia. The marriage, however, was never consummated, and in 1474 Pierre married the King's eldest daughter, Anne [Paul Pélicier, *Essai sur le gouvernement de la Dame de Beaujeu, 1483–1491* (Chartres, 1882; repr. Geneva: Slatkine, 1970), pp. 36–38].

4. Ziliolo Oldoini, Milanese ambassador at the Savoyard court. In his letter to the Duchess of Savoy [Orléans, 17 April 1466, BN, *Fonds Italien*, Cod. 1591, fol. 337; Vaesen, *Lettres*, 3:51–52], the King reproached the Duchess for having sent the Abbot of Casanova to Venice and Monferrat for the purpose of inciting war against Milan, and urged her to end this activity against a state which he meant to defend at all costs.

5. Giovanni Vagnone, Majordomo of Philip of Savoy from 1462 to 1467, and co-Lord of Trofarello, near Moncalieri, approximately nine kilometers south of Turin [Daviso di Charvensod, *Filippo II*, p. 186].

6. This letter has not been found.

7. This letter has not been found.

8. The King had written to the Treasurer of Dauphiné, Claude Cot [Jargeau, 3 April 1466, Vaesen, *Lettres*, 3:43–45], to pay the sum of 6,000 écus to the Milanese troops so that they could return to Lombardy. Part of this sum, which later was reduced to 4,000 écus, was to be raised through a loan from the Medici Bank in Lyon. See the documents relative to this payment in BN, *Fonds Français*, Cod. 20,420, nos. 33–34, 37, published by Vaesen, *Lettres*, 3:352–62. Cf. P. F. Visconti, Giovanni Andrea Tizzoni, and Giovanni Bianchi to the Duke, Lyon, 5 April 1466, and Panigarola to G. Bianchi, Meung-sur-Loire, 22 May 1466, *Francia*, cart. 532.

9. Antelme de Miolans, influential Savoyard baron. One of the other Savoyard ambassadors may have been Aymon de Seyssel, Count of La Chambre. The King had requested Duchess Yolande to send both of them to him on this mission [Marco Corio to F. Sforza, Chambery, 4 March 1466, *Savoia*, cart. 481]. The Chancellor of Cyprus has not been identified.

10. See doc. 16, n. 4.

The Magnificent Lord Garcia Betes,[1] ambassador of His Serene Highness King Ferrante, is going to His Most Christian and Most Serene Highness the King [of France] regarding matters of great importance to us and to our state. Since the late Most Illustrious Lord, our husband and father of happy memory, had great trust in Lord Garcia, clearly recognizing that he was ardently devoted to him and to his affairs, he used to discuss all his affairs with him.[2] After his death, he [Garcia] likewise took part in our councils and was aware of all our business. Therefore, we want you to share everything openly with Lord Garcia and to have faith in him, as he richly deserves, not keeping anything at all hidden from him, since his Most Serene Highness King Ferrante and we might [as well] be considered one and the same.

HISTORICAL NOTES

1. In his letter to Louis XI, relating the measures he was taking in support of Milan [Castronovo in Naples, 22 March 1466, *Registri Missive*, Reg. 77, fols. 66–67v], King Ferrante announced that he was sending Garcia Betes on a mission to the French court, the nature of which was not specified. The purpose of his mission, however, is revealed in docs. 33 and 42.

2. Betes had been on missions to Milan in 1460 and in 1462 [Santoro, *Gli Uffici*, pp. 154, 273].

22 · *The* DUKE *and* DUCHESS OF MILAN *to*

EMANUELE DE IACOPO *and*

GIOVAN PIETRO PANIGAROLA

Reg. Missive 74, fol. 63v. Copy

El M.co D. Grassia Bethes,[1] oratore del Ser.mo Re Ferrando, se transferisse da quello Christ.mo et Ser.mo S.re Re per alcune cose molto importante ad nuy et Stato nostro. Et perchè la felice memoria del Ill.-mo quondam nostro consorte et patre d'esso D. Grassia grandemente se confidava, et per haverlo chiaramente cognosciuto ad luy et cose soe ardentemente affectionato cum essa, ogni soa facenda communicava;[2] et così dappoy la morte soa, è intervenuto ad li nostri Consigli et ha inteso ogni nostra cosa. Pertanto volemo che cum lo prefato D. Grassia communicate ogni cosa, et de luy prendiate quella fede che meritamente se debbe, non tenendoli nesuna cosa ascosta, perochè lo Ser.mo S.re Re Ferdinando et nuy semo una cosa medesma.

Ci[chus]

We have until today delayed answering your letters of the twenty-fifth, twenty-sixth, and thirty-first of last month and of the first of this month,[1] because from day to day we have been expecting the Most Christian King's magnificent ambassadors to learn in greater detail what they had to say to us in the name of His Majesty; and also because we were awaiting to have news from Franceschino Nori who, as you know, went to France some days ago. Now that the royal ambassadors have arrived and have related to us His Majesty's messages,[2] we inform you that we are incapable of expressing orally or in writing how much we appreciated and welcomed their visit, and how much favor and reputation it has contributed to your affairs; for in truth they spoke both publicly and privately so freely and so aptly of the King's supreme goodwill and propensity toward us, our state, and for the safety of our possessions, that one could neither say, think, nor wish any more. Wherefore, it seems to us that our obligations toward His Serene Highness have so increased and multiplied, in addition to those of the past, that we are not at all able to find the right words of thanks. Nevertheless, we are answering the King by writing the letter herein attached, as you may see from the enclosed copy.[3] You will present the letter to His Majesty together with our apologies for not having written more to him, since we rely on what his ambassadors will write him, and also because in two or three days we

23 · *The* DUKE *and* DUCHESS OF MILAN *to*

EMANUELE DE IACOPO *and*

GIOVAN PIETRO PANIGAROLA

Francia, cart. 532. Minute

Siamo tardati fin ad questo dì ad fare altra risposta alle vostre littere de dì XXV, XXVI et ultimo del passato, et del primo del presente,[1] expectando de dì in dì la venuta de li M.ci ambassatori dela M.tà del Christianissimo S.re Re per intendere più particularmente quanto ce havessero ad exponere in nome d'essa M.tà, et item expectando havere qualche aviso da Francischino Nori zà più dì venuto in quelle parte como sete informato. Essendo mo venuti li dicti ambassatori regii, et exposto le ambassate dela prelibata M.tà,[2] dicemo che non vi porressimo dire nè scrivere quanto ne sii stata cara et acceptissima questa loro venuta, et quanto favore et reputatione el habii dato alle cose nostre, perchè in vero hano parlato in publico et in privato così largamente et degnamente dela optima voluntà et dispositione dela prelibata M.tà verso nuy et questo nostro Stato, et salveza de cose nostre, che più non se poria dire nè pensare nè desyderare; donde ne pare essere cresciuti et moltiplicati in tanti oblighi verso Sua Ser.tà ultra tanti altri passati, che non siamo puncto sufficienti ad trovare convenienti parole de ringratiare quella. Pure nuy li respondemo et scrivemo per le alligate, como vederete per l'inclusa copia,[3] quale littere presentarete ad Sua M.tà, facendo similiter nostre scuse se non gli scrivemo per longo, remettendone ad quanto gli scriveno li predicti suoy regii ambassatori, et etiamdio perchè fra duy o tre dì rimandaremo uno nostro cavalaro con nostre littere et de inde uno di

will send another courier with our letters. Thereafter we will send His Majesty one of our men who will be fully instructed regarding our needs and necessities, so that His Majesty, as well as yourselves, will be more fully informed.

There is no necessity for us to reply to all the matters raised in the letters you sent us, except to say that we have taken note of them and that you should continue to be solicitous and attentive in endeavoring to commend us to the Most Christian King, together with our sons and brothers, our state, and all our possessions which are more his than ours, so that he can dispose of them [as he wishes]. Assure him that, as we wrote, all our hope and safety are placed in His Serenity, through whose grace and protection we fear no harm or failure.

We expect to hear from you concerning daily noteworthy occurrences as they come along.

HISTORICAL NOTES

1. Docs. 12–14, 16.

2. The royal ambassadors, Gaston du Lyon and Giovanni Filippo da Trecate, traveling with more than fifty horses, had first gone to the Savoyard court to insure proper treatment of the Milanese troops passing through Savoy on their way to Lombardy [Cristoforo da Bollate to the Duke, Grenoble, 18 April 1466, BN, *Fonds Italien*, Cod. 1593, fols. 245–46]. They arrived in Milan on 24 April, and the next day they were given an audience by the Duke before the Secret Council and in the presence of other envoys. The Florentine ambassadors reported that the Duke gave a long and eloquent reply [Bernardo Giugni and Luigi Guicciardini to the Signoria of Florence, Milan, 26 April 1466, ASF, *Signori, X di Balia, VIII di Pratica, Legazioni e Commissarie, Missive e Responsive*, Reg. 63, fols. 87–88].

3. On the same date of this letter, the Dukes wrote to the King [BN, *Fonds Italien*, Cod. 1591, fol. 338], thanking him profusely for his support, etc., repeating much of what is written in this letter.

nostri ad Sua M.tà, informatissimo de quanto ne occorre et de ogni nostro bisogno, dal quale Sua M.tà et cusì vuy intenderete più ad pieno.

Ale cose che per dicte vostre littere ci havete scritto non accade dire altro, se non che havemo inteso tutto et che de continuo solicitate et attendete alla presentia della M.tà del Christianissimo S.re, recommandandogli le persone nostre, de nostri figlioli et fratelli et questo nostro Stato et cose che sono più sue che nostre, et così ne ha ad disponere, certificandone como gli scrivemo che ogni nostra speranza et salute consiste in la Ser.tà Sua, et mediante la gratia et protectione sua, non dubitamo de alcuno sinistro o mancamento.

De le cose che acadeno alla zornata degne de aviso expectamo ne avisate.

We reply to your letters of 31 March and 1¹ April in which you indicate that His Majesty, and you yourselves, are astonished that we did not write to you. We can well understand [your astonishment]. We [wish to point out], however, that we had written the enclosed letters² addressed to you and the one that we, Galeazzo, addressed to His Majesty (of which we enclose a copy for you), but we have delayed forwarding them until today because we were waiting every day to understand better the attitude of the Venetians toward us. From what we have come to know after we had written the enclosed letters, both from the Venetian ambassador who is here and from our ambassadors who have returned from Venice, we believe they are willing to be good neighbors, to live in peace, and to continue in the same manner as they did during the lifetime of our Most Illustrious husband and father of happy memory.

Bartolomeo da Bergamo still continues to give his soldiers money, and he also insists on the demand he wrote to Pietro de Pusterla, as you will learn from the enclosed copy; nevertheless, he has not undertaken anything new. The Venetians say what we have communicated to you, although we are not at all sure about their ways and intentions, above all because they have not sent an ambassador as the Pope and the other

---

a. Crossed out: XXIII.

24 · *The* DUKE *and* DUCHESS OF MILAN *to*

EMANUELE DE IACOPO *and*

GIOVAN PIETRO PANIGAROLA

Francia, cart. 532. Minute

Respondendo ad quanto per le vostre de ultimo del passato et primo del presente[1] ne scrivete, che la M.tà del Re et vuy ve maravigliati non ve habiamo scripto, dicimo che ne siamo certi; ma havendo scripte le aligate[2] che scrivemo a vuy et quelle nuy Galeazo scrivemo alla M.tà del Re, de le quale ve mandamo inclusa la copia, havemo soprasseduto fino al dì de hogi ad mandarle expectando ogni dì intendere meglio l'animo de Sig.ri Venetiani, quali per quello semo venuto intendendo alla giornata, da poy facte le aligate, et dal ambassatore d'essi Venetiani, quale è qui et dali nostri ambassatori, che sonno retornati da Venetia, ne pareno ben disposti ad volere ben vicinare con nuy et vivere in pace et perseverare como facevano con la bona memoria del Ill.mo quondam S. nostro consorte et patre. Et Bartolameo da Bergamo continue più ad dare dinari alli suoy,[b] etiandio persevera in le domande fece per soe littere scripte ad Petro da Pusterla, secondo intenderete per la copia inclusa in l'aligate; ma non ha però facta novità alcuna et loro parlano como intenderete. Tamen non ne havemo certeza alcuna de loro modi et intencion, maxime non ne havendo mandato alcun ambassatore como

---

b. Crossed out: tamen non ha facta novità alcuna contra nuy, né Stato nostro, né anche dapoy scrisse [ad Petro da Pusterla] per più littere de la domanda ne faceva [secondo intenderete per la copia inclusa in l'aligate], non ha de tale domanda facto altro caso et forse speramo che forse [*sic*] né la Signoria né luy farano altra novità contra nuy et Stato nostro. The words enclosed in brackets are part of the text as transcribed above.

Italian states have done.[3] We shall continue to inform His Majesty about what we hear and what happens daily. We are quite sure he will help and protect us against the Venetians or others that might in any way molest us.

We have postponed sending the enclosed letters also in order to wait for Franceschino Nori to give us answer concerning what we had charged him to do. Now, seeing he does not write, we think it best not to delay any longer in sending you these letters.

We will not dwell further on the subject of the marriage because as you will learn from the enclosed letter[4] which we, Galeazzo, wrote to His Majesty, we shall soon send there Pietro da Gallarate, who is to leave immediately and who will without doubt give satisfaction to His Majesty. Nevertheless, we wish you to inform His Majesty the King that concerning the kinship with My Lord of Charolais, it is our intention that it should completely be passed over in silence, because we do not want to venture into anything that we know might not please and satisfy His Majesty, even if he wished to give us all his state and dominion—which was also the thought and disposition of the late Lord, our husband and father.

As we, Galeazzo, wrote to the King, the Most Illustrious Marchioness was here to pay us a visit of condolence, and for no other reason: she started her return journey home on the twenty-fifth of this month.[5]

There is nothing else new here; everything is going on peacefully and quietly.

From Venice, we have heard what you will gather from the enclosed letter, which we wish you to show His Most Serene Majesty.

hanno [facto] el Papa et l'altre potentie de Italia.[3] Et pur de quello in-
tenderemo et seguirà alla giornata, continue ne daremo adviso alla M.tà
de quello S. Re, la chuy M.tà tegnamo per certissimo et constantissimo
che quando da Venetiani, o da altri, ne fosse facta molestia alcuna ne
aiutarà, et conservarà da caduno. Havemo ancora soprasseduto in mandare dicte alligate, expectando che Franceschino Nori ne respondesse
qualche cosa de quanto gli commettessemo. Mo vedendo de lá non
scrive altro, non ne è parso ad noy soprassedere più in mandare dicte
alligate nostre littere.

Del facto del parentato non ne extenderemo altramente, perchè
como per la ligata[4] nuy Galeazo scrivemo alla M.tà del Re, presto mandaremo de là Petro da Galarà, quale partirà de subito, et non dubitamo
satisfarà alla M.tà prefata. Ben volemo avisati la M.tà del Re che al
parentato de Mon.re de Chiarloes nostra intentione è che in tutto se li
metta silentio, perchè non metteressemo boca ad cosa non sapessemo
fosse grata et de bon contentamento de quella, etiam se ne vollesse dare
tutto el su stato et dominio suo, como ancora fo mente et dispositione del
quondam S. nostro consorte et patre.

La Ill.ma Madona Marchesana, quale è stata qui, como nuy Galeazo
scrivemo al S. Re, era per visitarne et condolersi del caso et non per altro.
Partì[c] alli XXV del presente per retornare ad casa soa.[5]

De qua non gli è altro de novo, ogni cosa passa pacificamente et
quiete.[d]

Da Venetia havimo quanto per l'inclusa copia intendereti, quale
volimo monstrati alla M.tà de quello Ser.mo S. Re.

---

c. Crossed out: partirà posdomane.
d. Crossed out: né alcuno de li nostri populi hanno facte novità alcuna, ma caduno sta obediente
commo facevano al tempo che viveva lo prefato quondam S. nostro consorte et patre.

HISTORICAL NOTES

1. Docs. 14, 16–17.

2. Doc. 23 and Appendix, doc. VIII.

3. The fact that Venice, unlike the other Italian states (except Savoy), never sent an embassy of condolences for the death of Francesco Sforza, created suspicion everywhere about its intentions, particularly in view of Colleoni's hostile moves. When it was learned in Milan that Venice had finally decided not to send such an embassy because it would be the last to arrive, the Dukes, eager to have this demonstration of support, sent an unofficial message to the Venetians, assuring them that their ambassadors would be received as if they

had been the first to arrive [The Dukes to Friar Simone de Camerino (who was to deliver the message on his own initiative), Milan, 8 May 1466, *Venezia,* cart. 353].

4. Appendix, doc. IX.

5. Marchioness Barbara Gonzaga's departure is also confirmed by her letter to Lodovico Gonzaga [Pizzighettone, 26 April 1466, ASMA, *Lettere Originali dei Gonzaga,* B. 2099]. The date of her departure further establishes the fact that all or portions of this letter were written on 23 April [cf. notes a and c].

So that you may know what to respond if the Most Christian King or others were to ask of the conduct of His Most Serene Majesty King Ferrante toward us and our state, we notify you that immediately upon hearing of the death of the late Illustrious Lord, our husband and father, King Ferrante wrote and sent envoys to His Holiness the Pope, the Venetians, the Florentines, and to all the other rulers of Italy, giving them to understand his excellent disposition and goodwill toward us. That is, with his troops, realm, and his very person, [he was determined] to help in our defense and in the preservation of our state, just as he would do for his own state, since he felt that all that pertained to his would be the same for ours. He gave everyone to understand that whoever did anything against us and our state would so act against His Majesty. Therefore he immediately sent his fleet composed of twelve galleys to Genoa, where they still are, having thus accomplished the salvation of the [present] government of Genoa. Then he had money distributed to all our troops that are in the Abruzzi to put them at the ready; he did likewise for those of the Illustrious Lord Alessandro, Grand Constable, our brother-in-law and uncle, in order to have him come here; and similarly he had ten of his own squadrons put at the ready, which within two or three days, along with ours mentioned above, ought to be leaving the Abruzzi to come here. Furthermore, His

25 · *The* DUKE *and* DUCHESS OF MILAN *to*

EMANUELE DE IACOPO *and*

GIOVAN PIETRO PANIGAROLA

Francia, cart. 532. Minute

Perchè, quando per quello Christianissimo S. Re o altri ve fosse domandato deli portamenti dela M.tà del Ser.mo S. Re Ferrando verso
nuy, et Stato nostro, sapiati che respondere, ve avisamo como esso S. Re
Ferrando, immediate ch'el intese della morte del quondam Ill.mo S.
nostro consorte et patre, scrisse et mandò suoy oratori ala S.tà del Papa,
Venetiani, Firentini, et tutte l'altre potentie de Italia, ad farli intendere
la soa optima dispositione et voluntà verso nuy, quale era con le gente,
Reame, et propria persona, aiutare, defendere et conservare nuy et questo
nostro Stato, non altramente ch'el suo proprio Stato, del quale deliberava omnino fosse quello medesmo seria del nostro; et facendo intendere
ad caduno che chi faria contra nuy et Stato nostro, tenesse fare contra
la M.tà Soa. Cossì subito mandò l'armata soa che sonno XII galee ad
Zenoa, dove sonno ancora, quale sono state cason de salvare quello
Stato de Zenoa. Deinde fece dare dinari ad tutte le nostre gente sonno
in Apruzo per metterse in ordine et cossì ad quelle del Ill. S. Alexandro
Gran Conestabile, nostro cognato et barba, per venire de qua. Et similiter ha facto metterne in ordine X squadre de quelle de Soa M.tà, quale
con dicte nostre fra duy, o III dì se debbeno partire de Apruzo per venire
de qua. Et più Soa M.tà ha poste in ordine tutte l'altre soe gente, con le
quale in propria persona, et con lo Ill.mo S. Duca de Calabria suo
primogenito, nostro genero et cognato,[1] vene in Aprucio alle confine

Majesty has put all his troops at the ready and, with them in person, together with the Most Illustrious Duke of Calabria, his first born and our son-in-law and brother-in-law,[1] he came into the Abruzzi to the borders above the Tronto River in order to be closer at hand for our support; and if there were need, he would even come in person or would send his first born together with his troops for the preservation of our state. In addition, he sent money to the Most Illustrious Count of Urbino, who also came to us, to help him put his troops at the ready for our aid and support. He also took action and sent his envoys to conclude an agreement with the Illustrious Marquis of Mantua and his first born, whom he took in his service and ours; he paid half the expenses simply for our defense and for no other reason. In fact, he has made and continues to make all those real demonstrations of support for our preservation and that of this state—more than we would know how to ask or desire. So it seemed wise to us to notify you of this so that, as we said, you might know how to respond to those who might speak to you of this matter.[2]

HISTORICAL NOTES

1. Alfonso, married to Ippolita Sforza, sister of Galeazzo Maria.
2. For the measures taken by King Ferrante in support of Milan, see also doc. 15 and n. 7.

sopra el Tronto per essere più vicino alli favori nostri, et bisognando venirà in propria persona o mandarà el prefato suo primogenito con dicte sue gente per conservatione del Stato nostro. Ha ancora mandati dinari al Ill.mo S. Conte de Urbino, quale *pure* è venuto da nuy, per mettere in ordine li suoy pur per *nostro* favore et subsidio. Preterea se è operato et mandato suoy messi per l'acordio del Ill. S. Marchese de Mantoa et il figliolo suo primogenito, quale ha tolto alli servici de Soa M.tà et nostri, et pagò la mità delle spese solamente per defensione nostra, et non per altro; et ha in effeto facto et fa continue tutte quelle effectuale demonstratione per conservatione nostra et de questo Stato, quale nuy più non saperessemo dimandare nè desyderare, del che ne è parso darne notitia perchè, come è dicto, sapiati che rispondere ad chi ve parlasse de tale cosa.[2]

From Emanuele de Iacopo[1] and from letters that I sent by means
of the courier Deserto on the twenty-eight of last month, Your Lordships
will have learned how things stand here and how the King, from all
that can be gathered, shows sign of wanting to do everything possible
with no reservations for the preservation of Your Lordships and of your
state. Recently, Franceschino Nori and I have gotten the King to dispatch
his present pursuivant, who will go with the King's letters to all the
rulers of Italy, of which I sent you copies. He will say and do whatever
Your Lordships tell him since those are the instructions he received
from His Majesty; having been dispatched for a period of two months,
Your Lordships can dispose of him as you see fit, and he will obey.

Moreover, since here it is being said that His Holiness the Pope is
amassing troops to make war against the Bolognese, and because His
Majesty fears he might have an understanding with the Venetians,[2] and
might be a joint effort on their part, the King is thinking of writing His
Holiness a letter along lines that would indicate that His Majesty knows
of the preparations being made by the Pope and recognizes that His
Holiness cannot make war against the Bolognese without harm to Your
Excellencies. [The letter would] serve notice that if he were to make
war and take up this enterprise, he would have no oath of obedience
whatsoever from His Majesty, who furthermore would become his

26 · GIOVAN PIETRO PANIGAROLA *to the*

DUKE *and* DUCHESS OF MILAN

Francia, cart. 532. Orig.

Per Emanuel de Iacoppo[1] et per littere manday per el Deserto cavalaro a dì XXVIII dil passato, haverano le Vostre S. inteso in che termine si trovano le cose di qua et como questo S. Re dimonstra, per quanto si pò comprehendere, volere fare ogni cosa possibile et nulla sparagnare per conservatione de le V. S. et de vostro Stato. Al presente Franceschino Nori et io habiamo facto expedire da la M.tà Soa el presente suo Prosuvano, quale andarà cum le littere di quella, di le quale vi ne manday copia, a tute le potentie de Italia et dirà et farà quanto per esse V. S. li sarà ordinato; et così ha commissione dala prelibata M.tà, havendo da qui spazamento per doy mesi. Si chè Vostre S. haveranno a disponere di luy como li parerà expedienti, che obedirà. Ulterius perchè qui si dice che la Sanctità de Nostro Signore fa gente per far guerra a Bolognesi, et dubita essa M.tà che non habii intelligentia cum Venetiani[2] et sii una practicha ordita a manno, dice di far scrivere una littera ala p.ta Sanctità di tal tenore, che essendo la M.tà Soa avisata dile preparatione fa essa Soa S.tà, et cognoscendo quela non potere guerezare a Bolognesi senza preiuditio de le Vostre Ex.tie, li notificha che facendoli guera, o pigliando questa impresa, da la prelibata Soa M.tà non haverà obedientia alchuna dal lato di qua, ma oltra che li sarà inimica, temptarà ogni cosa possibile contra di quella, sforzandosi farli intendere tal cosa esserli molto molesta et haverla a core. La quale littera si farà di fare spazare et

enemy and try every conceivable action against him; it would forcefully give him to understand that such an action would be greatly displeasing to the King, and he takes the matter to heart. We will see to having this letter dispatched and sent to you so that Your Excellencies can make use of it if the need arises.

We are constantly attending to the preparations for the dispatch of those ambassadors who are to come there [in Italy], as they are making many requests relative to their departure. I hope that within four days Francheschino Nori, who is working with great success on these arrangements, will have arranged the departure of My Lord of Gaucourt, and then we will see to the dispatch of the others. All efforts will be made to expedite their journey so that they lose as little time as possible in going straightaway to Venice and wherever there is need. Of what is accomplished daily, I will always notify Your Lordships, to whom I humbly commend myself.

Postscript. His Majesty has ordered Franceschino to write to merchants in Rome, Florence, and wherever seems best to him, saying that the King has indicated that he wished to engage in every action for the defense of Your Lordships, without failing you in any way. The King intends to gain more support for the affairs of Your Excellencies by the publication and spread of this information. Franceschino has already begun writing, and so I make note of it to you.

HISTORICAL NOTES

1. See Emanuele's letter of credence, issued to him by the King and addressed to the Duke of Milan [Meung-sur-Loire, 23 April 1466, *Francia*, cart. 559; *Lettres*, 3:55], announcing his impending departure for Milan.

2. Since the preceding year, Pope Paul II had been making attempts to secure a more direct control over the papal city of Bologna, which had an oligarchic regime under the influence of Giovanni Bentivoglio, a friend of

mandarola, ació che bisognando possanno V. Cel. operarla. Circha el spazamento de li ambassatori che debeno vegnire di là, et quali per questa loro andata dimandano di molte cose, continue si atende ala expeditione loro. Spero che fra IIII° giorni Franceschino Nori, quali in questi acordi si travaglia et giova assay, haverà acordato l'andata di Mons.re di Gocurt et poy si attenderà al spazamento de li altri, ali quali tuti si sforzarano provedere, che al venire suo perdano mancho tempo che sii possibile per potere di bona hora andare a Vinesia et dove bisognarà, tenendo di quanto a la giornata si concluderà, V. S. sempre avisate, ale quale humilmente mi riccomando.

Post scripta. La p.ta M.tà ha commisso ad Franceschino predicto, che scriva a Roma, a Firenza et dove li parerà a mercadanti, quella haverli dicto volere pigliare ogni impresa et defensione per le V. S. et in nulla volerli manchare, ació che publicando et spargendosi questa voce, sia più favore a le cose di Vostre Ex.tie; et già Franceschino ha commenzato a scriverne, si chè gli ne aviso.

the Sforza. Although a seemingly satisfactory accomodation between the Pope and the city was reached in January 1466, with Francesco Sforza's mediation, Bentivoglio feared an attack by Bartolomeo Colleoni with the secret connivance of Venice and the Pope [Cecilia M. Ady, *The Bentivoglio of Bologna: A Study in Despotism* (Oxford: Oxford University Press, 1937), pp. 60–63].

My Lord of Miolans went to the King of France with a letter of credence in the Illustrious Madame of Savoy's own hand; on her behalf he entreated His Majesty to give her support and aid in making war against Your Lordships on general grounds but especially to recuperate Bassignana, Valenza,[1] *and certain other territories that belong to her and which were unjustly taken from her. Since she is His Majesty's sister,* [she thus hopes] *that His Majesty will be happy to have her, rather than another, gain benefits, because once she has them, he will always have them at his disposal. She pointed out that she would have many troops at her service, and for this very reason she was going into Piedmont in order to make preparations. When His Majesty responded that these seemed to him castles in the air and not very likely to succeed, My Lord of Miolans replied that they were pursuing their claims by taking steps on a very solid foundation and they had come to a real understanding with the Venetians, the Duke of Modena, the Pope, the Bernese, the Swiss, the League, and other rulers who would help them and give them a hand. Wherefore His Majesty answered that it seemed to him, and he thus counseled his sister, that for her own good and that of her country she not begin or try such undertakings, for from them there would only come forth great scandal and trouble. Rather, he encouraged her to be neighborly and live on good terms with Your Lord-*

27·GIOVAN PIETRO PANIGAROLA *to the*

DUKE *and* DUCHESS OF MILAN

BN, Fonds Italien, Cod. 1593, fol. 249–49v. Orig.

Monsignor de Miolan hé stato da questo Signor Re de Franza con una littera di credenza de propria mano dela illustre Madama de Savoia, et per parte di quela ha pregata la M.tà Soa che voglia darli favore et adiuto a fare guerra ad le S.rie V. in genere et maxime ad recuperare Basignana, Valenza[1] et certe altre terre che li apertieneno et che indebitamente li furono tolte; et così voglia essere contenta che, essendo quela sorela de essa Soa Maiestà, più tosto habii del bene cha uno altro, perché havendone ne porà sempre disponere, notificandoli che haveria gente assai al suo servitio et per questa casone andava in Piemonte a fare le preparatorie. Rispondendo la M.tà Soa parerli questi foseno desegni facti in aere et non apti ad reuscire, disse esso Monsignor de Miolan oltra le ragione pretendevano, moverse con fondamento et havere strecta intelligentia con Venetiani, Duca de Modena, Papa, Bernesi, Suiceri, la Ligha et altre potentie che li adiutarano et li tegnirano la mano. Donde essa Maiestà rispose che li pareva et consigliava soa sorela, per el bene et utile suo et del paise, ad non intrare né temptare simile imprese, essendo maxime per parturire grande scandalo et inconveniente, ma la confortava ad vicinare et vivere bene con le S.rie V.; et in questo haveva ad studiarse non a fare guerra che, così facendo, conseguiria la fidelità del Marchese de Monferrà et del Marchese de Saluce[2] et seria temuta, riverita et obedita da tuti li subditi soi che, essendo in guerra, non se ne poria

*ships, and it was in that that she should place her zeal rather than in
making war. In so doing, she would assure herself of the loyalty of the
Marquis of Monferrat and of the Marquis of Saluzzo;[2] she would then
be feared, revered, and obeyed by all her subjects whom, were she at
war, she could make no use of. Nor should she be so willing to place
her faith in dealings with the Venetians, etc., because they are in no
way to be believed, and when it comes to deeds she will find that they
are nothing but smoke. He advised her that for his part he intended to
help and sustain Your Lordships without fail for it seemed to him that
he was thus obliged, and so she should consider well her position. On
the matter of giving help, he [said] that shortly he would send an embassy there through which he would let them know his intentions and
what he means to do on this and many other matters; and in this connection he said some very rude words, whereby My Lord of Miolans left
in great confusion and ill content, from what I understand. Indeed, My
Lord Filippo recently told me that if it were someone other than Your
Lordship, who had served the King of France in his hour of need, and
you are thus regarded by His Majesty as his brother to be protected, the
House of Savoy would certainly press its rights and would indeed find a
way for taking care of them.*

*I dutifully relate these things to Your Lordships, faithfully remind-
ing you that, although My Lord Filippo might say such things in order
to clarify, if he can, the question of the marriage, as he indicated to me
and to Emanuele de Iacopo at other times, it could do nothing but good
if Your Lordships in whatever ways you saw fit were to seek to keep
My Lord Filippo friendly, because he can do a great deal in Savoy and
each day presently he becomes more powerful. I will make every effort
to see that His Majesty sends as soon as possible an embassy to Madame
of Savoy to obviate whatever dealings she has and keep things on an even
keel for Your Lordships over there; I will give detailed notice of whatever happens daily.*

*Furthermore, I notify Your Lordships that the King of France has
secretly sent for Duke John by means of the Bailli of Rouen,[3] who is*

valere, nè anche si voglia fondare sopra practiche de Venetiani etc.,
perché nulla ne crede et al effecto trovare non sono cha fumo; avisandola
che dal canto dela prelibata Soa Maiestà intende adiutare et mantenire le
S.rie V. et in niente mancharli, parendoli così essere obligata, si ché
avisi bene el facto suo. Ala parte de darli adiuto, che in breve mandarà
lì una ambassata per la quale li farà sapere in questo et in molte altre
cose l'intentione sua et quelo che delibera fare. Et li disse alchune parole
molto rude in questo proposito; donde esso Signor de Miolan si hé
partito con tal conclusione et malcontento, sicondo intendo. Ben me disse
questi dì Filippo Mon.re, che se fusse altro cha la S.ria V. che haveva
servito el Re de Franza in el suo bisogno, fratelo de la M.tà Soa[a] *et quale*
quela voleva defendere, che fosse certa la Casa de Savoia precazaria el
drito suo et trovaria bene a fare el facto loro. Le quale cose per el debito
mio significo ad le S.rie V., ricordandoli fidelmente quanvis existimi esso
Filippo Mon.re dire tal parole per volere, se pò, essere chiaro del paren-
tato, come ad Emanuel de Iacop et a me altre volte ha dimonstrato, non
seria forse cha bene con le vie che le S.rie V. parerano, cerchare de tegnirse
el prefato Filippo Mon.re amico, perché pò assai in quela Savoia et al
presente hé per divenire ogni dì più grande. Sforzarome etiam che più
presto si porà la prefata Maiestà mandi ambassata dala prelibata Madama
de Savoia per obviare ad qualonche practiche et tegnire le cose bene
hedificate dal canto delà per esse Vostre Signorie, ale quale di quanto
ala giornata se operarà, darò particulare aviso. Ulterius aviso le S.rie V.
che el signor Re de Franza ha mandato secretamente ad tore el Duca
Iohanne che vegni da la M.tà Soa per el Bailì de Roano,[3] *che hé uno de*
più fidati che quela habia, et fra pochi[b] *dì serà qui. Se dubita serà forza*
la M.tà Soa lo acarezi et piglii la banda de Angiò, facendo dele cose che
mai non haveria facto vivendo la felicissima memoria del condam
Signore vostro consorte et patre, come ad Emanuel predicto ho comisso
notoficare ad le S.rie V. aciò che, parendoli, li possano fare pensiero. Et
pure anche se dice che el matrimonio dela sorela del Re Odoardo haverà

---

a. C. C. reads: "la chuy M.tà ve reputa fratello," which is Panigarola's intended meaning.
b. C. C. incorrectly reads: octo.

one of the most trusted men that he has; he will be here shortly. It is feared that His Majesty will flatter him and take up with the Angevin clique, doing things that he would never have done were the late Lord, your husband and father of happy memory, alive. I asked Emanuele to relate this to Your Lordships so that you might give it some thought as you see fit. It is also being said that the matrimony of King Edward's sister to My Lord of Charolais[4] will take place and that there will be an alliance between them, especially since they are saying that My Lord of Charolais fears that in time the King of France will take Piccardy from him and wage war against him. However, we are not yet sure that it has been agreed to; but if it does take place, His Majesty will necessarily be constrained to adhere to the House of Anjou. I will stay alert and bend every effort to learn what follows, and I will give detailed notification to Your Excellencies, to whom I devotedly commend myself.

HISTORICAL NOTES

1. Bassignana and Valenza, two localities on the southern edge of the Po River, about 17 and 14 kilometers northeast of Alessandria respectively. Both had come under Milanese control during the Visconti sweep into Piedmont in the middle of the fourteenth century, and since then they had become a bone of contention between Milan and Savoy.

2. Lodovico I. Both he and the Marquis of Monferrat, Guglielmo VII, were feudatories of the Duke of Savoy.

3. Jean de Montespedon, called Houaste.

4. The marriage of Margaret of York and the Count of Charolais was concluded in 1467 after the latter succeeded his father, and was celebrated a year later. Louis XI did everything possible to prevent this union between his two enemies [Richard Vaughan, *Charles the Bold. The Last Valois Duke of Burgundy* (New York: Harper and Row), pp. 44-48.]

loco con Mon.re de Chiarlois[4] et fra loro sarà ligha, maxime perché dicono Mon.re de Chiarlois dubitare che con tempo questo Re de Franza non li toglii Picardia et li fazi guerra; ma peranche non siamo certificati che così sia concluso, ma se havesse efecto saria necessario constrecta la M.tà Soa adherirse ad al Casa de Angiò. Strarò atento, sforzandomi intendere che seguirà et distinctamente ne avisarò le Vostre Ex.tie, a le quale devotamente me ricommando.

MILAN [MEDIOLANI], 9 MAY 1466

We have received joint letters of the tenth, eighteenth, and nine-teenth of last month[1] from you and from Emanuele, and we reply to various portions as seems necessary. First, regarding the tardy com-munication of our, Galeazzo's, return, we will not say anything more because you will have learned the reasons from the letters carried by the other courier.

Regarding the King's pronouncements in the presence of King René's envoys about his excellent disposition toward us, and the pro-visions made in having additional letters sent to the rulers of Italy, the offers he makes of troops and of all that he can do for the preservation of our state, and sending here My Lords of Vienne and of Gaucourt to go to the lords of Italy, and so forth, we instruct you to thank His Majesty as much as you possibly can for these provisions and offers. And were the need to arise, we would use them, because our every hope is in His Majesty; thank God our affairs are in such a state that we do not have any need of them. Since His Majesty has already done a great deal, so much so that we do not know how we may ever be able to pay back even the minimal part, were it to please His Majesty, it seems to us that he might cancel the dispatch of his ambassadors; and in case they have al-ready left, and have not traveled therefrom more than two days, he

28 · *The* DUKE *and* DUCHESS OF MILAN *to*

GIOVAN PIETRO PANIGAROLA

Francia, cart. 532. Minute

Havemo recevute le littere comune de ti et Emanuel de dì X, XVIII, et XVIIII° del passato,[1] ale quale responderemo ad quelle parte ne pareno necessarie; et primo alle parte del nostro tardo scrivere de l'intrata de nuy, Galeazo, che per le littere portate per l'homo mo haveray intese le casone, sichè circa questo non ne extenderemo altramente.

Alla parte del parlare ha facto quello S. Re in presentia de quelli oratori del Re Renato della soa optima dispositione verso nuy, et dele provisione facte in fare replicare quelle littere ale potencie de Italia, et offerte ne fa de quelle lanze et de tutto quello possa per conservatione de questo nostro Stato, et de mandare de qua Mon.ri de Viane et de Gocurt per andare alli S. de Italia etc., dicimo regracy Soa M.tà quanto te sia possibile de dicte provisione et offerte, et che quando accada el bisogno ne usaremo, perchè ogni nostra speranza consiste in Soa M.tà; ma per Dio gratia le cose nostre sonno in tale termine che non ne havimo bisogno. Et perchè la M.tà Soa ha facto assay, et tanto che non sapiamo quanto may poterli satisfare ad niuna minima parte, quando sia de piacere de Soa M.tà ne pare faza restare la venuta de dicti suoy ambassatori, et quando sianno partiti, et non siano venuti in qua per più che due giornate, li faza retornare in dreto; et cossì volimo dighi alla prefata M.tà da nostra parte, sforzandote però de sporgeli questo humanamente

might have them recalled. We want you to tell this to His Majesty on our behalf, but making every effort to relay the message as courteously and as pleasantly as possible, since they are presently not necessary, submitting everything however to His Majesty's pleasure.

We want you to thank His Majesty and also My Lord Filippo for the letters written and the envoys sent to Madame of Savoy reminding and advising her to live with us on friendly terms.

We affirm that what was told to the King regarding the Marquis of Monferrat is not true. Having heard of the passing of the Most Illustrious late Lord, our husband and father, the Marquis only came to visit and offer his services, and then returned home, as you will have learned from our other letters. You will therefore assure His Majesty that he has received from us no office or honor of any sort, except that of friendly relations and neighborliness.

We say nothing more regarding Lord Roberto and Asti, since we are sure that His Most Serene Highness will stand firm in the decision and the terms arrived at with the late Lord, our husband and father, to the effect of having us possess it.[2] When you have occasion to speak of it, make every effort to have His Majesty adhere to this decision and end.

We say nothing else about the marriage with Savoy because Pietro da Gallarate, who is leaving immediately, will tell orally His Majesty all that is necessary, as you will also have learned fully from our letters.[3]

We are very happy about His Majesty's declaration that he would never give the Pope his oath of obedience until he learns that the Pope is our friend, etc., and we want you to thank His Majesty. We will immediately advise His Majesty of the way in which the Pope behaves with us. We want you to stay alert regarding Duke John and My Lord of Charolais, to learn how they behave, what their dealings and developments are, constantly notifying us of whatever you learn.

et piacevelmente perchè al presente non sonno necessarii, remettendo però tutto in arbitrio de Soa M.tà.

Dele littere scripte et messi mandati ad Madama de Savoya per Soa M.tà et per Filippo Mon.re per recordarli et confortarla ad ben vivere con nuy, et piace et volimo ne regracy la M.tà del Re et cossì el prefato Filippo Mon.re.

Del S. Marchese de Monferrato dicimo non è vero quello è stato referto ad quello S.re Re; et solo esso S. Marchese, inteso ch'el hebbe el caso del Ill.mo quondam S. nostro consorte et patre, ne vene ad visitare et offerirse, et poy tornò ad casa como per altre nostre haveray inteso. Et cossì ne certificaray Soa M.tà che da nuy non ha havuto officio nè dignità alcuna, se non de ben vivere et vicinare con nuy.

Del facto del S. Roberto et de Asti non dicimo altro, perchè siamo certi quello Ser.mo Re stii fermo nel proposto et pratiche facte con Soa M.tà per lo prelibato quondam S. nostro consorte et patre de farnelo havere;[2] et ad questo proposto et fine, quando te accada parlarne, sforzate mantenere Soa M.tà.

Del facto del parentato de Savoya non dicimo altro perchè Petro da Galarate, quale de subito partirà, dirà ad boca alla M.tà del Re quanto bisogna et anche per altre nostre haveray inteso ad compimento.[3]

De quello ha dicto el S. Re che non darà may al Papa obedientia finchè non intenda sia nostro amico etc., dicimo che regratii Soa M.tà et questo molto ne è piaciuto; et alla giornata avisaremo Soa M.tà in che modo se portarà con nuy.

Del Duca Iohanne et de Mon.re de Chiarlois, volimo staghi attento de sentire como se portano, et tutte lor pratiche et progressi, et continue ne avisi de quanto sentiray.

HISTORICAL NOTES

1. Docs. 19–21.

2. In the fall of 1463, during the negotiations for the confirmation of the alliance between Louis XI and Francesco Sforza, the King had suggested that Francesco could purchase from the Duke of Orleans the County of Asti and his claims to Milan for the sum of 200,000 ducats. Francesco reluctantly agreed, but the Duke of Orleans refused to give his consent and the matter, though frequently discussed, was never settled. Later, the purchase of Asti by the

Duke of Milan was used by the King as an additional inducement to gain his consent to the Savoyard marriage [Mandrot, *Dépêches*, 1–4 passim, and particularly, 1:425–26, 344–45; 3:37–38; Vaesen, *Lettres*, 2:170–71]. In April 1466 Louis was apparently still pursuing this tactic by signifying that he desired to purchase Asti himself [doc. 21], while Galeazzo Maria is here reminding him of the previous offer made to his father.

    3. Doc. 24, and Appendix, docs. VIII–IX.

My Lord of Crussol, Seneschal of Poitou, recently returned from Savoy. He had gone to the Illustrious Madame of Savoy for Your Excellency's release,[1] and upon his return he made a long and noteworthy report to the King. From what can be gathered from his actions, he has continually shown and shows himself to be a partisan of Your Lordship. Whenever he had the chance, he spoke with love and fidelity of Your Lordship's affairs. He can be of great service, for he is first in His Majesty's chamber, most trusted and most depended upon. His brother, the venerable Deacon of Grenoble, who assists His Majesty in reciting the Office, has been faithfully in his service for a long time; thus His Majesty, by way of recompense for his service, is presently giving him the Archbishopric of Tours. In this connection he has written warmly to His Holiness the Pope, with the intention that he alone have it and no one else.[2]

My Lord of Crussol and the Deacon have asked me to commend them to Your Excellency, which I do as much as possible, beseeching on their behalf that it may please Your Highness to write to His Holiness and intercede with him and with others as you see fit, so that the aforementioned Archbishopric may be conferred upon him, as is the intention of His Majesty. They are confident that Your Lordship's intercession together with what the King is writing will be of great help, and they entreat you to assist them with every help and favor possible, for besides

29·GIOVAN PIETRO PANIGAROLA *to the*

DUKE OF MILAN

BN, Fonds Italien, Cod. 1593, fol. 250. Orig.

Questi dì ritornò di Savoya Mons.re di Corsol, Senescalcho di Poyto, quale era andato da la Ill. Madama di Savoya per la liberatione de la V. Ex.tia;[1] al ritorno di quella ha facto una grande et digna rellatione ad questo S. Re, et per quanto si pò comprehendere et a li effecti, si hé continue monstrato et monstra partesano dela V. S. et, dove hé achaduto, ha parlato con amore et fede dele cose de essa V. S.; et pò servire che hé el primo in camera con la M.tà dil p.to S. Re, più fidato et più operato. El venerabile Diano di Granoble, suo fratelo, che adiuta dire l'offitio ad la p.ta M.tà, gran tempo fa hé in li servitii di quella fidatissimo; alsi essa M.tà al presente, in recompensatione dil suo bon servire, li ha donato lo Arcivescovato di Tors et hanne scritto affectuosissimamente ala Sanctità di Nostro Signore, intendendo che costuy solo lo habii et non altro.[2] Havendomi li p.ti Mons.ri di Corsol et Diano riquesti che li ricomandi ala V. Ex.tia, quanto più posso gli ricomando il facto loro, pregando per parte di quelle la V. Cel. che li piacia in favore suo scrivere ala Sanctità p.ta intercedendo apresso quela et dove vi parirà, ita che dicto Arcivescovato li sia conferito como hé intentione de la prelibata M.tà; et confidandose loro che le intercessione de la V.S. apresso quanto questo S. Re scrive di là, li debiano molto giovare, pregano quela li volia asistere d'ogni favore et ayuto a quela possibile, et oltra che servireti a questo S. Re, fariti etiam piacere a persone che meritano essere favoriti et che

serving the King, you will do a favor for people who merit it and who love Your Lordship. The bearer of this letter will be the Most Reverend My Lord of Cahors,[3] who is going to Rome at His Majesty's orders, and he has special instructions in this matter. He will pass by Milan, and through him Your Highness can write to Rome and make provisions in favor of the Deacon, thus fulfilling his desire, as he has perfect faith and hope in you. I always commend myself to Your Illustrious Lordship.

HISTORICAL NOTES

1. See docs. 7–8.

2. Gerard de Crussol, in fact, became Archbishop of Tours on 9 June 1466 [Eubel, *Hierarchia catholica*, 2:258].

3. Antoine Allemand or Alleman, formerly Abbot of Ambronay, and Bishop of Cahors since 1465 [ibid., 2:123], who left the royal court on 14 May [see next doc. 30].

amano essa V. S. El presente exhibitore sarà el Rev.mo Mons. de Caors,[3] che va a Roma mandato da la p.ta M.tà et ha commissione speciale di questo facto; passarà per Milano, et per luy porà V. Cel. scrivere a Roma et provedere in favore dil p.to Diano, ita che conseguisca el desyderio suo et como in quela ha perfecta fede et speranza. Me ricommando sempre a la Ill.ma V. S.

Recently the Seneschal of Poitou, called My Lord of Crussol, returned from Savoy where he had been sent for the liberation of Your
Excellency. Upon his return he made a worthy and excellent report on
Your Lordships, and with regard to the actions taken here in your favor,
he has behaved in a most friendly manner. He could be a very useful
person, since he is first in the King's chamber and His Majesty confides
to him a great number of his secrets, and considers him very trustworthy.
Furthermore, he has great influence in Savoy and also upon My Lord
Filippo, because he was one of the staunchest supporters of his release.
For these reasons it would be a good thing, if Your Lordships see fit,
to write to him and try to cultivate him, now more than ever, as he
can be useful in many things, *above all because Duke John is trying to
augment his influence in the Court and upset all our affairs, as you will
learn from my letters.*

I have delayed so long in writing to Your Lordships because I was
waiting to be able to inform you as to the conclusions and consequences.[1]
Since His Majesty had ordered, several days ago, the dispatch of his ambassadors there,[2] I thought things were taking too much time, owing to
certain *Angevins who had told him that your circumstances were different from what Your Lordships wrote.* [They pointed out that] this
would be a great enterprise that His Majesty was undertaking, and ex-

30·GIOVAN PIETRO PANIGAROLA *to the*

DUKE *and* DUCHESS OF MILAN

Francia, cart. 532. Orig.

Questi dì ritornò di Savoya el Senescalcho de Poytò, appellato Monsignor di Corsol, mandato là per la liberatione de la Vostra Ex.tia. Al ritorno suo ha facto una digna et optima rellatione de le V. S., et in le cose che qui hè acaduto fare per favore di quelle, se gli hè portato molto amorevelmente: hè persona che pò servire, et primo in camera di questo S. Re, con el quale Soa M.tà comunicha molto li soy secreti, et a quela fidatissimo. Ulterius in Savoya pò assay, et con Filippo Monsignore, havendo luy maxime sollicitato la liberatione soa; per questi rispecti non saria cha bene, parendo a le V. S., che quelle li scrivesseno et cerchasseno di intertenerlo al presente più cha may, perchè pò giovare in molte cose, *maxime cercando el Duca Iohanne como fa de ingerirse in questa Corte et rompere ogni nostra practicha, como per mie littere intenderite.* Io ho differito tanto tempo de scrivere a le V. S. expectando avisarle de conclusione et effecti.[1] Havendo più dì fa la M.tà prelibata ordinato mandare li ambassatori soi di là,[2] mi pareva le cosse andasseno in longo, et procedeva che certi *Angiovini havevano significato ad quela le cose vostre non essere in el termino che scrivevano* le Signorie Vostre, et questa essere una grande impresa che Soa M.tà pigliava, et di grandissima spessa, essendo Venetiani potenti como sono de dinari et di gente d'arme, et essere alligati cum molte potentie che vi dariano da fare, *cercando con ogni via licita et illicita de interompere che quela non mandasse persona*

cessively expensive, the Venetians being powerful both financially and militarily, besides being allied to many powers, so that they would give you trouble. *They tried in every way, lawful and unlawful, to prevent the King from sending anybody to Venice, Rome, or elsewhere.* Having learned this, I begged His Majesty, in the best way and with fitting words, to send the said ambassadors, pointing out that the most important service that he could do for you was to take with great celerity those measures which he thought suitable, above all as good weather was approaching. For this reason, and especially because he heard that the Pope wanted to go to war against Bologna and so was in contact with the Venetians, he then decided he would send the other embassy afterward; but in order to save time, he sent the Bishop of Cahors[3] (formerly Abbot of Ambronay) to Rome in great haste. The King added that he was doing this because two embassies would be more useful to Your Lordships than one alone, and the Bishop, traveling swiftly, might interrupt the negotiations that might have begun already. Members of the Council, Franceschino, and I made out the instructions, of which herein enclosed I send Your Excellencies a copy in Italian.

The Bishop, however, was reluctant to bear to the Pope what was a challenge to the oath of obedience, pleading that a courier rather than a cleric was more apt for the office, because in the instructions there is a paragraph where it is said, that if the Pope should make war on Bologna or otherwise be hostile to Your Lordships, His Majesty serves notice that he will not render him any act of obedience at all.[4] Thereupon, the King in my presence commanded the Bishop (since we had told the King that this point was absolutely necessary) never to set foot within the kingdom if he would not serve in this capacity. He declared that he wanted the Bishop to indicate that paragraph and frankly tell the Pope that before making the act of obedience, he wanted to know how His Holiness would behave with him, his friends, relations, supporters, and allies, in order that there should not be a repetition of what had happened with the late Pope Pius, to whom the King had trustingly made the act of obedience and then was deceived.[5] Moreover, if the Pope

ad Venetia, a Roma nè altrove. Le quale cose intendendo, pregay la p.ta Soa M.tà cum quelli migliori modi et parole che mi parse, ad expedire dicti ambassatori, notificandoli ch'el più relevato servitio che vi poteva fare, si era cum cellerità fare quelle provisione li parevano, maxime aprossimandosi el bon tempo; et per questa casone deliberò poy di mandare el Vescovo di Cahors,[3] altre volte Abbate di Ambronay, a Roma volando per anticipare tempo, potissimum intendendo ch'el Papa voleva far guera a Bologna, et così teneva practiche cum Venetiani, dicendo che mandaria l'altra ambassata apresso; et disse facevalo per questo rispecto, che doy ambassate fariano più favore a le V. S. cha una, et andando presto el p.to Vescovo saria casone di interompere tale practiche che fusseno commenzate. Per questi dil Consiglio, Franceschino et me furono facte le instructione, de le quale ne mando copia in italiano qui alligata a le p.te V. Ex.tie. Et facendo resistentia esso Vescovo di non volere portare al Papa desfindanza dil hobedientia, ma più tosto dicendo essere offitio de uno cavalero cha di homo di giexia, perchè in le instructione hè uno capitulo che se la Sanctità Soa fa guera a Bologna o altramente sii contraria a le V. S., Soa M.tà li notifica che non li farà obedientia alchuna.[4] Essa Soa M.tà in mia presentia alhora li commandò, perchè già li havevamo dicto questo poncto essere necessaryssimo, che may non tornasse in el Reame se non la serviva a questo tracto; et che voleva portasse dicto articulo, et liberamente lo dicesse al Papa, che prima che li facesse obedientia, voleva intendere como et in che modo la Sanctià Soa si governaria cum Soa M.tà, soy amici, parenti, adherenti et alligati, ad ciò che non li achada como ha facto dil quondam Papa Pio, che havendoli liberamente facto la obedientia, da poy se ne trovò inganato.[5] Et quando pure ad Bologna deliberi far guera, o interprendere cum Venetiani o per qualonche altro modo guera che torni a danno o preiuditio de le V. S., certifica Soa Sanctità che mandarà socorso a Bolognesi, et dove bisognarà, et farà passare Filipo Monsignore cum octo o X.M. persone, monstrando cum effecti che ha questa cosa a core, et che delibera fare ogni cosa possibile per mantegnimento dil Stato vostro, replicando a dicto Vescovo che parlasse chiaro a la p.ta Sanctità, et non

were to decide to wage war against Bologna, or undertake hostilities together with the Venetians, or in any other way that might harm Your Lordships, the Bishop should notify His Holiness that the King will send aid to the people of Bologna or wherever it is necessary, and will let My Lord Filippo, with eight or ten thousand soldiers, cross the Alps, thus showing with this act that the King has this matter at heart and means to do everything possible to support your state. He instructed the Bishop once again to speak quite bluntly to the Pope without sparing anything, as this was the King's firm intention. At this point he turned around, and in the presence of many lords, spoke as much in favor of Your Highnesses as one could say, adding that the Pope had no reason to please the Venetians, since in the past they had banished him from Venice and deprived him of his benefices.[6] As a consequence, the Bishop left already four days ago with the above instructions. He will stop in Lyons six or eight days in order to get ready. Then he will come through Milan to share his mission with Your Excellencies, and if Your Excellencies want the Bishop to emphasize one thing more than another, he will do so, as if it were a part of his instructions, because he has strict orders to that effect from His Majesty.

Several days ago, through the ambassador of My Lord of Charolais, who left from here, I forwarded the letters that Your Lordships had written to the Duke of Burgundy and to the Count of Charolais.[7] While I was speaking to the King recently, he told me to exhort Your Excellencies to maintain an understanding and alliance with My Lord of Charolais, without any regard for His Majesty, for he is most happy about it, and aside from the fact that you will be doing him a great favor, he thinks that you should do this for the good of all parties.

On the sixteenth of this month at Tours, My Lord the Admiral of France[8] left this life; his death is greatly mourned by the King because he had been very faithful. The King distributed the Admiral's responsibilities in the following fashion: he appointed the Bastard of Bourbon, who is His Majesty's son-in-law, Admiral of France; he gave My Lord Filippo the hundred lances;[9] to the Angevin, My Lord de la Forêt [Louis

sparagnasse cosa alchuna, perchè così era soa ferma intentione. Et qui poy si voltò, presente molti Signori, parlando in tanto favore de Vostre Cel. quanto dire si potesse, subgiongendo ch'el Papa non haveva casone di compiacere a Venetiani, perchè per el passato lo havevano tenuto bandito da Venetia et cazatolo fori de li benefitii soy.[6] Sichè in questa conclusione et cum tale commissione dicto Vescovo zà quatro giorni hè partito; starà a Lione VI overo VIII giorni a metersi in poncto, et deinde passarà per Millano, comunicharà con V. Ex.tie la commissione ha, et se quele vorano dicha più una cosa cha una altra lo dirà, como se fusse in le soe instructione, perchè così ha expresso commandamento da la p.ta M.tà.

Insuper le littere che V. S. scrivevano a li Ill.mi Duca di Bergogna et Conte de Chyarolloes,[7] più dì fa le manday per uno ambasatore di esso Mons.re Chyaroloes che de qui partite; et trovandomi questi dì a ragionamenti cum questo S. Re, la M.tà Soa mi disse che vi confortava et laudava a tenire ligha et intelligentia cum el p.to Mons.re Chyaroloes, non havendo rispecto a ley, perchè oltra che li fareti cosa gratissima, ne hè contentissima, et li pare lo habiati a fare per utile di tute le parte. A dì XVI dil presente a Tors Mons.re l'Armiraglio di Franza[8] passò dela presente vita, la cui morte per esserli stato fidatissimo, hè molto doluta da questo S. Re. Li offitii soy ha distribuito essa M.tà, in questo modo. El Bastardo di Borbon, zenero de la prelibata Soa M.tà, ha creato Armiraglio di Franza. Le lanze cento[9] ha dato a Filippo Monsignore, el governamento de la Rozella a Mons.re da la Forest, Angiovino. La maystrissa de li boschi, aque et rivere dil Reame a Mons.re de Chiatilion,[10] che fu Governatore a Zenoa, Angiovino; alsi *et a tuta brida*[a] *cercano Angiovini di meterse al presente in questa Corte, ma non intendo peranche chiaro come seguirano loro desegni.* El Seneschalcho di Giena,[11] quale poy che questo S. Re hè in Stato, et inanti, dormiva con la M.tà Soa continue, hè stato trovato doe leghe qui apresso stravestito che se ne andava, et del loco dive[rsa]mente se ne parla. Essa M.tà, suspectosa

---

a. C. C. incorrectly reads: tutta via.

de Beaumont], he assigned the government of La Rochelle; to another Angevin, My Lord de Châtillon,[10] who had been governor of Genoa, he gave the administration of the forests, waters, and beaches of the realm. *Thus in an unbridled fashion the Angevins are now trying to make headway in this Court, but I do not yet see clearly what issue their plans will have.*

The Seneschal of Guyenne,[11] who before and after the King's accession to the throne shared sleeping quarters with him, has been found two leagues from here, leaving in disguise—there are many versions of where he was going. The King, being suspicious about this disguise, had him arrested along with [some others?], who have been put to the rope. It is feared that he was arrested in order to discover [certain?] intrigues, owing to the suspicion that His Majesty has had of him in the last few days. Up to now *it is said he was [leaving?] to find [a certain] girl whom he loved, and who is in the King's graces.* Of what I subsequently learn concerning this matter, I will make every effort to keep Your [Lordships?] informed, [to whom?] I commend myself.

HISTORICAL NOTES

1. This explains the absence of dispatches after 12 May up to the present one.

2. See doc. 26.

3. See preceding doc. 29.

4. This threat is expressed in the penultimate paragraph of the Italian version of the instructions, dated 13 May [*Francia*, cart. 532]. The Bishop was also charged to tell the Pope that the King was bound by his alliance with Milan, now strengthened by the imminent marriage of Galeazzo Maria with Bona of Savoy, to defend at all costs the Duchy and its allies, such as Bologna. Finally, the ambassador was instructed to pass through Milan, show his instructions to the Duke, and follow whatever additional instructions he received from him with regard to his mission at the papal court.

5. In 1461 Louis XI had abolished the Pragmatic Sanction of Bourges, which gave control of all Church benefices in France to the monarchy, in the

per tal habito, lo ha facto pigliare et poy alch[uni altri?],^b quali sono
stati missi ala corda. Si dubita che questa soa presa sia per discoprire di
[certe?] practiche per el suspecto che più dì fa la M.tà Soa ha di luy.
Fino qui *se dice an[dava da certa?] damisela trovare dela quale era
inamorato, la quale hè in gra[tia di questo?] Signor Re di Franza.* Di
quelo che più oltra sentirò in questa materia, sforzarome tenere avisate
esse V. [S., ale quale?] me ricomando.

---

b. The lower right margin of this dispatch is torn off, resulting in several missing words, some
of which have been tentatively supplied.

hope that Pius II would end his support of King Ferrante and recognize Duke
John of Lorraine as King of Naples. When these hopes did not materialize,
the King felt deceived by the Pope, who in effect had outmaneuvered him.
The question of the Pope's alleged duplicity, however, has not been definitely
established. Cf. Christian Lucius, *Pius II und Ludwig XI von Frankreich,
1461–1462* (Heidelberg: Winters, 1913), pp. 40–76; Charles Fierville, *Le
cardinal Jean Jouffroy et son temps (1412–1473)* (Coutances: Salettes, 1874),
pp. 109–32; Joseph Combet, *Louis XI et le Saint-Siège (1461–1483)* (Paris:
Hachette, 1903), pp. 2–54; and Pastor, *Storia,* 2:101–17.

6. That is, in 1459, when the Venetian government prevented the then
Cardinal Pietro Barbo, later Pope Paul II, from taking possession of the
Bishopric of Padua, which had just been granted to him by Pius II [Pastor,
Storia, 2:348].

7. These letters [Milan, 20 March 1466, *Borgogna,* cart. 515] contained

an account of Galeazzo Maria's return to Milan and general expressions of friendship toward the Duke of Burgundy and his son.

8. Jean de Montauban, who had been one of the Dauphin's principal councillors and apparently had remained faithful to the King through the war of the Public Weal, contrary to Mandrot's statement [*Dépêches*, 1:48, n. 2].

9. Panigarola seems to be in error. The one hundred lances were assigned to Montauban's successor, Louis, Bastard of Bourbon [Philippe Contamine, *Guerre, état et société a la fin du Moyen Âge. Études sur les armées des rois de France, 1337–1494* (Paris: Mouton, 1972), p. 408].

10. Louis de Laval, who governed Genoa from 1459 to 1461 while Duke John of Lorraine was waging war against King Ferrante in the Kingdom of Naples.

11. Antoine de Castelnau, Lord of Lau, was arrested for his intrigues with the lords of the League of the Public Weal. Two years later he escaped from prison, and finally regained the King's favor in 1471 [Bernard de Mandrot, ed., *Mémoires de Philippe de Commynes*, vol. 1. (Paris: Picard, 1901), p. 76, n. 1; cf. doc. 39].

As it seems my duty to keep Your Excellencies continually informed
of what is happening here, I advise you that My Lord of Charolais has
sent an embassy to request and entreat His Majesty to be so kind as to
help, favor, and give him aid against the people of Liège, who have
completely repudiated and broken the agreement they once made with
him.[1] Moreover, they had the mediator of this agreement, the most emi-
nent man in Liège, decapitated. Therefore, Charolais now means to go
to war against them and if possible oblige them to obey him. On the
other hand, the exiled Bishop of Liège,[2] brother of the Duke of Bourbon,
has summoned the secular arm, and with eclesiastic censures interdicted
them, seeking to make headway and regain the stature rightfully due
to him. His Majesty, who seeks with all means and every craft to keep
My Lord of Charolais's friendship (since he once favored the other side),
has promised to give him two hundred lances, and wants to aid him in
every way in order to preserve this new friendship. He was giving this
his every thought as the ambassador left with this decision.

The Earl of Warwick came to our Lady of Boulogne and there he
met My Lord of Charolais, whom the King of France is using to negotiate the truce and peace with the English;[3] as His Majesty told me, they
are willing to make peace with him, and he hopes that it will be concluded. Furthermore, the Earl of Warwick has made His Majesty many

31·GIOVAN PIETRO PANIGAROLA *to the*

DUKE *and* DUCHESS OF MILAN

Francia, cart. 532. Orig.

Parendomi essere mio debito tenere Vostre Ex.tie continuo avisate de le occurentie di qua, li significo che Monsignor Chyaroloes ha mandato da questo Signor Re una ambassata ad requirire et pregare la M.tà Soa che li piacia darli adiuto, favore et socorso contra queli di Legia, quali dil tuto hanno refudato et romputo l'acordo altre volte facto con luy.[1] Et più hanno facto tagliare la testa al principal homo di Legia, el quale fo mediatore ad esso acordo. Si chè hora intende farli guera, et si potrà, tirarli ala hobedientia soa. Da l'altro canto el Vescovo di Legia,[2] fratello dil Duca di Borbon, fori inscito, ha facto venire el brazo seculare et cum censure eclesiastice li tene interdicti, cerchando de introdursi et rimetersi al primo et debito suo stato. La p.ta Soa M.tà, quale cum ogni via et ingenio cercha di conservarsi esso Mons.re Chyaroloes amico, poy ché una volta ha acollato ad quela banda, li ha promisso darli adiuto lanze ducento et volerli fare ogni favore possibile per mantenimento de l'amore commenzato, et in questo mette ogni suo pensiero, essendo dicto ambassatore cum questa conclusione partito. El Conte de Vervic era venuto a nostra Dama di Bologna, et lì si hé trovato cum Mons.re Chyaroloes, per mezo dil quale si tracta tregua et pace cum Englesi;[3] et per quanto questo S. Re mi ha dicto, sono contenti di far pace con la M.tà Soa, et spera quela che haverà effecto. Ulterius esso Conte di Vervic ha facto di molte offerte ala p.ta Soa M.tà, così etiam fa Mons.re Chy-

offers, and so has My Lord of Charolais, who says he neither wants nor means to do anything that might displease His Majesty, but rather puts himself and all his possessions at his service. The Count of Saint Pol, Grand Constable [Louis de Luxembourg], is to come here to confer with His Majesty. Concerning the marriage of the King of England's sister, it is said it has been concluded with Don Pedro of Portugal, since it could not be arranged with My Lord of Charolais.[4] From hour to hour we are expecting confirmation from someone the King has sent on purpose in order to ascertain the truth. The King of Aragon, from what is reported in letters received by his ambassador, has conquered a certain seaport near Barcelona, driving away the Count of Pallars [Huc de Roger]. He has also conquered certain other localities, raising the hope that this summer he may take back Barcelona.[5] The ambassadors of the above mentioned Don Pedro, who were going to My Lord of Charolais, and to the Count of Armagnac, have been captured by His Majesty, who said he would deliver them to the King of Aragon so that he might examine them and dispose of them as best as he thought.[6]

[The Count of Armagnac has recently taken a locality which was disputed between the Duke of Bourbon and himself. His Majesty sent him an ambassador, asking that things be resettled as they once were. But this he would not do. Now the King is sending another ambassador to the Count of Armagnac, and it is feared that he may bring things to such a point as to provoke war against himself, owing to his bad behavior and evil conduct in the past, which His Majesty takes to heart. His Majesty is at the point of giving a caning both to him and the Duke of Nemours, uncle and nephew,[7] as the King has more ill-feelings toward them than toward the others. My Lord of Beaujeu, the Duke of Bourbon's brother, is to marry the late Duke of Orléans's daughter and receive as a dowry Asti and all the lands belonging to the late Duke except those territories which cannot be divided or alienated from the Crown. This promise was made when the late Duke had only this one daughter. Now, there are negotiations to have Madame of Orléans assign Asti, with its territory and the county of Blois, to My Lord of Beaujeu, thereby

aroloes, dimonstrando in parole non volere né intendere fare cosa che aliqualiter habia ad turbare la mente di quella, ma volere in servitio suo exponere ogni soa facultà et propria persona.

El Conte de Sanpolo, Grande Connestabile, debbe vegnire qui a parlamento con la M.tà Soa. Del matrimonio de la sorella dil Re de Inglitera si hé dicto essere concluso a Don Pietro di Portogallo, et non havere potuto havere loco cum Mons.re Chyaroloes;[4] de hora in hora ne aspeciamo novelle certe per uno, quale questo S. Re ha mandato aposta per saperne la verità. El S. Re d'Aragon, per quanto ha qui littere el suo ambassatore, ha guadagnato certo porto di mare verso Barzalona et cazato el Conte de Palliazes, et così ha conquistato certi altri loci in modo che si spera questa estate debia recuperare Barzelona.[5] Li ambassatori del dicto Don Pietro presi per questo S. Re, che andavano a Mons.re Chyaroloes, Conte d'Armignac, et Soa M.tà ha dicto li rimetterà in mano dil p.to S. Re d'Aragon, a fine che siano examinati et ne dispona como meglio li parirà.[6] [ᵃEl conte d'Armignac questi dì prese di facto una terra, che era in differentia tra el Duca di Borbon et luy. La prelibata M.tà li mandò uno ambassatore che volesse restituire la cossa al primo stato. El che non ha voluto fare. Hora quella gli ne manda uno altro, et si dubita che ala fine non si saperà guardare che non se li fazi guerra per li soy mali portamenti, et maxime havendolo essa M.tà molto a pecto per li disgoverni passati. Et contra luy et el Duca di Nemors, barba et nipote,[7] si tracta di darli una bastonata, dolendosi più di loro essa M.tà cha de altri. Mons.re di Biogin, fratello dil Duca di Borbon, debbe havere la fiola del quondam Duca de Orliens per mogliere, et per dote Ast et tute le terre haveva esso quondam Duca, excepto quelle che non si ponno partire né separare da la Corona. Et questa promissione fo facta essendo quelo cum questa unica fiola. Di presente si tracta che Madama d'Orliens assigni Ast cum le pertinentie et el Contato di Bles al p.to Mons.re di Biogin, liberando luy el presente Duca de Orliens, dapoy nato,[8] de ogni drito che più oltra potesse consequire, al quale rimagnerà

---

a. Bracket-like signs appear in the text.

excluding the present Duke of Orléans, who was born after [the daughter],[8] from any rights that he might acquire in the future; but he will [nevertheless] have the remainder of the dominion. It is believed that these negotiations will be successful, owing to the influence the Duke of Bourbon enjoys in Court.] I will stay alert to what follows and will inform Your Excellencies, to whom I continually commend myself.

HISTORICAL NOTES

1. The Treaty of St. Trond of 22 December 1465, which shortly after was repudiated by the powerful, extremist anti-Burgundian faction in Liège, headed by Raes de Rivière [Vaughan, *Philip the Good*, p. 396].

2. Louis de Bourbon, who in 1456 had been appointed Bishop of Liège, but had not been able to occupy his see owing to the opposition within the city. Louis XI supported the anti-Burgundian faction, but abandoned it after the Peace of Conflans (October 1465) [ibid., pp. 391–97].

3. On these negotiations, see docs. 16 and 21. This meeting at Notre-Dame of Boulogne, 34 kilometers southwest of Calais, between the Earl of Warwick and the Count of Charolais, led to the signing of the Anglo-French truce at Calais on 24 May. This meeting is not mentioned by Calmette-Périnelle, *Louis XI*.

4. This report is false. See doc. 27, n. 4.

5. Already in March 1466, Barcelona, besieged by the troops of John II of Aragon, was desperately short of food, infested by the plague, and demoralized [Leonardo de Sarathico to the Dukes, Genoa, 27 March 1466, *Aragona e Spagna*, cart. 652]. In the following months, the Count of Pallars,

el resto de la Signoria. Et questa practicha si crede sortirà effecto per el favore che ha el Duca di Borbon in questa Corte.] Di che seguirà starò attento, dandone notizia ad esse Vostre Ex.tie, a le quale continuamente me ricommando.

Captain General of the Catalans, tried unsuccessfully to defend the city while Don Pedro was gravely ill [Calmette, *Louis XI, Jean II*, pp. 261–64; Jaime Vicens Vives, *Juan II de Aragon (1378–1479). Monarquia y revolucion en la España del siglo XV* (Barcelona: Teide, 1953), pp. 294–96].

6. The ambassadors were arrested in March [doc. 1]. Immediately after, Louis XI offered to place them in the hands of John II of Aragon [Dispatch by Leonardo de Sarathico cited in preceding note].

7. Actually the Count of Armagnac, Jean V, and the Duke of Nemours, Jacques d'Armagnac, were cousins. They had both taken part in the League of the Public Weal, and still remained hostile to the King, who in return supported the territorial claims of Duke Jean II of Bourbon against the Armagnacs [Bernard de Mandrot, "Jacques d'Armagnac, Duc de Nemours, 1433–1477," *Revue historique* 43 (1890); 315–16; 44 (1890); 241–42].

8. Louis of Orleans, later Louis XII, born at Blois on 27 June 1462. The marriage between Pierre de Bourbon, Lord of Beaujeu, and Marie of Orleans, was never consummated [see doc. 21, n. 3].

A few days ago His Most Serene Majesty, perceiving that My Lord Philip wished to have his rightful share of the state of the Most Illustrious Duke of Savoy and of his brothers,[1] and conscious of Philip's realization that this objective could, with the support of His Majesty, be better satisfied at present than at any other time, the King was prevailed upon by him to write to Gaston instructing him to pay a visit to the Illustrious Madame of Savoy on his way home from Milan. From here the King sent to Savoy a doctor [of law] and his secretary, Baude [Meurin], as ambassadors, so that all three will plead and press on behalf of His Majesty that a proper portion be assigned to the aforementioned Philip, bringing about his effective possession of it.[2] In this regard they have broad and ample mandate and as many appropriate letters as one could wish.

As soon as these ambassadors had gone, it struck My Lord Philip that he would better execute his intention if he too were there with the said ambassadors. So he induced His Majesty to give him leave and departed shortly thereafter.[3] Since I knew that Lord Philip placed too much faith in the words of the Savoyards, it seemed to me in every respect wise to have the King verbally recommend to Lord Philip the interests of Your Lordships. Thus, at the departure of Lord Philip, His Majesty pressed him and most insistently charged him, if ever he desired to do the

32·GIOVAN PIETRO PANIGAROLA *to the*

DUKE *and* DUCHESS OF MILAN

Francia, cart. 532. Orig.

Questi dì la M.tà di questo Ser.mo S. Re, intendendo Filipo Monsignor di havere la parte soa dil Stato de lo Ill.mo Duca et fratelli di Savoya,[1] como li apartiene, et parendoli al presente cum spala de la p.ta M.tà meglio potere conseguire l'intento suo, cha aspectare ad altro tempo, ad soa instantia scrisse ad Guastoneto, che al suo ritorno de Milanno pasasse per quella Ill. Madama di Savoya. Et da qui li ha mandato uno doctore et Baldizon suo secretario ambassatori, li quali tuti tre haverano ad pregare et instare, per parte di essa M.tà, che parte conveniente sii assignata al p.to Filippo, operando che cum effecto ne sii misso in posessione di quella.[2] Et circha questo hano tanto ampla et forte comissione, et così littere quanto dire si potesse. Partiti che furono essi ambassatori, parse a Filipo Mons.re che ritrovandosi anche luy di de là cum dicti ambassatori, che meglio exequiria l'intento suo; et così induse la prelibata M.tà a darli licentia, et questi dí si ne hè partito.[3] Cognoscendo io dicto Filipo dare molto fede a parole de Savoyni, mi parse per ogni rispecto da questo S. Re farli di bocha ricommandare le cose de la V. S. di là. Et così la Soa M.tà, ala partita dil p.to Filippo, lo strinsse et caricò instantissimamente, se may desyderava farli cosa grata, che in Savoya da quela Ill. Madama et dove bisognasse, interprendesse et operasse talmente, che favore et ayuto fosse dato ale V. Ex.tie et Stato loro, et bisognando se ne andasse da quelle cum socorso, gente d'arme et quanto

King a favor, that with the Duchess as well as with others in Savoy he set about working in such a manner as to gain support and aid for Your Excellencies and for you state—if need be he would come to your aid with troops and whatever else he could manage. Similarly, if he [Philip] found some negotiations in progress inimicable to your interests, he should endeavor to have them annulled, because he could not do a greater favor for His Majesty, closely concerned as the King is with the protection and defense of your state, and not wishing to spare it anything at all.

Philip gave his promise and offered to do wonders for Your Excellencies, to the extent that His Majesty will recognize that he has served him well. As he took leave, he assured me that, if needed, he will bring succor to you and will conduct himself in such a manner that you will acknowledge him as your good relative. Thus in his words did he show himself excellently disposed toward Your Highnesses. Of which matters it seemed to me proper to advise you, adding that the King, beside the hundred lances and pension already given to Philip, intends to raise his status: he has promised him the governorship of Guyenne, a great and honorable office, one of the best of this realm, which at present is held by My Lord of Comminges, Marshall of France [Jean, Bastard of Armagnac].

Furthermore, the King has found fitting, while he dispatched his embassy, to send ahead to the Venetians as ambassador Messer Luigi Valperga, brother of the late Messer Giacomo, Lord of Roppolo. Although Franceschino [Nori] and I are certain that Messer Luigi will do the best he can and work willingly and with good heart, we have nevertheless reminded His Majesty that since Luigi himself was not a learned man, it would be a good idea to send with him an individual who was—a doctor—Venice being the place that it is, of great importance, requiring for its honor and reputation an intelligent and well-educated man. His Majesty, pressed by others as it has been confided to me, decided to send him alone on this mission; he said to us that he wanted him to go and that he deemed him adequate. Today it is already four days since his departure for Lyon, where he will make preparations to leave.

li fosse possibile; et similiter dove qualche practicha fosse contraria fazi tuto revocare, perchè non li poria fare cosa più grata, maxime atendendo Soa M.tà, come sa, a la tuitione et defensa di quelo Stato, non volendo sparagnarli cosa alchuna. Esso Filipo ha promisso, et si hè offerto de fare maraveglie per esse V. Ex.tie et talmente che Soa M.tà cognoscerà la haverà bene servita. Et al partire suo mi disse che bisognando menarà socorso a quelle, et si governarà in tal forma che cognoscereti serà vostro bono parente, monstrandose in parole benissimo disposto verso esse V. Cel. De le qual cose mi hè parso dargline aviso, notificandoli che questo S. Re, oltra le lanze cento et pensione che ha dato ad esso Filipo, delibera di farlo grande, et li ha promisso el governo de Ghiena, quale al presente tene Mons. re di Cominges Marescalcho di Franza, che hè uno grande et digno offitio et de li migliori di questo Reame. Ulterius hè parso ad questo S. Re tanto che spachia questa soa ambassata, di mandare inanzi ad Venetiani Miser Loyse de Valperga, fratello dil quondam Miser Iacomo, Signor di Ropol, suo ambassatore. Et quamvis siamo certi, Franceschino et io, che esso Miser Loyse farà et operarà quanto saperà et porà di bon core, non dimancho havendo noy ricordato ala p.ta M.tà luy non essere letterato, Venesia essere quelo loco hè et di grande importantia, havere bisogno per honore et reputatione di quella, di homo intelligente et saputo, che saria bene la M.tà Soa havesse mandato con luy uno doctore. Essa M.tà a preghere, per quanto mi hè stato riferto da alchuni, lo ha voluto mandare solo, et a noy disse che voleva gli andasse et che li pareva assai suffitiente. Si chè hogie quatro giorni partite per andare a Lione a metersi in poncto. Le soe instructione conteneno in effecto, che notifichi ad Venetiani la ligha, amore et intelligentia, che la M.tà Soa ha auto et ha con le V. S., per le quale per el parentato et per li benefitii ricevuti in le soe necessitate, essa Soa M.tà hè tenuta et obligata adiutarle; che li prega non voliano instigare el Papa a fare guera a Bologna, perchè saria preiuditio al Stato vostro, contra el quale non vogliano etiam in modo che sia temptare cosa alchuna, perchè non se poria la M.tà Soa excusare che non li deffendesse, et a questo vole exponere Regno et ogni soa facultà, dimonstrandosi in fine essa M.tà

His instructions direct him in effect to notify the Venetians of the alliance, love, and understanding that His Majesty has had and has with Your Lordships, by virtue of which and because of kinship and benefits received by him in times of necessity, His Majesty is held and obliged to help you. Wherefore, he begs the Venetians not to instigate the Pope to wage war on Bologna, because it would be prejudicial to your state, against which nothing at all should be attempted, for His Majesty could not excuse himself from defending it, being ready to dedicate his realm and every other means for this purpose. Finally, His Majesty revealed his willingness to aid the Venetians against the Turks. Verbally, moreover, the King commissioned him to make broad promises to the Venetians and to utter all possible ample and general expressions in order to prevent them from molesting Your Lordships. He charged him most insistently to work on this matter as if the King's soul were at stake, for he could do him no greater favor in the world.

If besides these instructions Your Lordships wish that he say or do one thing more than another, he is charged to do it exactly as if he had it in the above instructions. Luigi will thus pass through Milan,[4] unless it were to seem better to Your Excellencies that he not pass through Milan and go directly to Venice, in order to have it appear that this embassy originates from the pure and sincere feelings of the King. In that case, Your Lordships can arrange that which seems best.

The letters of Gaston and that which you have written to the King[5] arrived and in good time. His Majesty was very happy about them, saying to me in the presence of many lords that he found himself quite comforted by the fact that the affairs of Your Excellencies had gone better than he had thought, adding that you can do him no greater favor than to keep him informed frequently of successes there. With regard to the other affairs, we expect hourly a specific answer, as is announced in your letters.

Duke John arrived here today at supper time, to whom it was necessary that the aforementioned Majesty *send two thousand francs for his journey, because the Duke claimed not to have a groat. It seems that His*

volonterosa ad adiutare dicti Venetiani contra el Turcho. Di bocha etiam li ha commisso che prometta largamente a Venetiani, et dica tute quelle parole ample et generale si porano per obviare che non diano disturbo ale V. S., carichandolo cum ogni instantia ad operare in questa materia como per l'anima propria di Soa M.tà, perchè cosa al mondo non li poria fare più grata. Et se oltra le instructione esse V. S. voleno ch'el dica o faza più una cosa cha una altra, che lo fazi ita et taliter como s'el lo havesse in le instructione, et così esso Miser Aloyse farà et passarà per Millanno.[4] Salvo se forsi paresse ad esse V. Ex.tie che per dimonstrare questa ambassata procedesse dal mero et sincero core di questo S. Re, che non pasasse per Millanno, ma di longo andasse a Vinesia. In el qual caso V. S. disponano quello che li parirà el meglio. Le littere di Guastoneto, et quelle che haveti scrito ad questo S. Re,[5] sono zonte et in tempo. La M.tà Soa si ne hè molto realegrata dicendomi, presente molti Signori, trovarsi reconfortata assay che le cose de le V. Cel. pasasseno meglio che non pensava, et non pono quele farli cosa più grata como spesso tenerla avisata de li successi di là. De le altre cose aspeciamo di hora in hora particular risposta, como in le vostre littere si contiene. El Duca Iohanne hogie a cena hè arivato qui, al quale hè stato neccessario la p.ta M.tà *per la soa venuta habii mandato franchi doamillia, che dice non haveva uno grosso; et così in questa soa venuta pare la M.tà Soa non se fidi bene de lui. Ale provissione che quela ha facto, et primo ha* ordinato lanze cinquanta cum soldo duplicato del usatto per la guardia de la persona de la M.tà Soa, li quali continuo, quando quela andarà ala caza o altrove, circuirano oltra li arcieri el loco dove quela se ritrovarà. Ulterius ley in persona ha visitato el castello di questa terra dove hè logiata, di parte in parte, et trovandoli certo adito secreto, quale non si sapeva, lo ha facto stopare. Item ala parte de la salla ha misso arcieri ala guardia, che non haveva acostumato, quali omnino lassano intrare se non persone cognoscente. Et queste tale provisione non dimonstrano però *signo de grande nè efficace amore fra la prelibata Maiestà et esso Duca Iohanne, quale credo domane la andarà ad visitare et* io interim di quanto intenderò, ne avisarò le Vostre Ill.me S., ale quale sempre me riccomando.

Majesty is apprehensive about his presence and has taken several precautions. First, he has engaged fifty lances with double the usual pay, who, together with the archers, will surround him and constantly guard his person at the hunt or in whatever place he may happen to be. Furthermore, he personally inspected every angle of the castle of this zone, where he is lodged, and, having found there a certain secret opening up to now unknown, he had it closed up. Also, at the entrance to the hall he has placed archers on guard, contrary to custom, who allow absolutely no one to pass except known individuals. Obviously, these precautions do not demonstrate any *sign of great or efficacious love between the aforementioned Majesty and Duke John, who, I believe, will go tomorrow to visit him, and* of what will transpire I will then give notice to Your Most Illustrious Lordships, to whom I always commend myself.

HISTORICAL NOTES

1. Philip, the ablest and fifth in line of succession among the nine sons of Duke Louis I of Savoy, on the day this dispatch was written was invested with the County of Bresse by his brother, Duke Amédée IX. Sixteen years earlier, his father had made him Count of Bagé, Valbonne, and Reversmont, comprising a great part of the County of Bresse, which had been assigned to his brother, Amédée, then Prince of Piedmont. The nickname, *sans terre,* assigned to him later by sixteenth-century chroniclers, is thus not entirely accurate, but it is descriptive of his restless career as an ambitious younger son searching for a larger role commensurate with his abilities. After more than thirty years of feverish and aggressive activity, he finally satisfied his longing for power when, in 1496, he became Duke of Savoy as Philip II, but died nineteen months later [Daviso di Charvensod, *Filippo II,* pp. 5–6, 53–54, and passim].

2. Louis XI wrote to Gaston du Lyon and to Baude Meurin [Meung-sur-Loire, 21 May 1466, *Francia,* cartelle 532 and 559 (Italian copies); published by Edith Thomas, "Cinq lettres inédites de Louis XI," Société de l'Histoire

de France, *Annuaire-Bulletin* (1941), pp. 82–83], referring to a previous letter in which he had instructed them to go to the Savoyard court and press the Duchess to allow Philip to take possession of his alloted share of the Duchy. He also instructed them to urge the Duchess and her Council to desist from any anti-Milanese activity, and support the new rulers of Milan. The third ambassador is possibly Jean Aubert [See doc. 46]. Meurin was well versed in Savoyard and Italian affairs, having carried out prolonged missions earlier in Italy for the Dauphin [vol. 2, passim]. He knew Italian well, and the Doge of Venice once addressed him in that language during a mission to Venice [Memorandum by Meurin, 14 April (1461), *Venezia*, cart. 1314].

3. Philip must have left around 11 May, for on this date the King wrote to officials in Lyon that he was coming to that city, evidently on his way to Savoy [Vaesen, *Lettres*, 3:57]. It was immediately upon his arrival that Philip was invested with the County of Bresse [see n. 1].

4. For Luigi di Valperga's instructions, see Appendix, doc. XI.

5. Letters of 13 April and 1 May, Appendix, docs. VIII–IX.

The Magnificent Lord Garcia Betes, ambassador of the Most Serene King Ferrante, arrived here a few days ago. Having related to His Most Christian Majesty what Your Lordships wrote to me about his mission,[1] the King had him escorted by My Lord of Clermont-Lodève [Pons] and the Governor of Montpelier [Guillaume Cousinot], seeing him willingly and twice granting him most gracious audience. In a friendly manner, the King inquired about the welfare of His Majesty, King Ferrante, of his kingdom, and of diverse other matters, remaining most content and satisfied with the manners and attitudes of Lord Garcia, who explained, always in my presence, both the positions of King Ferrante and those of Your Lordships. God knows with what cordial affection and love he expressed all that Your Excellencies had commissioned him to say, especially of the love and faith placed in this King by my late and unvanquished Lord, your husband and father of happy memory. He spoke so eloquently on this subject that His Majesty kept him for almost half an hour. In effect, His Majesty encouraged King Ferrante to persevere in his efforts to support and aid Your Lordships, because of past services received from you. His Majesty added that he was even more obligated for having had Your Lordship at his services, thus offering himself for you and your state with his usual ample and dignified offers.

He then thanked the aforementioned King Ferrante for his message

33·GIOVAN PIETRO PANIGAROLA *to the*

DUKE *and* DUCHESS OF MILAN

Francia, cart. 532. Orig.

Questi dì zonse el Mag.co Domino Grassia Bethes, oratore dil Ser.mo S. Re Ferando. Et havendo io dicto a la M.tà di questo Chrystianissimo Re quanto circha la venuta soa mi scriveno V. S.,[1] la M.tà Soa lo ha facto acompagnare da Mons.re da Chyaramont et lo Governatore di Monpelieri, halo visto volontieri, et doe volte li ha dato gratissima audientia; et molto familiarmente li ha domandato di la p.ta M.tà del Re Ferando, de le cose dil Reame et varie et diverse altre facende, rimanendo certo molto contenta et satisfacta de li modi et costumi di esso Domino Grassia. El quale expose tanto le ambassate dil Re Ferando como de V. S., in mia presentia sempre. Et Dio sa con quanta affectione et amore cordiale parlò, quanto V. Cel. li havevano commisso a dire, de l'amore et fede che quela felicissima memoria dil quondam invictissimo mio S., vostro consorte et patre, portava a questo S. Re. Ne parlò tanto altamente, che la M.tà Soa lo tene circha meza hora a questa parte; et in effecto la M.tà Soa confortava el S. Re Ferando ad perseverare in li favori et adiuti contribuiti a le V. S. per li oblighi recevuti da quele, et più diceva la M.tà Soa essere obligata havendo auto voy, Signore, a li soy servitii, offerendosi per voy et vostro Stato con le solite soe ample et digne offerte. Ringratiò poy el p.to S. Re Ferando di quanto li mandava a dire. Et in mia presentia li disse molte cose che a me altre volte havea dicto di esso Re, dimonstrandoli amore et affectione, concludendo che per rispecto de

and in my presence told the ambassador many things that at other times he had said to me about King Ferrante, showing love and affection toward him. He concluded by saying that out of respect for the happy memory [Francesco Sforza] and for Your Excellencies, he loves and would continue to love King Ferrante, and would serve him where he could, even though his duty as King of France demanded that he ought to love Duke John instead. Thereupon he recounted all the deceits and bad actions committed this year by the House of Anjou against His Majesty.

We stayed together a good piece and many things were said, of which you will learn from letters separately written by Lord Garcia to the Magnificent Lord Fabrizio [Carafa], [Neapolitan] ambassador there. By my faith, Lord Garcia properly responded to all the questions posed by the King, so that I will not tarry in explaining them further. Yet I do notify Your Lordships that according to what His Majesty told me at this hour in the presence of Franceschino [Nori], he doubts for many good reasons that the ambassador can long remain here because of the hostility of Duke John. In any case, within two or three days we shall see at what decision His Majesty will arrive, and I will advise Your Lordships of it.

For the rest, since Gaston and Baude are going to the Illustrious Madame of Savoy, and since they are not pressed to leave there soon, it has seemed to me abundantly proper that His Majesty write them a letter to the effect that they stay alert in favor of your interests. I have sent them the letter, of which, in case it should be of use, I enclose a copy[2] to Your Excellencies, to whom I always commend myself.

HISTORICAL NOTES

1. Doc. 22.
2. See preceding doc. 32, n. 2.

quela felicissima memoria et de le Vostre Cel. ama et amaria el Re Ferando, et dove potesse lo serviria, quamvis per debito dil Reame più tosto doveria amare el Duca Iohanne. Et poy commemorò li ingani e mali portamenti che la Caxa di Angiò questo anno haveva facto ad essa Soa M.tà. Furono molte cose dicte, che bon pezo stetemo insieme, le quale intenderiti per le littere che distinctamente scrive D. Grassia al Magn.co D. Fabritio lì oratore. Et per mia fede dignamente respondete esso D. Grassia a tute le parte domandate per questo S. Re, si chè non mi extenderò in più oltra explicarle. Ben notifico a le Vostre S. che per quanto Soa M.tà mi ha dicto questa hora, presente Franceschino, per le infestatione fa el Duca Iohanne, dubita esso ambassatore non porà stare qui longamente per boni rispecti; tuta volta fra doy o tre giorni se vederà la conclusione che Soa M.tà pigliarà et de quela ne sarano V. S. avisate.

Ceterum, andando Gastoneto et Baldizon da la Ill. Madama di Savoya et non havendo così presto a partire di là, mi hè parso ex habondanti che Soa M.tà li scriva una littera, aciò stiano atenti al favore de le cose vostre. La qual littera gli ho mandata, et ad esse V. Ex.tie ne mando la copia qui inclussa,[2] aciò che, bisognando, se ne posseno valere, a le quale sempre me ricommando.

After allowing Lord Philip to leave, the King had second thoughts about his mission and doubted that the Savoyards would counsel or allow him to return to His Majesty. He therefore has decided to send Franceschino Nori over there so that he might help Philip expedite his mission, staying with him as long as he is there, to keep him well disposed in supporting Your Excellencies' interests and accomplishing all that must be done. His Majesty has no doubt that, with Franceschino there, Philip will conduct himself well in your favor and will even give you aid if needed. Since Franceschino is most trustworthy, knowledgeable of the country's ways, and fit to accomplish this particular mission, it seems to him that for the good of everyone concerned he could not find his better, and so he is dispatching him.

For the rest, in order to better serve Your Lordships, His Majesty has informed me that he has ordered Philip and Franceschino to come to Milan and negotiate the marriage, giving them power of attorney to negotiate, conclude, and formally obligate His Majesty with regard to the dowry. He also told me that he ordered Franceschino, who will be leaving in two days[1] to join Philip, to do all that is necessary in this matter, since the King desires this matrimony to be concluded in the name of God. I will not continue further in this regard, making no more mention of it, especially since I am not aware of what instructions Your

34·GIOVAN PIETRO PANIGAROLA *to the*

DUKE *and* DUCHESS OF MILAN

Francia, cart. 532. Orig.

Pensando questo S. Re sopra la partita de Filippo Monsignor, si dubita hora che lo ha lassato partire, che Savoyni non lo lassino nè lo consiglieno ritornare da la M.tà Soa; et per questo ha deliberato di mandare Franceschino Nori di delà, el quale adiuti esso Filippo a la expeditione de la parte soa et con luy stia tanto, che sarà là, per tenerlo etiam bene hedificato a dare favore a le cose de le V. Ex.tie et provedere ad quanto li sarà da fare. Et per essere esso Franceschino fidatissimo, practico in el payse, et apto a dovere exequire quanto di sopra si contiene, non facendo dubio essa M.tà che essendo lì Franceschino, esso Filipo si governarà bene a li favori vostri et se bisognarà daravi etiam adiuto. Li pare per el bene et utile de le parte, non possi mandare el migliore di luy, et così lo va spazando. Ceterum mi ha dicto la M.tà Soa che per dare magiore favore a le V. S., vole et ha ordinato, che essi Filippo et Franceschino venganno a Milanno ad concludere el parentato, et a loro ha facto procura di acordarlo, concluderlo et di obligare la M.tà Soa in forma per la dote; et a Franceschino, quale fra doy giorni partirà[1] per andare a trovare lo p.to Filipo, mi ha dicto havere ordinato quanto in questa materia sarà da fare, desyderando che questo matrimonio con el nome de Dio si metta ad effecto. In le qual cose al presente non mi extenderò in dire più oltra, neanche mi hè parso farne altra mentione, maxime non sapendo che commissione habia el Mag.co Domino Pietro

Lordships may have given to the Magnificent Lord Pietro da Gallarate,[2] who should be here soon; but as soon as he arrives, we shall speak of the matter with His Majesty, and thereafter notify Your Excellencies more specifically of what remains to be done.

Regarding the departure of My Lord of Gaucourt and of the embassy, Franceschino and I press continuously, and in fact agreement has already been reached in the matter of his departure; but it is a pity that these Collectors of Revenue are so busy with so many tasks that all such matters take a long time. Nonetheless, before Franceschino leaves, he and I will make every effort to terminate the affair and have them depart as soon as possible, and Your Lordships will be advised of the outcome.

Duke John has spoken to the King *on the subject of living at Court, offering to reconcile the Duke of Berry with His Majesty, and asking for the sister[3] of the Queen to be his wife (or so they say), and proposing many other dealings, in which up to now very little faith is placed.* In any case, yesterday in conversation His Majesty told Duke John that he was allied, bound, and obligated to Your Excellencies and to Your House, and that he would do all within his knowledge and power for the good, preservation and exaltation of Your Lordships. His Majesty admonished Duke John to take it for certain that he would in no way abandon you, nor would he, in so far as he could, suffer that any harm be done to you, being well disposed to defend you as his very self. Last night, these very same declarations were repeated to Duke John by Franceschino upon order of His Majesty. Therefore, with regard to what follows on this matter, I will bend every effort in notifying Your Excellencies, to whom I always commend myself.

HISTORICAL NOTES

1. The King had already issued a letter of credence to Franceschino Nori, addressed to officials in Lyon [Meung-sur-Loire, 11 May 1466, Vaesen, *Lettres*, 3:57], in connection with the departure of Philip of Savoy for that city.

da Gallarà[2] da le V. S., el quale doveria presto essere qui, ma gionto ch'el sarà ne parlaremo cum la p.ta M.tà, dandone poy di quello si haverà a fare più particulare aviso ad le V. Ex.tie. Circha el partire di Monsignor di Gaucurt et de l'ambassata, continue Franceschino et io sollicitamo et già hè facto l'acordo de l'andata soa, ma questi Maestri de Intrate et Spazi di questa Corte per le molte occupatione sono così longhi, che hè una pietà. Tutavolta ananzi che Franceschino parta, si sforzaremo metere la cosa in termino che più presto sii possibile partano, et de la conclusione sarano V. S. avisate. El Duca Iohanne ha parlato ad questo S. Re. *Cercha di meterse ad stare in questa Corte, oferendo che farà acordare el Duca de Berrì con la M.tà Soa; domanda la sorella[3] dela Regina per mogliere, sicondo se dice, et mette molte altre practiche inanzi, ale quale fino qui se dà pocha fede.* Che se sia heri la p.ta M.tà li disse in discurso di parlare che era alligato, tenuto et obligato ad le V. Ex.tie et a la Casa loro, et che non li mancharà dove saperà et poterà al bene, conservatione et augumento di quelle; et di questo fusse certo, che a modo alchuno non vi habandonarà, nè a suo potere soffrirà esserve facto offensa alchuna, essendo disposta di defenderve come sè medesima. Et queste tale parole heri sera di comandamento di essa M.tà repplicò Franceschino al p.to Duca Iohanne. Sichè di quanto in queste cose seguirà, sforzarome tenerne V. Ex.tie avisate, ale quale sempre me riccomando.

2. His impending departure for the royal court had been announced by the Dukes of Milan [See doc. 24 and Appendix, docs. IX–X].

3. Marie of Savoy, whom the King had already promised to Louis of Luxembourg, Count of Saint-Pol. Their marriage took place on 1 August 1466 [Mandrot, *Dépêches*, 2:320–21, n. 3].

We have received and noted the contents of your letters of May first and second,[1] and we hereby reply. By the hand of His Majesty's Pursuivant,[2] we have received the letters he wrote to the Lords and states of Italy, which were most pleasing to us, and for which we thank His Majesty. By means of the same Pursuivant, we have sent them on to those whose address they bear, and we do not doubt that they will bring us great favor and esteem. With regard to the letter, His Serene Highness intends to write informing His Holiness the Pope that he is well disposed toward us in the matter of the preservation of our state, and that he will not pledge obedience to him, etc., we observe as follows. The Pope is of such a peculiar opinion and nature, and has set in his mind to do things in his own way, as can be gathered from his current actions, such as his engaging Lord Napoleone [Orsini], whom he wishes to send into the Marches together with other troops of the Church. This he does under the fiction, guise, and pretext of fearing that Lord Sigismondo [Malatesta][3] will make trouble, and in so doing the Pope will see if he can occupy Forlì and Rimini, then proceeding as far as Bologna, which is to say that he can then arrange matters as he chooses. All of which, there is no doubt, the Pope does with the connivance of Venice. Considering, moreover, that the Pope greatly fears for [Church] affairs

---

a. Crossed out: XXVII.

35 · *The* DUKE *and* DUCHESS OF MILAN *to*

GIOVAN PIETRO PANIGAROLA

Francia, cart. 532. Minute

Havemo recevute le toe littere del primo et II del presente,[1] et inteso quanto per quelle ne hay scripto. Respondiamo, che per el Persivanto[2] della M.tà de quello Christianissimo Sig.re Re havemo recevute le littere, che Soa M.tà scrive ali Sig.ri et potentie de Italia, quale molto ne sonno state grate et ne regratiamo la prefata M.tà. Le havimo mandate ad chi se drizano per dicto Persivanto et non dubitamo ne darano gran favore et reputacione. La littera, dice quello Ser.mo Re de scrivere alla Sanctità del Papa, con fargli intendere la soa bona disposicione verso nuy per conservatione de questo nostro Stato, et che non li darà obedientia, etc., dicimo che, essendo questo Papa de quello cervello et natura che l'è, et havendo animo de fare dele cose ad suo modo como hè, secondo pare per le demonstratione fa al presente in havere tolto el S. Napolione, el quale con l'altre gente de la Chiesa vole mandare in la Marcha, con fictione et sotto collore et pretesto de dubitare ch'el S. Sigis[mondo][3] faza qualche novità, et con questo vedere s'el potesse tore de mezo Forlì et Arimino per potere poy trascorere fino ad Bologna, che non saria ad dire altro ch'el potesse poy fare dele cose ad suo modo; le quale cose non è dubio le fa con intelligentia de Venetia. Poy consydrando che ha gran paura de quelle cose de Franza et che non possa haver l'obedientia, ne pare tale littera seria molto utile. Et volimo preghi Soa M.tà li piaza farla fare uno poco gagliarda con fare intendere al Papa che, finchè non intenda

in France and for obtaining the pledge of obedience [by the King], we think that such a letter would be most useful. Therefore, we want you to entreat His Majesty, if it please him, to word it a bit strongly, so as to make the Pope understand that as long as His Holiness does not intend to be a friend and supporter, His Majesty will not pledge his obedience. We are sure the King in his great prudence will know how to arrange the letter in the most apt and efficacious manner—better than we would ever know how to ask or conceive. Thus, it could do nothing but good to have His Majesty defer pledging his obedience to the Pope until such time as it becomes clearer what path His Holiness means to take—this you will solicit by every good and honest means you see fit, for it should be done quickly because the Pope is now sending the afore-mentioned troops into the Marches with the intention of having them proceed afterward to the Romagna in order to accomplish what was mentioned above. Surely, he can make no move in Romagna that would not be against us and unfavorable to our interests.

Regarding His Majesty's resolve to send his ambassadors to the Italian powers, there is no need to say more, since from our other letters[4] you will have understood our intention and all that is suitable thereto.

We will not dwell on the King's having sent for Duke John, since we are most certain that what is done by His Majesty is well thought out and directed to a good end, as will be related more thoroughly to His Majesty by Pietro da Gallarate, whom we are presently sending to him.

About the dealings of My Lord of Charolais with King Edward regarding the marriage and alliance, of which we too have received notification by way of a merchant, we are thoroughly sorry, because all that which is apt to displease the King of France cannot but be a great disturbance to us. We are dispatching an ambassador[5] both to the Most Illustrious Lord Duke of Burgundy and to My Lord of Charolais with instructions to be made known to you by the said Pietro, to wit: he is to go to the aforesaid Lords and inform them that our state, thank God, is in good condition and entirely dedicated and disposed to devotion,

Soa S.tà essere amico et favorevelle,[b] non li prestarà l'obedientia, in quella migliore et più efficace forma parerà alla M.tà Soa, quale per soa summa prudentia saperà molto meglio ordinare, che non saperessemo chiedere nè pensare. Et cossì non poria altro che giovare che la M.tà Soa diferisca el prestare l'obedientia al Papa fino ad tanto che se intenda meglio ad quale via se drizarà Soa S.tà. Et questo solicitaray con quello bon modo et honesto te parerà che se expedisca presto, perchè el Papa manda de presente dicte gente in la Marca con intentione de mandarle poy in Romagna ad far quanto è dicto, et non porà fare novità alcuna in Romagna che non sia contra nuy et in nostro desfavore.

De la expedicione deli ambassatori voleva la M.tà del Re mandare alle potentie de Italia, non accade dire altro perchè per altre nostre[4] haveray inteso la intentione nostra, et quanto bisogna.

Del havere quello S. Re mandato per el Duca Iohanne, non ne extenderemo più oltre, perchè siamo certissimi Soa M.tà tutto quello fa, el faza maturamente et ad bon bon [*sic*] fine, como più largamente ad Soa M.tà dirà Petro da Galerà, quale expedito de subito partirà per venire da quella.

Alla pratica de Mon.re de Chiarlois con el Re Odoardo, de parentato et intelligentia, dicemo che ancora nuy per via de mercadante havemo questo medesmo aviso, del che ne recresce, perchè tutto quello habia ad essere in dispiacere de quello Sig.re Re de Franza, non pò essere senza nostra gran molestia. Nuy mandamo uno nostro[5] dal Ill.mo S. Duca de Bergogna et dal prefato Mon.re de Chiarloys, con la commissione che dal dicto Petro intenderay, che è de visitare dicti Sig.ri et fargli intendere le condicione del Stato nostro per Dio gratia essere bone, et tutte dedicate et disposte ala devocione, amore, et reverentia dela M.tà Soa et ali suoy comandamenti; deinde starà in sul generale et seguirà poy quello serà el parere et voluntà de Soa M.tà.

---

b. Crossed out: alla conservatione de questo nostro Stato, per lo quale Soa M.tà intende exponere le gente, Stato et propria persona, may non li prestarà obedientia, nè li sarà amico, et farà de le cose [for the preservation of our state in defense of which His Majesty intends to proffer his troops, his state, and his very person; he will never pledge his obedience to him, nor will he be his friend, and will do things].

love, and reverence for His Majesty and ready to obey his orders. Thereafter, he is to keep a general approach and to follow whatsoever opinion and policy His Majesty may formulate.

Regarding those requests made of His Majesty by My Lord of Miolans on behalf of the Illustrious Madame of Savoy, we have understood that they are groundless dreams and fantasies, and in that vein His Majesty the King has prudently and wisely made response; nor do we deem it necessary to say more about them since we are certain that His Majesty will opportunely provide in the matter.

On the subject of the Turks, we have the news that you will read in the enclosed copy of a part of a letter written to us by Lord Agostino Rossi, our ambassador with His Holiness the Pope.

There is nothing else new here. All our subjects both in Lombardy and in Genoese territory are calm and properly obedient, while the fleet of His Majesty King Ferrante is continuously at our service in support of our interests at Genoa.

Regarding My Lord Philip, we say nothing more at present, since Pietro da Gallarate will arrive completely briefed.

HISTORICAL NOTES

1. Docs. 26–27.

2. The Pursuivant named Grenoble, who was back in France by 26 August [Panigarola to the Dukes, Briare, 26 August 1466, *Francia*, cart. 532].

3. In 1463 Pius II had stripped Sigismondo Pandolfo Malatesta of his vicariate over several places in the Romagna except for Rimini, which he was allowed to retain during his lifetime [Giovanni Soranzo, *Pio II e la politica italiana nella lotta contro i Malatesti, 1457–63* (Padua: Fratelli Drucker, 1911), pp. 449–55]. Sigismondo, who had recently returned from campaigning against the Turks in the Morea in the pay of Venice, hoped that with the death of his mortal enemy, he would be reinstated in his possessions by Paul II. The new Pope, however, was determined to exclude both the Malatesta and Venice from any interference with papal authority in Romagna. Contrary to what is stated in this letter, this policy created a bitter contest between

De quelle cose ha domandate Mon.re de Miolan alla M.tà del Re per parte dela Ill. Madama de Savoya, havemo inteso sonno tutte sogni, fantasie, et cose senza fundamento, como prudentemente et saviamente la M.tà del Re ha risposto; nè circa ciò accade dire altro, perchè siamo certi la prefata M.tà provederà oportunamente al tutto.

Del Turco, ne havemo quanto intenderay per la copia de una parte de una littera ne scrive D. Augustino Rosso, nostro oratore presso la S.tà de el Papa. De qua non gli è altro de novo. Tutti li populi nostri, tanto de qua in Lumbardia como del Zenoese, stano quieti et in bona obedientia, et l'armata dela M.tà del Re Ferando sta continue ali servicii nostri et favori per le cose de Zenoa.

De Filippo Mon.re non dicemo altro, perchè Petro da Galarate vene informato del tutto.

the Pope and Venice, while Milan opposed both and sought above all to preserve the independence of Bologna under its friends, the Bentivoglio [Pastor, *Storia*, pp. 350–51, 393; P. J. Jones, *The Malatesta of Rimini and the Papal State. A Political History.* (Cambridge: Cambridge University Press, 1974), pp. 240–43].

4. Doc. 28.

5. The envoy chosen for this mission was Tommaso Tebaldi da Bologna [B. Giugni and L. Guicciardini to the Signoria of Florence, Milan, 24 May 1466, ASF, *Signori, X di Balia, VIII di Pratica, Legazioni e Commissarie, Missive e Responsive*, Reg. 63, fols. 94–94v]. Tebaldi was a Milanese diplomat of vast experience, who had discharged several missions in France [vol. 1, Introduction, xlvi]. His mission, however, was postponed, and it appears that it never took place [The Dukes to Antonio da Trezzo, Milan, 3 September 1466, *Napoli*, cart. 215].

Pietro: In God's name you will go to His Holy Majesty the King of France, conferring with Giovan Pietro Panigarola when you arrive, before doing anything else, to come to an understanding of timing and tactics to be employed, since he has full instructions and can inform you as to the disposition of the Court, so avoiding any errors; then at the proper time (having first dutifully extended suitable greetings from our part) you will explain your embassy to said Majesty, to whom you will make our excuses for having so delayed in sending you to do our duty toward him, as was, however, always our intention ever since the departure from this life of the dearly beloved Illustrious Lord, our husband and father of happy memory. This caused the delay, along with our desire to send you clearly and fully instructed with regard to the conditions both in Italy and in our state, so that His Majesty could verbally learn everything from you that has occurred to date, even though he had been previously informed by us. And, likewise, you could now inform him of what is necessary for the preservation of our state, His Majesty being the person in whom we have every hope and place our every expectation, both for the safety and preservation of ourselves and of our state. Since we could not see clearly how things stood, not knowing whether we would be attacked from any quarter, your departure was delayed from day to day until now.[2]

36 · *Instructions of the* DUKE *and* DUCHESS OF

MILAN *to* PIETRO DA GALLARATE[1]

BN, Fonds Italien, Cod. 1593, fols. 252–56v. Minute

Petro. Con el nome de Dio tu andaray da la Sacra Mayestà del S.re Re de Franza et quando seray gionto, inanti che faci altro, conferiray con Zohannepetro Panigarola per intendere el tempo et el modo che haveray ad tenere, perché luy come instructo d'ogni cosa et de li modi de la Corte, te informarà in modo che non haveray errare. Et tolto el tempo idoneo, explicaray la tua ambaxata a la prefata M.tà, ala quale (facte prima de debite reccomendatione da nostra parte con parole conveniente), faray l'excusa nostra in esserne tanto tardati ad mandarti per fare el debito nostro verso Sua M.tà, come fu però sempre el nostro proposito de fare depoy che passò de questa vita la recolenda memoria del Ill.mo S.re nostro consorte et patre; de la quale tardanza ne é stata casone per volerti mandare bene instructo et ben chiaro et de le condicione de Italia et de questo nostro Stato, adcioché Sua M.tà, benché sii stata da nuy advisata de le occurrentie de qui indrieto, intendesse ad bocha per ti ogni cosa. Et cossì quello ne fusse necessario per la conservatione de questo nostro Stato, come quella in la quale havemo ogni nostra speranza, et facemo ogni nostro fondamento per la salute et conservatione nostra et d'esso nostro Stato. Et per non poter havere le cose chiare, se doviamo essere offesi da veruno canto o non, la tua partita de dì in dì é retardata fin mo.[2]

Deinde rengratiaray la Sua M.tà tanto quanto più ad ti sii possibile

Following that, you will thank His Majesty as much as is humanly possible for all that which, through his clemency and grace, he has deigned to do in our regard once he learned of the death of the Most Illustrious Lord, our husband and father. First, thank him for the excellent and most worthy provisions made by His Majesty for the liberation of us, Galeazzo, when he learned of our detention in the country of My Lord the Duke of Savoy; truly, he could have made no better provisions, nor greater show of support, nor with greater speed, than if it had been to keep from death a brother or son of his own, or to save his own life. Then, you will thank His Majesty for writing duplicate letters to the rulers of Italy and to our people, for sending his ambassadors, the Quartermaster of Cavalry and My Lord of Crussol [Louis], to Savoy, subsequently dispatching My Lord Gaston [du Lyon], Seneschal of Saintonge, and Master Giovanni Filippo to us with so many worthy offers for the preservation and stabilization of our state. Next, you will extend our gratitude for his having quickly ordered our troops, who were in Dauphiné, to return here, allotting to them the monies he did, so that these troops could leave and come in good order. Finally, express our thanks for the ambassadors whom His Majesty ordered to be sent to the rulers of Italy, bearing those worthy and favorable commissions for our benefit and for that of our state, it not being possible for him to have done more even if it had been for the preservation of his own kingdom.

Wherefore, we recognize that so great is our obligation to His Majesty, that if he and we were to live hundreds of years, we could not properly redeem our debt to him. It does not seem possible to us to make satisfaction for even a minimal part of the love, benevolence, and charity that His Majesty through his grace always had for the Illustrious Lord, our husband and father, without regard for merit extending to him, and subsequently to us, his successors, immense and undying benefits. These were so many and of such a nature that, as we have said, we do not know how to render satisfaction for them in accordance with what would have been the duty, desire, and will of the Illustrious Lord, our husband

in questo mondo de quanto Sua M.tà, per sua clementia et gratia, si é dignata de fare verso nuy dapoy che intese la morte del prefato Ill.mo S.re nostro consorte et patre; prima de l'optime et dignissime provisione facte per essa Sua M.tà per la liberatione de nuy, Galeazo, quando intese la nostra detentione nel paese de Monsig.re Duca de Savoya, che veramente non haveria possuto fare né mazor provisione, né mazor demonstratione né con più celerità s'el fusse stato per campare da la morte uno proprio fratello o figliolo o per salute de la sua propria persona; et cossì in scrivere per sue littere dupplicate et ale potentie de Italia et ad questo nostro paese, et poy in mandare Monsig.re de Logis et Mon.re de Cursol in Savoya, deinde Monsig.re Guaston, Senescalco de Santogna, et Maestro Zohanne Filippo soy ambaxatori ad nuy con tante digne offerte per la conservatione et stabilimento de questo nostro Stato; et in mandare subito ad ordinare che le nostre gente, che erano nel Delfinato passassero de qua, et far dare li denari che li ha facto dare, adcioché dicte gente se potessero levare et venirsene in ordine; et anche de li ambaxatori, che la prefata Sua M.tà haveva ordinato de mandare a le potentie de Italia con quelle digne et favorevole commissione per beneficio nostro et de questo nostro Stato, che se fusse per la conservatione del suo Reame proprio non haveria possuto fare più. Onde cognoscemo tanta essere la grandeza de li oblighi che havemo verso Sua M.tà, che se vivessemo centenara d'anni et la M.tà Sua et nuy, non poressemo renderne digno merito ala M.tà Sua, perché non ne pare poter essere sufficienti ad satisfare ad una minima parte de lo singular amor et benivolentia et carità, che la M.tà Sua per sua gratia sempre hebbe verso el prefato Ill.mo S.re nostro consorte et patre, et de li immensi et immortali beneficii recevuti per luy da Sua M.tà, senza veruno merito, et successive verso nuy soy servitori, li quali sonno stati tanti et tali che non cognoscemo, come havemo dicto, poter satisfare ad quello che seria stato el debito et desyderio et voluntà del prefato Ill.mo S.re nostro consorte et patre, et seria etiandio el nostro. Ma pregamo Dio, che é remuneratore d'ogni bene, se digni per sua clementia de satisfare ad quello che nuy non possemo.

and father, and which would be ours also. But we pray God, remunerator of every good action, that He in His clemency will make satisfaction for all that we cannot.

We also wish that you assure the king that he can, and must, and we so intend, dispose of this state, of all our powers, and of us, his servants, as he sees fit at any time and at his pleasure or need, as if it were his own kingdom or one of his most disposable possessions; for he will always find us most prompt and willing to do all that we know is the pleasure and will of His Majesty. You should make clear to the king that not only in the case where there is need for the good of his state, which we hope will never occur, but also at his pleasure, as soon as things have settled down in our state, as we hope they must through the favors of His Majesty and of other friends, we will always send to him as many troops as His Majesty desires—and not the troops alone, but also, we, Galeazzo, in person shall come without hesitation or reservation of any sort. Communicate to His Majesty that one of our greatest displeasures, after the death of the Most Illustrious Lord our father, is that we, Galeazzo, have not been blessed with the good fortune of being able to go visit and pay our respects to His Majesty—as was indeed the consuming desire of said Most Illustrious Lord our father and ourselves. And if we believed that in our allotted days it were not to be possible to personally see His Majesty and do our duty toward him, in some way, we would disconsolately live out the remaining time of our life.

Item: in an orderly fashion you will explain to His Majesty the sequence of events that followed the demise of said Lord, our husband and father, just as you yourself have known and seen everything. Even before we, Galeazzo, reached Milan, Bianca [Maria], who was destitute of men of authority and of capability in war, was quickly visited, comforted, and counseled in what was to be done for the preservation of this state by the Illustrious Lord Guglielmo, Marquis of Monferrat. Then came the Illustrious Lord Ercole, sent by his brother, the Most Illustrious Lord Duke of Modena, to offer his possessions, his state, and his very person, all for the preservation of our state. Their presence gave

Volemo bene certifichi el prefato S.re Re, ch'el può et deve, et cossì intendemo ch'el possa non altramente disponere et deliberare de questo Stato, d'ogni nostra facultà et de nuy soy servitori in ogni tempo et in ogni suo piacere et bisogno, come può del suo Reame proprio, et de quelle cose de le quale può più disponere, perché sempre ne troverà promptissimi et dispositissimi ad fare tucto quello che cognosceremo sii piacere et voluntà de la M.tà Sua; chiarendola che non solamente per bisogno che li occorresse per bene del Stato suo, che speramo non occorrerà may tal caso, ma per suo piacere, quando siano assettate le cose de questo nostro Stato, come speramo se debiano assettare mediante li favori de la M.tà Sua et de li altri amici, nuy li mandarimo sempre quello numero de gente dal canto de là che ad Sua. M.tà piacerà; et non solo li mandaremo le gente, ma li andaremo nuy Galeazo in persona con esse, senza reguardo né reservo alcuno, dicendo a la M.tà Sua che uno de li mazori dispiaceri che nuy Galeazo habiamo, dapoy quello de la morte del prefato Ill.mo S.re nostro patre, si é che non havemo possuto havere tanta gratia che fussemo possuti andare ad visitare et reverire la M.tà Sua, come era lo ardente desyderio del prefato Ill.mo S.re nostro patre et nostro. Et se nuy credessemo a li dì nostri de non poter vedere personalmente la M.tà Sua et fare el nostro debito verso ley per qualche modo in l'advenire, nuy viveressemo malcontenti tucto el tempo de la vita nostra.

Item, diray a la prefata M.tà del Re, adcioché ella intenda per ordine tucto quello che qui é seguito depoy ch'el prefato S.re nostro consorte et patre passò de questa vita, come tu medesmo hay inteso et viduto ogni cosa, che inanti nuy Galeazo giongessemo qui in Milano subito vene da nuy Bianca, la quale eramo nuda de homini maxime de auctoritate et apti ala guerra, lo Ill. S.re Gulielmo Marchese de Monferrà ad visitarne et confortarne et consigliarne in quello era da fare per la conservatione de questo Stato. Et poy li arrivò lo Ill. S.re D. Hercules, fratello del Ill. mo S.re Duca de Modena, mandato per esso S.re Duca ad offerirne et le facultate, et el Stato, et la persona sua propria, pur per conservatione de questo nostro Stato. La venuta de li quali dete grande conforto ad questi

great comfort to our people. After the arrival of us, Galeazzo, there came two ambassadors, chosen from among the foremost citizens of the Magnificent City of Florence. They are still here to offer their condolences and, with broad mandate and commission from the Signoria, to promise and do all that might be expedient, within the extent of their powers, for the preservation of this state, not otherwise than they would do for the good of their own.[3] Then came the Illustrious Count of Urbino [Federico III], followed by the Illustrious Lord Alessandro [Sforza], Grand Constable of the Kingdom of Naples, our brother-in-law and uncle, and also the Magnificent Lord Roberto [Sanseverino], our nephew and cousin,[4] all of whom stayed with us night and day in watchful vigilance and zeal to determine and make all necessary provisions for upholding this state of ours. In a similar manner, envoys were sent here from Siena, Bologna, Lucca, and other Italian states, to offer their condolences with greatest love and charity. His Holiness the Pope, too, sent here a worthy prelate, the Bishop of Leon in Spain, as his ambassador, to extend condolences and generously offer all that which pertained to the apostolic faith and all that which His Holiness could do for the preservation of this state. Thus he [the Pope] sent briefs to all the rulers of Italy, exhorting them to persevere as effectively as possible in preserving peace and the Italian League.

Above every other ruler and lord of Italy, however, His Majesty King Ferrante made every demonstration and every possible provision for the well-being of this state, just as the dear departed Lord, our husband and father, would have done. As soon as King Ferrante heard of the death of said Lord, he sent his galleys to Genoa for the preservation of that state, and made all other provisions to our benefit, of which we want you to be aware, and regarding which we have also informed His Majesty by means of our letters to Giovan Pietro Panigarola.

To both our resident ambassador in Venice and to those we especially sent there, the Venetians have continued to say that they are disposed to persevere and live with us in that peace, friendship, and meeting of minds that prevailed while the dear departed Lord, our husband and

nostri populi. Da poy che nuy Galeazo gionsemo, lì venero duy ambaxatori de la Excelsa Comunità de Firenza, de li primi reputati cittadini de quella città, li quali sonno ancora qui de presenti ad condolersi, et deinde con amplo mandato et commissione da quella Signoria de poter promettere et fare tucto quello fusse expediente per quanto se extendessero le loro facultà per conservatione de questo Stato et non altramente che fariano per el bene del Stato loro.[3] Dapoy gionse lo Ill. Conte de Urbino, et deinde lo Ill. S.re D. Alexandro, Gran Conestabile del Reame de Napoli, nostro cognato et barba, et cossì el Mag.co S.re D. Roberto, nostro nepote et cusino,[4] li quali sempre sonno stati con nuy con grandissima vigilantia et studio ad recordare et fare dì et nocte tucte le provisione sonno state necessarie per mantenimento de questo nostro Stato. Similmente hanno mandato qui Senesi, Bolognesi, Luchesi et altri Signori de Italia, ad condolersi et offerire con grandissimo amore et carità. La S.tà de Nostro Signore ancora mandò qui uno digno prelato, Vescovo de Lion in Spagna, suo ambaxatore ad condolersi et offerire largamente tucto quello che perteniva a la fede apostolica, et posseva la S.tà Sua per conservatione de questo Stato. Et cossì scripse per soy brevi ad tucte le potentie de Italia, che ciascuno dovesse perseverare a la conservatione de la pace et Liga Italica molto efficacemente. Ma sopra ogni altra potentia et signoria de Italia, la M.tà del Re Ferando ha facto tucte quelle demonstratione et tucte quelle provisione per la salute de questo Stato, che haveria facto la bona memoria del prefato S.re nostro consorte et patre. La M.tà del quale, subito che intese la morte del prefato S.re, mandò le sue galee ad Zenova per la conservatione de quello Stato, et fece tucte le altre provisione in beneficio nostro, de le quale tu sii informato et ancora ne havemo dato notitia a la M.tà Sua per nostre littere directive ad Zohannepetro Panigarola. Venetiani hanno sempre dicto ali nostri ambaxatori, et ad quello che tenemo là continuamente et ad quelli che li mandassemo, et cossì hanno scripto ad nuy per sue littere, respondendo ale nostre, et resposto etiandio ala S.tà de Nostro S.re, al prefato Re Ferando in principio, et cossì ad S.ri Firentini per littere che li hanno scripto, che la loro disposicione é de perseverare et vivere con

father, was alive. They have reiterated this same position in response to letters we wrote them, answering likewise to His Holiness, the Pope, to said King Ferrante earlier, and also to the Florentines. Since the aforementioned Majesty [King Ferrante] a few days ago sent them an ambassador,[5] to better learn of their disposition toward us, especially in light of the warlike moves continually made by Bartolomeo of Bergamo since the death of our husband and father, claiming that he was free [from his contract with Venice], and so forth, that Signoria [of Venice] therefore responded to the said royal ambassador that its intention was to live and act with us as it did during the lifetime of our husband and father, as mentioned above. On the matter of Bartolomeo, they declared and explained that having had him under firm contract for one year and under option for yet another, they have now exercised their option and placed him under contract, binding him therefore for this year as their man and soldier, so that there will be no trouble at all coming from him. Nevertheless, what causes talk and much wonderment in all is that, up to now, they [the Venetians] have not sent, nor do they show sign of sending, an ambassador to us as all the other powers in Italy have done.

You will also point out that through the intervention of King Ferrante, the Illustrious Lord Marquis of Mantua renewed his contract of service with His Majesty [King Ferrante] and with ourselves, for three contractual years and one optional, with payment of thirty-six thousand ducats per annum in time of peace, and seventy thousand ducats in time of war, payable in equal shares by His Majesty and by us. The Marquis of Mantua is bound to do all that might be expedient for the defense of our state, by means of his own state, troops, and his very person itself, against whomever might wish to harm us, as required and ordered by us without waiting for other orders from King Ferrante. You will tell His Majesty [the King of France] that we have willingly engaged the said Marquis into our service and support because he is most useful for the preservation of this state in the event that the Venetians were to attack. Even more willingly have we done so because of what was recalled to us by Messer Alberico [Maletta] regarding His Majesty's con-

nuy in quella pace, amicicia et coniunctione d'animi che facevano vivendo la bona memoria del prefato S.re nostro consorte et patre. Et perché
la M.tà del prefato Re li ha mandato pochi dì fa uno suo ambaxatore[5]
per intendere bene la disposicione loro verso nuy, et maxime el fato de
Bartholomeo da Bergamo per le demonstratione che continuamente ha
facto dapoy la morte del prefato S.re nostro consorte et patre, che sonno
state tucte de guerra, dicando ch'el era in sua libertà etc.; quella Signoria ha resposto a dicto ambaxatore regio, che la disposicione sua era
de vivere et fare con nuy, come faceva con el prefato S.re nostro, come é
dicto. Et circ'al facto de dicto Bartholomeo hanno dicto et chiarito, che
havendolo loro conducto l'anno passato per uno anno fermo et un altro de
beneplacito, mo novamente l'hanno reconducto per questo anno de beneplacito et mettutolo in obligo, dicendo che per questo anno é loro homo
et soldato, et da luy non se receverà molestia alcuna. Et nientedemanco
may fin qui ad nuy non hanno mandato né monstrano mandare ambaxatore, come hanno facto l'altre potentie de Italia, che ad ogniuno ha
dato da dire et admiratione assay.

Diray ancora che per interposicione del prefato Re Ferando si
é reconducto a li servitii de Sua M.tà et nostri, lo Ill. S.re Marchese de
Mantua per tre anni fermi et uno ad beneplacito, con la provisione de
ducati XXXVI.M. per anno in tempo de pace, et in tempo de guerra de
ducati LXX.M., da pagarsi per mittà per la M.tà Sua et nuy; el quale é
obligato de fare tucto quello serà expediente per la defesa de questo
nostro Stato con lo Stato, gente d'arme et persona, contra chi ne volesse
offendere secondo li serà ordinato et commandato per nuy, senza expectare altra commissione del prefato Re; dicendo a la M.tà Sua che nuy
havemo conducto volentieri dicto Marchese a li servitii et favori nostri,
peroché l'é molto utile a la conservatione de questo Stato quando fussemo offesi da Venetiani. Et tanto più l'havemo facto volentieri, quanto
per Misser Albrico ne é stato recordato che la M.tà Sua sempre fu de
parere, trovandosi luy presso ley, et cossì confortò per suo mezo la bona
memoria del S.re nostro consorte et patre, ch'el se reconducesse a li
nostri servitii, et n'el conservassemo per amico, intendendo la M.tà Sua

currence with this point of view, when he was there at his court, and he [Louis XI] thus advised, through him, the dear departed Lord, our husband and father—that the Marquis put himself at our service and that we maintain him as our friend. In his great prudence His Majesty had comprehended just how important and useful the Marquis, together with his state, is for the preservation of our state, as mentioned above. Having concluded the pact as described, the Marquis sent here his wife, the Marchioness [Barbara], to visit and offer condolences; she remained here a few days and then returned home.

When you are presenting the preceding part of these instructions to His Majesty the King, you will say openly, as he may have heard from Garcia Bethes[6] who was sent to His Majesty a few days ago by King Ferrante, that he would do well to form a good opinion and make capital of King Ferrante as a fine friend and son; for we have in the past, and now even more so, always recognized him to be most friendly toward His Majesty, and extremely well disposed to place all his possessions and his kingdom itself, both on land and on sea, at the service of His Majesty in any and every need, not otherwise than he would do for the preservation of his own kingdom. And if His Majesty were to wish to make trial of this, he would find that the deeds match the words, since King Ferrante has both the will and the means, considering that at present his kingdom is totally calm and obedient, and that he has so settled his affairs that he in no way fears they can be disturbed from any quarter or by anyone either from within or without his kingdom.

Since His Majesty a few days ago amiably put forth some propositions[7] (as was written to us by Giovan Pietro Panigarola), to effect some agreement between King Ferrante and Duke John, whether by way of money or other recompense, naming Avignon whenever the Pope might wish to concede it to Duke John in exchange [for another city to be given to the Pope] by King Ferrante, you will point out to His Majesty that King Ferrante heartily thanks him for the thoughts and labors undertaken in his behalf with love and charity. King Ferrante, however, has sent word through his ambassador, who is here with us, that he would

per la sua summa prudentia quanto dicto Marchese con lo suo Stato importa et é utile a la conservatione de questo Stato come é dicto; el quale Marchese, concluso che fo el facto suo, come é dicto, mandò qui Madonna Marchesana soa consorte ad visitarne et condolerse con noy, et stecte qui alcuni dì et poy se retornò a casa sua. Quando seray ad exponere questa parte a la M.tà del S.re Re, diray etiandio largamente a la M.tà Sua, come porà havere inteso per Gratia Bethes,[6] mandato pochi dì fa per esso Re a la M.tà Sua, ch'ella ha ad fare bono concepto et bono cavedale del prefato Re come de bono amico et figliolo, perché l'havemo per lo passato sempre cognosciuto, et cossì mo de presenti più che may affectionatissimo a la M.tà Sua, et dispositissimo ad mettere ogni sua facultà et lo suo Regno in beneficio de Sua M.tà ad ogni suo bisogno, et non altramente che faria per conservatione del suo Reame proprio, et per mare et per terra. Et quando la M.tà Sua ne vorà fare experientia, troverà che li facti corresponderanno a le parole, perché li ha la voluntà et lo potere, consyderato che ha al presente el suo Reame in grande tranquillità et obedientia et ha talmente assettate le cose sue, che non dubita che li possano essere perturbate da veruno canto né per persona che fusse dentro del dicto suo Reame né che venesse de fuora. Et perché la M.tà Sua amorevolmente porchi dì fanno ha mosso alcuni partiti,[7] ad nuy scripti per Zohanne Petro Panigarola, per mettere qualche accordio fra el dicto Re Ferando et el Duca Zohanno, come seria o per via de denari o recompensa, nominando Avignono, quando el Papa el volese concedere al dicto Duca Zohanne havendo contracambio dal dicto Re Ferando, denoteray a la M.tà Sua che esso Re Ferando grandemente rengratia essa Sua M.tà de li pensieri et fatiche che prende per luy con quello amore et carità, come ella fa, et che non li pare al presente intrare in tal praticha, né li pare expediente trovandosi maxime la M.tà Sua nel stato che se trova in quello Reame pacifico et reintegrato, come é dicto. Et questo ne ha facto dire per lo suo ambaxatore che é qui presso nuy.

Questo nostro Stato et questi nostri populi tanto de qua in Lombardia, quanto de là in Zenovese, sonno stati et stanno in bona tran-

rather not at present enter into such negotiations, regarding them inexpedient, especially since the King finds himself in the position he is in, with his kingdom pacified and reintegrated, as was said above.

Our State and our peoples both here in Lombardy and in Genoa have maintained and are maintaining calm, union, and obedience. In order to give them reason for continuing in their proper conduct, constancy, and fidelity, we have remitted them, both in ordinary duties and in some few extraordinary taxes, more than 100,000 ducats in all. You can communicate to the King that we consider this good fortune to proceed first from God, and then from His Majesty, because of the great show of support given us by him both in word and deed for the preservation of this state, which was a most powerful reason for keeping everyone on the mark, and careful to avoid committing actions against the state, that might be harmful to us.

You will next inform His Majesty that even though our affairs are in the state and condition such as we mentioned, nevertheless we cannot place any faith at all in the Venetians or in the aforementioned Bartolomeo, since by means of information that we receive continuously from many sources, we have no doubts regarding their hostile and threatening attitude toward us, because of their cupidity and ambition to possess all or part of this state. If they were to see a chance to make a strong attempt upon this state, they would make it, with no regard for peace, for alliance among us, or for the friendly words exchanged with us on the subject of remaining our good neighbors and tending to their own business. For they have no other desire and appetite, nor do they think of anything else both day and night, except that of usurping this state—convinced as they are that once they had conquered it, then they would in short order be lords of Italy, and then with Italy, lords of the world, as the Romans did. It is their fantasy to consider their commonwealth immortal, and that therefore they must in time rule and have sway over all the world.[8]

Wherefore, to avoid being at their mercy and risking some great reversal, it is necessary (as we are so urged and pressed consistently by

quillità, unione et obedientia, ad li quali perché habino casone de vivere bene et essere fideli et constanti a la devotione nostra, havemo remesso tanto de datii ordinarii, quanto de alcune poche intrate extraordinarie più de C.M. ducati, dicendo a la M.tà Sua che questa gratia reputiamo havere primo da Dio, et poy da essa Sua M.tà, perché le grande demonstratione facte per ley con parole et con facti verso nuy per la conservatione de questo Stato, sonno state potissima casone de far stare ogniuno ad segno in guardarsi ad non commettere cosa alcuna contra questo nostro Stato, che ne fusse molesta.

Diray appresso a la M.tà Sua, che quantuncha le cose nostre siano in li termini et condicione che havemo dicto, nondimanco nuy non possemo prendere veruna fede de dicti Venetiani né de dicto Bartholomeo, perché non dubitiamo per li advisi che havemo continuamente da molti canti de la cattiva et pessima loro disposicione verso nuy, per la cupiditate et ambitione hanno de havere o tucto o parte de questo Stato, quando se vedessero fare uno bello tracto in questo Stato el fariano senza reguardo alcuno, né stariano per pace, né liga che é fra nuy, né per le bone parole hanno dicto de voler ben vicinare con nuy ad fare el facto loro, perché non hanno altro desyderio, né appetito né pensano dì et nocte in altro nomma de usurpare questo Stato, parendoli che, conquistato ch'el fusse per loro, se fariano poy signori in poco tempo de tucta Italia, et deinde con Italia se fariano signori del mondo, come fecero Romani. Et hanno questa fantasia che, siando la loro Comunità immortale, che con el tempo debiano ancora havere la monarchia et imperio de tucto el mondo.[8] Onde per non stare a discretione loro et ad periculo de recevere qualche gran danno, ne é necessario, et cossì siamo tucta volta confortati et strecti da questi Signori che sonno qui et tucti quelli che ne vogliono bene, che nuy mettiamo in puncto le nostre gente d'arme et stare provisti, non altramente che se expectassemo la guerra, perché siando provisti se farà fugire li mali pensieri, ad chi li havesse, de far male. Et stando nel modo che facemo adesso, se faria venire voglia de malignare ad chi non l'havesse, perché se dice ch'el bello furare fa l'homo ladro. Et ad voler mettere in puncto queste nostre gente da cavallo, le quale de

the lords who are present here and by all those that wish us well) that we place our troops at the ready and be prepared as if we were expecting war; for being so prepared will cause the dissolution of evil intentions to do us harm in those who might harbor them. Remaining in our present posture [i.e., unprepared] will generate the will to do us harm in those who might not have it, for it is said that easy stealing makes man a thief.

We would want to get our cavalry at the ready, two-thirds of which at present are without mounts. The elements that are best prepared are those that were with us, Galeazzo, in His Majesty's service in the Dauphiné, just recently returned here; and also those that we are awaiting from the Kingdom [of Naples], which were made ready by His Majesty King Ferrante; together with another force of approximately a thousand horses to whom our Lord [Francesco Sforza] had given monies in order to send them quickly into the Dauphiné. We have calculated that a great deal of money will be necessary, and we find ourselves neither with money nor the means to raise any, given our current income. For, in his last days, the said Lord, our husband and father, left no money at all, but instead left many debts. These His Lordship had incurred, first, to preserve peace in the state of the Church, at the cost of many thousands of ducats, to defend it from the aggressions of Count Iacopo [Piccinino] and of other lords, both during the reign of Pope Calixtus and of Pope Pius; and second, to help His Majesty King Ferrante, at great cost over several years, as well as for the acquisition of Genoa and for many other expenses that occurred.

These things His Lordship principally did in order to preserve peace and the Italian League, it being his obligation to so act—thereby leaving us many friends,[9] and firmly establishing this state in good will. From these friends and from our own officials, we have received, and continue to receive, aid by various means, including loans of money. We have made do with that money and have taken care of the most necessary things. So finding ourselves in this situation, we have asked some friendly lords and commonwealths of Italy to support us with

le tre parte le due se trovano essere ad piede, et quelle che siano meglio in puncto sonno quelle, che erano con nuy Galeazo in adiuto de la M.tà Sua nel Delfinato, quale sonno tornate novamente de qua, et quelle che expectiamo del Reame, quale ha facto mettere in puncto la M.tà del Re Ferando, et circa altri mille cavalli, ad li quali havia dato denari el prefato S.re nostro per mandarli presto de là nel Delfinato, havemo facto rasone che li bisogna uno grande numero de denari. Et nuy non se troviamo havere né denari, né el modo de haverne sopra queste nostre intrate per al presente, perch'el prefato S.re nostro consorte et patre in questo suo fine non ha lassato denaro alcuno, ma debiti assay sì. Li quali debiti la Sig.ria Sua ha facti, primo per conservare el Stato de la Chiesia in pace, dove spese molte migliara de ducati per defenderla da le oppressione del Conte Iacomo, tanto al tempo de Papa Calisto quanto de Papa Pio et de altri Signori, et per adiutare la M.tà del Re Ferando, dove spese grande numero de denari in più anni, et etiandio per l'acquisto de Zenoa, et per molte altre spese che li sonno occorse. Et tucte queste cose la S.ria Sua le fece principalmente per la conservatione de la pace et Liga de Italia, per la quale era obligato ad cossì fare; ne ha bene la S.ria Sua lassato de molti amici,[9] et questo Stato bene edificato et benivolo, con li quali amici et con de li nostri servitori de questo Stato, nuy ne siamo adiutati et adiutamo per molte vie; dali quali havemo havuto alcuni denari in prestito. Et con questi ne siamo reparati et provisto ad quelle cose che sonno state più necessarie. Onde trovandone in questi termini, havemo rechiesto de li Signori et Comunità de Italia nostri amici ad subvenirne de alcuna quantità de denari,[10] et cossì haveressemo etiandio rechiesta la M.tà Sua, che ne havesse subvenuto de qualche summa de denari, per poter mettere in puncto dicte nostre gente, le quale quando siano in puncto con le altre che vengono del Reame, et quelle sonno venute de Franza, non haveremo poy dubio che veruno ne possa offendere. Et quando la M.tà Sua desyderasse havere et operare o de là o altrove qualche parte de dicte nostre gente o per qualche altro respecto, quando le cose nostre de qua siano assettate et quietate come havemo dicto, sempre seranno apparechiate al suo commando, cossì come

sums of money,[10] just as we would have asked His Majesty for some sum of money, in order to be able to ready the said troops. Having done so, and bolstering them with those that come from the Kingdom [of Naples] and those that have returned from France, we would then have no fear that anyone could do us harm. If His Majesty then desired to have and use, there or elsewhere, some part of these troops in whatever regard, as soon as things are settled and quieter here, as we said, they will always be ready and at his disposal, just as if they were his own. Considering, however, that His Majesty must be in difficult straits with regard to money, because of the intolerable expenses he had to meet during the past year due to the disturbances and great warfare that occurred in his kingdom, it has not seemed proper to us to burden him with aiding us monetarily. We are, of course, certain that had he the means, then he most willingly would have come to our aid, as he has done in all things for the well-being of this state.

On the subject of the marriage [with Bona of Savoy], you will tell His Majesty that he must certainly have thoroughly understood our intent and attitude in this matter, from what we committed to Emanuele de Iacopo, member of our household, at our, Galeazzo's, departure from Beaurepaire; and then also from a letter in our own hand to His Majesty on 1 May.[11] Nevertheless, having learned of what Emanuele had to report upon his return from the King, we wish you to certify once again to His Majesty that the Most Illustrous Lady our mother and we ourselves have unanimously made a firm decision to execute and accomplish the aforesaid marriage—just as it was the intent and design of the late Lord our father, whose will we intend thus to execute afer his death, as when he was alive, through the love and reverence we bore him always, as was our duty. In this regard, His Majesty can place his mind at rest and his spirit in repose, for to bring this matter to a proper end, whenever it seems correct to His Majesty considering the death of our father, we will send to the King Messer Alberico Maletta, our Counselor, who is most experienced and informed of all that must be done in the matter, giving him instructions and appropriate mandates in order

sonno le altre sue; ma consyderando nuy che la M.tà Sua deve havere mal el modo al denaro, per le intollerabile spese che li occorseno fare l'anno passato per li disturby et guerra grande che hebbe nel suo Reame, non n'é parso dargli carico de adiutarne de denari, rendendosi però certi, che quando havesse havuto el modo, ne haveria subvenuto cossì volentieri come ha facto tucte le altre cose per salute de questo nostro Stato.

Circ'al facto del parentato, diray a la Sua M.tà che ben per quanto commettessemo ad Emanuele de Iacopo nostro fameglio a la partita de nuy Galeazo da Belrepparo, la M.tà Sua debbe assay havere inteso la mente et firma disposicione nostra circa ciò, et dapoy ancora per una littera scripta de nostra propria mano a dì primo de mazo[11] directiva a la prefata Sua M.tà. Nondimeno, havendo nuy inteso quanto dicto Emanuele ne ha referto per parte de quella in questa sua ultima venuta, volimo de novo certifichi la prefata Sua M.tà come la Ill.ma Madonna nostra matre et nuy havemo unanimiter facto firma deliberatione de exequire et mandare ad effecto dicto parentato, secondo era la mente et disposicione del prefato quondam S.re nostro patre, la voluntate del quale intendemo cossì exequire dapoy che l'é morto, come quando l'era vivo, per l'amore et reverentia che sempre li portassemo, come era nostro debito. Et de questo la M.tà Sua ne staghi con la mente et animo quieto et reposato. Et per darli el debito fine, mandaremo quando parerà a la M.tà Sua che sia decente a la morte del S.re nostro patre, Misser Albrico Maletta, nostro consigliero, da Sua M.tà, come quello che l'ha praticato et é informato de quanto é necessario de fare, con le commissione et mandati opportuni per concludere tucto quanto serà expediente. Ben pregamo Sua M.tà ch'ella se digni per honore nostro et per nostro singulare contentamento essere contenta, ch'el tempo in lo quale se haverà ad menare la donna de qua ad casa nostra se differischi, finché sii passato l'anno che morite el prefato S.re nostro patre. Nientedemanco nuy se remettemo et in questo et in tucte le altre cose al parere et voluntà de Sua M.tà, la quale seremo sempre prompti ad exequire, rendendosi però certi che la M.tà Sua haverà bona consyderatione et reguardo al honore del prefato S.re nostro patre, el quale li fu tanto

to conclude all that is necessary. However, we entreat His Majesty that he deign, for the sake of our honor and for our especial consolation, that he be willing to defer the time when the lady is to be conducted to our house in order to allow one year to have passed since the death of our father. Nevertheless, in this as in all other things, we submit ourselves to the pleasure and will of His Majesty, which we will always be ready to fulfill; yet knowing with certainty that His Majesty will take into fullest consideration and regard the honor of said Lord our father, who was such a dedicated and affectionate servant of the King, as is manifest to all the world.

You will further inform His Majesty that in order to continue the ancient friendship which our forebears, especially the dear departed Lord, our husband and father, have had with My Lord of Burgundy, with his son, My Lord of Charolais, and with their House, and also in order to implement His Excellency's decision (taken a few days before leaving this life with His Majesty's advice and full consent)—to wit, sending to the said lords one of his ambassadors together with one of His Majesty King Ferrante[12]—now we, Galeazzo, as soon as we returned to Milan, thought of sending an ambassador to the said lords to notify them of the decease of our father and communicate to them our intention to persevere in that very same friendship with their lordships that our father contracted with them. But before dispatching the said ambassador, we wanted you, Pietro, to notify His Majesty, so as to have the King's opinion and wishes in this, and ascertain what posture he prefers us to assume, since we do not intend to depart from what we learn to be his pleasure and will. In the midst of these deliberations, the aforesaid Emanuele returned and, among other things, related to us that His Majesty advises and heartily agrees with our sending one of our men to visit the said lords, in the interest of maintaining good relations with them.

Therefore, without further delay, we have decided to send to these lords our ambassador,[13] who will simply have the commission to visit with their lordships on our behalf, informing them of conditions here

deditissimo et affectionatissimo servitore, come é manifesto ad tucto el mondo.

Ancora diray a la M.tà Sua, che per continuare in l'amicicia con Mon.re de Borgogna et Mon.re de Ciarloys suo figliolo, la quale ab anti-quo hanno havuto li nostri antecessori con quella Casa et maxime la felice memoria del S.re nostro consorte et patre, et per seguire etiandio quello medesmo che la Soa Excellentia pochi dì inanzi ch'el passasse de questa vita con bono consentimento et parere dela Soa M.tà haveva deliberato, zoé de mandare uno suo ambaxatore insieme con uno de quelli de la M.tà del Re Ferrando ali prefati Signori,[12] fin da principio che nuy Galeazo giongessemo qui in Milano, deliberassemo de mandare uno nostro ambaxatore da quelli Signori per notificarli el decesso del prefato Signore nostro, et dirli che la disposicione nostra era de perseverare in quella medesma amicicia con le Sig.rie loro, che havia facto el prefato S. nostro; ma prima che mandassemo dicto ambaxatore, volevamo noti-ficarlo per ti Petro a la M.tà Sua, per essere da quella advisati del parere et voluntà sua, et se havevamo ad servare più uno modo che un altro, come quelli che non intendemo partirsi da quello che cognosceremo essere suo piacere et voluntà. Ma siando fra questo mezo arrivato el predicto Emanuele, et referitone tra le altre cose per parte de la Sua M.tà che li pare et é molto contenta che nuy mandiamo uno de li no-stri ad visitare li predicti Signori, et che interteniamo bona amicicia con le Sig.rie loro, havemo determinato de mandare da essi Signori, senza expectare altro, el dicto nostro ambaxatore,[13] el quale haverà solamente commissione de visitare le Sig.rie loro per parte nostra, et dirli de le condicione de qua in generale et perseverare in la principiata amicicia con loro, come faceva el prefato S.re nostro consorte et patre; et confortare et pregare li prefati Signori ad vivere bene et havere bona intelligentia cum la M.tà Sua. Et se per caso le Sig.rie Loro intrassero con dicto nostro ambaxatore in alcuna cosa particulare de intelligentia o altra coniunctione, dicto ambaxatore haverà solamente ad intendere et non intrare in altra pratica, ma advisare nuy d'ogni loro motivo. Et in questo caso chiariray molto bene la M.tà Sua, che nuy non veneremo

in general and of our desire to persevere in the friendship initiated with them, as did our Lord, husband and father. The ambassador will urge and entreat their lordships to live peaceably and in good understanding with His Majesty. If by chance their lordships were to broach some particular question with our ambassador, regarding an alliance or some other entanglement, he will simply lend an ear and not enter into any negotiations, but advise us of their proposals. You will make very clear to His Majesty that in such a case we would not entertain any negotiations for an alliance with these lords without participation, advice, and consent of the king, for we want nothing in such a matter except that which may be good, useful, honorable, and in accord with the king's will.

You will also tell His Majesty that, as we have heard, he was thinking of having Duke John[14] come to his court, and of dealing with him kindly in order to win him over, and so forth. This idea and plan of the king pleases us, because we are certain that His Majesty, in his wisdom and prudence, does all for a good end and for the benefit of his state. Certainly, all that redounds to the benefit of his state is considered by King Ferrante and by us as favorable and acceptable as if it were in benefit of our states, since the more firm and secure His Majesty finds himself in his own state, just so much more freely and powerfully could he aid us in time of need here. Thus, we are bound to consider and hold his good or bad fortune as our own, and King Ferrante feels likewise. We noted the firm and constant conviction that, as His Majesty has said and in effect acted in the past, he will not do or permit anything prejudicial to King Ferrante and to us, since no harm could be directed against the said king that would not also be aimed against us. As we said above, His Majesty can expect from King Ferrante in his every need all the favor and aid that one could hope for were that kingdom [Naples] governed by His Majesty's own son.

Item: mention to His Majesty that, if he agrees, you will visit on our behalf the Most Serene Madame the Queen [Charlotte], together with some lords of his court, such as My Lord of Bourbon, the Count of

ad alcuna pratica de intelligentia con essi Signori senza participatione, parere et consentimento de Sua M.tà, perché nuy non volemo puncto in tal cosa nomma quello che sia bene, utile et honore et voluntà d'essa M.tà.

Ancora diray a la M.tà Sua come nuy havemo inteso, ch'essa Sua M.tà deliberava far venire da sì el Duca Zohanne[14] et ben tractarlo per farselo benivolo etc., et che tale deliberatione et proposito de la M.tà Sua ad nuy é molto piaciuto, perché semo certissimi che la M.tà Sua, come sapientissima et prudentissima, faza tucto ad optimo fine et per ben del Stato suo, et tucte quelle cose che redundano in beneficio del Stato suo, sonno a la M.tà del Re Ferando et ad nuy non altramente grate et accepte, che se fusseno in beneficio de li Stati nostri, però quanto più la M.tà Sua é secura et ben ferma nel Stato suo, tanto più liberamente e con più possanza poterà subvenire ad nuy in li bisogni ne potesseno occorrere de qua; onde havemo ad reputare et tenere el suo bene et el suo male nostro, et lo simile reputa et tene el prefato Re Ferando, tenendo per fermo et constante come sempre ha dicto et facto con effecto per lo passato, ch'el non farà, né consentirà may cosa alcuna che sia in preiudicio del prefato Re et nostro, perché non se poria fare cosa molesta al dicto Re, che non se facesse ancora ad nuy; dal quale Re, come havemo dicto de sopra, la M.tà Sua ne ha ad expectare quello favore et adiuto in ogni suo bisogno, che poria sperare se fusse in quello Reame uno suo figliolo.

Item, diray a la M.tà Sua, che parendoli habii ad visitare da nostra parte la Ser.ma Madamma la Regina et de quelli Signori de la sua Corte, come é Mon.re de Borbon,[a] Conte de Dunoys, et de li altri principali, et dire qualche cosa ad alcuno de loro del facto del parentato, che tu faray in questo quello che serà de sua voluntà et piacere. Et cossì portando littere de credenza ad caduno de loro, li visitaray da nostra parte et li diray quello che per Sua M.tà te serà ordinato.[b]

---

a. Crossed out: Filippo Mon.re.

b. This paragraph follows and is entirely crossed out:

Ancora pregaray la prefata M.tà del Re, che ne voglia fare uno presente ad nuy Galeazo, el quale ad nuy serà tanto grato et accepto, quanto più dire se potesse in questo mondo El quale presente intendemo sia Cigles, castello nel Delfinato presso ad Susa; et piacendo ad Sua M.tà

Dunoys, and some other important individuals, to express something to each of them regarding the marriage, doing so according to his will and pleasure. Thus, bearing letters of credence to each of them, you will visit them on our behalf and express to them that which His Majesty will instruct you.

Then, after you have expounded to His Majesty the King our embassy, according to your commission and the present instructions, you will make every proper effort to have His Majesty's reply. Having done so and having observed that nothing compels further sojourn on your part, taking courteous leave of His Majesty, you will return well informed and apprised regarding affairs in France. If for whatever reason, however, it should seem better, or please His Majesty, that you remain there a few days, you will do precisely as the King orders you, in your recognition of his pleasure and will.

Regarding news of Italy, inform His Majesty that already some days ago the Pope pressed to have the Italian League[15] reconstituted, which we believe came about perhaps through the insistence of the Venetians, who fear being attacked in Italy while they are already at war with the Turks. Recently the Pope has again pressed us that the League be reconstituted, even according to the old articles. He has not, however, sent us ambassadors or letters on this matter, but instead he has conferred with our ambassadors and those of other powers meeting in Rome. As is our duty, we wish to inform His Majesty of this, and we shall continue to keep him apprised of all further developments. We believe that now, because of the Turkish attack on Christendom, as His Majesty has been informed by our letters, His Holiness will apply greater pressure for the confirmation of this League, because he greatly fears a Turkish attack against the states and lands of the Church, and also out of regard for the Venetians—with Italy at peace, he could better provide against the Turks.

Postremo, quando haveray exposto la nostra ambaxiata a la M.tà del S.re Re, secondo hay in commissione et se contiene in la presente instructione, te studiaray con bono mode de havere la resposta da la Sua M.tà. Et facto questo, non parendoti lo tuo demorare là altramente necessario, togliendo bona licentia dal prefato S.re Re, te ne retorneray bene informato et bene instructo de le cose de là. Et se a la M.tà Sua paresse o piacesse che te demorasti alcuni dì de là per qualche respecto, faray et exequiray quanto per la prefata Sua M.tà te serà et ordinato, et che tu cognosceray essere de suo piacere et voluntà.

De le novelle de Italia, diray a la prefata M.tà che già più dì passati el Papa ha facta instantia de reformare la Liga de Italia,[15] et questo credemo forsi sii ad instantia de Venetiani, li quali dubitano, che havendo la guerra del Turco, gli fusse mosta guerra de qua; et novamente ne fa grande instantia, che la dicta Liga sii reformata pur secondo li capituli vechy. De ciò non n'ha però ancora mandato ambaxatori, né scripto littere, ma solo conferito con li ambaxatori nostro et d'altri che se sonno retrovati ad Roma. Del che per nostro debito ne habiamo voluto dare adviso a la Sua M.tà. Et de quanto più oltra se farà, de continuo la teneremo advisata. Et credemo che adesso per questo conflicto che ha dato el Turco ad Christiani, come la M.tà Sua haverà inteso per le nostre littere, la Sua San.tà farà molto mazore instantia de la confirmatione de la dicta Liga, perch'el dubita grandemente del Turco per lo Stato et per le terre de la Chiesia, et anche per respecto de Venetiani, et essendo Italia in pace poterà meglio provedere contra el Turco.

---

de farne dicto presente, la pregamo non ne voglia fare altra demonstratione né parola alcuna con veruno, ma concedere ad nuy solamente licentia ch'el possiamo tore, et sopra ciò farne littere opportune ch'el possiamo tore, quando parirà ad nuy, adcioché li Delfinenghi non ne impedissero, et sopra ciò diray la casone de tal rechiesta. [This paragraph is translated at the beginning of the following document 37, p. 253].

1. Influential ducal adviser frequently utilized for diplomatic missions throughout Italy. His biographical sketch will be published in the Introduction to the next volume.

2. There were additional, and apparently more compelling, reasons for the postponement of Pietro's mission. The Florentine ambassadors, B. Giugni and L. Guicciardini, wrote to the Signoria of Florence [Milan, 18 May 1466, ASF, *Signori, X di Balia, VIII di Pratica, Legazioni e Commissarie, Missive e Responsive*, Reg. 63, fols. 92–92v] that the Duke wanted first to receive the latest report brought by Emanuele de Iacopo, who had recently returned from France. The Mantuan ambassador gave other reasons. The continuing struggle between Louis XI and the nobles gave the Milanese rulers cause to pause, wishing to evaluate the King's chances of success. The amount of the dowry to be given to Bona of Savoy was still uncertain and demanded a cautious approach. Finally, while Pietro da Gallarate was favorable to the Savoyard marriage and was pressing to leave as soon as possible, another adviser, P. F. Visconti, ws arguing before the Secret Council in favor of the Mantuan marriage. Although Galeazzo Maria seemed inclined toward the Savoyard marriage, he showed such a degree of indecision and volubility that there was widespread amazement at court: "vedendosse tante varietade in lui, ogniuno se ne stupisce" [Marsilio Andreasi to Marchioness Barbara Gonzaga, Milan, 3 June 1466, ASMA, *Carteggio-Milano*, B. 1623]. Later, Andreasi, in reporting that Pietro da Gallarate was scheduled to leave on 11 June [Cf. doc. 44], still commented on the Duke's volubility as follows: "Non vidi mai tante mutatione né volubilitate. La Ill.ma Modonna Duchessa dice che se pur el tolesse la prefata Madonna Dorothea, la crederia ch'el Nostro Signore Idio ge lo havesse servato per una sua grande disciplina" [Andreasi to Marchioness Barbara, Milan, 10 June 1466, ibid., B. 1623].

3. This flattering passage about Florence and its ambassadors, the first to arrive at Milan after the death of Francesco Sforza, pleased Giugni and Guicciardini, who had seen these instructions as early as 24 May [Giugni and Guicciardini to the Signoria of Florence, Milan, 24 May 1466, ASF, *Signori, X di Balia, VIII di Pratica, Legazioni e Commissarie, Missive e Responsive*, Reg. 63, fols. 94–94v]. After repeated requests, the Florentine ambassadors

were given permission to leave Milan on 9 June [Giugni and Guicciardini to the Signoria of Florence, Milan, 4 June 1466, ibid., Reg. 63, fol. 95].

4. Roberto Sanseverino, a leading condottiere, was the son of Leonetto Sanseverino and Elisa Sforza, sister of Francesco Sforza.

5. Giovanni Antonio Buccharelli, Bishop of Ascoli. Originally the attitude of Venice was unfriendly, claiming that it had no control over Colleoni, whose *condotta* had expired, and contending that it had no obligations under the Italian League because Francesco Sforza had violated it with his occupation of Genoa in 1464 [Buccharelli to King Ferrante, Venice, 11 March 1466, BN, *Fonds Italien*, Cod. 1591, fol. 282–82v]. Ferrante warned the Signoria through his ambassador [Naples, 25 March 1466, ibid., Cod. 1591, fols. 312–13v], not to attack Milan directly or indirectly through Colleoni, and expressed his view that Venice was obligated under the Italian League, which remained in force. Additional copies of both letters are in *Registri Missive*, Reg. 77, fols. 53–56v. Cf. Perret, 1:446.

6. See docs. 22 and 33.

7. See doc. 14.

8. The alleged inordinate ambition of the Venetians to dominate Italy and the world was a common charge made against them by contemporaries. See for example *The Commentaries of Pius II*, Book III, pp. 233–50, trans. F. A. Cragg, ed. L. C. Gabel, *Smith College Studies in History*, 25 (1939–1940). However, the Dukes are here purposely exaggerating the threat posed by Venice, for by this time they knew that there was little danger from that quarter [Cf. docs. 28 and 41].

9. Francesco Sforza's active role as principal champion of the Italian League had raised the prestige of the Duchy to its highest level, but the consequent heavy expenditures for diplomacy and military campaigns had depleted its rich resources [Caterina Santoro, *Gli Sforza* (Milan, Dall'Oglio, 1968), pp. 32–33, 148].

10. One such request was made to Florence when the Milanese rulers sent a special emissary to solicit a loan of 40,000 florins [B. Giugni and L. Guicciardini to the Signoria of Florence, Milan, 26 April 1466, ASF, *Signori, X di Balia, VIII di Pratica, Legazioni e Commissarie, Missive e Responsive*, Reg. 63, fols. 87–88].

11. Appendix, doc. IX.

12. The decision of Francesco Sforza and Ferrante to send ambassadors to the Burgundian court is revealed in the Duke's instructions to his son for his projected trip to the court of Louis XI [Milan, 2 March 1466, BN, *Fonds Italien*, Cod. 1591, fols. 274-77].

13. See doc. 35, n. 5.

14. See doc. 27.

15. In late April Paul II had appointed a committee of three cardinals to determine his obligations under the Italian League. The committee produced a secret report on 30 April, which held that the Pope was no longer obligated

by the provisions of the League since the compact itself was no longer in force, having already been violated several times by other members. The cardinals, however, advised the Pope to consult Italian rulers about steps to be taken for the reconstitution of the League so as to preserve peace in Italy and proceed against the Turks [Agostino Rossi to the Dukes, Rome, 27 April and 1 May 1466, *Roma*, cart. 59]. The Milanese rulers, on the other hand, felt that the League was still in force and that the process of negotiating a new one would plunge Italy into confusion and turmoil, leaving the peninsula disunited against the Turks [The Dukes to Agostino Rossi, Milan, 12 and 17 May 1466, ibid., cart. 59].

Memorandum to you, Pietro, separate from the instructions also to be executed with His Majesty, the King:

Pietro, first we want you to beseech His Majesty that he make us, Galeazzo, a gift which would be as pleasing and well-received as anything in this world—we mean the castle of Cigles,[1] in the Dauphiné near Susa. Were it to so please His Majesty, we pray him not to make any move or say a single word to anyone, but simply issue appropriate letters authorizing us to take possession of it when it suits us, so that those of Dauphiné will not impede us; and you will explain to the king the reasons for this request.

Then, you will recommend for us the Illustrious Marquis of Monferrat to His Majesty the King, choosing suitable and adequate language, as we also have done in our letters to him; mention to His Majesty that you yourself are aware of just how affectionately and charitably he conducted himself both with our dear departed husband and father, and then with us upon the death of the said lord, coming here personally to offer his state and person, counseling and aiding us in that which was necessary for the good of this state both before and after the return of Galeazzo, so that we are perennially obliged to him. Wherefore we would esteem it a most gracious, welcome, and kindly act if His Majesty were to consider him highly in every possible way and enroll him among

37 · *Memorandum of the* DUKE *and* DUCHESS OF

MILAN *to* PIETRO DA GALLARATE

BN, Fonds Italien, Cod. 1593, fols. 261–62. Minute

Memoriale ad ti, Petro, separato dala instructione da exeguire etiandio cum la M.tà del Re.

Petro. Primo volemo che tu preghi la M.tà del Re che ne voglia fare uno presente ad nuy Galeazo, el quale ad nuy serà tanto grato et accepto, quanto più dire se podesse in questo mondo. El quale presente intendemo sia Cigles,[1] castello nel Delphinato presso ad Susa; et piacendo ad Soa M.tà de farne dicto presente, la pregamo non ne voglia fare altra demonstratione né parola alcuna con veruno, ma concedere ad nuy solamente licentia ch'el possiamo tore et sopra ciò farne lettere opportune ch'el possiamo tore, quando parirà ad nuy, adcioché li Delphinenghi non ne impedissero, et sopra ciò dirai la casone de tal rechiesta.[a]

Item, recommendarai da nostra parte alla p.ta M.tà del Re cum parole accommodate et conveniente lo Ill. S.re Marchese de Monferrato, secundo etiandio per nostre lettere li l'havemo recommendato, dicendo alla p.ta Soa M.tà como tu medesmo sei informato quanto amorevelmente et caritativamente se é deportato, et cum la recolenda memoria del S.re nostro consorte et patre et poi cum noy in questo caso dela morte del p.to S.re nostro, in venire qui personalmente et offerirne

---

a. In the left-hand margin of this paragraph there is the Chancery's notation, "vacat." It seems that having been crossed out in the preceding instructions [doc. 36, n.b, p. 245], it was then eliminated from this memorandum as well [cf. n. 1].

his faithful and good servants, as we always have known him to be. We would be singularly thankful if, for our regard, His Majesty were to demonstrate his goodwill toward him.[2]

Item: next, you will thank His Majesty for having deigned, through love for us and also because of our intercession, to take into his good grace Lord Antonio di Romagnano, for which we are indeed glad. To all the other great obligations we have toward His Majesty we add all that which he has done for Lord Antonio as if he had done it for us, considering the aid he gave us, as His Majesty has been informed by him and by others of his house. We also pray His Majesty that in the future he deign to number him among his servants, and that he be well treated by the illustrious Lords, the Duke and Duchess of Savoy, and taken in to their service.[3]

Item: You will take singular care, in the case where the [Royal] Council or others on behalf of His Majesty ask to read your instructions, that under no circumstances should a copy be made of a part or of the whole; the reason for this you have already been told by us orally.

Item: when you relate the part of the instructions dealing with the Marquis of Mantua and with the coming here of the Marchioness, you will remember to mention what we told you verbally; that is, she modestly spoke of [our] marriage with her daughter, but always subordinating her own interests and desires to the good of ourselves and our state. She was answered in such a manner that she clearly understood our intention to execute what had been arranged, and what was the last wish of our husband and father.[4]

Item: regarding your visit to My Lord Philip and your verbal communication touching on [our] marriage with his sister, you will say that we are ready to do all that is the pleasure and will of His Majesty the King of France in this as in every other matter.

Item: when you have joined the King, you will make every effort, both through Giovan Pietro Panigarola and through every other means, to investigate and inform yourself as well as you can regarding the situation of that envoy[5] that the King holds in prison, as the Duke

et lo Stato et la persona, et così in consigliarne et aiutarne in quello fo necessario per lo ben de questo Stato inanzi et poy che nuy Galeazo giongessemo, per modo che nuy gli ne restiamo per sempre obligati. Unde ad nuy serà molto grato, caro et acceptissimo che la M.tà Soa lo habia per recommendato in ogni suo facto et lo habia nel numero deli soi fideli et boni servitori, come sempre lo habiamo cognosciuto, et haveremo ad singulare gratia che per nostro respecto gli ne facia qualche bona demonstratione.[2]

Item, regratiarai appresso la M.tà Soa che per amore et intercessione nostra se sia dignata tore ad gratia el Spectabile D. Antonio da Romagnano, del che ne retrovamo molto contenti, et ne restiamo obligati alla Soa M.tà inseme cum le altre obligatione havemo cum essa grandamente, perché tutto quello ha facto verso esso D. Antonio reputamo haverlo facto verso nuy proprii, attento el beneficio recevuto per noi, come é informata la M.tà Soa dal dicto D. Antonio et dala casa soa; pregando essa Soa M.tà che etiandio per lo advenire ella se degni haverlo nel numero deli soi servitori, et ch'el sia ben tractato dali Ill. Mon.re Ducha et Madonna Duchessa de Savoya et operato nelli loro officii.[3]

Item, haverai singulare advertentia, che se per caso el te fosse domandata la instructione o per lo Consiglio o per altri dela M.tà del Re per legerla, che non se ne possa cavare copia né de tutta né parte per conditione alcuna del mondo, et questo per lo respecto che hay inteso a boccha.

Item, quando dirai quella parte che toccha el Marchese de Mantoa et la venuta dela Marchesana qui, te recorderai de dire ancora le parole che te havemo dicto a bocha, zoé che modestamente fece pur qualche mentione del parentato per soa figliola, anteponendo però sempre quello era el meglio per noi et per lo Stato nostro al facto suo et desiderio suo. Al che li fo resposto in modo che assai intese la dispositione nostra essere de exeguire quello era stato ordinato et fo ultima voluntà del S.re nostro consorte et patre.[4]

Item de visitare Filippo Mon.re et de le parole gli haverai ad dire a bocha del parentato con soa sorella, zoé che semo disposti de fare tutto

of Modena's man. Ascertain if the envoy was truly sent by the said Lord or not, since you are aware of the great excuses being made by His Lordship, and by Ugolotto de Facino[6] in his name, insisting that it will never be proven that the envoy is his man, nor that he sent him; adding that this man must be a trickster who, in order to extract money from Duke John or from others, has pretended to be sent and commissioned by the aforementioned Duke, as did Frosano,[7] and so on.

Postscript: You also will tell His Majesty that we are advised by way of our ambassador in Venice that the Venetians, being eager to know the state of affairs in France, have a few days ago sent an envoy with appropriate letters to the court of His Majesty. He is to be in touch with that friend you know of, with whom he seems to have an understanding, in order to be fully advised of matters over there.[8] The Venetians are widely broadcasting that His Majesty will never be in decent accord with my Lord of Charolais, who they say is taking the sister of the King of England as his wife. When they hear of some news unfavorable to His Majesty, they are most willing to repeat it, wishing as they do, through the great hatred they bear him, that he never have any peace but rather be always at war and in tribulation.

HISTORICAL NOTES

1. Presumably it is Aiguilles, located about 150 kilometers south of Susa. Apparently this request, which was eliminated both from the preceding instructions [doc. 36] and from this memorandum [see n.a], was not made or was expressed orally. In any case, no mention of it has been found in Pietro's dispatches, which will be published in next volume.

2. This general request of support for the Marquis of Monferrat is con-

quello serà de piacere et voluntà dela M.tà del S.re Re de Franza, et tanto in questo quanto in ogni altra cosa.

Item, quando seray dove serà la M.tà del Re, te sforzeray de investigare et informarte molto bene, et per la via de Zohampedro [*sic*] Panigarola et per ogni altra via, dela conditione de quello messo[5] che tene im [*sic*] presone el prefato S. Re, come homo del S. Duca de Modena, et chiarirte s'el dicto messo é homo veramente mandato dal dicto S.re o non, perchè tu say le grande scuse fa la S. Sua et cossì Ugolocto de Fazino[6] in suo nome, dicendo ch'el non se troverà may che sia suo homo né che la S. Sua l'habia mandato; et che indubitatamente crede questo homo debbia essere uno qualche ribaldo che, per cavare denari dal Duca Zohanne o d'altri, habia facto fictione de essere mandato et commissionato del dicto S.re, come fece Frosano[7], etc.

Post datum. Diray etiandio ala M.tà del Re come noy semo advisati per la via del nostro ambaxatore da Venexia che Venetiani, desiderosi molto de sentire come passano le cose de Franza, hanno mandato pochi dì fa uno loro messo cum littere in la Corte de Soa M.tà, el quale deve far capo con quello amico sapete, con lo quale pare habiano intelligentia, per essere a pieno advisati de quelle cose dellà.[8] Li quali molto divulgano che la M.tà Soa non serà may ben d'accordio con Mon.re de Ciarloys, el quale Mon.re dicono toglie per mogliera la sorella del Re de Ingliterra, et quando sentono una qualche novella desfavorevole ala M.tà Sua, la dicono molto volentieri, come quelli che per l'odio grande li portano, non vorrebeno havesse may bene, ma stessi sempre in guerra et tribulatione.

nected with his refusal to do homage to the Duke of Savoy. A month earlier both Savoy and Monferrat had sent envoys to Milan in an effort to solicit support for their respective positions [Marchioness Barbara to Lodovico Gonzaga, Milan, 21 April 1466, ASMA, *Lettere Originali dei Gonzaga*, B. 2099].

3. Three documents confirm once more Antonio di Romagnano's crucial role in the release of Galeazzo Maria in the Novalesa, and explain the Duke's

concern for him. The first is a dispatch by Giovanni Bianchi to the Duke [Lyon, 6 June 1466, BN, *Fonds Italien*, Cod. 1591, fol. 348], which relates that the Duke and Duchess of Savoy had intended to punish and destroy Antonio for his role, but had postponed taking action to a more propitious time, fearing to create suspicion about their complicity in the matter. The second consists of an undated memorandum (probably of late March 1466), presumably prepared by Antonio himself and addressed to the Milanese rulers, which lists the past services performed by the Romagnano for the Sforza, including Galeazzo Maria's release, and makes various requests for suitable concessions and privileges. [BN, ibid., Cod. 1591, fols. 323–24]. The third is an undated letter by Galeazzo Maria addressed to Louis XI, in which the Duke recounts Antonio's role in his liberation, and asks the King to accept him in his good graces [*Francia*, cart. 532, published by E. Colombo, *Iolanda, Duchessa di Savoia (1465–1478)*, in *Miscellanea di Storia Italiana*, 31 (1894): 220–21]. As a result of the Duke's intercession, the King wrote to Antonio, forgiving him for his part in the execution of Giacomo di Valperga [see Introduction, p. xliii], and asked the Duchess of Savoy to take him at her service [The King

to Antonio di Romagnano and to the Duchess of Savoy, Meung-sur-Loire, 18 April 1466, *Francia*, cart. 532; Vaesen, *Lettres*, 3:52–55]. The King's letter to Antonio was delivered by Emanuele de Iacopo on his return from France [Antonio di Romagnano to Giovanni Simonetta, Turin, 11 May 1466, *Savoia*, cart. 482].

4. Appendix, doc. VIII, n. 4.

5. Carlo de Corregio, who had been imprisoned by the King at the end of 1465 because of his pro-Angevin activity [Mandrot, *Dépêches*, 4:275]. Duke Borso d'Este's long-standing activity in support of the Angevin claims over Naples [ibid., 3:354–56] was being newly reported to the Dukes of Milan from various places [Battista and Gerolamo Spinola, Genoa, 12 April 1466, *Genova*, cart. 426; Agostino Rossi, Rome, 27 April 1466, *Roma*, cart. 59].

6. Ugolotto de Facino, ambassador of the Duke of Modena in Milan.

7. Presumably an earlier Ferrarese envoy in France [Cf. Mandrot, *Dépêches*, 3:354–56].

8. See Gerardo de' Colli to the Dukes, Venice, 27 May 1466, *Venezia*, cart. 353.

In my last letters[1] Your Lordships were informed of the misgivings the King had about the return [to Savoy] of my Lord Philip, and the decisions he had come to regarding the departure of Franceschino Nori. Thereafter, His Majesty wrote duplicate letters to Philip urging him to complete his mission there as quickly as possible, and to return here immediately after to take possession of the hundred lances he has given him, together with the other things he has granted him, because he needs him here. Therefore, he has dispatched Franceschino Nori, who left today, to go to Philip and help him in his embassy, so that he may return quickly. Depending upon how he finds Philip to have arranged things both for the marriage and for other matters regarding Your Lordships, he will perhaps come to Milan. But if he does not, he will write of what he learns, as he told me, and he will advise Your Excellencies of the King's excellent disposition toward you. He will also relate the kindly words His Majesty expressed at his departure to demonstrate and affirm the love he bears you, his firm intention and disposition to continue in the friendship undertaken, progressing from good to better.

In addition, His Majesty publicly declared and announced, in the presence of the Angevins, that if Duke John were to act against Your Excellencies, he would by necessity become his active enemy—for you supported His Majesty in adverse times and Duke John opposed him.

38·GIOVAN PIETRO PANIGAROLA *to the*

DUKE *and* DUCHESS OF MILAN

Francia, cart. 532. Orig.

Furono per le ultime[1] mie le Vostre Sig.rie avisate dil dubio haveva questo S. Re circha la ritornata de Filippo Monsignor, et de la deliberatione haveva facto de la partita di Franceschino Nori. Da poy la M.tà Soa per duplicate littere ha scritto ad esso Filippo che si spazi più presto che sii possibile di quanto ha a fare di là, ritornando subito di qua ad pigliare la posessione de le lanze cento gli ha dato, e così de le altre cosse che li intende di dare, et che qui de luy ha bisogno. Et così ha spazato Franceschino Nori, quale hogie hé partito. Se ne va dal dicto Filippo per aydare el suo spazamento, afine che ritorni presto, et sicondo che trovarà el p.to Filippo havere le cose disposite tanto dil parentato como altramente con le Vostre S., forsi vegnirà a Milanno, ma quando non vegna, scriverà quanto intenderà sicondo mi ha dicto. Et così avisarà esse V. Ex.tie de la bona et optima dispositione, et de le parole che a la partita soa questo Re li ha dicto in dimonstrare et dechiarare lo amore che porta a quelle, la bona soa intenzione et dispositione di volere tenere l'amore comenzato, et di perseverare di bene in meglio. Et così publice dice et predicha essa M.tà in presentia de li Angiovini, che si bene el Duca Iohanne fusse contra esse V. S., che saria forza la M.tà Soa li fosse et cum effecto li saria inimica, perché in le soe adversità voy la haveti servita et el Duca Iohanne la ha deservita, et li hé stato contrario. Ceterum el Marchexe di Monferrato ha mandato qui uno suo

The Marquis of Monferrat has sent here an ambassador, called Messer Guglielmo da Biandrà. I have not been able to ascertain the reason for his coming, nor has he yet had an audience [with the King]. I suspect that it has to do with the oath of fealty to [the Duke of] Savoy, or with some letters and secret promises that, as a friend tells me, were most surreptitiously made some time ago between His Majesty and the Marquis regarding this; but I have not been able to learn their tenor. So that for this reason, one cannot even learn the purpose of his mission. Your Excellencies will be advised of what I will learn later.

My Lord of Charolais's ambassador, who bore the letters Your Excellencies wrote to the Most Illustrious Duke of Burgundy and to My Lord of Charolais, has returned. On behalf of their Lordships he told me that these letters were most welcomed to them, especially since they intend to continue with Your Lordships that friendship they had established with the late [Lord Francesco Sforza], your husband and father of happy memory; they will shortly make response to these letters, sending one of their men to thank Your Lordships and express to you all that is necessary.

Madame of Orléans [Mary of Clèves] was here recently. The King cultivated and entertained her highly, I say highly indeed. The Duke of Bourbon and his brother [Pierre, Lord of Beaujeu] did likewise. At her departure I learned that she promised to turn Asti over to My Lord of Beaujeu, the Duke's brother, for the marriage of her daughter [Mary of Orléans] as was promised.[2] Since the girl is still only a child, I do not know if some other decision will be taken, but I will make every effort to stay alert in the matter. The other day I found myself in conversation with His Majesty, and I strove as best I could and with as much grace as was possible to persuade him along lines that Your Lordships last wrote me:[3] namely, to persevere in the original decisions and plans to which you think His Majesty also still adheres—to let you have Asti. His Majesty made a very succinct general answer to me, but not so that I could clearly understand that he had altered his original position. As soon as the proper moment presents itself, I will try to understand

ambassatore chiamato Misser Gulielmo da Biandrà. La casone de la venuta soa non ho potuto anche intendere né ancora ha auto audienzia. Dubito sia per la fidelità di Savoya, o per alchune littere et promesse secrete che uno amico mi ha dicto furono facte fra la p.ta M.tà et esso Marchese bon pezo fa molto secretamente circha ciò, et el tenore non ho potuto sapere. Si che per tal rispecto non si pò anche intendere la casone di la venuta di esso ambassatore. Di quello che più oltra intenderò, ne haverano le V. S. aviso.

Lo ambassatore de Monsignor Chyaroloes, che portò le littere che le V. Ex.tie scrisseno ad li Ill.mi Duca di Bergogna et Monsignor Chyaroloes, hé ritornato et per parte de le loro Signorie mi ha dicto che esse littere li sono state gratissime, maxime che intendeno di continuare con le V. S. quela amicitia che havevano con la felicissima memoria dil quondam vostro consorte et patre et che in breve farano risposta ad esse littere, mandando per uno suo ad ringratiare le Vostre S. et dirli quanto sarà necessario.

Madama de Orliens questi dì fo qui. Questo S. Re l'ha molto carezata et festezata, dico molto. El simile ha facto el Duca di Borbon et el fratello. Ad la partita soa ho inteso che ha promisso di dare Ast in le mane di Monsignor di Biogin, fratello di esso Duca, per el mariagio de la fiola, sicondo che li fo promisso.[2] Dapoy non intendo, essendo la fiola ancor zoveneta, se dia altramente forma ad tale materia, ala quale mi sforzo stare attento. Et ritrovandome l'altro giorno cum la M.tà Soa a ragionamento, me inzegnay persuaderli sicondo che ultimo V. S. mi hanno scritto,[3] quale perseverare in le prime conclusione et ragionamenti, in li quali penseno Soa M.tà etiam rimanere, che fo di farli havere Ast, dicendolo cum quelo migliore modo che mi parse in discurso di parlare. La p.ta M.tà me ne rispose in genere molto succintamente, ma non però che potesse intendere chiaro che sii rimosta da quelo primo proposito. Ma como prima mi ocorra el tempo, mi adaptarò intendere più oltra la mente de Soa M.tà, dandone statim particular aviso ad esse V. Ex.tie. Et questo farò, perché el Duca di Borbon et suo fratello cazano forte ad haverlo. A la partita di Franceschino, questo Re lo carichò ad farli subito

more deeply the King's mind in this, immediately giving special notification to Your Excellencies. I will do this because the Duke of Bourbon and his brother are seeking mightily to possess it [Asti].

As Franceschino [Nori] was leaving, the King charged him to procure for him quickly some silk material for two or three pairs of warm weather hose of the kind that the Most Illustrious Lord, your husband and father, used to wear—I had written[4] to His Excellency about this numerous times on His Majesty's behalf. So I gladly alert Your Lordship of this; if it seems fitting to you, you could have a courier bring material sufficient for two or three pairs, as I understand that a few days ago some was prepared in Milan to be sent here. I know that His Majesty would be most grateful to receive it now, in small rather than in large quantity.

Next, the magnificent Bailli of Lyons [François Royer] complained to His Majesty just the other day because, without repaying him the 1,200 florins that he had loaned, the castle and the supreme knighthood of Piedmont had been taken from him, which had previously been conceded to him for a set period of time by the Most Illustrious Duke and Duchess of Savoy. This was done by certain deputies of their Lordships, among whom it seems there was the Magnificent Lord Antonio di Romagnano. His Majesty, imagining that the said Lord Antonio was the instigator and prime mover in this because of his partisanship, and so forth, complained of it to me. He said that this was neither the undertaking nor the intention of which Your Lordships had written,[5] that Messer Antonio must serve His Majesty, and that he was pondering on going to the aid of the Bailli, who is his true and faithful servant.

I answered as seemed necessary, making excuses for Messer Antonio, telling [the King] that he would find in effect that Antonio, out of reverence for him, would attempt nothing that in any way could disturb the King's peace of mind or that of his servants. I said that he could be certain of this, adding that I could not believe that he had done such a thing, and His Majesty was sufficiently satisfied. I notify Your Lordships of this so that if they wish they may write [Messer Antonio] for his own

venire per doe o tre para di calze per questo caldo di quella saya che portava el p.to Ill.mo S. vostro consorte et patre, et de la quale più volte ne scrissi[4] ad Soa Ex.tia per parte de la M.tà Soa. Si che volontieri ne aviso V. S., aciò che parendoli possando volando per uno cavalaro mandarne per doe o III para, che ho inteso più dì fa a Milano fo facta per mandarglila. Et al presente mandandogline, cognosco la M.tà Soa lo haverà gratissimo, et per picola più tosto cha in grande quantitate.

Postremo l'altro giorno el Mag.co Baylì de Lione si dolse ad la prelibata M.tà che li era stato tolto el castello et offitio di Cavaler Magiore in Piemonti, altre volte concessoli per queli Ill.mi Duca e Duchessa di Savoya per certo tempo, senza restituirli fiorini mille ducento che li haveva prestato. Et questo per certi deputati da le loro Signorie, fra li quali pareva essere uno el Mag.co D. Antonio da Romagnano. Essa M.tà, imaginando che per la partialità, etc. dicto D. Antonio ne fosse inventore et principal casone, se ne dolse cum me, dicendo che questo non era el commenzamento né desyderio che V. S. li havevano scrito[5] che Misser Antonio prefato haveva di servire la M.tà Soa, et deliberava adiutare esso Baylì como suo vero et anticho servitore. Io li risposi quanto mi parse necessario, excusando esso Misser Antonio, el quale li dissi trovaria cum effecto che non atemptaria cosa che aliqualiter havesse a turbare la mente di Soa M.tà et per reverentia di quela soy servitori, et di questo ne fosse certa; né poteva io credere che quanto a luy ne fosse stato consentiente, in modo che essa M.tà ne restò assay satisfacta. El che notifico ad le V. S., aciò che parendogli gli possano scrivere, che per suo bene voglia ben tractare le cose del Baylì de Lione, che quando altramente fesse, daria disturbo et nocumento assay ad quanto V. Ex.tie hanno temptato in suo favore. Et così esso Baylì haverà caro et prega V. S., per le quale si confida el predicto D. Antonio farà assay gli ne scrivano, aciò habia casone di fare revocare quanto ha facto se ne ha casone, maxime che già la M.tà Soa ne ha scritto a quela Ill. Madama et a Filippo Monsignor; avisando le p.te V. S. che ogni favore et adiuto che fareti ad esso Baylì lo fariti ad uno, quale ho sempre cognoscuto di qua partesano et affectionato a le cose vostre, et dove ha cognoscuto cosa che aliqualiter habii

good, that he proceed carefully in his dealings with Bailli of Lyons, for if he were to do otherwise he would disturb and greatly upset all that Your Excellencies have attempted in his favor. The Bailli would be grateful, as he is confident that Lord Antonio would do precisely as Your Lordships write to him, bringing about the revocation of what he has been accused of having done. This is especially true, since His Majesty has already written to the illustrious Madam [of Savoy] and to My Lord Philip. I also wish to notify Your Excellencies that whatever favors and aid you extend to the Bailli, you extend to one whom I have always known as a partisan of yours here, and devoted to your interests.

Whenever he has come upon something that concerned the welfare, profit, and honor of Your Excellencies he has immediately notified me, ever zealous to serve you in whatever way he could. It would make the Bailli most unhappy, however, if, in order to protect his own interest, he were compelled to disturb the designs of Your Excellencies. Out of reverence for you, he says he would not want to do or say anything against Romagnano that would turn out badly; for his part, he will behave correctly with them when they do the same with him. So, on behalf of the Bailli, I alert Your Lordships, to whom I always commend myself.

HISTORICAL NOTES

1. Doc. 34.
2. See docs. 21, n. 3 and 31, n. 8.
3. Doc. 28.
4. See doc. 1.
5. See preceding doc. 37, n. 3.

concernuto bene, utile et honore di esse V. Ex.tie o altramente, subito me lo ha notifichato, et dove ha potuto et pò sforzassi con ogni studio servirle. Etiam saria mal contento esso Baylì, che per defensione de le rasone soe havesse a disturbare li dysegni de le V. S., per reverentia di le quale dice non voria fare né dire cossa contra li Romagnani che li havessero a tornare danno, et con loro dal canto suo si governarà bene quando loro fazano el simile con luy. Et così per parte di esso Baylì ne aviso esse V. S., ale quale sempre me ricommando.

As Your Excellencies will recall, this past November[1] I informed them that the King, having certain suspicions of the Count of Cominges, Marshall of France [Jean de Lescun], removed him from the royal presence and sent him to Bordeaux, where he was and is governor. The Marshall, like the sage individual he is, conducted himself in such manner that one can impute nothing to him, patiently living out this turn of fortune and persevering in the service of His Majesty, as he was inclined. From what I understand, there only remains to clear up the suspicion—they are saying that he is a partisan of his relative the Count of Armagnac [Jean V], who has formed a large army which he continues to augment, and with it he is scouring the countryside of Guyenne and Gascony where he has secret alliances. For this reason and also to ascertain the Marshall's position in this, His Majesty has written him, commanding that he immediately, fully armed and with numerous troops, ride for Guyenne and Gascony. Finding there any lord or nobleman ready for war or armed in any way, he is to subdue him, raze the fortresses to the ground, confiscate goods and personnel, without exception.

Moreover, as I wrote in other letters,[2] since His Majesty is most displeased with the Count of Armagnac and the Duke of Nemours [Jacques d'Armagnac], in order to keep them under control, he has stationed 300 lances in their country and now is sending 200 more,

39·GIOVAN PIETRO PANIGAROLA *to the*

DUKE *and* DUCHESS OF MILAN

Francia, cart. 532. Orig.

Como si debeno le Vostre Ex.tie recordare, questo novembre proximo passato[1] le avisay che questo S. Re, per certo suspecto haveva dil Conte di Comingia, Marescalcho di Franza, lo haveva da la M.tà Soa alongato un pocho et mandato ad Bordeos, dove era et hè Governatore. Esso Marescalcho pare che como savio se sii talmente governato che niente se li possi imputare, et patientemente ha passato et passa questa soa fortuna, perseverando in li servitii di essa M.tà como soleva. Resta solo, per quanto intendo, ad chiarire el dubio che dicono hè partesano dil Conte d'Armignac, dil quale hè parente, et essendo riferto ch'el p.to Conte d'Armignac ha facto grossa armata, et continue fa, et va scorrendo el payse di Giena et di Guascogna havendoli intelligentia secreta. Per dicto rispecto, etiam per cognoscere la volontà di esso Marescalcho, la p.ta M.tà li ha scrito che subito armata manu et cum multitudine di zente d'arme, cavalchi per Ghiena et Guascogna, et trovando signor alchuno o gentilhomo publice o secrete in poncto, o misossi in arme, che lo desfi, fazi spianare le forteze fino a piana terra confischando ad quela corpo et beni, rimosta ogni exceptione; et più, essendo essa M.tà como per altre[2] ho dicto, malissima contenta dil prelibato Conte d'Armignac et del Duca di Nemors, ha mandato a logiare in el payse loro lanze CCC, et hora gli ne manda ducento, fra li quali va el Conte Don Martino per tenerli in più subiectione. Ulterius questi dì ha facto fare publica crida

among whom will be the Count of Dammartin [Antoine de Chabannes]. Furthermore, several days ago he publicly announced and issued an edict[3] that, at the risk of grave punishment, all noblemen and francs archers of France arm themselves and be prepared by the fifteenth of this month to march against the English, who, it is said, are moving into Guyenne.

His Majesty is doing this either to keep the lords of the realm subjugated and fearful, or to see what aid he can expect from his subjects. Nevertheless, it is feared that he intends to undo the Count of Armagnac and the Duke of Nemours, who have vigorously opposed His Majesty—and he is angrier with them than with the others. I do not know what will come of this army, but it will certainly be very large; here they have mustered the archers and the King's guards, each day adding more men. If they set out on the march, Your Lordships will be notified.

The King and the English have concluded a truce for a period of twenty-two months, with four months notice for suspension; the Earl of Warwick [Richard Neville], in hopes of concluding perpetual truce,[4] is expected shortly at Calais. The Bishop of Langres [Guy Bernard] and the Bastard of Bourbon [Louis], ambassadors for this truce, have written of the negotiations mentioned above, and are returning. The Bastard of Bourbon, having been made Admiral, goes to take possession of the Norman lands assigned to him—the seaports, that is—and then he will return here.

It is confirmed that the marriage of King Edward of England's sister [Margaret, Duchess of York] to Don Pedro of Portugal has taken place. Nevertheless, I cannot certify it as true to Your Lordships. It has been written that for many reasons my Lord of Charolais refused her, especially because she is not of particularly noble blood on her mother's side, and also because she had already found a good match.[5]

The Grand Constable, Count of Saint-Pol, scheduled to come here at His Majesty's request, has in fact not come despite having written to the contrary many times. He has recently sent his excuses to the King, mentioning the question of Liège, with whom my Lord of Charo-

et commandamento,[3] che tuti li nobili et franchi arcieri di questo payse siano in arme et in poncto ad li XV dil presente sotto grosissime penne, per andare contra li Englexi, che dicono veneno a descendere in Ghiena. El che o fazi essa M.tà per tenere li Signori dil Reame in subiectione e timore, o per vedere como si adiutarà de li soy subditi. Nientedimancho si dubita sarà per desfare li p.ti Conte d'Armignac et Duca di Nemors, che sono stati molto contrarii ad la M.tà Soa, et de li quali essa si dole più cha deli altri. Non so quello seguirà de questa armata perchè sarà grossa, et qui si sono etiam facte le monstre de li archieri et gente d'arme de la guardia de soa persona, facendosene ogni dì de altre gente; sicondo prenderano camino, ne sarano le V. S. avisate, ad le quale notifico fra questo S. Re et Englexi essere concluso tregua per spatio di mesi XXII cum mexi IIII di contrabando, et in breve debe ritornare a Cales el Conte de Vervic sperandose per concludere tregue perpetue.[4] El Vescoco di Langres et Bastardo de Borbon, ambassatori per queste tregue, havendo scritto de le cose di sopra agitate, se ne ritorneno, et esso Bastardo essendo facto Armiraglio, va ad pigliare la posessione de le terre di Normandia sottoposite al offitio suo, cioè porti de mare, et poy vegnirà qui. El mariagio de la sorella dil Re Odoardo de Inglitera si conferma essere facto a Don Pietro di Portogallo, peranche tamen io non lo certifico ale V. S.; et per molti rispecti hè stato scritto Mons.re Chyaroloes haverla refutata, maxime per non essere de matre tropo nobile, et per havere già facto bona compagnia.[5] El Conte di Sanpolo, Grande Connestabile, dovendo vegnire qui domandato da la prelibata M.tà, peranche non hè venuto, quamvis più volte havesse scritto l'opposito. De presente si ha mandato ad excusare ad quella, che per questo facto di Legiesi, con li quali Mons.re Chyaroloes fa guera, non si pò partire, che bisogna sii lì cum le gente d'arme, ma factoli fine che vegnirà. La quale excusatione fa ad essa M.tà suspicarre di molte cose, et così ad altri che intendeno che dubiti di vegnire.[6]

Essendo publicata voce in questo payse circumstante, che ogniuno como ho dicto si metta in arme, batando Mons.re Chyaroloes ha mandato qui Ghio de Ussi[7] da questo S. Re, dubitando non convochi questa armata

lais is at war, so that he cannot leave, as he must remain with the troops
—adding that he will come as soon as all that is over. This excuse causes
His Majesty and others to suspect many things, including his fear
to come.[6]

The call to arms having gone into the countryside here, as I said,
and fearing that His Majesty has assembled his army to make war
against him, take Picardy from him, and thwart his plans, My Lord of
Charolais sent Guiot d'Usie[7] to the King in order to say that Charolais
was willing and happy to marry His Majesty's daughter [Anne] as he
had promised.[8] He asked to know the reasons for preparing and assembling such an army. His Majesty's answer to this embassy was a laugh,
and he has made practically no other reply. From what I hear, the Burgundians are quite fearful that the King may attack them and make war
on them; for their part, they are already taking countermeasures. The
Seneschal of Guyenne [Antoine de Castelnau] is still a prisoner, and each
day some of his servants and gentlemen are tortured with the rope.
Even though it is not certain as yet, from what I have heard His Majesty
say, I understand that there is some secret plot, which makes me suspect
that it will all come to a not so happy end.[9]

Regarding recent news received by the King, the King of Aragon
[John II] is making headway: he has gained certain villages and lands
of modest size around Barcelona, about ten or twelve in number. Within
the present month he hopes to have Tortosa,[10] and once that is accomplished, he writes that nothing stands between him and the gates
of Barcelona. He reports that he is strong both on land and sea, and finds
his enemy weak. He awaits Your Excellencies' ship, which will give him
strong support, and thereby hopes soon to regain Barcelona.

My Lord of Charolais has intervened with great pressure on the
King, to prevent him from giving aid, favor, and succor to the King
of Aragon. Rather, with great fervor, he entreats His Majesty to abandon that alliance and adhere to the aforementioned Don Pedro: he caused
a great deal to be said in order to arrive at this end. His Majesty responded conclusively that he will not abandon the King of Aragon, nor

per farli guerra, torli Picardia et rompere li soy disegni, dicendo che sta in proposito et hè contento di tore la fiola de la M.tà Soa como ha promisso,[8] et manda ad sapere la casone di metere in poncto et congregare questa armata. Dela quale ambassata essa M.tà si ne hè riso, et peranche non li ha facto altra risposta; ma per quanto intendo, dicti Bergognoni hanno auto paura che sii per corere sopra di loro et farli guera, et già comenzavano dal canto loro a provedersi. El Senescalcho di Ghiena ancora hè prisoniero, ogni dì hè dato de la corda ad alchuni soy servitori et gentilhomeni; pure anche non si ragiona di cosa alchuna certa, ma per quanto ho odito parlare essa M.tà, comprendo esserli certa trama secreta che mi fa dubitare la fine non sarà tropo bona.[9]

Per le nove che di presente ha auto questo S. Re, el Re d'Aragona prospera li progressi soy. Ha guadagnato certe ville et terre non tropo grosse intorno a Barzalona numero da X in XII. Per tuto el presente mese spera havere Tortosa,[10] et havuto quela, scrive havere nullo obstaculo fino ale porte di Barzalona, trovarsi forte in campo et per mare, et aspectare la nave dele V. Ex.tie, che li darà grande adiuto, et lo inimico suo fievole, in modo che spera presto recuperarà dicta Barzalona. Monsignor Chyaroloes ha facto fare grande instantia et opera ad questo S. Re, che non li voglia dare adiuto, favore nè socorso alchuno, ma prega la M.tà Soa cum grande fervore ad lassare quella ligha et adherire al p.to Don Pietro, havendo facto dire molte efficace parole per vegnire ad questo effecto. Conclusive la M.tà Soa ha risposto non abandonarà el Re d'Aragona, nè cum honore suo poterse ritrare nè desviare da la ligha nè promesse fra loro facte, le quale vole et intende observare, confortando Mons.re Chyaroloes ad non dare favore ad esso Don Pietro. Et poy ha dicto al ambassatore[11] dil p.to Re d'Aragon, che li pareria che esso Re mandasse da Mons.re Chyaroloes ad stringerlo et coniurarlo per l'Ordine di Bergogna et sacramento dela Tosone che portano comune ad essi doy, che nullo pacto volesse dare favore a Don Pietro suo inimico, ma per li capituli di esso Ordine adiutarlo. Et già intendo sarà qui presto uno di quelli dil prelibato Re d'Aragon, che andarà per dicta casone in Bergogna.

El Conte di Foys hè in Navarra, et pare ch'el Grande Connestabile

could he with honor withdraw or deviate from the alliance and promises between them, which he wishes and intends to observe. He counseled
My Lord Charolais not to favor Don Pedro. Then His Majesty told the
King of Aragon's ambassador[11] that it would seem to him wise if that
monarch were to dispatch someone to My Lord of Charolais, to press
and conjure him, by the Order of Burgundy and the sacrament of the
Toison [d'Or], common to them both, that he form no pact in favor of
Don Pedro, his enemy, but rather come to Aragon's aid according to
the provisions of that Order. And I understand that one of the King of
Aragon's men will be here soon, and will go to Burgundy for that very
task.

The Count of Foix [Gaston IV] is in Navarre, where the Grand
Constable, it seems, has placed in his hands certain castles and even his
own person, if he accepted a certain agreement offered to him by the
King, as is being said: namely giving him a pension and twenty thousand écus—which was proposed some time ago in line with His Majesty's
intention of reaching an understanding with the King of Castile [Henry
IV].[12] Now the Count of Foix has sent request that this accord be observed, since he has put into effect his part of the agreement. At present
no conclusion or action has been taken, because, as I wrote Your Excellencies at other times, the King is not well pleased with him.

The Duke of Bourbon [Jean II] will leave shortly to go see his
wife [Jeanne of France], with whom he will stay a few days and then
return. The Duke's influence grows each day with His Majesty and with
the Court. As far as can be gathered, he shows a friendly and partisan
attitude toward Your Excellencies; saying that he wishes to do everything possible for you, he has declared his support with a thousand
kindly words. In the course of these conversations, since he likes warlike pursuits and the hunt above all else, he entreated that you deign
to provide him with a fine steed and a set of horse armor, repeating to
me numerous times that you could neither give him anything more de-
sirable nor make him a finer present. Having made to him a suitable and
seemly response, I notify Your Lordships so that you will provide as best

di là li habii rimesso certe castelle et la persona soa in le mane acceptando certo acordo, che dicono li offerse questo S. Re, cioè di darli certa pensione et scudi XX.M., et questo fo già bon pezo, intendendo la M.tà Soa havere intelligentia cum el Re di Castiglia.[12] Hora el Conte di Foys ha mandato a domandare dicto acordo sii observato, poychè lo effecto de la domanda hè seguito; per anche non li hè stato facto conclusione nè spazamento alchuno, perchè como altre volte scrissi ad le Vostre Ex.tie, questo Re di luy non hè bene contento.

El Duca di Borbon in breve partirà per andare a vedere Madama di Borbon, soa consorte, con la quale starà qualche pochi dì, et poy ritornarà. El p.to Duca ogni giorno cresce in auctorità con la prelibata M.tà et questa Corte, et per quanto si pò comprehendere, si monstra amico et partesano de le V. Ex.tie, dicendo volere fare per quelle quanto li sia possibile. Et a me ha dicto mille bone parole, tra le quale prega quelle si degneno, perchè ama cosse di guera et di caza più cha altra cosa, provederli de uno bono corsero et uno payro di barde, che non li potriano donare cosa più grata nè farli magiore piacere, et questo più volte me ha replicato; al che, havendoli facto quella risposta mi hè parso conveniente, ne aviso le V. S. aciò che li provedano como meglio li parirà.

Ceterum in camera di questo S. Re hè uno secretario zoveneto, nutrito con luy et fidatissimo, et de chi molto la M.tà Soa se ayuta, chiamato Metre Loyse Touten,[13] el quale in le cose de la felicissima memoria dil quondam S. vostro consorte et patre et de Vostre Cel., continue se li hè monstrato et governato cum grande amore, diligentia et affectione. Et perchè di luy la p.ta M.tà si vale assay, ha auto a fare più spazamenti di littere et altre cosse, in le quale se li hè molto bene governato, ricordo fidelmente ale V. S. scriverli una bona littera, perchè non pò cha giovare et servire, essendo continue como hè in la camera di essa M.tà ale cosse de le prelibate Vostre Signorie, ale quale sempre me ricomando.

seems fit. Also, there is a young most trustworthy secretary, who is quartered in the king's own chambers, by name Master Louis Toustain,[13] of whom His Majesty frequently avails himself. He has comported and governed himself with great love, diligence, and affection in the affairs of both the late Lord, your husband and father of happy memory, and of Your Excellencies themselves. Since His Majesty employs him frequently, he has had to dispatch many letters and other matters, in which he has conducted himself very well. I faithfully remind Your Lordships to write him a kind letter, for it can serve and do nothing but good, being that he is constantly in the King's chambers and attending to the affairs of Your Lordships, to whom I always commend myself.

HISTORICAL NOTES

1. See the dispatch of Panigarola and Cristoforo da Bollate to the Duke of Milan, Orléans, 29 November 1465, Mandrot, *Dépêches*, 4:123, n. 1.

2. Doc. 31. Cf. Vaesen, *Lettres*, 3:62–63.

3. The edict was published in Paris on 24 May [Calmette-Périnelle, *Louis XI*, p. 73].

4. The Franco-English truce was also concluded on 24 May, to take effect on land on 15 June and at sea on 15 July. It was due to expire on 1 March 1468. During the truce the plenipotentiaries for both parties were to meet at Dieppe to negotiate a permanent peace [ibid., p. 73].

5. This report is false both with respect to Don Pedro and the Count of Charolais [See doc. 27, n. 4].

6. Louis de Luxembourg, Count of Saint-Pol, had taken part in the Battle of Montlhéry at the service of Burgundy against the King. On 12 October 1465, Louis XI appointed him Constable of France as a gesture of conciliation

[Mandrot, *Dépêches*, 4:10–11]. This report again demonstrates the fragility of that conciliation.

7. Guiot d'Usie, Lord of Vaudrey and equerry of the Count of Charolais, had been a frequent envoy of Burgundy to Louis XI, but later in 1466 he passed to the service of the King [ibid., 4:178, n. 1].

8. See doc. 4, n. 4.

9. See doc. 30, n. 11.

10. Tortosa lies about 150 kilometers southwest of Barcelona. It was captured by John II of Aragon in August 1466 [Calmette, *Louis XI, Jean II,* p. 263, n. 8].

11. Pere Forner [Joseph Calmette, *La question des Pyrénées et la Marche d'Espagne au Moyen-Âge* (Paris: Janin, 1947), p. 143].

12. For these negotiations with the Count of Foix, in process since the preceding year, see Courteault, *Gaston IV,* pp. 297–304.

13. His countersignature appears on a great number of royal letters from 1461 to 1486 [Vaesen, *Lettres,* 3:103–4, n. 1].

A few days ago my man delivered five letters from Your Lordships, to which I had made a partial response in my last communications, so that for the rest I will make supplementary reply as seems necessary. I sought out the King immediately after I received them, and so I presented him with a letter in Your Excellency's own hand,[1] which was most pleasing to him. Having read it completely through, with great show of appreciation, he said that the next day he would speak to me, since at that moment he was quite busy.

Finding myself with His Majesty the other day, I thanked him, insofar as I could, on behalf of Your Excellencies for the generous offers and cordial show of support that His Majesty had given and continued to give in your affairs, having treated them as if they were his very own. I thanked him also for the esteem and honor he had bestowed upon you in sending his ambassadors there, and so forth; which so multiplied the debt of Your Lordships that you considered yourselves unable to render worthy retribution—elaborating on this with the best, sweetest, and most grateful expressions at my command. His Majesty replied that such thanks were not needed, because he felt himself so obligated that he was bound to exhibit and put into effect much more than he would ever be able to, in return for the infinite benefits received from the late Lord, your husband and father of happy memory, and then from Your

40·GIOVAN PIETRO PANIGAROLA *to the*

DUKE *and* DUCHESS OF MILAN

Francia, cart. 532. Orig.

Ho recepute questi dì cinque littere da le Vostre Sig.rie per lo homo mio, a le quale havendo per le ultime mie facto risposta in parte, per queste suplirò al resto dove mi pare bisognare risposta. Me ritrovay cum questo S. Re statim aute quelle, et li presentay la littera scritta di propria mano de la V. Ex.tia,[1] la quale li fo molto carissima, et havendola cum grande dimonstratione di haverla auta grata, lecta tuto al longho, disse el sequente giorno parlaria cum mi, che per alhora era molto occupatto.

L'altro giorno ritrovandomi cum la M.tà Soa, la ringratiay per parte de le Vostre Ex.tie, quanto mi fo possibille, de le grande offerte et cordiale dimonstratione che Soa M.tà haveva facto et faceva ad le cose vostre, havendole per riccomandate come soe proprie, et così de la reputazione et honore vi haveva datto in mandare li ambassatori soy di là etc., per il che acrescevano tanto obligo ad esse V. S. che si vedevano inhabile ad renderli condigne gratie, extendendomi cum quele migliore, dolce et grate parolle che mi fo possibile. La M.tà Soa mi rispose non bisognare tale gratie, perché si sentiva talmente obligata, che era tenuta ad fare dimonstrare cum effecti molto et assay più, che non poteria né saperia fare per li infiniti benefitii receputi da la felicissima memoria dil quondam S. vostro consorte et patre; dil quale, dicendo queste parole, stete alquanto sopra di sè et cambiose di colore, et poy da le V.S. Et se non haveva fino qui facto quele opere et effecti tuti, che saria tenuto o

Lordships—saying this for a piece, he became pensive and pale. He added that if up to now he had not been able to do all he ought, or rather felt in his very heart he should do, he hopes Your Excellencies will excuse him, pointing to the many serious preoccupations he continues to have about the lords of the realm, whom he has not as yet put in their proper place. Nevertheless, he feels that the realm is in reasonably good order, and he hopes that within the year he will be in complete control of it, whereby His Majesty will then be better able to show his own mind. He assures Your Highnesses that he will spare nothing in the interest of preserving your state, since you have already done the same for His Majesty; with many kind and humane words, he exhibited his displeasure with not having been able to do more.

It above all pleases His Majesty that the Genoese persevere in their devotion, loyalty, and obedience, even though the Angevins here make many allegations to the contrary. He is also well pleased with the Archbishop's having turned back and taken refuge in the territory of the Duke of Modena, for the King says that it is all work of the Venetians and he will finish badly. The King took especial great pleasure in the provisions made and in the coming of the lords in support and defense of our state, which I explained to him at length. He took particular interest in the show of good conduct on the part of Lord Alessandro [Sforza], the Count of Urbino, and of Lord Roberto of Sanseverino, whom in His Majesty's opinion Your Lordships ought to cultivate and treat well, so that as relatives and friends one may place faith in them and make use of them in time of need. He added that it seemed to him that up to now worthy and excellent remedies had been taken, so that your ship of state had reached a safe port, and he hoped your affairs would proceed from good to better. Taking off his cap and hat as is his custom, he prayed God for His grace, asking to receive the good news for which he hopes; again, he offered his services to you, as mentioned above.

I already knew something of King Ferrante's public show of support for you, but Your Lordships' last letters brought me completely up to

l'animo de la M.tà Soa richiederia, vogliano V. Ex.tie haverla per excusata, atribuendola ad molte et grande occupatione che continue ha de
li Signori dil Regno, et per non havere quelle dil tuto ben stabilito;
pure per hora esso Regno stare assay bene, ma questo anno sperare dil
tuto assicurarsi, dove potrà molto più poy monstrare l'animo suo. Certificando V. Cel. che per conservatione di quelle non li sparagnarà cosa
alchuna, havendo già quelle facto el simile per essa Soa M.tà, cum molte
bone et humane parole, dimonstrando havere despiacere che più non
habii potuto fare.

Piacie insuper molto ad la M.tà Soa che Genovesi persevereno in
bona devotione, fede et obedientia, quamvis per questi Angiovini fossero
allegate molte cosse al opposito. Così etiam del Arcivescovo tornatto
indrieto et redutosi in quello dil Duca di Modena, molto li piacie, dicendo
che farà la mala fine, et che tuta hé practicha de Venetiani. Et de le altre
provisione et Signori venuti al favore et conservatione dil Stato vostro, li
quali ad longum li explicay, ha auto grandissimo piacere, maxime dil
bon governo et dimostratione che hanno facto el S. Alexandro, Conte
de Urbino et Signor Roberto di Sanseverino; li quali, dice essa M.tà,
parerli le V. S. habiano ad carezare et bene tractare, adciò che como de
soy parenti et amici ne posseno prendere ogni fede, et in li bisogni valersi
di loro. Disse etiam fino qui parerli essere facto digni et optimi remedii,
et le cosse vostre collocate in bon porto et sperare quele procedere di bene
in meglio, cavandosi el boneto et el capello, pregando Dio a modo usatto
di la Soa M.tà, che li conceda questa gratia, et li mandi bone novele,
como spera, offerendose ut supra.

De le demonstratione ha facto el Ser.mo S. Re Ferando in favore vostro, de le quale parte ne hera informato, ma per le ultime de le V. S.
molto amplamente ne sono avisato, havendole tute facto intendere ad
essa M.tà particularmente, rispose quella piacerli molto; et el p.to Re
Ferando havere facto cosa digna da Re, et sicondo che hé obligatto,
monstrando al bisogno essere cognoscente de li servitii receputi, et anche
essendo vicino como hé, confortando esso Re Ferando ad perseverare in
questo proposito, como etiam ha dicto al ambassatore[2] suo qui, perché

date, and I have discussed their contents with His Majesty in detail. He said that he was well pleased and that King Ferrante had behaved in a truly kingly manner, showing in time of need his appreciation for services received, both because he is obligated to do so and also because of his proximity. He has urged King Ferrante to continue in such a manner, adding that for his part His Majesty intends to do likewise and not be lacking to you in any way, as he also informed his ambassador[2] here.

Thereafter, being at table with His Majesty the other day, and speaking of Italian affairs in the presence of many lords, among them Angevins, I openly related King Ferrante's show of support and his honorable comportment. Although this displeased many, I believe that in his heart His Majesty took pleasure in it, for from time to time he would pretend to ask me for information as if he had never heard of it—despite his previous knowledge.

I gave the King to understand everything about the maneuvers of the Venetians—even though they say they wish to be good neighbors—and everything about Bartolomeo Colleoni's request which the Magnificent Pietro da Pusterla, your counselor, is making on his behalf. His Majesty laughed at this, concurring in Your Lordships' opinion that Bartolomeo would never attempt this on his own, but that it is all the doing of the Venetians, who search out these subtleties in order to terrorize your subjects and incite some of them to revolt. Using this as a starting point and as a way of gaining time, they first expect trouble to arise either from your territory or from elsewhere in order to provoke a war. The King said that in his opinion *these villainous Venetians ought to have some day so much on their hands that they would not know how to extricate themselves, in order to curb their overweening pride. His Majesty has a good mind to drive them into the sea because they are so anxious to gobble up their neighbors, never returning anything once they have taken it. Once his own realm is in order, he would most willingly help do this, for over here he has got the worst possible impression of the Venetians in the world, detesting them heartily.*

His Majesty concludes, however, that since your subjects are peace-

la M.tà Soa intende di fare così, et dal canto suo non li manchare in cosa alchuna. Poy, essendo l'altro giorno a tavola essa M.tà et parlandomi de le cosse de Italia, presente molti Signori et Angiovini, publice recontay le demonstratione facte per el p.to Re Ferando, et quanto dignamente se li hera operato. El che, quamvis a molti despiacesse, credo in l'animo suo essa M.tà ne havesse piacere, perché di parte in parte monstrava informarsi da me como se may non ne havesse odito parlare, et già lo sapeva.

De le demonstratione che fanno Venetiani, quamvis dicano volere ben vicinare, et così de la domanda fa fare Bartolameo Collione per mezo dil Mag.co Piero da Pusterla, vostro Consigliero, quale li feci tuta intendere, la M.tà Soa se ne risse, concorendo in la opinione de le V. S. che da luy esso Bartolameo non la faria, ma che siano practiche di Venetiani, che vanno cerchando queste subtilitate per dare terrore ali subditi vostri et dare materia ad qualche terra di ribellarsi, per potere poi commenzare guerra cum questo principio, et che così vadano dilatando tempo, expectando che da altrove o in le vostre terre commenzasse differentia. Et dice parerli *che essi vilani Venetiani per la loro superbia debiano havere una volta tanto da fare che non saperano como scrimirse, et havere la M.tà Soa grande desiderio de cazarli ad la marina, perchè voleno mangiare li soi vicini, et cosa che una volta pigliano may non restituisseno, al che fare adiutaria volontieri, stabillito questo suo Regno; et qui de essi Venetiani ha quelo malo concepto che se possi havere de homini del mondo, havendoli molto ad pecto.* Conclude però essa M.tà che, essendo li populi de le V. S. in pace et quiete, et non havendo fino qui loro, nè terra vostra facto novità alchuna, dicti Venetiani debiano bene avisare el facto loro né così presto farvi guerra, havendo presertim el Turcho da l'altro canto. Ma pure quando rompano guera, dice essa M.tà dal canto suo farà ad le Vostre Ex.tie ogni adiuto et favore possibille, non manchandoli in cosa alchuna che ley possa. Et el vostro stare proveduto et in arme, per ogni rispecto molto li piacie et lo collauda.

Quanto etiam le V. S. mi scriveno sopra el facto dil Turcho, ho monstrato et lecto ad questo S. Re, de verbo ad verbum. Lo quale ha poy

ful and quiet, and no one has made any hostile move, the Venetians must indeed reconsider their position and not be quick to wage war on you, especially since they have the Turks at their back. All the same, if they were to declare war, His Majesty says that he would for his part extend all help and support possible to Your Excellencies, and not be lacking insofar as he can. He commends the fact that you are keeping your state armed and ever ready, which pleases him in every respect.

To His Majesty I have shown and read word for word what Your Lordships wrote me about the Turks. He then requested that I read all this at table in the presence of many lords, and he spread the news throughout the court, it pleasing him exceedingly that the Venetians are threatened from another quarter, so that they cannot disturb Your Excellencies. He [goes so far as] to say that if the Turk were to pour a spoonful of water on his head professing, "I am a Christian," he would help him and go to his aid against the Venetians. Were it not out of respect for the faith, he declares that now would be the time for Your Excellencies, King Ferrante, and the Florentines to make league with the Turks against the Venetians and completely undo them. In a similar manner, he is glad that the Venetians are not exactly friendly with the Pope. If anything else develops, His Majesty would consider it a favor to be kept constantly informed.

I made excuses for Your Excellencies' tardiness in writing, according to the reasons you had elaborated in your letters. Becoming pensive upon learning this, His Majesty considered it reasonable and said that it had been the correct thing to do.

On the matter of the marriage contract with Savoy, His Majesty is quite satisfied that Your Lordship adhere to the agreement and take his sister-in-law. He anxiously awaits the magnificent Pietro da Gallarate, as mentioned in your letters, so that all can be correctly managed and the marriage concluded. He very much desires this matrimony, and he counsels it to Your Lordship. *He added, however, that if your marriage to My Lord of Charolais's [daughter] could have been arranged, he would have urged you to contract it, but now such ne-*

voluto lo habii etiam lecto a la tavola, presenti molti Signori, et ha pub-
licta per tuta la Corte questa tale novella, piacendoli molto che Venetiani
siano urtati da altro canto, in modo che non diano disturbo ad le Vostre
Ex.tie. Et s'el Turcho volesse tore uno cuchiaro di aqua sopra la testa,
dicendo, "io sono Chrystiano," dice lo adiutaria et si voria adiutarlo contra Venetiani. Et se non fusse per la fede, dice saria al presente tempo
che Vostre Ex.tie, Re Ferando et Fiorentini festino ligha con el Turcho
contro Venetiani et dil tuto disfarli. Così etiam li piacie che non siano
bene amici dil Papa. Et se altro sarà dapoy seguito, haverà caro la M.tà
Soa esserne continue avissata.

Excusay etiam la tardatione di scrivere de le V. Ex.tie essere stata
per la casone, che in esse vostre littere si contiene. Le quale intese,
rimase la M.tà Soa tacita et contenta, dicendo che hé stato bene a così
fare.

Circha el facto dil parentato di Savoya, la M.tà Soa resta contenta
et satisfacta che la S. V. resti in proposito di tuore soa cognata; et cum
desyderio aspecta el Magnifico Piero da Gallarà, como in le vostre littere
si contiene, ad ciò che a tuto si possi dare bona forma et dil tuto concludere esso parentato, quale assay desydera, consigliandolo ad essa
Vostra Signoria. *Ben dice, che quando quelo de Mons. de Chiarloys
havesse potuto havere loco, che lo haveria sempre consigliato, ma hora
sono cose longhe et el fine non si sa anchora quale sarebe. Al che, rispondendo io che la M.tà Soa li metesse silentio per le ragione che ne
scriveno le S. Vostre, mi disse parerli che quele pigliavano bon camino,
et quanto più presto se venisse al efecto tanto meglio.*

De la Ill. Madona Marchesana di Mantoa stata a Milanno, et del
S. Marchese conduto ad li servitii del S. Re Ferando et vostro, imitando
el consiglio di la M.tà Soa più volte dicto al Magnifico D. Albrico, essendo luy qui, li piace molto tale acordo; et persevera in quelo primo
consiglio, parendoli che meglio stia esso Marchese a li servitii de la V.
Cel. cha de altri per ogni rispecto. Et ad conservarlo in questo fino che
almancho le cose vostre siano stabilite, conforta et lauda molto la p.ta
Soa M.tà.

gotiations would be lengthy and their outcome uncertain. When I responded that His Majesty could forget all of that since Your Lordships had expressed their viewpoint in writing, he answered that in his opinion you have chosen the right way, and the sooner it was done the better.

[We discussed] the Illustrious Marchioness of Mantua's visit to Milan, and the King is quite pleased that the Marquis has contracted to serve King Ferrante and you, in accordance with His Majesty's advice repeatedly given through the Magnificent Lord Alberico when he was here. He renews that advice, for in his opinion it is better in all respects that the Marquis be in Your Highness's service than in that of others. His Majesty urges and highly recommends that you keep him so engaged, at least until your affairs are settled.

At all occasions whenever and to whatever extent possible I have commended Your Excellencies, your state, children, and brothers to His Majesty, for in him you have placed your every hope; in the future I will do likewise when the occasion presents itself.

As you will have learned from Emanuele de Iacopo, one of the Cardinal of Pavia's men was here regarding the Abbey near Avignon, about which Your Lordships gave me strict orders. Before his arrival, having been informed of the matter from the beginning and being apprehensive, I had spoken of this to the King in order to safeguard Your Excellencies' honor. His Majesty assured me that he had no intention of revoking anything that had been done out of respect for your husband and father of happy memory, and for Your Lordships. Thus, he has rescinded his revocation and has ordered that the Cardinal be reinstated with no further discussion. His Majesty told the Duke of Bourbon, who was pursuing the matter with his every cunning, that he should on no account meddle any further, for anything the King had done or might do during his lifetime at the behest of Your Excellencies was never to be undone. Therefore the Cardinal has Your Lordships to thank, for it is out of respect for you that all was expedited, despite great opposition.[3]

Regarding Giovanni Boydo and Gianelo dal Castellazo, who are

Continue etiam, tanto stretamente quanto mi hé stato possibile, ho riccomandato le V. Ex.tie, loro Stato, fioli et frateli ad la M.tà Soa, in la quale hanno quelle collocata ogni soa speranza, et per l'avenire quando achada farò el simile.

Del Abbatia apreso di Avignone dil R.mo Monsignor el Cardinale di Pavia, la quale le V. S. tanto stretamente me ricomandano, dico che como da Emanuel de Iacop haverano inteso, fu qui uno di quelli dil p.to Cardinale per essa casone, et ananzi ch'el venisse, havendone io che dal principio ne sono informato, presentito non so che parlato cum questo S. Re per honore de le Vostre Ex.tie, la M.tà Soa mi disse che non intendeva cosa havesse facto ad contemplatione de la felicissima memoria dil quondam S. vostro consorte et patre et vostra aliqualiter fusse revocata; et così tuto concesso al opposito ha facto revocare, et mandato che esso Cardinale sii rimeso in posessione, ponendo a tuto silentio. Et al Duca di Borbon, quale cazava questa cossa cum ogni ingegno, la M.tà Soa li disse che nullo pacto se ne impachiasse più oltra, perché cosa che havesse facto o facesse ala riquesta de le Vostre Ex.tie in soa vita, may non intendeva fosse revocata. Dil che el p.to Cardinale ne ha ad ringratiare esse V. S. che per loro reverentia, quamvis de gli opositi li fusse assay, el tuto hé stato expedito.[3]

De Iohanne Boydo et de Gianelo dal Castellazo, prisonieri in Ast, più dì fa scrissi che la Ill. Madama de Orliens, a contemplatione di questo S. Re, era stata contenta di farli rillassare, e così commise al Governator de Ast quando partì de qui. Resta solo che cum esso Governatore si solliciti, perché li farà rillassare, et così mi mandò a dire quando partì che faria infallanter.[4]

De Villagio che roba quanto trova, vederò la provisione che la p.ta M.tà mi ha dicto di fare, et per el primo la mandarò a le prelibate Vostre Ex.tie, ale quale sempre mi ricommando.

prisoners at Asti, I wrote a few days ago that the Illustrious Madam of Orléans out of respect for His Majesty saw fit to set them free and so instructed the Governor of Asti when she left here. There only remains to expedite the matter with the Governor, which, as she was leaving, she said she would do without fail.[4]

Regarding [Jean de] Village, who steals all he comes upon, I will look to the measures His Majesty told me to take, as soon as possible explaining them to Your Excellencies, to whom I always commend myself.

HISTORICAL NOTES

1. Appendix, doc. IX. For the other four letters written by the Dukes, see docs. 22–25.

2. Garcia Betes.

3. Shortly before his death (15 August 1464), Pius II had assigned the Benedictine monastery of St. Andrew near Avignon in benefice to his confidant, Cardinal Iacopo Ammannati-Piccolomini (1422–1479). When local opposition prevented his taking possession of the benefice, the Cardinal obtained, in April of the following year, empowering letters from Louis XI through the intervention of Francesco Sforza and his ambassador, Alberico Maletta [Mandrot, *Dépêches*, 3:125–26]. Apparently forgetful of this concession, the King made the same commitment to another candidate, who was backed by the Duke of Bourbon. Although this dispatch states that the King revoked the

second concession and confirmed the first, the Cardinal was never able to obtain possession of the monastery, owing to royal opposition which developed in the following months [Giuseppe Calamari, *Il confidente di Pio II. Card. Iacopo Ammannati-Piccolomini (1422–1479)*, vol. 2 (Rome–Milan: Augustea 1932), pp. 293–97].

4. Giovanni Boido and Janello de Castellazo, two Milanese subjects, had been arrested earlier for plotting in Asti against the government of the Duchess of Orleans. Francesco Sforza had intervened with Louis XI to have them released. Now the Dukes pledged that they would no longer be a threat to the Orleans if they were released [The Dukes to Regnault de Dresnay, Governor of Asti, Milan, 9 May and 27 August 1466, *Registri Missive*, Reg. 74, fols. 69–69v, 103].

ORLÉANS [ORLIENS], 4 JUNE 1466

There arrived recently here to me a courier, Piero da Sesto, bearing a letter from Your Lordships dated the ninth of last month.[1] I do believe that omnipotent God inspired you to write me because it could not have come at a better time, one where the need was great, with opportunity to bear fruit and bring benefit and honor to you. For the King, having ordered the dispatch of My Lord of Gaucourt and of the ambassadors, could on no account, no matter how diligently he tried, get action out of those he had placed in charge of dispatching them. He had words with them and, seeing the iron grow cool, His Majesty had become angry. Yet, there was no remedy to be found. All of which came about through intrigue of the *Angevins and Duke John, who are bitter about whatever support His Majesty extends you, and with all* diligence and guile seek to increase their power in the Court and take control of it, so that everything need pass through their hands.

I received Your Lordships' letter at about midnight; immediately I went to His Majesty, who was having his boots removed in preparation for bed, with certain Angevins present. I notified him of what Your Excellencies communicated to me on the matter of the ambassadors no longer being necessary, since your affairs were in safe haven and properly concluded, placing everything, however, at His Majesty's discretion. Knowing full well the noxious guile and extreme pressure exerted [by

41·GIOVAN PIETRO PANIGAROLA *to the*

DUKE *and* DUCHESS OF MILAN

BN, Fonds Italien, Cod. 1593, fols. 263–64. Orig.

Zonse da me questi dì Piero da Sesto, cavalaro, con una littera de le Vostre S. de dì VIIII° dil passato,[1] la quale credo lo omnipotente Idio inspirasse quelle a farmi scrivere, perchè non poteva vegnire in migliore tempo et dove essendone bisogno fusse per fare magiore fructo et el bene et honore di quelle, perché havendo ordinato questo S. Re la expeditione di Mons.re di Gaucurt et deli ambassatori, nullo pacto per diligentia che sapesse fare li poteva fare expedire da quelli ad chi la M.tà Soa lo havea commisso et cum li quali essa M.tà a chi haveva parlato, vedendo le cose rinfredate, si era corozata; pure non erat dare remedium. El che procedeva per opere de questi *Angiovini et del Duca Iohanne, li quali sono malissimi contenti de ogni favore che la M.tà soa ve fazi, et con ogni* studio et diligentia cerchano di ingerirsse in questa Corte et havere el governo di quella, adciò che tuto passi per le loro mane. Io receveti le littere dele V. S. circha ad hore IIII.to di nocte; subito anday da la M.tà p.tà, la quale si faceva descalzare per andare a dormire et gli eranno certi Angiovini. Li notificay quanto le V. Ex.tie mi comettevano sopra el facto de li ambassatori non essere necessaria la loro andata, rimetendo tuto però in arbitrio dela Soa M.tà, et le cosse vostre collocate in bono porto et termine. Et cognoscendo io le infestatione, arte et bataglie che si davano ad questo S. Re per li effeti che di sopra si contiene, mi perdonarano le V. S. se usay un pocho di presomptione,

the Angevins] upon the King to bring about what I mentioned above, I exercised a bit of presumption, which I hope Your Lordships will forgive me, since I did it for a good end. I told His Majesty, as was written in the letters of Pigello[2] to Franceschino, that Bartolomeo Colleoni had declared himself soldier of the Signoria [of Venice] and there was no longer need to fear him.[3] I also told him that the Venetians wanted to be friends with Your Lordships, that you were on good terms with them, and there was no longer need to fear war. I added that now Your Lordship would be swift and ready to constantly serve His Majesty, with your own person, state, brothers, troops, and all means at your disposal. So would the King find, in fact, for Your Lordship had no other desire but to serve him, mirroring the will of your late father of happy memory. I assured His Majesty that he should make capital of you, since you were willing and able to serve him, as any lord in the King's own country.

His Majesty immediately took off his cap and hat, thanking God for this good news. He stood up and said in a loud voice: "This is the best and finest news I have received all year, which pleases me and gives me great joy." And in the presence of all he repeated the news about the Venetians. He then began to catch his breath and almost sighing said: "Since my uncle [Francesco Sforza] passed from this life and my brother-in-law, the Duke of Milan, was captured, I did not at all feel free or at ease with myself; now I feel that all has turned out well. God be praised! This is fine news." The King took much comfort that night.

When I had left, the Angevins began to say that such news could not be true, because it was not like the Venetians to turn so handily to peace, and similar trash—but His Majesty declared he believed what I had said.

The next morning when Duke John came to him, His Majesty, in the presence of the Duke of Bourbon and certain chamberlains, said the following: "I have news from my brother, the Duke of Milan, whose state is tranquil, quiet, and in accord with the Venetians, who have sent

che lo feci ad bon fine, dicendo ad essa M.tà, et così contenevano le littere di Pigielo[2] a Franceschino, che Bartolamio Collione si era dechiarato soldato dela Signoria et de luy non bisognava dubitare.[3] Li dissi etiam che Venetiani volevano essere amici con le Vostre Signorie et che con loro eravati d'acordo et non bisognava dubitare di guera. Item che hora la V. S. con la persona, Stato, fratelli, gente d'arme et ogni soa facultà saria prompta et aparechiata servire sempre la Soa M.tà et così trovaria cum effecto, non havendo altro desyderio essa V. S. cha di servire quella et de imitare la volontà che verso quella haveva la felicissima memoria dil quondam S. vostro padre, certificandola che V. Ex.tia era così apta et disposta a servirla, como signor che essa M.tà habia di suo Stato et grado, havendo di quella a farne capitale. La p.ta M.tà statim si cavò el boneto et el capello, ringratiando Dio di questa bona novella, et si levò in piede dicendo alta voce: "queste sono le migliore et più grande novelle che habii auto questo anno, le quale molto mi piaceno et mi realegrano." Et disse palam le novelle de Venetiani, et comenzò ad prendere fiato quasi suspirando, dicendo:" dapoy ch'el mio bel barba passò dela presente vita et mio bel fratello, Duca di Millano, fo distenuto, may non mi sono sentito libero né bene de la persona; al presente mi pare che tuto sia refacto. Idio ne sia laudato! Queste sono grande novelle." Et molto si reconfortò per quella sera. Poy che io foy partito, essi Angiovini disseno che non potevano essere vere queste novelle, perché Venetiani non erano giente da condure così presto ad pace, dicendo mille zanze; et essa M.tà disse credere quello che io li haveva dicto. La matina sequente, essendo venuto el Duca Iohanne da quela, la M.tà Soa li disse, presente el Duca di Borbon et certi soy camereri, queste parole: "Io ho novelle de mio fratello el Duca di Millano, el quale hé de la soa Signoria pacifico et quieto et d'acordo con li Venetiani, li quali hanno mandato ad offerire la pace et hanno mandato le gente d'arme a le stantie, et mi ha facto dire che non hé neccessario che io mandi più di là ambassatori, perché ha le cosse sue in boni termini. Fiorentini, Bolognesi, Senesi, el Papa et tuta Italia hé per luy et più mi manda ad offerire la soa persona, soy fratelli, Stato, Signoria, facultate et gente

offerings of peace and have sent their troops to their quarters. He has sent me word that I need not send ambassadors there, because his affairs are in good order. The Florentines, Bolognese, Sienese, the Pope, and all of Italy are on his side, so he offers me his own person, his brothers, state, government, all means at his disposal and his very army, to come into my service. Take note of his great desire, in addition to his already having served me in person in Bourbonnais; his father previously had served me so well and had sent me many fine troops at his own expense. These indeed are friends. Such as these one does not forget. My Lord of Calabria, does it seem to you that these are friends that one abandons?" Duke John making no response to the query, His Majesty asked again: "Do you consider them friends?" Then the Duke answered: "If it is as you say, it is very fine news, but if the Turks are not pressing the Venetians, certainly they cannot have come round so soon." His Majesty observed: "You ought simply to consider whether they have served me or not—for what I say is completely true."

The Duke and many other important personnages of this Court were astounded, since it appeared that things were not going as they had hoped. They had said that everyone would leap upon your back, and it seems strange to them that you no longer have need of their embassies. This has gained greater reputation, glory, and honor for Your Highnesses than you could imagine; and, moreover, it has dismayed those who would have rejoiced in your difficulties, giving them little hope of accomplishing their designs.

Duke John is presently here and he strives to win over the Duke of Bourbon and certain others who have influence in the Court, in order to gain more control. From what the Duke of Bourbon told me, he will stay here at Court a few days. *Since little faith is given to his* [Duke John's] *words* and proposals, the Duke of Bourbon intends *to test him and see how patient he remains and learn the outcome of the propositions he offers.* His Majesty also told me that he will continue to temporize [with Duke John] for a few days. As the Duke of Bourbon openly told me, *he will oppose his* [Duke John's] *staying here at Court, because*

d'arme et che mi vegnirà servire. Avisate el grande suo desyderio, oltra che già mi ha servito con la propria persona in Borbonesse, ulterius suo patre mi ha facto tanti servitii et mi mandò tante belle gente d'arme a soe spese. Questi sono amici. Questi non sono da domentichare. Mons.re di Calabria, vi pare che questi siano amici da abandonare?" Ad le qual parole, niente rispondendo el Duca Iohanne, replicò la M.tà Soa dicendo: "Vi pare che questi siano amici?" Alhora risposse esso Duca: "Se così hé como diciti, sono bone et grande novelle, ma s'el Turcho non caza li Venetiani, per certo non si debbeno essere acordati così presto." Disse la p.ta M.tà: "Voy dovete sapere se mi hanno servito o non, et questo che dico hé verissimo." Per le quale cose el prelibato Duca et molti principali di questa Corte sono rimasti stupefacti, parendoli le cose non essere succedute come speravano, che dicevano tuto'l mondo saria adosso ad le V. S. et parli stranio che quelle più non habiano bisogno de loro ambassate. El che ha acresciuto tanta reputazione, gloria et honore ad esse V. Cel. che non lo poriano pensare, et più fa stare sbigotiti queli che dil male di quele si volevano realegrare, dandoli pocha speranza de li loro desegni. El *Duca Iohanne hé qui, et cercha farse propitio el Duca de Borbon et certi altri che hano adito in questa Corte per meglio governare;*[a] *et per quanto me ha dicto el Duca de Borbon, starà* qualche di a questa Corte, perché dandose *pocha fede ad le soe parole et* proferte, si delibera un pocho *de asazarlo et vedere come sta patiente et come reinsceno li partiti soi che ofere, et così me ha dicto la M.tà Soa che* andaralo temporizando qualche dì. El Duca di Borbon, per quanto mi ha dicto molto liberamente, *sarà contrario che non stia qui dentro perché, come li ho dicto, non conveneno insieme et così* mi ha dicto servirà le V. S., dil che mi tegnirò ad li effecti. Quanto ad la p.ta M.tà, le cose pareno assere assay bene disposite et per queste bone novelle pare essere rotto un grande colpo; dove intenderò et saperò, sforzaromi como vero vostro servitore, sicondo el potere mio, obviare che cosa non si fazi che cum tempo possi tornare preiuditio ad le Vostre Ex.tie. Ma fidelmente ricordo ad quele, *hora che el primo colpo hé ribatuto, perseverare in le oferte* o fare qualche

---

a. C. C. incorrectly reads: governarse, et per quanto se hé dicto, el Duca Iohanne.

they do not get along (as I have told you), and in so doing he declares that he will serve Your Lordships—which I will believe when it actually happens.

Regarding His Majesty, affairs seem to be very well ordered, particularly since this good news seems to have broken an important coup. As best I know how within my powers, I will make every effort as your good servant to prevent anything from being done that in time might turn to Your Excellencies' disadvantage. But I faithfully remind you, now that *the first coup was beaten, to continue in your offers*, or make some other show of your affection for the King, writing to him in the best manner that seems fit to you, in order to insure that His Majesty persevere in this direction, *especially since Duke John will be here a few days, as I mentioned. For if at present His Majesty abandons him, it may last as long as the Duke lives.* All these things I leave to Your Lordships, however, for in your prudence you will dispose and arrange as you see most fit. All that I have said and done has been for a good end, and in the future I will strive within my powers to keep things on the right track.

I note further that a spice-laden Venetian galley was shipwrecked recently at Marseilles; King René and Duke John gave the wreck and all the cargo, which had been confiscated, to the Venetian merchants. Since these two lords are as poor as they are, it is not credible that they have done this for any other end but to please the Venetians, with whom they must have an understanding. From a good and trustworthy source I have it that *Antonello Scaglione*[4] *and certain others were sent by Duke John, and have gone into Italy to Bartolomeo Colleoni.* I alert Your Lordships of *this because they have gone to stir up disputes if they can*; here it is said publicly that they have *an understanding with Bartolomeo*.

On behalf of Your Lordships I have thanked His Majesty for letters written to the Illustrious Madame of Savoy, which the King had my Lord Filippo write in your favor. He observed that he would like to do much more, and hopes that God grant him the grace to be able to satisfy the obligations he has toward you, and so forth.

altra demonstratione de l'afectione vostra verso questo S. Re, scrivendoli in el miglior modo che ad quele parirà, adciò che la M.tà Soa habii casone di perseverare in questo proposito, *maxime havendo el Duca Iohanne, come ho dicto, ad stare qui qualche dì, perché se al presente la M.tà Soa lo abondona, sarà facto durando la vita di quela.* Le quale cose però rimetto ad le V. S., che como prudentissime disponeno et ordineno quanto cognoscerano più expediente; et quanto io ho facto et dicto, hé stato a bon fine, et così per l'avenire sforzarome tegnire le cose ben disposite a mio potere.

Insuper, essendo questi dì romputa per naufragio una gallea caricha di spetie di Venetiani a Marsiglia, el Re Renato et Duca Iohanne hanno donato tuto el naufragio e le robe ad essi mercatanti venetiani, le quale li erano confiscate. El che essendo essi Signori poveri como sono, non si pensa lo habiano facto ad altro fine, se non che cerchano fare piacere ad Venetiani, et cum loro habieno intelligentia. Et da bon loco et digno di fede sono avisato, *che Antonello Scarlione*[4] *et certi altri mandati dal Duca Iohanne, sono passati in Italia verso Bartolameo Colleone.* El che significo ad le V. S., *perché sono andati per suscitare debato se pono, et qui* publice dicano havere *inteligentia con el prefato Bartolameo.* De le littere scripte ad la Ill. Madama di Savoya, et che ha facto questo S. Re scrivere da Filippo Monsignor in vostro favore, per parte de le V. S. ho ringratiato la M.tà Soa. Rispose voria fare magiore cossa, et Dio li presti gratia che possi satisfare ad li oblighi che ha verso quelle etc. Così etiam ho certificato la prelibata Soa M.tà, che de le Vostre Cel. *el Marchese de Monferrato non ha auto dignità alchuna salvo de ben vicinare. Al che* hé rimasta satisfacta, ben ché dicesse non lo potere credere, et hé contenta et prega le V. Ex.tie *che de tale cosa non se ne fazi altra mentione.* Se altro acaderà, ne avisarò le prelibate Ill.me V. S., ad le quale sempre me ricommando.

I also assured His Majesty that from Your Highnesses *the Marquis of Monferrat has received no honor save that of neighborliness. Which* satisfied the King, even though he said he could not believe it; but he is pleased and asks Your Excellencies *that no further mention be made of this business.* If anything else occurs, I will advise Your Lordships, to whom I always commend myself.

HISTORICAL NOTES

1. Doc. 28.

2. Pigello Portinari, manager of the Medici Bank in Milan.

3. This report is not entirely accurate. Venice had not yet renewed the service contract with Colleoni, although by this time it had signified its intention to retain him at its service [Belotti, *La vita di Bartolomeo Colleoni*, pp. 354, 359; cf. also doc. 36].

4. Antonello Scaglione, a long-time agent of the Angevins, made a trip in disguise to Venice in late May, and it was believed that he was traveling throughout Italy in an effort to gain support for Duke John's schemes against Ferrante of Naples [Gerardo de' Colli to the Dukes, Venice, 27 May 1466, *Venezia*, cart. 353].

Document 42. G. P. Panigarola to the Duke and Duchess of Milan. Orléans,
5 June 1466. Partly ciphered.

While speaking with the King just recently, His Majesty, of his own volition, told *me that Duke John was making him many impressive offers, including serving the King with his own person and with friends;* and many similar propositions, *to which the King gave little heed. Nevertheless, Duke John kept after him,* waiting for *His Majesty to request his services. But the King said that he does not much want to do that,* so he has given him very little attention *up till now since he does not feel that he can really trust him.* Nevertheless, within four or six days he will speak to him to see what he has to say, and he will advise me of the outcome.

I thanked His Majesty for his goodwill, which I always recognized as such. I besought him that if it please His Majesty, he would always look benevolently upon Your Lordships, and upon your affairs, which are equally those of His Majesty. I assured him that Your Lordships would serve him with their persons, state, troops, and with whatever he might ask within their powers—of this His Majesty could be sure, and on it he could place his trust. The same would also hold true, *whether publicly or privately, with regard to help from King Ferrante, from whom he could expect help in the shape of galleys, cavalry, and all* else within his powers. Since his kingdom is well provisioned and at peace, King Ferrante desires to put his riches to His Majesty's service,

42·GIOVAN PIETRO PANIGAROLA *to the*

DUKE *and* DUCHESS OF MILAN

Francia, cart. 532. Orig.

Ritrovandomi ultimo ad parlare cum questo S. Re, la M.tà Soa da sé medexima mi disse *che el Duca Iohanne li faceva de molte et grande oferte, et se oferiva servirla con la persona et amici, et* sporgeva di molti partiti, ad li *quali dava pocha orechia. Tutavolta che esso Duca Iohanne stava molto sopra de lui* expectando che *la M.tà Soa lo pregasse; del che dice ha pocha volontà, et fino qui* li haveva dato pocha audienza, *non cognoscendo de lui poterse ben fidare.* Ma fra quatro o sey giorni parlaria con luy distinctamente, vedendo quelo che voria dire, et di che seguiria me ne avisaria. Io ringratiay Soa M.tà di questa soa bona volontà, havendola sempre cognoscuta tale, pregandola che li piacesse havere sempre le Vostre Ex.tie et le loro cose, che sono però di essa M.tà Soa, per ricomandate; notificandoli che le S. V. la servirano con le persone, Stato, gente d'arme, et quanto li saperà domandare per la loro possibilità, et di quelle essa M.tà sapeva ne era sicura et potevasene fidare. Così etiam *dal Signor Re Ferrando publice o secrete haveria adiuto de galee, cavalli et de quanto* potesse, el quale essendone fornito, pacifico et quieto Re, richo et desyderoso di servirla, volontariamente et per introductione de la felicissima memoria dil quondam S. vostro consorte et patre et de le V. S., si offeriva ad farlo et haveria caro spendere dil suo in grande somma per farli cossa grata, et che una volta cognoscesse l'animo che ha verso la Soa M.tà; ricordando fidelmente a quela, che

most willingly thereby continuing the service to which he had been led by the late Lord, your husband and father of happy memory, as well as by Your Lordships. He would enjoy spending some great sum of his money to do the King a favor, in order to show his feelings toward His Majesty. I faithfully reminded His Majesty that such friends were to be well received, especially when they come forward of their own will as does King Ferrante, on whom His Majesty could always count in time of need, as he can on Your Lordships.

I added that I wished to say nothing to him about Duke John, since the King in his prudence will select and choose the best side in the matter, for he was fully aware of the *treatment he had received from the house of Anjou and from Duke John, who beside taking from His Majesty so many thousand écus, had attempted also to undo him of both his state and of his very life*, as His Majesty well knows, *and they did not spare themselves in this effort. Moreover, Duke John was the first to march against His Majesty at Paris; certainly the aforementioned Duke John can in no way be useful to His Majesty*, but rather a constant great drain, who would incessantly be after the King to make requests.

I did, however, put to His Majesty *whether he can trust him* [Duke John], which caused the King to pause for a moment. Then he said that all of these things were true, but that after having spoken with him [Duke John], he would inform me further; *for if he were to come to an understanding with King Ferrante, he would make an enemy of the entire* realm. I responded by saying that *he could if he wished make use of Your Lordships' name to mask the benefits of King Ferrante's aid—saying* nothing more at that time.

Six days later, *the King and Duke John having spoken together*, it seems to me that *His Majesty was not happy with him*, so that in light *of his not wishing and not being able to trust Duke John*, the [King] told Franceschino Nori,[1] at his departure *to come here* to Orléans to speak with the Magnificent Lord Garcia Betes, *ambassador of the aforementioned King Ferrante. The purpose would be to inquire about his authority to negotiate an agreement with His Majesty; to inquire about*

tali amici erano da aceptare, maxime offerendosi da sé *come fa esso Re Ferrando, delo quale et de le S.rie V. in ogni suo bisogno se* ne poteria valere sempre. *Del Duca Iohanne non li voleva dire niente, perché come* prudentissima disponeria et elligeria el migliore partito, essendo assay informata del *tractamento che li era stato facto per la Casa de Angiò et per el Duca Iohanne, che oltra tante migliara de scudi che li hano tolti, hano cercato, come sa la M.tà Soa, de desfarla del Stato et dela persona, et per loro non hé manchato; etiam esso Duca Iohanne essere venuto el primo contra la M.tà Soa ad Parise, né poterli dicto Duca Iohanne essere utile in* cosa alchuna, ma continue di grandissima spessa, et standoli apresso non faria may altro cha domandare oltra, che mi rimeteva ad essa Soa M.tà *se de lui se poteva fidare.* Ad le qual parole la p.ta M.tà stete un pezo suspessa et mi disse tute queste cose essere vere, ma parlato che l'haveria con luy, che mi diria più oltra, *et che se pigliasse inteligentia con el Re Ferrando se inimicaria tuto questo Regno.* Io li risposi che *se vorà soto nome dele S.rie V. se ne valerà, pure che quela intenda sii opera del prelibato Re Ferrando, et per* alhora non fo dicto altro. Da poy sey giorni in qua mi pare intendere che, havendo *questo Re de Franza et el Duca Iohanne parlato insieme, la M.tà Soa de lui non sii rimasta contenta. Et per questo,* a la partita di Franceschino Nori,[1] li dissi[a] *che del Duca Iohanne non si voleva né poteva fidare, che venisse qui* ad Orliens ad parlare cum el Mag.co D. Grassia Bathes, *ambassatore del prefato Re Ferrando, et intendere da lui che possanza ha de pigliare inteligentia con la M.tà Soa, che fondamento ha dele promesse, parole et oferte che fa fare dicto Re Ferrando ad la M.tà Soa, et che secureza haveria che quela la adiutasse;* intendendo tuto particularmente *et investigare se esso ambassatore diceva cosa, perché con ragione se li potesse dare orechia, et trovandoli fondamento li desse speranza de inteligentia, ma publice non la voria fare, perché dice se inimicaria questo Regno. Ben dice prometeria in presentia de testimonii de adiutare esso Re Ferrando, maxime ala destructione del Duca Iohanne, et quando el Re Ferrando mandasse le soe galee in Provenza, che faria andare Mons.*

a. Read: disse.

the foundations which exist for the promises, utterances, and offers King Ferrante extends to His Majesty; about guarantees he would receive that [King Ferrante] would help him. He should learn all particulars and *investigate if the ambassador said things to which [the King] could reasonably lend an ear, and, finding himself on reasonably secure ground, he could extend the possibility of an agreement, but not publicly, because he states he would then have the realm as an enemy.*

Nevertheless, he says that he is willing to promise in the presence of witnesses to aid King Ferrante, especially for the purpose of undoing Duke John; and whenever King Ferrante sends his galleys to Provence, then he would have My Lord Philip, enemy of said Duke John, go by land toward Nice with support troops in order to completely undo him. Franceschino was instructed to write immediately how things stood, *because the King would send a trusted man to speak with Lord Garcia and to confer with me on this matter.*

Franceschino did precisely that, and as he and I arranged, *he wrote in good order to His Majesty* regarding *the position of the ambassador who* prudently had made a good and appropriate response. *Having grasped all this, His Majesty told the Seneschal of Poitou to advise me* in no way to allow *said ambassador to leave, because he would come here to speak with him* in detail. Franceschino, however, *could leave, as he did.*

While recommending this alliance to the Seneschal of Poitou (who is very much trusted by His Majesty), seeking to understand *a bit more, he said to me that the King of France was of a mind to form an agreement with King Ferrante, and that he would put so many proposals before said ambassador as to make him content—repeating to me that* on no account should I let him *leave.* It has seemed to me proper to advise Your Excellencies of all these things so that you may attend to them as you see fit.

The King has come to Orléans; *I will bend every effort to see that His Majesty speak with said ambassador, and according to what is said, every attempt will be made to issue the most suitable response possible.*

Filippo de Savoya, inimico del dicto Duca Iohanne, de verso Niza per terra con secorso de gente per desfarlo del tuto; rescrivendoli subito como trovava la cosa, *perché mandaria uno suo fidato ad parlare con esso Domino Grassia, et che con me comunicasse de questa materia.* Così ha facto Franceschino, et sicondo che luy et io ordinamo, *rescrisse in bona forma ad la prefata Maiestà* circha la *dispositione de esso ambassatore, el quale come* prudente ha risposto in bona et optima forma. Donde *la M.tà Soa, havendo el tuto inteso, disse al Senescalcho de Poitò che* mi dicesse che a modo alchuno non *lassasse partire dicto ambassatore, perché vegniria in questa tera et parlaria con lui del* tuto particularmente, et che Franceschino *se ne poteva andare. Et così ha facto. Et confortando io questa ligha ad esso Senescalcho de Poitò, el quale hé fidatissimo ad la M.tà Soa, et* cerchando di intendere *più oltra*, mi disse che *l'animo del Signor Re de Franza era de prendere inteligentia con el prefato Re Ferrando et che si meteria tanti partiti inanzi ad dicto ambassatore che seria contendo, replicandomi che* nullo pacto lo lasasse *partire.* Dele quale tute cose mi hé parso darne aviso ad le Vostre Ex.tie adciò che intendano el tuto, et li possano fare quelo pensiero che li parerà. El S. Re hé venuto in questa terra; *sforzarome fare che la M.tà Soa parli con dicto ambassatore, et sicondo che quela dirà, si ingegnarà farli quela più conveniente risposta che sarà possibile, et de che se concluderà o seguirà, ne* sarano per meso[b] volando le V. Ex.tie avisate.

Ad la littera che Misser Archaselles,[2] Capitanio del armata del S. Re Ferando per mare, scrisse ad questo Ser.mo S. Re, la M.tà Soa haveva ordinato che li fosse facto risposta ringratiandolo etc. de le offerte. Mi hé parso di soprasedere ad farla expedire, per vedere se al presente li ordinarà altro o cambiarà proposito per le cose da poy seguite.

Circha li scudi II.M. che manchano ala soma de li scudi VI.M., che questo S. Re disse di donare ad le gente d'arme, questi Maystri de intrate che hanno la commissione, dicono che ultimo l'acordo fo facto per Monsignor de Chiastronovo con li Mag.ci Piero Francescho et Iohanne de Scipione ad scudi IIII.M., oponendo el Tesoriero dil Definato che era

---

b. Read: messo.

Your Excellencies will be advised *of the outcome and consequences* by means of rapid messenger. In reply to the letter of Messer Archaselles,[2] captain of King Ferrante's fleet, sent to His Most Serene Highness the King, His Majesty had instructed that response be made thanking him, and so forth, for the offers. It seemed proper to me to have its dispatch delayed, in order to ascertain if at present he gives other orders or otherwise changes opinion in view of what has since happened.

On the subject of the two thousand écus that are short in the total of six thousand that the King promised to give to the [Milanese] troops, the revenue officers here who are commissioned in the matter say that the accord was finally arrived at by My Lord of Chateauneuf with the Magnificent Pier Francesco [Visconti] and Giovannui di Scipione [Pallavicino] in the sum of four thousand écus, the Treasurer of the Dauphiné opposing that he was not able to pay six thousand.[3] So did My Lord of Chateauneuf communicate, and moreover, presently he writes that the troops remained quite content and satisfied with said sum, thanking His Majesty for it. To my contrary observations, when they do not know what else to answer, they in effect say that nothing else can be done, having reached such agreement, since the revenues of the Dauphiné have already been allocated and spent (over and above what is available), and the Treasurer can do nothing. So that I have little hope, with the troops already there and considering, moreover, with what extreme labors and sweat one dredges money from such as them, it seeming as if their very soul were being wrenched from their bodies. Nevertheless, when the moment presents itself, I will have a word of my own with His Majesty the King, doing whatever I can, but safeguarding the honor of Your Lordships. I will inform you of the answer I receive.

Learning yesterday morning that a courier from the Signoria of Venice was coming, and fearing that he was coming to Duke John, I found the means to have him sent to me. I spoke to him and, as the King was returning from morning mass, I had presented to him a letter[4] addressed to His Majesty. He immediately went into Council, which he had called; when he was seated in his regal chair he immediately had

inhabile a pagare li scudi VI.M.[3] Et più che esso Mons.re de Chiastronovo così scrisse, et etiam di presente ha scritto che esse gente d'arme sono
rimaste ben contente et satisfacte a dicta somma, et ne ringratiano la
M.tà Soa. A le qual parte, allegando io quelle rasone che sono in prompto
a l'oposito, quando non sanno che più oponere, dicono in effecto non si
pò fare altro che una volta così hé convenuto, et che le intrate dil Delfinato sono già assignate et spexe più che non li hé, et el Tesorero inhabile,
in modo che gli ho pocha speranza, consyderato che già le gente d'arme
sono di là, etiam cum quante fatiche et extremi sudori si cavano dinari da
costoro, che pare li sia tolta l'anima dil corpo; nondimanco captato tempore, ne dirò una parola ala M.tà dil Re como da me, et faroli quelo mi
sarà possibile cum honore però de le V. S., et de la risposta che haverò
ne serano avisate.

Heri matina, intendendo io che veniva qui uno corero de la Signoria
di Venesia, dubitando venisse al Duca Iohane, trovay modo di farlo
drizare a me, parlay con sì, et heri matina ritornando questo S. Re da
la Messa, li feci presentare una littera[4] haveva directiva ad la Soa M.tà.
La quale subito andò in Consiglio che haveva facto congregare, et asse-
tata che fo in sedia regale, statim mi fece domandare et ley propria legete
in mia presentia essa littera, de la quale ne mando qui inclusa copia ad
le V. S. La quale lecta, ne fece festa assay ad esso Consiglio e a me,
dicendome molte cose, presertim che tanto che Venetiani seriano amici
de le Vostre Ex.tie, seriano de la M.tà Soa, et li adiutaria contra el Turcho,
et faria quanto li fosse possibile tenendoli per soy spetiali amici. Quando
fosse altramente, o che al Stato vostro volesseno tochare, che li haveria per
inimici, et ogni male et danno che li potese fare, lo faria per cazarli a la
marina et destruerli dil tuto. Ma invero al presente piacerli molto che
rimagnano amici et boni vicini con le Vostre Cel., sicondo che scriveno,
et per tale bona novella voleva donare de li dinari al corero che era venuto, et farli un presente, comandando che fusse festezato. Poy mi dete
essa littera, dicendo che la vedesse, et commandò al Grande Canzellero
che li fesse far risposta, como luy et io avisaressemo fusse expediente.
Volse etiam la M.tà Soa che io stesse presente ad odire la rellatione che

me called and he himself in my presence read this letter, of which herewith enclosed I send a copy to Your Lordships.

Having read it, the King made great show of it to the Council, saying many things to me, especially that as long as the Venetians were Your Excellencies' friends they would also be His Majesty's; he would help them against the Turks and do all he could for them, treating them as special friends. Were it otherwise, however, or were they to touch your state, he would consider them enemies, doing every evil and damage he could to drive them into the sea and destroy them totally. But in truth it pleases him greatly that at present they are friends and good neighbors with Your Highnesses, according to what they write—for such good news he wished to bestow money on the courier who had come, giving him a present and ordering that he be entertained.

Then he gave me the letter so that I might see it, and ordered the Grand Chancellor [Guillaume Jouvenel des Ursins] to make that response to it which he and I would consider suitable. His Majesty also wanted me present to hear the report of his ambassadors, who were returning from the Count of Armagnac. Since there is not sufficient time for this one, I will, with another courier, separately relate the report to Your Most Illustrious Lordships,[5] to whom I always commend myself.

Postscript: As Your Lordships know, it is already a long time that I am here; and to uphold your honor I have suffered many extraordinary expenses with these French, receiving no funds at all, even my stipend. We are presently in the third month that I await it. I supplicate Your Excellencies to deign to consider me kindly, allotting me funds so that I can continue to uphold your honor—for I am in great need. And were I in my own house, I would mortgage it up to the last roof tile in order to serve you. Being far off, however, and in a foreign land, I entreat you to be mindful of me, making provision for me as I hope and trust you will. I assure you that the treatment I receive, beyond bolstering the honor of Your Lordships, can be said to be given to your true and loving servant.

fesseno li soy ambassatori, che vegnivano dal Conte d'Armignac. De la quale, non havendo tempo per questo cavallaro, distinctamente per uno altro ne avisarò le Ill.me V. S.,[5] ale quale sempre me ricommando.

Post scripta. Como sanno le Vostre S., hé tanto tempo che io sono di qua, et per fare lo honore de quelle ho patito molte spesse extraordinarie cum questi Franzosi senza provisione alchuna, item dil soldo mio. Al presente corre el terzo mese che lo ho ad havere. Supplico V. Ex.tie se degneno havermi per ricomandato, facendomi fare provisione de dinari, et che possi fare lo honore di quelle, che mi trovo in grande bisogno. Et quando io fusse a casa mia, voria fino ali copi impegnarla per servirle. Si che essendo di longhi et in payse ignotto, supplico quelle habieno di me memoria, provedendomi como in quele ho speranza et fede, certificandole ch'el tractamento mi farano, oltra che sarà per fare lo honore di esse V. S., ponno dire farlo ad uno suo vero et affectionato servitore.

HISTORICAL NOTES

1. Nori left the royal court on 1 June [doc. 38].

2. Galcerán de Requesens, corrupted into Archaselles, Count of Trivento, Avellino, and Ruvo, Governor of Catalonia and Captain General of the Aragonese fleet, who served King Alfonso V in Italy and later John II of Aragon and Ferrante of Naples [Irma Schiappoli, *Napoli aragonese: traffici e attività marinare* (Naples: Giannini, 1972), p. 46]. In March 1466 he had been sent with twelve galleys by Ferrante to help keep Genoa faithful to the Sforza [Leonardo de Serathico to the Dukes, Genoa, 26 March 1466, *Genoa*, cart. 425]. Before he left Genoese waters on 25 June [Leonardo de Serathico to the

Dukes, Genoa, 26 June 1466, ibid., cart. 426], the Captain apparently wrote to Louis XI offering his services against the Angevins.

3. On the payment made to the Milanese troops returning to Lombardy, see doc. 21, n. 8; cf. also Giovanni Bianchi to the Duke, Lyon, 8 June 1466, *Francia*, cart. 532, in which Bianchi blames Panigarola in part for the non-payment of the additional 2,000 écus.

4. Doge Cristoforo Moro's letter of 3 May, cited in Appendix, doc. XI, n. 2. The Venetian courier had left Venice around the middle of May [Gerardo de' Colli to the Dukes, Venice, 27 May 1466, *Venezia*, cart. 353].

5. See doc. 45.

At this hour, the King, returning from his pleasures, asked for me, and told me to cultivate, entertain, and treat well the Venetian courier,[1] since he wished to welcome him affably. He also told me to draft a reply to the letter he had delivered, responding in the most advantageous and favorable terms for the interests of Your Lordships, and he would sign it exactly as I wrote it. Furthermore, the King would give to the courier whatever I saw fit, so that he would make good report to the Venetians and speak of this show of His Majesty's mind. He says he wishes to do this so that all may understand the love he bears Your Excellencies, and be made to realize that anyone who seeks to disturb you will act against His Majesty as well. Thus, the Venetians, realizing how much the King loves Your Highnesses and understanding that he wishes to spare you nothing, in fear of this have reason to be good neighbors.

His Majesty spoke these words to me with such a cheery countenance, with such cordial show of love and heartfelt sincerity, as I ever have seen in his talk of your affairs. He obviously takes and has taken great pleasure and joy in this response made by the Venetians. I am certain you will derive great pleasure and consolation from this action, and so it has seemed proper to inform Your Highnesses, to whom I always commend myself.

43·GIOVAN PIETRO PANIGAROLA *to the*

DUKE *and* DUCHESS OF MILAN

Francia, cart. 532. Orig.

Ritornando questa hora questo S. Re da solazo, la M.tà Soa mi domandò, dicendomi che facesse carezare, festezare et ben tractare el corero de Venetiani,[1] perchè li voleva fare bona chiera, et che facesse la risposta de la littera che luy haveva portato al avantagio et più favore si potesse de le V. S., perchè tale quale la faria, tale la signaria. Et ulterius donaria ad esso corero quello che mi pareria, ad fine che ad Venesia potesse fare bona rellatione, et dire de la demonstratione del animo de la M.tà Soa. Et questo dice volere fare, a fine che ogniuno intenda l'amore che porta ad esse Vostre Ex.tie, et chi a quele cercharà dar disturbo, lo darà ad la M.tà Soa, et che Venetiani cognoscendo quela talmente amare V. Cel. et per quele niente volere sparagnare, habiano casone di vicinare bene, stando sotto questo timore. Et queste parole mi disse la p.ta M.tà con viso alegro, con una tanta cordiale dimonstratione di amore et sincerità di core, quanto may vedese quela parlare de le cose de V. S.; et di questa risposta de Venetiani ne ha monstrato et monstra havere grande piacere et alegreza. De le quale cose mi hè parso darne notizia ad esse V. Cel., rendendomi certo che di tal acto ne haverano piacere et consolatione assay, ale quale sempre me riccomando.

HISTORICAL NOTE

1. See preceding doc. 42.

In the enclosed letter[1] we have communicated to you all you need to know about affairs here, so that we wish to add nothing else, except that Pietro da Gallarate left here today at 2 P.M. He is proceeding to His most Serene Highness the King as quickly as possible without delay along the way. We want you to send a courier to meet him a day's journey away, who will be able to inform him regarding the manners and customs of the court, so that he know how best to conduct himself in all matters.

Our present courier bearing this note you will keep there until said Pietro has presented his embassy and has an audience [with the King]; afterward, send him back with letters explaining fully all that occurred up until then.

HISTORICAL NOTE

1. The letter of 25 May, doc. 35.

44 · *The* DUKE *and* DUCHESS OF MILAN *to*

GIOVAN PIETRO PANIGAROLA

Francia, cart. 532. Minute

Per l'aligata[1] te havimo scripto quanto bisogna dele cose de qua. Per questa non volimo dire altro, se non che Petro da Galarate è partito de qui hogi alle XVIII hore, et se ne venne ad quello Ser.mo S. Re, quanto più presto li serà possibile non perdendo tempo in veruno loco; al quale volimo mandi uno cavallaro al incontro per una iornata, quale el sapia informare deli modi et maynere della Corte, aciò che luy sapia meglio como governarse in ogni cosa. Questo nostro cavalaro, presente portatore, lo teneray lì, tanto che dicto Petro haverà exposta la imbassata soa et havuta audientia, et ne lo remandareti scrivendone per luy ad compimento de tutto quello fin alhora sarà accaduto.

With the last courier, I did not have time to notify Your Lordships of the report made by the King's ambassadors upon return from the Court of Armagnac. So with this letter I inform you that, the [Royal] Council having been assembled these past few days, and with His Majesty sitting upon his throne as if he were in judgment or concluding some very important matter, the said ambassadors made their report [as follows].

When His Majesty had sent them to the Count of Armagnac, the latter received them with all the submission, reverence, and humility one could expect, honoring them and sending them back with the [following] message: the Count would serve His Majesty with his person and with his possessions for or against all others. He would go wherever the King wishes and do whatever he commands, obeying him as his sovereign lord. He would never serve any other but him, nor would he make any moves against him, or consent to such, asserting this with as many agreeable expressions as possible. Regarding His Majesty's request that the Count come to him, he excused himself, saying that at present he could not come because he finds himself destitute and without money on account of the wars that occurred and the great expenses he suffered this year—adding that he would make provisions and without fail come to His Majesty as soon as he could. When the ambassadors

45·GIOVAN PIETRO PANIGAROLA *to the*

DUKE *and* DUCHESS OF MILAN

Francia, cart. 532. Orig.

Non havendo auto tempo per lo ultimo cavalaro di notificare ad le Vostre Signorie la rellatione, che feceno li ambassatori di questo S. Re venuti dal Conte d'Armignac, per questa le aviso che essendo questi dì passati el Consiglio congregato et la M.tà Soa in sedia regale, como si fusse per iudicare o terminare qualche importantissima facenda, dicti ambassatori feceno tale rellatione; che havendoli la M.tà Soa mandati da esso Conte d'Armignac, dicto Conte cum tanta submissione, reverentia et humilità quanto dire si potesse li ha ricolti, honorati et expediti in questa forma: che servirà la p.ta M.tà di corpo et beni verso tuti et contra tuti; andarà et farà dove quella vorrà et commandarà, et obedirà como a suo soprano Signore, nè may servirà altri cha quela, nè li temptarà nè consentirà contra cosa alchuna, cum tante humane parole quanto extimare si possa. Circha el venire de la M.tà Soa, che quella lo haveva mandato a domandare, si excusa al presente non potere venire per trovarsi disproveduto et senza dinari per le guerre ocorse et grande spesse che ha patito questo anno, ma che farà provisione et più breve che potrà vegnirà infallanter da essa M.tà. Volendo essi ambassatori intendere el termino particulare et non stare suxo tale parole generale, tolse termino ad tardius di presentarsi da la prelibata M.tà ad mezo luglio proximo, dicendo che non fallaria esso termino. Così etiam havendoli mandato a dire questo S. Re che ben che li havesse promisso per l'acordo de Paris

wished to establish a particular date rather than merely accepting a general intention, the Count fixed the middle of next July as the latest date for presenting himself to His Majesty, adding that he would not miss that deadline.

Although by the Paris agreement the King had promised him a yearly pension of 16,000 francs, His Majesty nevertheless also sent word that this year the Count would have to be satisfied with 12,000 francs, considering the great expenses he has had during the year and the augment in pensions. To which the Count responded that he was happy to do as the King desired; he would accept lesser or greater allotment as the King wished, for his dominion and all he possessed, he had by the grace and liberality of His Majesty who had given them to him. When it would please His Majesty, the King could do more for him, and he imploringly commends himself to him. In addition, the Count of Armagnac asked His Majesty if it pleased him to arrange a match for him, or let him marry according to his own desires, however he thought best. He mentioned matrimony with Mademoiselle Maria, the King's sister-in-law, about whom there already had been dealings last year in Auvergne, with the agreement that she be wed to him, although afterward the Count did not observe the steps necessary for its conclusion as he was obliged. His Majesty had told his ambassadors to point out that he was willing to send a mission to Savoy to ascertain their wishes in respect to this match, but the Count should advise the King which one pleased him most, the Savoyard or the Duke of Bourbon's sister,[1] regarding whom negotiations had already been in progress for a long time.

The Count of Armagnac replied that he kneels at the King's feet, who may dispose of the matter as best he sees fit, for he will obey. He is certain that His Majesty will advise only what is for his best interests; and so he concluded by saying that he will immediately dispatch an embassy to give initial shape to what must be done, and also to give the King to understand what is on his mind.

Thus, this embassy did arrive here, but up to now there is no word of it taking a position, except that of pressing the King, on the Count's

franchi XVI.M. l'anno di pensione, nondimanco pareva ad la M.tà Soa
che, consyderate le gran spese che ha auto questo anno et le pensione
acrescute, esso Conte havesse questo anno ad contentarse per franchi
XII.M. Ad che risponde dicto Conte essere contento di fare quanto quela
voleva, et più e meno haveva a disponere como li piaceva, perchè la Signoria et quello haveva, lo haveva per gratia et liberalità de la Soa M.tà
che gli lo haveva donato, et quando li piaceria, li poteva ben far magiore
bene, pregandola che lo volesse havere per riccomandato. Postremo,
perchè el prelibato Conte d'Armignac richiedeva la p.ta M.tà che li
piacesse maritarlo, o che altramente si maritaria ad suo piacere e dove
li metesse meglio, et ricordava el matrimonio di madimisella Maria,
cognata di Soa M.tà, de la quale hora uno anno in Alvergna fu parlato
et concluso di darghela, quamvis li effecti perchè si faceva non siano da
poy stati serviti per esso Conte como era obligato; havendoli la prelibata
M.tà facto dire per essi ambassatori che mandaria in Savoya per sapere la
volontà di Savoyni circha tal matrimonio, ma che avisasse qual più li
piaceva o quela di Savoya o una sorella dil Duca di Borbon,[1] de la quale
se ne hè stato gran tempo in practicha: risponde che si mette in zeno-
chione ad li piedi di Soa M.tà che ne dispona quello che li parirà meglio,
perchè luy obedirà, et hè certo non li consiglierà se non el suo bene,
concludendo che subito mandaria una sua ambassata per dare forma ad
quanto fusse da fare, et farli intendere più oltra l'animo suo. Et così
questa ambassata hè venuta, et fino qui non se intende fazi fondamento,
se non de instare per parte dil p.to Conte ad questo S. Re, che li piacia
maritarlo o che si maritarà ad suo modo; dicono bene havere etiam altre
commissione, ma peranche non le hanno explicate. Le quale cose per chi
intende si conclude, che essa M.tà le fa per vedere como si potrà valere
dil p.to Conte, et per rimonstrarli lo errore et fallo che ha commisso
verso quella, et forsi per darli una bastonata se li parerà, et etiam per dare
terrore et exempio ad altri, perchè di luy como per più altre mie ho dicto,
la M.tà Soa hè mallissimo contenta. Di quello che in questa materia più
oltra succederà, mi sforzarò ad la giornata darne particulare aviso ad le
V. Ex.tie.

behalf, that he deign to make a match for him or allow him to marry according to his own wishes. The ambassadors do indeed insist that they have additional instructions, but up until now they have not even broached them.

Whoever understands the situation can clearly see that His Majesty behaves in this manner to test if he can depend upon said Count, and to reprimand him for the error and fault he committed against the King— perhaps even to give him a blow if he sees fit, and also to instill fear and give example to others. For, as I reported in other letters, His Majesty is sorely unhappy with him. Of what subsequently occurs in the matter, I will do my best on the very day to give special notice to Your Excellencies.

The Duke of Nemours has decided that for now he will go to Jerusalem, saying that he had made a vow to do so, because the King has stationed troops in his territory and is also sorely displeased with him. Before leaving, he sent to ask the King what his intentions were and to gain some assurances, for he fears that His Majesty will take from him certain fortresses he holds. The King gave him permission to go, promising him that as long as he was abroad on this journey, none of his fortresses would be touched, and so he could go freely whenever he pleases.[2] Some say that the King remitted and pardoned him of all offenses committed and perpetrated against His Majesty, but Your Lordships can form your own opinion of this from what His Majesty said to me. That is, the King [feels] that the Duke was the prime mover in gathering together the lords of this realm, causing the Battle of Montlhéry with my Lord of Charolais, tricking him in Bourbonnais; so that such things will never lift away from His Majesty's heart.

The Venetians' courier was dispatched on the fifteenth of this month. His Majesty responded to their letter in the manner which Your Excellencies can gather from the enclosed copy:[3] His Majesty himself verbally had given me the general form to follow. He gave the courier thirty écus and had him regaled; at his departure he had him instructed to tell the Venetians that His Majesty would help them and be their

El Duca di Nemors, per havere questo S. Re logiato in el payse suo certe gente d'arme, et per essere la M.tà Soa di luy malissimo etiam contenta, ha deliberato per el presente di andare in Hyerusalem, dicendo che ha così voto. Et prima che sii partito, dubitando che essa M.tà non li toglia certe castelle forte che tiene, ha mandato da quella ad intendere la mente soa et assicurarsi. La quale gli ha dato licentia che se ne vadi, promettendoli che tanto che starà de fori in questo suo viagio, non li tocharà forteza alchuna, et che liberamente se ne vadi quando li piacerà.[2] Alchuni dicono che etiam li ha rimesso et perdonato ogni offensa facta et perpetrata contra quela; ma per quanto la M.tà Soa mi ha dicto, fazone iudice le V. S. di tal remissione, che dice luy fu casone di redunare insieme li Signori di questo Reame, et de la bataglia di Monleri cum Monsignor Chiaroloes et in Borbonesse la inganò, et che may tal cose non li cascharano dal core.

Ceterum el corero de Venetiani ad li XV dil presente fu spazato. La M.tà p.ta ha risposto ad le littere loro in la forma che per la inclusa copia[3] porano le V. Ex.tie vedere, el tenore de la quale mi commandò essa M.tà di propria bocha. Ad esso corero ha donato scudi trenta, factoli bona chiera, e a la partita li fece dire che dicesse ad Venetiani per parte de la M.tà Soa, che tanto che stesseno boni amici con le V. S. che li saria amica et li adiutaria, facendoli tuti quelli piaceri et commodità che li fusse possibile, quando altramente che li saria inimica. Et questo tale spazamento fecelo la M.tà Soa molto volontieri et alegramente; dil quale ringratiandola io per parte de le V. S., maxime del honore che piaceva ad quella di farvi, mi rispose era obligata di fare molto più, et questo essere una picola cosa; ma guardasse se mi pareva la M.tà Soa havesse ad fare altra cosa ad esso corero, per dimonstratione del amore che porta ad le V. Ex.tie, et che Venetiani intendano habii auto cara et grata questa loro novella di vicinare bene cum quele, che lo faria di bonissima voglia. Le quale tute cose ho voluto significare ad le V. Ex.tie, rendendomi certo che haverano piacere et consolatione assay de la dimonstratione ha facto queso S. Re ad esso corero, et ad quele humilmente sempre me riccomando.

friend, doing for them every favor and kindly act that was within his powers, as long as they remained on good terms with Your Lordships—just as in the contrary case he would be their enemy. His Majesty dispatched the courier most willingly and with high spirits. When I thanked him on Your Lordships' behalf for the honor he deigned to show you, he responded that he felt obliged to do much more, this being a small thing. He told me to see if there was more in my opinion that His Majesty could accomplish with this courier, and he would do it with excellent goodwill, to demonstrate the love he bears Your Excellencies, so that the Venetians might understand how dear and welcome to him was the news of their intent to be good neighbors with you.

I am sure that you will take great pleasure and consolation from this show of regal support exhibited to the courier, and so I decided to report it to Your Excellencies, to whom I always humbly commend myself.

HISTORICAL NOTES

1. Neither the marriage with Marie of Savoy nor that with Jeanne de Bourbon, both of which had been discussed a year earlier, took place [Mandrot, *Dépêches*, 3:221–22, n. 1]. These negotiations between Louis XI and Count Jean V of Armagnac are briefly mentioned by Charles Samaran, *La maison d'Armagnac au XVᵉ siècle et les dernières luttes de la féodalité dans le Midi de la France* (Paris: Picard, 1907), pp. 154–55, and Mandrot, "Jacques d'Armagnac," *Revue historique* 44 (1890): 243.

2. This projected voyage to Jerusalem by Jacques d'Armagnac, Duke of Nemours, did not take place, owing to his suspicions about the King's true intentions during his absence [Mandrot, "Jacques d'Armagnac," pp. 242–43].

3. The King to the Doge of Venice, Montargis, 15 June 1466, BN, *Fonds Italien*, Cod. 1591, fol. 352; Vaesen, *Lettres*, 3:59–60. The King expressed satisfaction with the Doge's intention to continue the alliance with Milan, and reaffirmed his resolve to defend the Duchy against any attack.

From what I was given to understand, the King upon his departure from Orléans sent François de Briand, Captain of Susa, to the Illustrious Madam of Savoy, with the commission to speak with her regarding the marriage of the Count of Armagnac[1] and ascertain from her and from the Savoyards their views on this matter. He was also instructed to say to the duchess that the King was not pleased nor would he in any way suffer it, if the long term servants of His Majesty were deposed from their offices in Savoy and in Piedmont—as the Savoyards were in fact attempting to do, having taken the Supreme Knighthood from the Bailli of Lyons, which displeases the King of France.

Moreover, he instructed Briand to put a strong garrison in the castle of Susa, which is in his possession, and so furnish it that it could not be wrested from him were someone to attempt taking it; he should neither give or consign it to anyone in the world without His Majesty's knowledge.[2] Similarly, he then sent word to My Lord Filippo, requesting that he not allow the servants and friends of His Majesty to be demoted and removed from their offices, but rather promoted. He also sent Briand to Filippo in order to notify him that His Majesty asks and urges him to leave [Savoy] as soon as possible, to return here since he has need of him. Beside the hundred lances, the government of Guyenne, and the 6,000 francs (which were presently given to him at Lyons by Frances-

46·GIOVAN PIETRO PANIGAROLA *to the*

DUKE *and* DUCHESS OF MILAN

Francia, cart. 532. Orig.

Questo S. Re al partire de Orliens mandò Francescho di Briand, Capitanio de Susa, ala Ill. Madama di Savoya cum commissione, per quanto mi hé stato riferto, di parlarli dil facto dil mariagio dil Conte d'Armignac,[1] et sapere da ley et da Savoyni el parere loro; et che dicesse ad essa Madama che non li piaceva né sofriria a modo alchuno, che li servitori vechy de la Soa M.tà fusseno deponuti de loro offitii in Savoya et in Piemonti, como cercavanno di fare Savoyni, havendo etiam di presente tolto Cavaler Magiore al Baylì de Lione. El che non li piaceva. Ulterius, che esso Briando metesse bona guarnissone in el Castello de Susa, el quale ha in le mane, et talmente lo fornissa, che non li possa essere tolto; et quando gli lo volesseno tuore, che a modo alchuno non lo dagha né consigni a persona dil mondo senza saputa di Soa M.tà.[2] Et così dapoy ha mandato a dire a Filippo Monsig.re che lo prega non lassi li servitori et amici di Soa M.tà essere rimosti né desgraduati de loro offitii, ma più tosto elevati. Etiam ha mandato esso Briand dal p.to Filippo per dirli che la M.tà Soa lo prega et conforta ad spazarsi el più presto sii possibile, et ritornare de qua, perché di luy ha bisogno. Et oltra le lanze cento, el governo di Giena et franchi VI.M., che li ha facto dare di presente a Lione per Franceschino, per parte de li franchi XVIII.M. che li dà di pensione annuale, lo augumentarà a tale honore, stato et dignità, facendoli etiam tanto bene che se ne contentarà. Et in questo

chino [Nori] from the 18,000 francs assigned as annual pension), the King would elevate [Filippo] to such honor, position, and dignity, doing so much good for him that he would be content. [Briand] should use his every skill in getting him to return, for he fears that he may not, having been instigated by the Savoyards and by enemies of His Majesty, who have sought to divert [Filippo], as His Majesty has already been advised.[3] Therefore, His Majesty sends letters each day in this connection to Filippo; so that he might obtain his share in Savoy, he has given and still gives him every support, favor, and aid. Wherefore, upon the return of Baude [Meurin], whom His Majesty had sent there for this reason, he dispatched him and made him return to the meeting of the Three Estates in Geneva, congregated for said reason on the eighteenth of this month, as Your Lordships doubtlessly know. He also sent him a lawyer, called Master Jean Aubert,[4] to provide him further support and bring the matter to an end.

I notify Your Excellencies that Madam of Savoy has written the King about the support Filippo had there, fearing that in the end he might take control of the country, which it seems to her is what he is seeking, and so forth. I have it from a good source that discord has already arisen between Filippo and Madam, there not being much love between them for the aforementioned reasons; and if this is true, one can reach a true judgment at the conclusion of the meeting of the Three Estates. At present, however, the preponderant opinion is that the Three Estates will be favorable to Filippo, because of the faction he controls, rather than to Madam—about which the King of France secretly is not too happy. In addition we have news here that the Count of Saint-Pol, Grand Constable of France, was sending his daughter to Geneva to marry the Count of Geneva,[5] to whom she was previously promised, accompanied by three hundred horsemen and with great festive preparations. Until now the Constable, preoccupied in part by this matter, had used it as an excuse not to come to His Majesty: now no one knows what excuse he will take up, since the other no longer applies, so that now by necessity his spirit and intentions toward His Majesty will be known.

ussa ogni arte, a fine che ritorni, che dubita instigato da Savoyni et inimici di la M·tà Soa non retorni, como già hè avisata hanno cerchato di preverterlo.[3] Et però essa M.tà ogni giorno repplica littere in tal proposito al dicto Filipo; et perché consegua la parte soa in Savoya, li ha facto et fa ogni spala, favore et adiuto. Donde, essendo ritornato Baldizon, quale Soa M.tà haveva mandato di là per questa casone, lo ha spazato et facto ritornare ad la convocatione de li Tre Stati ad Ginevra, congregati per dicta casone ad li XVIII dil presente, como le V. S. debeno essere informate. Et etiam li ha mandato uno doctore, chiamato Metre Gian Aubert,[4] per darli più favore et che se li metta fine. Notificando ad le V. Ex.tie che Madama di Savoya ha scritto ad questo S. Re dil favore che esso Filipo ha di là, dubitandose che non toglia el governo dil payse ala fine, et che li pare che lol cerchi etc. Et per quanto da bon loco sono avisato, tra esso Filippo et la p.ta Madam già hé nata discordia, non li essendo fra loro tropo amore per le dicte rasone; che se sia, ala conclusione di questi Tre Stati se ne potrà fare vero iuditio. Di presente però la magiore parte indicha che li Tre Stati sarano più favorevelli per esso Filippo per la parte che li ha, cha per la p.ta Madama; *donde al secreto questo Signore Re de Franza non se ne trova tropo contento.*

Insuper qui si ha novella ch'el Conte di Sanpollo, Grande Conestabile di Franza, mandava ad Ginevra a marito la fiola soa promissa altrevolte al Conte di Ginevra,[5] acompagnata cum trecento cavali, et li erano aparechiate gran feste. Et essendosi fino qui in parte esso Conestabile ocupato a questo, excusato non potere venire da la M.tà Soa, non si sa che excusatione prenderà al presente che questa tale occupatione cessa, et sarà forza si cognosca l'animo et intentione soa verso quella.

Monsignor di Buel, Armiraglio di Franza al tempo dil Re Carlo ultimo trapassato, questi dì in publico Consiglio, ingenochiato ad li piedi di questo S. Re, li fece el sacramento di fidelità, domandandosi [*sic*] malissimo contento di essere stato contra la M.tà Soa et al sacramento che altre volte li haveva facto.[6] El Grande Canzellero li dete tale sacramento, dicendo che giurasse per el Dio quale haveva pergiurato, contando una historia di Romani che dete da ridere a la brigata.

My Lord of Bueil [Jean de], Admiral of France during the time of the late King Charles, recently in public Council while kneeling at the King's feet, swore an oath of fealty, declaring himself heartily sorry for having been against His Majesty contrary to the oath he had previously sworn to him.[6] The Grand Chancellor administered the oath, making him swear by the God he had perjured, and recounting an anecdote from Roman history which made the entire group laugh.

An English embassy was here to confirm the truces which were proclaimed and confirmed for a period of twenty-two months on land and on sea, as I previously wrote[7] Your Excellencies. On land, they begin on the fifteenth of this month; on sea, they begin the middle of July— upon confirmation of which, the embassy left. Now His Majesty plans to attend to the matter of the Duke of Berry, and he has sent the Bishop of Évreux[8] [Jean Balue] and certain Bretons to the Duke of Brittany to see if his brother desires to come to terms. If he does so, as was discussed at other times, then may it please God. But if not, he in no way wishes him to remain in Brittany, and he orders the aforementioned Duke not to keep him, and let him go wherever he desires—even if he wishes to go to England, His Majesty is happy to allow him, as long as he does not remain in Brittany. From what has been learned since the King ordered to arms this province and surrounding lands, the Bretons have also fortified their cities and put themselves at the ready, fearing that His Majesty, blaming them, might perhaps wish to attack them—and so they are taking precautions.

His Majesty, moreover, is having many extremely large springals and bombards cast here; and he is having constructed many pavises in order to approach walls; and certain portable wooden barricades, which when they are completed will be a most worthy piece of work, in number sufficient to surround a rather large city; and, in like manner, he is having many other war engines made. He puts a great deal of effort into these matters, almost every day going personally to inspect what is being done, taking great pleasure in it. Between here and Orléans he has all his artillery brought together, which in truth is a stupendous sight; but

Qui hé stata una ambassata di Englexi per confirmare le tregue, le quale sono state publicate et confermate per mesi XXII per terra et per mare, como per altre[7] scrissi ad le V. Ex.tie. Per terra commenzono ad li XV dil presente, per mare comenzarano ad mezo luglio poximo; et cum la confimatione predicta hé partita essa ambassata. Ora intende la prelibata M.tà atendere al facto dil Duca di Berri, et ha mandato el Vescovo di Evros[8] et certi Bertoni dal Duca di Bertagna per vedere s'el fratello si vole acordare. Se si acorda, sicondo che altre volte hé stato ventillato, sia con Dio. Quando che non, non vole a modo alchuno stia in Bertagna, et manda al p.to Duca che non lo tegni, ma lassilo andare dove vorrà; et si bene volesse andare in Inglitera, hé contenta la M.tà Soa che li vadi, pure che non stii in Bertagna. Et per quanto qui hé stato riferto, per havere questo S. Re facto commandare questo paese et qui dentorno che si metesseno in arme, in Bertagna hanno fortificato le loro terre et missosi loro alsi in poncto, dubitando che forsi la M.tà Soa, como offessa da loro, non li volesse dar impachio, et però si provedevano.

Insuper essa M.tà qui fa fondere di molte springarde grosse oltra mesura et bombardele, et fa fare di molte pavesine per aprosimare a le muraglie, et certe bastie di legnami per portare apresso sé, che quando siano fornite sarano digne opere, et in tal numero che porano circuire una cità assay grande; et così fa fare molti altri instrumenti di guera. A le qual cosse mette gran studio, andando ley quasi ogni giorno in persona a vedere quanto si fa, et li prende grande piacere; et tra qui et Orliens fa congregare tuta la soa artigliaria, che in vero hé stupenda cosa, ma qui si fa el più grande amasso. Così etiam ha facto commandare in el Ducato di Berri et Contato di Poytò ch'el payse et nobeli si mettano in arme. Et al presente si hé facto le monstre; pure peranche non si movano, né se intende per questo anno habiano ad fare grossa novità, ma che solo tal nova congregatione sii facta per dare terrore a la brigata et per tirare, se possibili sarà, li desegni di questo Re ad effecto como di Mons.re Chyaroloes et del Duca di Berri, et vedere de chi la M.tà Soa pi potrà valere.

Monsig.re de Comingia, Marescalcho di Franza, ha discorso et discorre armata manu per Ghiena et verso el payse d'Armignac senza trovar-

the greatest concentration of it takes place here. And he has also ordered in the Duchy of Berry and the County of Poitou that the countryside and nobles take to arms. For the moment they have held reviews, even though they are not on the move, nor is there any intention for them to engage in anything notable this year—this new mobilization is made only to strike terror and to bring to effect, if possible, the designs of the King relative both to My Lord of Charolais and to the Duke of Berry— thus His Majesty can ascertain whom he can trust.

My Lord of Comminges, Marshall of France, has ridden and is riding with his troops through Guyenne toward the territory of Armagnac without meeting any opposition, doing all that the King has ordered, so that His Majesty says he is well content with him, being a good man whom the King has always found to be tractable. Recently [the King] sent [word] to the King of Aragon to bring about the matrimony of the natural daughter of the King of Aragon to the aforementioned My Lord of Comminges, as had been discussed before;[9] moreover, he said to his advisers that for now he will not relieve him of the governorship of Guyenne but that even if he does, he will give him equal compensation from the Dauphiné, so that he will be well satisfied. This pleases many at court, where he is well loved for his good conduct.

My Lord of Candale [Jean de Foix], Governor of Perpignan and of Roussillon, is ill here, and, because of certain privileges which the King has confirmed to the people of Perpignan, says that he does not wish to remain governor under those conditions. He also requests the observance of certain agreements[10] he has made with His Majesty— Your Excellencies will be advised as to the form they take.

The Aragonese ambassador says he was notified that the King of Aragon had made certain agreements with Don Pedro of Portugal, who was to renounce his pretended rights over Barcelona and return to Portugal, with the compensation of a certain sum of money. There only remains that the Count of Prades [Juan Ramon Folch II] consent to this accord, and then the agreements could be drawn up, the news of which

li opposito; et fa quanto questo S. Re li ha commandato, in modo che la M.tà Soa dice contentarsi di luy, et che hé bono homo et sempre lo ha trovato perdomo.[a] Di presente ha mandato dal S. Re d'Aragon per concludere el matrimonio de la Bastarda di esso Re d'"Aragon al p.to Monsig.re de Comingia, como altre volte fu ragionato.[9] Et più ha dicto a li soy che ancora non li tolle el governamento de Ghiena, ma quando pure gli lo toglia, che li darà altratanta recompensatione in Delfinato et farà che sarà bene contento. El che piace a molti in questa Corte, perché li hé ben amato per el suo bon deportamento.

Mons.re di Candela, Governatore di Parpignano et di Rossiglione, hé qui amalato, et per certi privilegii ch'el Re ha reconfirmato a quelli di Parpignano, dice non volere el governo in quella forma. Etiam domanda la observatione di certi capituli[10] ha cum la M.tà Soa; sicondo che prenderano forma, ne sarano V. Ex.tie avisate. Lo ambassatore dil p.to Re d'Aragon dice essere avisato che la M.tà Soa haveva facto certi capituli con Don Pietro di Portogallo, che doveva renontiare al drito pretendeva havere sopra Barzalona, et se ne doveva ritornare a Portogallo mediante certa somma de dinari che li dava. Restava solo ch'el Conte di Prades consentisse ad questo acordo et deinde si dovevano concludere dicti capituli, de li quali di hora in hora se aspecta sentire che sarà seguito.[11] Ben dice esso ambassatore che la nave de le V. Ex.tie era gionta là a salvamento.[12]

Monsig.re Chyaroloes tiene qui uno suo apresso la prelibata M.tà, el quale me ha dicto che Monsig.re Chyaroloes ha mandato uno suo dal Ill.mo Duca di Bergogna suo patre, per sapere la volontà de la Soa Signoria circha el matrimonio de la fiola di questo S. Re, perchè quando la tolse fu con promissione in quanto piacesse al p.to Ill.mo S. suo patre; et che a sapere questa conclusione la p.ta M.tà insta molto, et hali dicto che si el prelibato Monsig.re Chyaroloes la aceptarà in bona hora, quando anche non, che sempre li sarà amica se per luy non rimane. Ma per quanto si pò intendere, pare che la volontà di Monsig.re Chyaroloes sii inclina

---

a. This unusual word, never before encountered, perhaps means "docile" or "servizievole."

is expected here at any moment now.[11] This ambassador indeed says that Your Excellencies' ship arrived there safely.[12]

My Lord of Charolais is maintaining with the King here one of his own men, who told me that My Lord of Charolais sent an emissary to his father, the Most Illustrious Duke of Burgundy, in order to learn the Duke's will regarding his marriage to the King's daughter. For when he agreed to marry her it was with the condition that it please the Most Illustrious Lord his father, and the King is anxious to know the decision in this. The King said to Charolais that if he accepts her soon, or if he does not, that he would always be his friend if he is willing. But from what one can gather, it seems that My Lord of Charolais is inclined to observe this match as he did at Paris, and as he always said afterward; the opinion of those who are well informed is that for numerous reasons this match must come about, and so each day news is expected in that regard.

Charolais's man also reports that the Bastard of Burgundy has gone to bring together and assemble troops to march against Liège, who has completely broken the agreement made and in no way wishes to observe it. The Magnificent Bailli of Lyons is constantly at court, and he immediately notifies me of anything he learns, showing himself an affectionate servant of Your Lordships, to whom he commends himself: it would be prudent to have a gracious letter written to him, for it could only do good. There are many things in the wind and many plots are being woven for and against, that make me fearful of war; but of these I cannot yet give certain account to Your Excellencies, but will remain alert as they become clearer, giving particular notification of all that transpires to Your Most Illustrious Lordships, to whom I eternally commend myself.

ad observare esso matrimonio como a Parise fece, et sempre da poy ha dicto, et l'opinion de chi intende hé che per più rispecti debia havere loco, et ogni dì se ne aspecta novella. Dice etiam che el Bastardo di Bergogna era andato ad metere insieme et redunare le gente d'arme per andare contra queli di Legia, che dil tuto hanno romputo l'aponctamento facto et in nullo pare lo vogliano tenere.

El Mag.co Baylì de Lione continue hé a questa Corte, et quanto intende statim mi notifica, monstrandosi servitore affectionato de le V. S., ale quale si riccomanda; et saria bene che quele li facesseno scrivere una littera gratiosa, che non poria se non giovare. Molte practiche sono in ayre et si ordisse di molte tele pro et contra, che mi fanno dubitare di guera, de le quale non posso peranche darne certo aviso ad le V. Ex.tie; ma como se intendano più chiare starò atento, dando dil tuto particular aviso ad le V. Ill.me S., ale quale in eternum me riccomando.

HISTORICAL NOTES

1. See preceding doc. 45, n. 1.

2. In 1465 François de Briand had been deprived of his office as Captain of Susa by the Duchess of Savoy [Mandrot, *Dépêches*, 4:95–96].

3. After his arrival in Savoy around 20 May [doc. 32, nn. 1, 3], Philip of Savoy went to Vercelli in Piedmont where he arrived on 2 June [Antonio di Romagnano to the Duke of Milan, Vercelli, 2 June 1466, *Savoia*, cart. 482]. Here he met his aunt, Maria of Savoy, widow of Duke Filippo Maria Visconti of Milan, whose claims to the succession had been frustrated by the Ambrosian Republic and the subsequent rise of Francesco Sforza. It is believed that she was among those who chiefly influenced Philip to adopt an anti-Sforza policy, particularly with respect to the planned marriage of Bona of Savoy and Galeazzo Maria [Daviso di Charvensod, *Filippo II*, p. 52; cf. Gaston du Lyon and Giovanni Filippo da Trecate to the Dukes of Milan, Grenoble, 4 June 1466, and Panigarola to the Dukes, Montargis, 1 July 1466, *Francia*, cart. 532]. It is evident that these ominous reports had quickly reached the King.

4. On the earlier mission to Savoy by Baude Meurin and, possibly, Jean Aubert, see doc. 32, n. 2.

5. Giano of Savoy, son of the late Duke Louis I of Savoy and of Anne of Cyprus. The bride was Hélène, daughter of Louis de Luxembourg, Count of Saint-Pol.

6. Jean de Bueil, Count of Sancerre and Admiral of France since 1450,

had been deprived of his office in 1461 by Louis XI, and as a result, he had taken service with the Duke of Berry against the King. He had already been pardoned in February [Mandrot, *Dépêches*, 4:259].

7. Doc. 39.

8. Neither Forgeot, *Jean Balue*, nor Stein, *Charles de France*, mentions this mission by Balue.

9. This projected marriage between Jean de Lescun, Count of Comminges, and the natural daughter (who has not been identified) of John II of Aragon, did not take place. This report, if accurate, corrects Jean de Jaurgain's statement that the King negotiated the Count's marriage with Margherita of Saluzzo, daughter of Marquis Louis I of Saluzzo, toward the end of 1465 ["Deux Comtes de Comminges," *Bulletin de la Société Archeologique du Gers* (1915), p. 78].

10. Cf. Mandrot, *Dépêches*, 4:105–6, 310–11, and doc. 1.

11. This report is false. A few hours before dying of tuberculosis on 29 June, at the age of thirty-seven, Don Pedro dictated his will according to which he left his claims to the crown of Aragon to his nephew, Juan, first son of Alfonso V and of Isabel of Portugal [Jésus E. Martinez Ferrando, *Tragedia del insigne Condestable Don Pedro de Portugal* (Madrid: Diana, Arte Gráficas, 1942), pp. 166–72].

12. On 5 June Milan had sent a warship from Savona to aid John II in his campaign against Barcelona [doc. 50].

So that Your Excellencies may be advised of what happens daily here, I notify you that recently Duke John has had reasons to suspect the Neapolitans who are here with him, and he has become angry with them; he told them that he has not been able, nor is he able, to do anything in this court, his father's or his own court, that is not immediately known in Italy. This cannot come about except by their intervention, because as soon as things are done they broadcast them over there [in Italy]. It was one of them, called Giacomo Galeota,[1] that responded to him, saying that the French are good for nothing except to eat and to stay at their ease, nor do they care to spend a groat in maintaining a man who might inform them of what is going on; and he ought to realize that Your Lordships maintain me here, where he asserts very little happens that you do not know by my intervention. He added, moreover, that King Ferrante now has sent his ambassador here not in order to request anything from the King nor because he has any particular need, but rather in order to make offer of his services and offer him all that he has in this world, and to learn what is going on here and how things are proceeding. Wherefore, he should not be surprised if his business is known in Italy, which comes about for the aforementioned reasons, since as was said, they [the Angevins] do not wish to spend a groat in order to learn the business of other lords and especially of their enemies. As one can

47·GIOVAN PIETRO PANIGAROLA *to the*

DUKE *and* DUCHESS OF MILAN

BN, Fonds Italien, Cod. 1593, fols. 266–67. Orig.

Adcioché le Vostre Ex.tie siano avisate di quanto ala giornata di qua achade, li significo che questi dì el Duca Iohanne ha auto suspecto li Napolitani che qui sono con luy; et con loro si hé corozato, dicendoli che non ha potuto nè pò fare in questa Corte, a caxa dil patre né soa, cossa che statim in Italia non se sapia. El che non pò procedree se non per loro mezo, che subito facte le cosse le notificano di delà. Hé stato uno di loro, chiamato Iacomo Galiotto,[1] che li ha risposto che loro Franzesi non sono boni cha ad mangiare et stare ben assii, né ossanno spendere uno grosso di defori in tenere uno homo per sapere de le cosse; et che debbe sapere che le V. S. mi tegneno qui, dove dice si fa molto poche cosse che quele non sapiano per mio mezo. Ulterius, ch'el S. Re Ferando hora ha mandato questo suo ambassatore, non per volere requirere cossa alchuna ad questo S. Re, né che de luy habia bisogno, ma più tosto debbe existimare per offerirsse et presentarli quanto ha ad questo mondo, et intendere quello che si fa de qua et como passano le cosse. Donde non si debbe maravigliare se in Italia si sa li facti soy, che procede per le dicte rasone, ma loro come hé dicto non voleno spendere uno grosso per sapere li facti d'altri Signori, et potissimum de soy inimici. Et per quanto si vede, non fa però esso Duca tropo stima di questi soy Napolitani, che anche al vero hé impotente ad fare bene a tanti. Ulterius, havendo esso Duca posto in Consiglio certe soe facende particulare, essendo dicto ad la M.tà Soa in

see, the Duke does not have a very high opinion of his Neapolitans, because in truth he is not in a position to provide for so many.

Furthermore, Duke John had placed before the [Royal] Council certain particular business of his, and the Council in public session said to His Majesty that its opinion in this matter was that the Duke's request should not be conceded. His Majesty answered that he was of similar opinion as the Council and that it should be thus done, in order that the Duke not have any reason to complain that His Majesty does not consult the Council and does not follow either its advice or what is right,[2] ruling instead by his will, as the Duke complained when he was before Paris. Thus his requests were repulsed. Nevertheless, Duke John seeks in every possible way, *with every stratagem and guile, to increase his influence in the court and to take control of it; and already he has won over to himself certain of the principals beyond the many who were already partisan to him. Now the* [Royal] *Council has begun to meet in Duke John's house, in such fashion that one fears that it will take firm footing there, and once it has it will not be so easily dislodged. Wherefore I faithfully remind Your Lordships to take sound and* prudent thought in the matter, as you are most wisely accustomed to do in your other matters, in order to apply the most suitable remedy, as you see fit— *especially maintaining the King of France very well disposed toward you, as he continually has shown and still shows to be at the present. I also note that now the Count of Maine*[3] *has sent here one of his men to make his excuses for past actions imputed to him, and to speak his mind. His Majesty has assigned* auditors to hear the case. Also, from what I have heard from His Majesty and from many others, *Duke John does not have to leave here for a good while, wherefore, with the nature he has, being sagacious and astute as Your Lordships know, it is the opinion of some that thought should be given to these matters early and remedy made for them; therefore,* Your Excellencies will dispose of them as best they see fit and suitable. I also will faithfully make every effort to notify you of what happens. I intend within my powers to obviate that

publico Consiglio la opinion di quelo in tal materia essere, che non se li dovesse concedere quelo che domandava, la M.tà Soa rispose essere in la opinion dil Consiglio et che così si facesse, ad ciò che esso Duca non habii casone di lamentarsi che la p.ta Soa M.tà non vada per Consiglio, como faceva quando era dananti Parise, che diceva quela faceva le cose di soa testa et non voleva opinion di Consiglio né di rasone.[2] E così hé stato dato repulsa a le domande soe. Nondimancho dicto Duca Iohanne cum ogni via, ingegno et *arte cercha de ingerirse in questa Corte et haverne el governo, et già ha tirato ad sé alchuni deli principali, oltra che li ha di molti partesani. Et hora si comenza ad tenere el Consiglio ala casa d'esso Duca Iohanne, in modo che se dubita li prenderà piede, et quando li habii non così tosto se cazarà. Donde fidelmente ricordo ad le S.rie V. fare quelo savio et* prudente pensiero che in le altre soe cosse sapientissimamente sono acustumate di fare, et darli quelo più conveniente remedio che li parerà, *maxime in tegnire questo Signor Re de Franza benissimo hedificato, come continue ha monstrato et monstra etiam essere al presente verso le S.rie V.; ricordando ad quele che hora etiam il Conte di Humene*[3] *ha mandato qui uno deli soi per excusarse dele cose passate de che era imputato et dire la mente soa, et la M.tà Soa li ha dato* auditori. Etiam per quanto dala prelibata M.tà et da molti sono certificato, *dicto Duca Iohanne non ha ad partire de qua de bon pezo, donde essendo dela natura che l'hé, sagaze et astuto come sano le S.rie V., saria opinione de alchuni de farli pensiero in questi principii et farli reparo. Tamen* le V. Ex.tie ne disponerano como meglio a loro parirà conveniente. Io autem fidelmente mi sforzarò avisarle di quanto achaderà, e a mio potere dove intenderò obviare che cosa non si fazi, che cum tempo habii ad generare preiudicio o disturbo ad le V. Cel.

Fra le persone che intendeno, si dubita in questo Reame di guerra, né ragione evidente hé alchuna, perché così non debba essere, stando le cosse in li termini che sono. Et el Duca di Berrì, di Foys et questi dil Duca Iohanne publice dicono che sarà guera, maxime che non intendo peranche *el Duca Iohanne habii voluto presentialiter et solemnemente*

anything be done which in time might generate prejudice or disturbance to Your Highnesses.

Among knowledgeable people there is fear of war in the realm, and there is no apparent reason that it should not occur, things being in the state that they are. The Duke of Berry, [the Count] of Foix, and these partisans of Duke John publicly say that there will be war, especially since I understand that *Duke John has not even wanted at present to solemnly swear and promise to His Majesty that he would serve him against all and any, alleging that he cannot do it because he is in league with others and wants to die a loyal lord. There are many secret maneuvers afoot that I cannot* as yet well understand. May God dispose for the best, *because if it comes to war, many perverse and sinister things will be seen because of the hatreds nurtured in the hearts of these men.*

Regarding the ambassador of the Most Serene King Ferrante, who is presently here, His Majesty told me *through the Seneschal of Poitou* [Louis de Crussol] *that because of Duke John's opposition to his stay here it would be better if the ambassador were to go to Orléans and not leave there* under any circumstances; for the King would speak to him *regarding the understanding which had been discussed*[4] *and would have him leave most contentedly, deferring* these matters for the moment for good reasons. *And so the ambassador went to see Paris, and* he will return hereabouts to see if I send any further word to him, *and then he will go to Orléans in due time.*

Since then His Majesty has had word sent to me recently by means of the Governor of Montpellier [Guillaume Cousinot]—and the King himself also told me—*that Duke John has vehemently complained to His Majesty, insisting that the ambassador leave.* So in order to avoid trouble for His Majesty, it seems better that at present the ambassador *return there* [Naples], *because it is not now time to negotiate agreements: Duke John will not leave here for many days and His Majesty must entertain him for a certain period whether he wishes to or not. That is, at least until it becomes clear whether My Lord of Charolais will marry his daughter; for by this means he would try to win over My*

iuare et prometere ad la prelibata Maiestà de servirla contra tuti et sia chi si voglia, ma dice non lo potere fare per la ligha che ha con li altri et che morirà lial Signore. Et molte secrete practiche si menano che non posso ancora bene intendere. Idio voglia disponere el meglio, *perché si se vene ad guerra, si vederano di molte perverse et sinistre cose per li odii sconfiati in li animi de costoro. Circha lo oratore del Serenissimo Re Ferrando, che qui hé, la prelibata Maiestà mi fece dire per el Senescalcho de Poitò, che per la infestatione che li faceva el Duca Iohanne per el suo stare qui, era meglio andasse ad Orliens et non partisse de lì* a modo alchuno, che parlaria con luy circha *la inteligentia de che si era ragionato*[4] *et lo faria partire benissimo contento, diferendo* queste cose per bon rispecto. *Et così esso oratore andò a vedere Parise, et se redurà qui d'in-*torno per vedere se li mandarò a dire altro, *et poi andarà ad Orliens* passando tempo. Dapoy questi dì la p.ta M.tà mi ha facto dire per el Governator di Monpelieri, et ley etiam mi ha dicto, *che el Duca Iohanne instia molto che esso oratore se ne vadi; et molto si ne hé doluto con la M.tà soa che* li pare meglio, et per dare mancho graveza ad essa Soa M.tà, che al presente *se ne retorni di delà per non essere hora tempo di pigliare inteligentia, perchè dicto Duca Iohanne non partirà de qui de molti giorni. Et hé neccessario la M.tà Soa lo intertegna, voglia o non, per certo tempo almeno fino che sia ben chiaro de Mons. de Chiarolois se torà soa fiola o non; et con questo apozo vedere di fare venire al suo desegno dicto Mons. de Chiarolois, dal quale ha mandato Misere Ugon du Fò,*[5] *che non partirà de là senza portare la conclusione di questo matrimonio. Se si conclude, come pure spera, dice la M.tà Soa che sarà el maistro, et poterà comandare per tuto el Regno ad suo modo ad tuti li Signori, et prendere queli partiti et lighe che vorà, quando che non bisogna interteg-na questa banda de Angiò, et dice cognoscere non potere stare senza* guerra. Le qual ultime parolle *me disse suspirando et con uno animo sdignato, che per quanto* possi comprehendere mi parse *dubiti de havere guerra, et che intenda si ordineno qualche secrete practiche contra la prefata Soa Maiestà, le quale altramente non mi ha explicato. Ad le quale cose, havendo risposto quelo che mi hé parso conveniente, maxime*

Lord of Charolais, to whom he has sent Messer Yvon du Fou[5] *with instructions not to leave there without bringing about the conclusion of this matrimony. If it is arranged as His Majesty hopes, he says that he will be supreme and will be able to take command of all the lords throughout the realm as he sees fit and choose whatever sides and alliances he wishes, it being no longer necessary to cultivate the Angevin clique. The King added, however, that he knows war is inevitable.*

These last words *he said to me with a sigh and with a disturbed spirit, so that from what* I was able to understand it seemed to me *that he fears the outbreak of war, and that he has knowledge that some secret plots are being hatched against His Majesty, which he did not otherwise reveal to me. To these matters I responded what seemed most suitable to me, especially reminding him of the affection and singular attachment that King Ferrante had for His Majesty and the offers which he was making to him, which should not be refused especially since today few like him were to be found. He could expect aid from him and not from Duke John unless it be with great expense and trouble for His Majesty, who besides should know how trustworthy he is. All that the King would do for him would be to the Duke's advantage and aggrandizement, which in time might turn to the detriment of His Majesty and of his friends and servants. The King answered me that it was necessary to make use of Duke John if My Lord of Charolais were not to accept the marriage, regarding which he hoped to be enlightened shortly —adding that he would not elevate Duke John in such a way that he could harm or do damage to Your Lordships, whom he would never abandon even if there were a hundred Duke Johns. Moreover he would keep him on such short rope that he would be able to do little even against King Ferrante, with whom* at present *he cannot openly contract an alliance, because he feels he would make an enemy of the entire realm. And so he is constrained to make use of Duke John, as* I mentioned above, *but he says that he will write a good letter to King Ferrante which the aforementioned ambassador can take with him on his immediate departure.*

in ricordarli l'afection et singulare desiderio che el Signor Re Ferrando haveva ad la M.tà Soa, le oferte li faceva che non erano a refutare, perché hogii pochi tali si trovavano, et de lui se poteria valere, del Duca Iohanne non, se non con grande spesa et iactura de la M.tà Soa, oltra che quela sapeva come se ne poteva fidare, et quanto li faria saria in avantagio et in sua ellevatione che anche con tempo poria tornare in dano de la M.tà Soa, soi amici et servitori: mi rispose che bisognava se aidasse del pre-fato Duca Iohanne, quando Mons. de Chiarolois non acceptasse el paren-*tato, del quale in breve spera essere chiaro; et che non ellevaria esso Duca Iohanne in modo che potesse nocere né fare dano ad le S.rie V., quale mai non abandonarà, se ben fusseno cento Duca Iohanne. Et più lo teg-nia così curto che anche al Re Ferrando poterà fare pocho, con el quale* al presente *non pò prendere inteligentia apertamente, perché dice se inimicaria tuto el Regno, et etiam hé forza si vaglia di esso Duca Iohanne, come de* sopra ho dicto; *ma dice scriverà una bona littera al prefato Re Ferrando, con la quale dicto oratore partirà instando questa soa partita.* Signori mei, quamvis la venuta di questo *oratore habii rotto gran giazo et sia per parturire bon fructo, maxime in havere facto intendere la mente dela Maiestà del Re Ferrando ad questo Re de Franza, et intendere le cose de zà,* non dimancho perché le cose de qui se cambiano de hora in hora, *vado dilatando tempo* per vedere se altre novelle sopraveneno, *che poriano venire tale che esso oratore faria ancor magior fructo ananzi par-tisse.* Siché *dilatarò questo suo spazamento più che si porà, et de che seguirà,* sarano le V. Ex.tie ala giornata dil tuto avisate.

Lo ambassatore dil Marchese di Monferato peranche non ha auto audientia, continue cercha di haverla per mezo di Gastoneto. Per quanto sono avisato et maxime dal Spectabile Iohanne Filippo da Trecchà, che passò per Casale et che hé domestico del dicto ambassatore, la casone dela venuta soa si hé che havendo inteso el Marchese questo S. Re essere un pocho di luy malcontento, lo manda per gratificarsi ad la M.tà Soa, ringratiarla de la mogliere[6] che li ha dato, de la quale si trova conten-tissimo, offerirli el Stato, la persona etc. et farli intendere la bona et optima soa dispositione che hé di servirla, et sempre sicondare el piacere

My Lords, even though the arrival of this *ambassador has thoroughly broken the ice and seems about to bring forth good fruit, especially in having revealed the intentions of His Majesty King Ferrante to the King of France and in clarifying how things stand there, nevertheless, because matters here change from moment to moment, I am trying to gain time to* see if other news is forthcoming, *for it might be of such a nature that the ambassador might bring forth even greater fruit before he leaves.* Therefore *I will delay his departure as long as possible, and all of that occurs* subsequently Your Excellencies will be completely informed on the very day.

The ambassador of the Marquis of Monferrat has not yet had an audience [with the King], but constantly attempts to have one by means of Gaston [du Lyon]. From what I have been told, and especially by the Esteemed Giovanni Filippo da Trecate, who passed through Casale and who is an intimate friend of the aforementioned ambassador, the reason for his coming is that, the Marquis having heard the King was somewhat unhappy with him, he sent the ambassador in order to ingratiate himself with His Majesty, thank him for the wife[6] he has given him (with whom he is quite happy), and to offer him his state, his very person, and so forth. [The ambassador was to have] the King understand his good and excellent disposition to serve him, always observing the pleasure and will of His Majesty, and he should point out to him that he has put aside his own interests to please him. That is, when Alexandria[7] rose in arms after the death of the unvanquished late Lord, your husband and father, he did not lend an ear to anyone in the city, but came quickly to Milan to serve Your Excellencies. He used his every skill for the benefit of [Your Lordships], realizing that he would do a favor and a welcome thing for His Majesty, who he knew would bend every effort and use his every power for the conservation of that state, as if it were his own realm—and so he would always be ready to do His Majesty's pleasure. Regarding the oath of fealty to the Duke of Savoy, I do not take it that he has instructions to speak of it except just in passing, but after

et volere di essa M.tà et rimonstrarli como ha lassato la soa spetialità per farli cosa grata; cioè che essendose Alexandria[7] missa in arme dopoy la morte del invictissimo quondam vostro consorte et patre, non volse darli orechia né ad quelo né ad altro, ma venì subito a Milanno ad li servitii de le V. Ex.tie et in benefitio di quele misse ogni suo ingegno, cognoscendo che faria piacere et cosa grata ad la p.ta Soa M.tà, la quale sapeva che metteria ogni soa possanza et studio per conservatione di quelo Stato, como del proprio suo Regno, et che sempre sarà aparechiato ad fare li piaceri di quella. De la fidelità di Savoya non intendo habii commissione di parlarne se non legiermente, ma parlato che haverà con la prelibata M.tà, studiarome de intendere se altro li sarà et statim avisarone le V. Ex.tie, ad le quale in eternum me riccomando.

he has spoken with His Majesty, I will strive to learn if there is anything else and will immediately advise Your Excellencies, to whom I eternally commend myself.

HISTORICAL NOTES

1. Giacomo or Iacopo Galeota, a leading condottiere and scion of an ancient Neapolitan family, who had always followed the Angevin banner in the Kingdom of Naples. He continued to serve the Angevins after Duke John's defeat in 1464, and in 1472 he passed to the service of Charles the Bold [Benedetto Croce, *Vite di avventure di fede e di passione* (Bari: Laterza, 1936), pp. 69, 80–83, 93, 95–97; Walsh, "Charles the Bold," chap. 7, passim].

2. This was one of the principal charges levelled against the King by the lords of the League of the Public Weal [Pierre Champion, *Louis XI*, vol. 2 (Paris: Champion, 1927), pp. 61–66].

3. Charles of Anjou had been deprived of his Governorship of Languedoc because of his participation in the League of the Public Weal [Vaesen, *Lettres*, 2:71, n. 1; cf. doc. 4].

4. See doc. 42.

5. Yvon du Fou, Lord of the Ramenteresse and of Fou, and Captain of Lusignan since 1464 [Mandrot, *Dépêches*, 3:240, n. 3].

6. Marie de Foix. See doc. 1, n. 2.

7. The possession of the city of Alessandria had long been disputed by the Dukes of Milan and the Marquises of Monferrat. During the struggle for the succession of Milan, Francesco Sforza had promised to give the city to Monferrat, but upon becoming Duke he broke the promise, imprisoned Lord Guglielmo, brother of Marquis Giovanni of Monferrat, and forced them to renounce their claims to the city (1450) [Damarco, "Guglielmo I Paleologo," pp. 551–52]. There is evidence that after the death of Francesco Sforza the people of the city were growing increasingly restive against the Sforza government [Alessandro Visconti to the Duchess of Milan, Alessandria, 11 March 1466, *Carteggio Interno-Alessandria*, cart. 775]. Many other dispatches in this *cartella* attest to their rebellious mood.

As I sent word[1] to Your Lordships by Giovanni Bianchi, I advise you that Saturday night I arrived here at Lyon where much cordiality and many honors were extended to me by these officials and citizens, including Franceschino Nori, all of whom came to meet me. Since my horses were quite worn out and I needed to make some provisions for them, I was compelled to tarry here for one work day, that is, today. Tomorrow without fail I believe I will leave to continue my journey, in which I will waste no time whatsoever. Having found here a member of the Bailli's[2] household, who had come expressly to await my arrival, I sent him back with my letters addressed to the aforementioned Bailli and to Giovan Pietro Panigarola. In them I wrote that they advise me, either by letter or by messenger, whom I can meet at Bourges (where I will be Monday without fail), of the journey I must undertake and where I must head to meet His Majesty the King. I hear that the King will leave Montargis and I believe he will more than likely go to Paris than elsewhere. When I am with His Majesty, I will bend every effort to execute diligently Your Excellencies' instructions, keeping Your Lordships constantly advised of all that happens and of all I learn. You must have heard from the two couriers I met while on this trip just how things stand at the Court. Therefore, I will not dwell upon writing more regarding what I learned from Franceschino and also from Baude [Meurin],[3]

48 · PIETRO DA GALLARATE *to the*

DUKE *and* DUCHESS OF MILAN

Francia, cart. 532. Orig.

Como per Iohanne Bianco scripse[1] a V. S.rie, le aviso che sabbato de sera giunse qui a Lione dovi me sonno state facte molte careze e honori da questi Officiali e citadini, e cussì da Franceschino Nori, quali tucti me venero incontra. E perché li mei cavalli erano pure strachi e me li bisognava fare alcune provisione, me é stato necessario demorarme qui un dì da lavore, che é hoze. Domane infallanter credo me partirò per proseguire el viazo mio, al quale non perdarò tempo alcuno. Et havendo ritrovato qui uno famiglio del Bayli,[2] che era venuto per intendere la venuta mia, l'ho rimandato indreto con mie littere dirrective al dicto Bayli e a Iohanne Pedro Panigarola, per le quale gli ho scripto che me vogliano avisare per sue littere, o per messo che ritrova a Borges, dovi serrò lunedì infallanter, del viazo che io haverò a fare e dovi me debia drizare, per ritrovare la M.tà del Re, la quale intendo s'é de partire da Montrargis e credo andarà più presto a Paris cha altrove. E quando serrò da la M.tà Sua, me sforzarò con ogni diligentia exequire quanto ho in commissione da Vostre Ex.tie, e de quanto succederà e de ogni cosa che intenderò, ne avisarò continuamente le S. V., le quale haveranno inteso da duy cavallari quali ho incontrati per questo mio viazo, como passano le cose de la Corte. E per questo non me extenderò a scrivervi più ultra de alcune cose quale ho intese da Franceschino, e cussì da Baldizono,[3] quale va da Filippo Monsignore perché, come é dicto, son certo che le V. S.

who is going to My Lord Philip; for as I said, I am sure that Your Lordships will have heard from the aforementioned couriers how things stand at the Court. Moreover, I have also avoided writing you too expansively because I have no safe messenger going your way, so that I must hazard this present letter to Your Lordships, to whom I constantly commend myself.

HISTORICAL NOTES

1. Earlier, in several brief dispatches, Pietro da Gallarate had kept the Dukes informed of the progress of his journey to France, which was delayed at first by torrential rains and swollen rivers. Having left Milan on 11 June [doc. 44], he passed through Monferrat, where on 13 June he had an interview with Marquis Guglielmo. The Marquis gave him a full report on what Lord Philip intended to do in Savoy, a report to which Pietro merely alluded and deemed not fully credible. He spent the night of 15 June in Turin, and the next day he was at Novalesa ready to cross the Alps. On the nineteenth, he reached Aiguebelle, intending to proceed to Chambéry the same day. Saturday morning, 21 June, he arrived at La Verpillière, twenty-five kilometers southeast of Lyon, which he reached that evening, as this dispatch indicates [Pietro to the Dukes, Crescentino (near Vercelli), 14 June, *Savoia*, cart. 482; Novalesa, 16 June, *Carteggio Interno-Novara*, cart. 828 (here misfiled); Aiguebelle, 19 June, *Francia*, cart. 532; La Verpillière, 21 June, ibid., cart. 532].

2. Evidently, the Bailli of Lyon, François Royer.

3. See doc. 46.

haveranno inteso da dicti cavalari como passano le cose de la Corte. Non me sonno etiamdio voluto extendere troppo a scrivervi, perché non ho messo alcuno certo che vegna da V. S., ale quale me bisogna mandare questa a ventura, e a le quale continue me ricomando.

Your Excellencies should not wonder if I have not made earlier response to the letter you wrote me on the twenty-sixth of last month;[1] this came about because the King did not want anyone with him except a few chosen individuals while he was hunting in the woods eight leagues from here—he wanted to deal with no business at all, and moreover there was no lodging in the vicinity. But as soon as was possible I had audience with His Majesty and explained to him what Your Excellencies wrote me in this letter, to which he responded as follows.

First, regarding [the facts] that His Holiness the Pope has engaged in his service Lord Napoleone [Orsini], and is giving signs of wanting to undertake something, and so forth, and regarding the letters that Your Excellencies would want His Majesty to write in addition to deferring his pledge of obedience: he responds that it displeases him greatly that the Pope seeks such dissension, because in trying to execute his plans, it will be necessary that the identity of various parties be known, and perhaps a great deal of trouble will result. He is very happy to extend every favor to Your Lordships and write to the Pope as strongly as possible, believing, however, that the Pope will reconsider his position when the Bishop of Cahors will have arrived before His Holiness. The Bishop has been given instructions to that effect; that is, he is to tell the Pope that were he to try anything against Bologna or otherwise in

49·GIOVAN PIETRO PANIGAROLA *to the*

DUKE *and* DUCHESS OF MILAN

BN, Fonds Italien, Cod. 1593, fols. 270–72v. Orig.
Francia, cart. 532. Orig. [Postscript]

Non si maraviglieno le V. Ex.tie se più presto non ho facto risposta ad le littere che quelle mi hanno scritto de dì XXVI dil passato,[1] che hé proceduto per essere stato questo S. Re in certi boschi qui vicini ad leghe VIII ad cazare, et con luy non ha voluto cha persone ellecte et rare, né occupatione alchuna di che sorte si fusse, et anche non li era logiamento; pure più presto mi hé stato possibile mi sono ritrovato con la M.tà Soa, et havendo a quela explicato quanto V. Ex.tie per esse littere mi scriveno, mi ha risposto in tale forma.

Et primo, che la Sanctità de Nostro Signore habii soldato el S. Napolione et monstra di volere fare de le cose etc., et le littere voriano V. Ex.tie scrivesse la Soa M.tà, et ulterius differissa la obedientia: risponde quella despiacerli grandemente ch'el Papa cerchi tale discessione, perché, volendole mandare ad effecto, bisognarà che le parte se discoprano et forsi sarà per seguire di gran male; che hé contenta et vole fare ogni favore possibile ad le V. S. et scrivere al Papa più favorevelmente che si possa, credendo però ch'el Papa farà de novi pensieri, quando el Vescovo di Cahors sarà gionto da la Soa Sanctità, che ha le instructione di tale tenore, cioé de dirli che quando faza interpesa suso Bologna o altramente in preiuditio de le V. Cel., che non li mandarà la obedientia.[2] Pure di novo farà replicare ad esso Vescovo et etiam al Papa, et commandò a queli dil Consiglio di la soa camera, che facesseno fare queste littere, le

prejudice of Your Highnesses, the King would not extend him his pledge of obedience.[2] Nevertheless, he will have this repeated to the Bishop and also to the Pope, so he ordered those of the Royal Council of his chamber that they write such letters, which every day I seek to expedite. It seems [to His Majesty] that if the Pope *were to persist in these fantasies, that King Ferrante should immediately have some troops ride toward the church's territory, since he is quite close; for His Holiness would have greater regard for that, fearing of losing King Ferrante or that he may cause him some trouble given his proximity, than he would for any number of letters that might be written to him. Yet if he were to persevere in his notion of wanting to undertake something against Bologna, it seems to him that it would be useful to urge King Ferrante to do this, showing his face to the Pope by sending some cavalry towards the Marches; and since the troops of Your Lordships are on their return journey from the Kingdom of Naples, he says that it seems to him that they could try to overcome the troops of the Church or at least prevent them from passing;* yet he hopes that as soon as the ambassador of His Majesty has arrived there, His Holiness will change his mind.

Regarding *deferral of the pledge of obedience to the Pope, until it is better understood how His Holiness will proceed, His Majesty says that by his honor he cannot defer it much longer; perhaps such a dilatoriness has already displeased both God and the world. For the whole month of July His Majesty hopes that his ambassadors* might be ready to leave, including the Most Reverend Archbishop of Lyons [Charles], brother of the Duke of Bourbon. As his counselors keep reminding him, he should make [his pledge] in simple form according to the obligations of the Church [of France?], which he cannot avoid. So that it seems to him that in the meantime Your Lordships must make every effort to insure yourselves against the Pope, while the aforementioned embassy is being dispatched.

I besought *His Majesty to further defer this embassy of obedience* [to the Pope] *as a special favor to Your Lordships; reminding him that if His Majesty were to postpone it into October, the* [suitable] *time for*

quale ogni giorno sollicito. Et che li pareria quando el Papa *vada drieto ad queste fantasie, che el Signor Re Ferrando facesse subito cavalchare qualche giente verso le terre dela Giesia, perchè lui li hé vicino et più temeria la S.tà Soa, dubitandose de perdere el Re Ferrando o che li facesse qualche novità, essendoli propinquo come hé, cha de quante litere se li possa scrivere. Et quando pure perseveri in questa soa opinione di volere interprendere sopra de Bologna, li pare che se habii ad indure el prefato Re Ferrando ad farlo et monstrare el viso al Papa; et così che mandi qualche cavalli verso la Marcha, et essendo le gente de le S.rie V. in camino per ritornare del Reame de Napoli, dice parerli che si assazasseno de svalissare esse giente dela Giesia o di vetarli che non passasseno.* Pure spera, che gionto che sarà lo ambassatore di Soa M.tà di de là, che la p.ta Sanctità mutarà pensiero.

A la parte *de diferire de mandare la obedientia al Papa fino che se intenda meglio come la S.tà Soa se governarà, dice la M.tà Soa che con suo honore non la pò però diferire tropo più, et che forsi questa tale dilatione a Dio et al mondo li hé stata nociva, sperando che per tuto el mese de luglio l'ambassata de la M.tà Soa* sarà presta a partire; in la quale andarà el Rev.mo Arcivescovo de Lione, fratello del Duca di Borbon, et che questi soy Consiglieri gli lo ricordanno, cioé farla in simplici forma sicondo el debito de la Giesia, et che da questo non se ne pò retrare. Siché in questo mezo li pare che V. S. mettano ogni opera per assicurarsi dil Papa, tanto che la dicta ambassata si aparechiarà.

Et pregando io *la M.tà Soa a diferire più oltra questa ambassata del obedientia per favore de le S.rie V., ricordandoli che se la M.tà Soa tardarala verso octobre ad mandarla, sarà passato el tempo de campezare,* et paura de *non havere la obedientia la S.tà Soa lassarà l'impresa,* donde se poy uno altro anno vorà atemptare tale cosa, le V. S. meglio et più convenientemente provederano al bisogno. *Dice essa Maiestà che la diferirà più che li sarà possibille, et ulterius che* essa ambassata simpliciter portando la obedienzia de la Giesia, tantum quando andarà, parlarà al Papa tanto amplamente et favorevelmente per le V. Ex.tie quanto si porà al mondo, et così li darà commissione. Interim aviseno quele quanto li

making war would be over. *Then in fear of not receiving His Majesty's* pledge of obedience, *His Holiness would abandon the enterprise.* If in another year he should make another attempt, Your Lordships would then be better and more strongly ready for the task. *His Majesty replied that he will defer it as much as will be possible; moreover,* the ambassadors, while simply bearing the obedience of the Church [of France] whenever they go forth, will speak to the Pope amply and favorably on behalf of Your Excellencies as much as is humanly possible—and he will so instruct them. Meanwhile Your Lordships can advise us of what seems expedient; *and although His Majesty says that the embassy will be ready by the end of July, the opinion of knowledgeable people* is that it will not leave before September,[3] for these French fear the heat, and even now say that one cannot ride in these hot months in Italy, since there is a great danger of the plague, which they hold in great account. In addition, the Most Reverend Cardinal of Albi,[4] who is supposed to go to Rome in order to help and guide the embassy, will not leave until September according to what a man of his household told me who arrived here yesterday; and so I notify Your Highnesses of this.

Regarding the ambassador sent by Your Lordships to the Illustrious Duke of Burgundy and to My Lord of Charolais, and in reference to what he is to say to them in His Majesty's favor, and also regarding the instructions given him: it pleased the King greatly, and twice he thanked Your Excellencies for the very gracious service. Likewise it pleased him greatly that the aforementioned ambassador is to keep a general approach until it is more amply known how My Lord of Charolais will conduct himself. His Majesty says that it is not true that [My Lord of Charolais] has agreed to marry the sister of King Edward of England, but that rather he has completely repudiated that negotiation;[5] so that he would be very happy to be kept informed, when the aforementioned ambassador will have arrived there [at Burgundian court], so that he can give thought to what may be needed.

Regarding *the arrival* [here] *of Duke John, I told him all that* Your Excellencies wrote me. To which His Majesty once again replied that *it*

parerà expediente, *et benché la M.tà Soa dicha per tuto luglio l'ambassata sarà in ponto, la opinion de chi intende* hé che più presto cha el mexe di setembre[3] non partirà, perchè questi Franzosi temeno el caldo, et già dicono che non si pò cavalchare per questi mesi caldi di de là et che li hé gran periculo di peste, dil che tengono gran conto. Etiam el Rev.mo Cardinale d'Albi,[4] quale debbe andare a Roma per adiutare et drizare questa ambassata, non partirà fino dil mese di setembre, sicondo mi ha dicto uno suo, quale gionse qui heri, siché ne aviso le Vostre Celsitudine.

Del *ambassatore mandato per le S.rie V. ad li Illustrissimi Duca di Bergogna et Mons. de Chiarolois, et le parole ha a dire ad essi in favore de la M.tà Soa et* così dela commissione ha, li piaque molto et doe volte ne ringratiò le V. Ex.tie, monstrando havere grato el servitio. Et così li piaque assay che dicto ambassatore stia suxo el generale, fino che se intenda altramente como si governarà Mons.re Chyaroloes; el quale, dice essa M.tà, non essere vero che habii tolto la sorella dil Re Adoardo de Inglitera, ma dil tuto havere refudato quela practicha,[5] et sarà contenta essere avista quando el p.to ambassatore sarà di là, adciò che bisognando li possi far pensiero.

Circha *la venuta del Duca Iohanne, li ho dicto quanto* le Ex.tie V. mi scriveno. Ad che la M.tà Soa di novo mi replicò *essere necessario lo intertegna, ad fine che Mons. de Chiarolois* più tosto condescenda *al parentado dela fiola soa, vendendola carezare esso Duca Iohanne, ma che ben lo tegnirà in modo che non porà fare dano ad le S.rie V.*; notificandoli che se *el Duca Iohanne persevera ad metersi in questa Corte come fa, dubito le cose vostre del canto de qua non sarano così favorevele come prima, ad li cigni che vedo. El che* volontieri ricordo ad le V. Ex.tie adciò li posseno fare pensiero, *maxime che hora si cercha de metere persone al Consiglio de la M.tà Soa in camera tute Angiovine, aciò che quela non possi fare né disponere se non quanto ad queli parerà et consigliarano. Prego Dio per* soa gratia voglia provedere *ad la mala volontà deli homeni. Questo Duca Iohanne cercha de roversare*[a] *tuta questa Corte se*

---

a. C. C. incorrectly reads: governare.

was necessary to maintain him [here] *so that My Lord of Charolais* might more easily agree *to the match with his daughter, once Charolais saw him graciously treating Duke John; that he would treat* [*Duke John*] *in such a way that he could not harm Your Lordships.* I point out that if *Duke John perseveres in putting himself forward in this court as he does, I fear that your affairs here will not prosper as before, according to the signs I see.* I most willingly remind Your Excellencies *of this* so that they can give it thought, *especially since presently there is an attempt to place individuals, all of them Angevins, into the council chamber of His Majesty, so that he can do nothing nor dispose of anything except what they see fit to advise. I pray God that through* His Grace he may wish to ward off *the evil intentions of men. Duke John seeks to control the entire court if he can. Of all that* further occurs on a daily basis Your Lordships will be advised.

Regarding the news about the Turks sent from Rome by Messer Agostino Rossi, His Majesty was extremely grateful to hear it and says that it greatly pleases him; so that the Venetians will not have any reason to cause disturbances to Your Excellencies nor to attempt any new moves against you. He asked me if the league between Your Lordships and them [the Venetians] had been reconfirmed, since each hour seems to him a thousand years in hearing about this reconfirmation. He fears, however, that by using gentle words they might be hiding a new move, as might be gathered from what these Angevins are saying. I answered that I had no news at all about the above confirmation, but from what I understood, your dealings with the Venetians were on very good terms; Your Excellencies had no fear at all of them, having already been given assurances, and at present there could be no war with them for many reasons, especially since they have so much to do against the Turks.

Regarding the presence of [Jean de] Village in Genoese waters, sailing on that sea and pirating, and so forth, His Majesty says that Your Excellencies would do a very meritorious act in having him taken and relieving him of his galleys and all that he has in the world, thus punishing him for his vices, for he is a bad scoundrel.

potrà. Et che più oltra ad lo giornata seguirano, sarano continue le V. S. avisatte.

Dele novelle dil Turcho mandate per Misser Augustino Rosso da Roma, ha auto carissimo la M.tà Soa intenderle; et dice piacerli molto, adciò che Venetiani non habieno casone di dare disturbo ad le V. Ex.tie, né temptare altrove novità contra di quelle. Et domandome se fra esse V. S. et loro la ligha hé riconfirmata, parendoli un'hora mille anni di sentire che sii reconfirmata, che dubita pure sotto bone parole non fazano qualche nova practicha, et questo per le parole dicono questi Angiovini. Io li risposi non haverne novella alchuna di confirmatione, ma per quanto intendeva, le cosse vostre cum Venetiani erano in bonissimi termini, né le V. Ex.tie di loro dubitavano essendone già assicurate, né con loro potevano di presente havere guera per molte rasone, havendo etiam da fare como hanno contra el Turcho.

Che Villagio sia in Genoese et discora quel mare robando etc., la M.tà Soa dice, che si fa cosa alchuna indebita, che le V. Ex.tie lo fazano pigliare et torli le galee et quanto ha al mondo, che hé uno ribaldo et cativo, et in tal modo dice si vole punire el diffecto suo.

Circha li scudi II.M che mancavano ad le gente d'arme, ad questa hora sono certo V. Ex.tie haverano inteso da Zohanne Biancho la risposta mi fu facta, che li scrissi tuto el caso; et per non dare a quele graveza, non mi parse di passare più ananzi senza suo consentimento, dubitando etiam di perdere el tempo, donde non achade dire altro perché, como ho dicto, sono certo haverano inteso el tuto.

Circha al facto *de Ast et del parentato*, la M.tà Soa dice che si sforzarà con la Dio gratia atendere quanto ha promisso a tuta soa possanza, et voria che questo matrimonio si concludesse omnino dil tuto, quale dice consiglia ad le V. Ex.tie. Et li pare per ogni modo et conforta ad quele ad mandare da Filippo Mons.re ananzi parta di Savoya, ad concluderlo et acordare de la dotta con luy, perché non partirà così presto, ma debbe andare da le Lighe de Alamagna et de Suyceri ananzi ritorni qui; et che essendo Filipo grande et in reputatione et havendo el payse in mano como ha, dovendo etiam loro pagare la dote, perché dice el

Regarding the two thousand écus that are short in payment for the troops, by now I am certain that Your Excellencies will have heard from Giovanni Bianchi the answer made to me, for I wrote to him of the entire matter; so as not to give you any concern, it does not seem prudent to me to proceed further in this without his consent, for I greatly feared wasting any time. There is no necessity to say anything else, since as I said, I am sure that you will have heard everything in this connection.

Regarding the matter of *Asti and the marriage*, His Majesty says that he will bend every effort, with God's grace, to observe what he promised within his powers, wishing that this matrimony be concluded once and for all. And so he counsels and urges Your Excellencies above all to send [an envoy] to Lord Filippo before he leaves Savoy, to conclude the matrimony and negotiate the dowry with him. He will not be leaving so soon because he must go to the German and Swiss Leagues before returning here. Filippo is influential, having a considerable reputation and controlling the country as he does, so he is in a position to extract the dowry from them. His Majesty will then provide for the marriage of the other two sisters. He thus feels that it is better to negotiate with him than with others, because then Filippo will place a tax on the country and there will be no exception taken. Moreover, he has the power to do this from His Majesty himself, and therefore it seems [to the King] that this is what must be done in order to gain Filippo's goodwill: *who in the end*, says His Majesty, *will become the ruler* [of Savoy]. *Each day Madam of Savoy writes the King letters regarding the esteem and following that My Lord Filippo now possesses there, complaining that it seems he wants to control the country.* Now, she recognizes her error, in having insistently urged his release, which she presently regrets and will regret even more in the future, knowing to be true what His Majesty said; namely, that she and her children would regret this—but that His Majesty would always be able to handle him. Therefore, although at present she grieves over this, there is no remedy for it, since he has so much power. His Majesty added that he

payse di Savoya debbe pagare la dota di questa et Soa M.tà maritarà poy le altre due sorelle, meglio dice hé concluderlo con luy cha con altri, perché esso Filippo poy metterà la taglia al payse et non li sarà facto exceptione alchuna. Ulterius ha la possanza ad questo fare da la M.tà Soa, etiam li pare che così si debbia fare per captare benivolentia cum esso Filippo; el quale dice la M.tà Soa *che ala fine si farà Signore, et che Madama de Savoia li scrive ogni dì litere del credito et seguito che ha esso Filippo Mons. de delà, dolendose de lui che pare voglia el governo del paise.* Ma hora cognosce lo errore suo, che ley ha tanto infestato ad farlo relassare, che al presente se ne pente et più se pentirà per l'avenire, cognoscendo essere vero quelo che la M.tà Soa diceva che se ne pentiria ley et soy fioli, et la M.tà Soa di luy si deffenderia sempre. Donde al presente, quamvis ella se ne doglia, non se li pò dare però remedio, tanto hé elevato; et dice la p.ta M.tà che ley se servirà de dicto Filippo, et per servirsene bisogna lo adiuti ad fare grande, né per soa sorella li pò fare contrasto, dil qual *caso se ne hé doluto con me fino al anima, maxime che non li pò altramente provedere.* Et in effecto conclude essa M.tà che per queste rasone et per stare bene cum Filippo, quale sempre in uno vostro bisogno pò dar subito et grande adiuto, che V. S. debiano mandare ad concludere con luy questo parentato. Ad le qual cose, *perché intendo hé stato dicto ad la M.tà Sua, et pare che così etiam habii mandato a dire Filippo Mons., che le S.rie V. hano grande bisogno de la M.tà Soa et de lui et che li lassi el caricho, che ben quele mandarano ad suplicare et pregare de havere questo parentato, et con molto meno dinari cha queli ha oferto la M.tà Soa, che hé una summa exterminata,*[6] con molte altre parole: non ho voluto fare ad quella altra risposta, salvo dirli che V. S. mandavano qui el Mag.co Pietro da Gallarà, quale non dubitava circha questo faria bene contenta essa Soa M.tà et che sempre le Ex.tie V. deliberavano servirla a tuto suo potere. Dala quale, gionto che sarà, intenderò la commissione ha da quele in questa materia, et poy si sforzaremo drizare la cosa al miglior camino. Et di quanto sarà dicto et ventillato più oltra, ne haverano le V. S. continue aviso, a le quale fra tre o IIII.to

will make use of the aforementioned Filippo, and in order to make use of him it is necessary to help him become powerful. He cannot oppose him on account of his sister, and in this *connection he expressed his heartfelt bitterness to me, above all because he is unable to take action.* So in effect His Majesty concluded for these reasons and in order to be on good terms with Filippo, who always in time of need could give you swift and great aid, that Your Lordships must send to him to conclude this matrimony.

To all this—*because I have learned that it has been said to His Majesty (and it seems that in like manner My Lord Filippo had sent word) that Your Lordships have great need of His Majesty and of him himself; and if he were in charge, that indeed you would send word to him supplicating and entreating to have this matrimony take place and even with a much lesser sum of money than His Majesty had offered to you, which is indeed an inordinate sum*[6] (and many other similar utterances):—I did not wish to make other response except to tell him that Your Lordships were sending here the Magnificent Pietro da Gallarate, who undoubtedly would make His Majesty quite content in this regard, since Your Excellencies always intended to serve him well within your powers. When he has arrived I will learn from him the instructions that he has from you on this matter, and then we will bend every effort to put things on the right track. Of all that will be further said and discussed, Your Lordships will be continually advised. Within three or four days I will notify you of some negotiations that I understand have been put into practice regarding this matter.

I have delayed the present courier sufficiently so that I might give him the letters which the King writes to the Pope and to the Bishop of Cahors. As I said, they have been rewritten twice, and they have not yet been dispatched. Moreover, it seems that the council of the royal chamber, *which in Angevin,* sees it *as an act contrary to them when His Majesty does some little favor for Your Lordships, and they consider it with very bad will indeed.* Nevertheless, within two days I expect to have the letters[7] dispatched in the best form possible, and very swiftly I will send

giorni significarò alchune practiche, che intendo sono ordite sopra questa materia.

El presente cavalaro ho differito tanto ad mandarlo per volere che portasse le littere scrive questo S. Re al Papa et al Vescovo di Cahors. Como ho dicto, sono state rifate doe volte, et anche non sono spazate. Et più pare ad questo Consiglio di camera dela prelibata M.tà, *che hé angiovino, che quando quela fa un pocho de favore ad le S.rie V., che proprio sia facto contra de loro et lo vedeno mal volontieri.* Nondimancho fra doy giorni spero haverò le littere[7] spazate in la miglior forma mi sarà possibile, et quelle volando mandarò ad le V. Ill.me S., ad le quale sempre me riccomando.

Post scripta. *Qui hè venuto uno chiamato Gabriele de Paleariis da Varese,[8] che hè usato stare con el Magnifico Mesere Tomaso da Riete[9] et fo con lui di qua et in Bergogna, ad Genua et in molti altri loci, giovene aparisente et assai eloquente et scorto, di etate de anni circa vintiquatro. Per Gastoneto ha facto dire ad questo Signor Re de Franza che li haveva ad parlare, mandato dal prefato Meser Tomaso, pregandoli audientiare. Trovandose el prefato Iohane Filipo ad tale domanda, fece che Gaston li domandò se haveva littera de credenza; rispose che non, ma che Miser Tomaso lo mandava solo per parlare con la M.tà Soa tantum et non con altri, et che li diria cose che li piaceriano in effecto. La prelibata Maiestà li ha facto dire che li darà audientia et peranche non lo ha facto. El giorno che gionse esse Gabriel, io el cognosceti statim et li domandai quelo andava facendo. Mi rispose che voleva andare ad Roano per certe facende de uno suo parente che là hè morto, chiamato Iohane Delaven, che ha lassato certi beni. Domandandoli de Miser Tomaso, disse che era gran tempo che non stava più con lui et che non lo haveva visto, et che gran pezo fa esso Gabriel non era stato ad Millano. Costui hè venuto qui in compagnia de uno Lucha Damar,[10] genovese foriinscito che sta con el Duca Iohanne, che viene de Provenza, frequenta ogni dì con questi del prefato Duca Iohanne et da mesi guarda più che pò. Le quale tute cose, havendo generato qualche scropulo in la mente mia per le con-*

them to Your Most Illustrious Lordships, to whom I always commend myself.

Postscript: *There has arrived here a certain Gabriele de Paleariis da Varese,[8] formerly of the household of the Magnificent Messer Tommaso da Rieti[9]—he was with him here and in Burgundy, in Genoa, and in many other places—an attractive, very eloquent and alert youth of approximately twenty-four years of age. Through Gaston he sent word to the King of France that he had been sent to speak to him by Messer Tommaso and requested an audience. The aforementioned Giovanni Filippo happened to be present when the request was made and he had Gaston ask him if he had letters of credence, to which he responded that he did not, but that Messer Tommaso had sent him to speak only with His Majesty and not with others, adding in effect that he would say things that would please the King. His Majesty sent word to him that he would give him audience, but he has not yet done so.*

I immediately recognized this Gabriele the day he arrived and I asked him what he was doing. He answered me that he wanted to go to Rouen because of certain business of a relative of his who had died there, by name Giovanni Delaven, who had left certain possessions. When I asked him of Messer Tommaso, he responded that it was already a long time that he was no longer with him, he had not seen him and it was a long period that he, Gabriele, had not been in Milan. [Gabriele] came here in the company of a certain Luca De Mari,[10] a Genoese exile who lives in Provence, with Duke John, who for months has been daily frequenting Duke John's men here, searching about all that he can. All these things have generated some suspicion in my mind, because of the contradictions mentioned above, and out of duty I indicate them to Your Lordships. For my part I will use every zeal and diligence to learn to what end this Gabriele has come, what he will say, and the answer that he will have. Having learned it, I will immediately notify Your Lordships, to whom I always commend myself.

trarietà che de sopra si contiene, per el debito mio le significo ad le S.rie Vostre; et io de qua metterò ogni mio studio et diligentia per intendere ad che efecto esso Gabriel sarà venuto, quelo dirà et la risposta ne haverà, et statim intesa ne darò noticia ad le S.rie Vostre, ad le quale iterum me riccomando.

HISTORICAL NOTES

1. Doc. 35, which is dated 25 May, however. Unless Panigarola is in error, the date might have been changed in the original.

2. See doc. 30, n. 4.

3. The ambassadors, in fact, left in late October [Vaesen, *Lettres*, 3:99–100, n. 2].

4. Jean Jouffroy, Cardinal since 1461 and one of the most influential advisers of Louis XI. The King had written to the Duke of Milan [Meung-sur-Loire, 3 June 1466, *Francia*, cart. 532 (not in *Lettres*)], requesting the Duke to do all he could to facilitate the Cardinal's mission. Jouffroy, however, was still in France in the middle of July [Pietro da Gallarate and Panigarola to the Dukes, Sully, 14 July 1466, ibid., cart. 532], and did not reach Rome until 4 October [Pastor, *Storia*, 2:353].

5. There seems to be no evidence that this is so, although the marriage negotiations at this time were in abeyance [Vaughan, *Charles the Bold*, pp. 45–46].

6. 150,000 écus [Mandrot, *Dépêches*, 3:392].

7. In these letters, addressed to the Pope and to the Bishop of Cahors [Montargis, 3 July 1466, *Francia*, cart. 532; Vaesen, *Lettres*, 3:65–69], the King asked the Pope to recall Napoleone Orsini from any contemplated campaign against Forlí, Rimini, and Bologna, which was bound to threaten Milan and the peace of Italy, both dear to the King. The above letters were forwarded to Rome by the Milanese rulers, who by now felt that they were no longer necessary because the Pope was well disposed toward Milan. They left the matter of whether to present the letter addressed to the Pope to the dis-

cretion of the Bishop [The Dukes to Agostino Rossi and Giovanni Giacomo Ricci, Milan, 19 July 1466, *Roma*, cart. 60].

8. Gabriele de Palearis, Paleari, or Pagliari, was appointed, in 1472, *Maestro delle Entrate Straordinaire* by Galeazzo Maria [Cerioni, *La diplomazia sforzesca*, 1:xiv], and the following year, secretary in the Secret Chancery [Santoro, *Gli Uffici* xxiv]. Since such sensitive posts were given to persons of unquestionable loyalty, it is doubtful that his mission to the King was connected with any anti-Milanese activity, as it is implied here. Later Panigarola was assured on this score by Gaston du Lyon, but in such a way that left him perplexed [Panigarola to the Dukes, Montargis, 3 July 1466, *Francia*, cart. 532]. The matter remains a mystery.

9. Tommaso Moroni da Rieti, poet laureate, humanist, soldier, member of the ducal Secret Council, and experienced diplomat, had been on missions to France (1454, 1461–1462) and in many other places. As in the case of Paleari, it is unlikely that Moroni was engaged in any anti-Sforza activity, since he continued to be employed by the Dukes and fell in disgrace for other reasons only in 1474, two years before his death [vol. 1, Introduction, pp. xliii–xlv.].

10. Nothing has been found about this personage. The De Mari family dates back at least to the twelfth century, and was one of the most powerful of the semi-feudal Genoese clans [Antonio Cappellini, *Dizionario biografico di Genovesi illustri e notabili*, 3d ed. (Genoa: Tipografia Olcese, 1941), pp 84–86].

We have received six letters from you, Giovan Pietro, of the first, second, third, fourth, and fifth of the present month,[1] by which we were fully informed of what has occurred there up to that time. [We learned] of the good disposition of His Majesty, the Most Serene and Christian King, toward us and of the show that he makes each day both with Duke John and with all others most openly, of his love for us and of his desire to do all that he can to protect us and our state in every eventuality that might occur. You mentioned His Majesty's statement that we should excuse him if he has not done for us all that he wishes to do, because of the difficulties and continuous problems he has had and still has stabilizing and firmly establishing matters in his realm; and in like manner we have understood what you write about His Majesty having sent word to the magnificent Lord Garcia Bethes that he should not leave, and so forth; and what you learned from the Seneschal of Poitou, regarding His Majesty's desire to negotiate a secret alliance with the Most Serene King Ferrante. [We also learned] from your letters of the King's arrival at Orléans to be with the aforementioned Lord Garcia for that reason, and of the discussions about the marriage and of other matters.

On these matters we do not have anything else to say at present,

---

a. Crossed out: XXII.

50 · *The* DUKE *and* DUCHESS OF MILAN *to*

PIETRO DA GALLARATE *and*

GIOVAN PIETRO PANIGAROLA

Francia, cart. 532. Minute

Havemo recevute VI littere de ti Iohannepero, del primo, II, III, IIII, et quinto del presente,[1] per le quale restamo avisati ad compimento de quanto fino ad quello dì era occorso dellà, et dela bona dispositione della M.tà de quello Ser.mo et Christianissimo S. Re verso nuy, et dele demonstratione fa ogni dì con el Duca Iohanne et con caduno palesemente de amarne, et volere fare quanto li sia possibile per conservatione nostra et del Stato nostro, et per ogni cosa ne possa occorere; dicendo Soa M.tà la vogliamo havere per excusata se non ha facto per nuy quello saria soa voluntà, de che è stato casone l'affano et continue occupatione ha havuto et ha per stabilire, et bene firmare le cose de quello suo Regno. Et cossì havemo inteso quello ne scrivete che Soa M.tà havere facto dire al Mag.co D. Garsia Betes che non se parta etc., et quello hay inteso dal Senescalco de Poytò de la voluntà della prefata M.tà de fare intelligentia secreta con lo Ser.mo S. Re Ferrando, et come era venuta ad Orliens per essere con dicto D. Grasia per tale casone, et del facto del parentato et altre parte in esse se contengano. Ale quale non sapiamo che dire altro al presente, perchè tu Petro saray gionto alla prefata M.tà[2] et ad gran parte de queste littere, et precipue del parentato, haveray satisfacto. Et cossì la M.tà del Re serà poy stata con D. Grasia et havereti inteso più oltra, et expectamo che ne avisati de quanto haveray facto tu Petro, et quello sarà seguito con dicto Grasia. Et cossì ancora Frances-

because you, Pietro, will have reached His Majesty[2] and dealt satisfactorily with many of the concerns mentioned in the above letters, especially those regarding the marriage. Likewise His Majesty the King will subsequently have been with Lord Garcia, and you will have heard further. We expect to be informed, of all that you, Pietro, will have done and of what will have taken place with the aforementioned Garcia. Similarly Franceschino [Nori] will write to us from Piedmont, and when we have had all of this information, we will respond more fully and we will give our opinion regarding the alliance to be made with King Ferrante.

As best you know and are able, we wish you to convey our thanks to His Majesty for the great show he constantly makes with everyone of his most cordial love for us, and of his desire to help and protect us against all who might wish to molest us; [thank him] in addition for the immense benefits that he conferred upon our Illustrious late Lord, husband and father, and afterward upon us. You will entreat His Majesty that he indeed attend to the proper settling of matters in his realm and to establishing himself, because by building his authority on a firm base, His Majesty can give us more effective aid than in any other way; for, having placed every hope in His Majesty as we have, we understand that when affairs are settled in that realm, our own will be led into a good and safe haven. You can tell His Majesty that, to stabilize things in his realm, we shall always be ready to place our every faculty at his disposal without any reservation.

We are pleased to learn about the silence imposed upon those who were seeking to impede the Most Reverend Cardinal of Pavia in the possession of his abbey, and about the sumptuous treatment of the courier who brought the letters of the Signoria of Venice. We want you to thank His Majesty in whatever way seems suitable. We expect you will send us the letters written by the King to [Jean de] Village along with the response of the captain of King Ferrante's fleet.

The Most Christian King's ambassador directed to the Pope was here; we gladly gave him an audience and treated him well, learning all

chino ne scriverà de Piemonte qualche cosa; quali tutti avisi havuti, responderemo più chiaro et diremo el parere nostro circa el fare l'intelligentia con el prefato S. Re Ferrando. Ben volimo, che quanto più sapereti et poreti, in nostro nome rengraciati la M.tà prelibata de tante bone demonstratione quante continue fa con caduno, de tanto cordialmente amarne et volerne aiutare et conservare da caduno, che molestare ne volesse, ultra tanti immensi benefitii per quella conferiti nella bona memoria del Ill.mo quondam S. nostro consorte et patre, et successive in nuy. Et pregareti Soa M.tà de attendere pur ad assetare bene le cose soe in quello Regno et stabilirse, perchè firmando le cose de Soa M.tà, ne dà el megliore aiuto ne potesse dare per veruna altra via, perchè havendo colocate ogni nostra speranza in Soa M.tà, come havimo, tegniamo che assetate le cose de quello Regno, le nostre siano conducte in bono et securo porto; dicendo ad Soa M.tà, che per stabilire le cose de quello suo Regno, metteremo sempre ogni nostra facultà senza reservo alcuno.

Del havere posto silentio a tutti quilli cercavano impedire el Rev.mo Mon.re Cardinale de Pavia in quella soa abbadia, et dele careze facte al corero portò quelle littere della Sig.a de Venetia, havemo inteso et tutto ne piace, et volimo ne regraciati la M.tà del Re quanto ve parerà conveniente. Le littere scripte per el S. Re ad Vilagio expectamo ne ne [*sic*] le mandati, et cossì la resposta del Capitano de l'armata del S. Re Ferrando.

L'oratore de quello Christianissimo S. Re che va al Papa è stato qui; l'havemo carezato, veduto volentere et da luy inteso el tutto, et è partito[3] et segue el camino suo. Nuy li havimo dicto che l'ambassata ha ad fare in nostro favore, la faza con bona prudentia, et humanamente, et con dolce parole, con servatione però sempre del honore de Soa M.tà. Et perchè ad Roma s'è saputa l'andata de dicto ambassatore et le casone perchè va, prima giongesse da nuy,[4] come per la copia dele littere de D. Augostino inclusa intendereti, haremo caro vediati informarve et per quanto possibile ve sarà intendere donde è proceduto tale aviso.

De quello Metre Loys Teuton, Secretario del Sig.re Re, dicimo che tu Iohanne Petro informi Petro de quello te pare li habia ad dire, et luy

from him. He has left on his journey.[3] We told him that he should perform the embassy in our favor with much prudence, courtesy, and gentle
speech, but always mindful, however, of His Majesty's honor. Since the
scope of the ambassador's mission was already known at Rome before he
arrived here,[4] as you will see from the enclosed copy of the letter written
to us by Lord Agostino [de' Rossi], we would be happy if you could
learn and get as much information as possible, to ascertain what the
source of this information was.

Regarding Master Louis Toustain, the King's secretary, we instruct
you, Giovan Pietro, to tell Pietro what seems proper to say to him, and
he can then verbally supplement what seems expedient. We are sending
you the enclosed letter of credence for the aforementioned secretary,
made out to you, Pietro. Regarding the cloth requested by His Majesty
the King, we are sending you sixteen arm lengths of black cloth as a
sample which you can present to His Majesty, making our excuses in
whatever manner seems fit; and if he likes it, advise us so we can send
him some more, and tell us what color he would like; and let us know
if he should wish to have it in several colors, because we will make provisions accordingly.

We have understood what you write regarding the prosperous affairs of the Most Serene King of Aragon, the matrimony of King Edward's sister to Don Pedro, and the matters relative to the Count of
Foix and the Count of Armagnac, as well as other occurrences there.
We should be pleased to be kept informed of all these matters, and also
of the conduct of My Lord of Charolais, to whom we will soon send
one of our ambassadors, whose instructions we will communicate to
the King, to whose discretion we will submit all that our ambassador
must do. We have sent a ship to His Majesty the King of Aragon, which
left on the fifth of the present month[5] from Savona.

Try to learn the purpose of the mission of the Marquis of Monferrat's ambassador, and notify us especially regarding those secret
promises, if you can. Try also to learn if the perpetual truce between

suplisca ad boca quanto circa questo ve parerà expediente; et qui alligata ve mandamo una littera de credentia al dicto Secretario in persona de ti Petro. Della saya per la M.tà del Re ve ne mandamo braza XVI negra per una monstra, quale presentareti alla M.tà Soa, facendo la scusa nostra in quello modo ve parerà. Et s'el sarà piaciuta avisatene, perchè gli ne mandaremo de l'altra; et avisatine in quale coloro li piace, et se ancora havesse grato haverne de più collori, avisatine, perchè secondo l'aviso ne dareti, provederemo.

Deli prosperi successi del Ser.mo S. Re de Aragona, et del matrimonio dela sorella del Re Odardo ad Don Petro, et del Conte de Foys, et cossì delle cose del Conte de Armignaca, et de l'altre occurentie dellà havimo inteso quanto ne serve. Havimo caro ne certificati de tutte queste cose; et cossì como se porta Mon.re de Chiarloes, dal quale presto mandaremo uno nostro ambassatore et de l'instructione li daremo ne avisaremo quello S.Re, al quale remetteremo tuto quello esso nostro ambassatore habia ad fare. Ala M.tà del Re de Aragona havemo mandata una nave, quale partì de Saona ali V. del presente.[5] Del ambassatore del Marchese de Monferrato vedeti intendere la cason dela venuta soa et avisatene, et precipue de quelle promesse secrete, s'el poteti intendere; cossì avisatene se sonno concluse le treughe perpetue fra quello S. Re et Inglesi, aut se son per concluderse.

Dele parole hay dicte ti, Iohanne Petro, alla M.tà del Re, del facto de Venetia et Bartolomeo da Pergamo, dicimo che hay facto bene; et cossì è el vero ch'esso Bartolomeo è refirmato con Venetia per uno anno, et benchè habia facte dele demonstratione assay,[6] tamen non ha facta novità alcuna, nè credemo farà al presente. Et quando ben la facesse, tra l'aiuto haveremo da Soa M.tà, S. Re Ferrando, Firentini et altri nostri amici, et quello ne aiutaressemo da nuy stessi ne defenderessemo. Né sapemo ancora iudicare quale sia meglio per nuy, o che fazano novità o che non la fazano. Pur nuy ne siamo proveduti, et provedemo quanto possemo per nuy stessi et con l'amici, per ogni cosa ne potesse ocorere et per poterne defendere da chi molestare ne volesse.

the King and the English has been concluded, or if it is about to be concluded.

We feel, Giovan Pietro, that you performed well in your discussion with His Majesty the King regarding Venice and Bartolomeo da Bergamo. It is indeed true that Bartolomeo has extended his contract with Venice for another year, and although he has made a certain show [of force],[6] nevertheless he has not made a move nor do we think he will presently do so; and even if he were to do so, considering the help we expect from His Majesty, from King Ferrante, from the Florentines, and from other friends of ours, in addition to what we ourselves can do, we shall be able to defend ourselves. We cannot at this point judge whether it would be better for us that they make a move or not. Nevertheless, we are prepared and we will continue to make preparations on our own, and with the help of friends, for every contingency that might occur, in order to be able to defend ourselves from whomever might desire to do us harm.

On the matter of Asti, we commend you, Giovan Pietro, for all you said [to the King], and you, Pietro, should repeat the very same to His Majesty according to the instructions[7] given to you, exerting yourselves with tact in having the King stand firm in his decision to let us have it. In this you must not spare your efforts.

Things here proceed well and tranquilly. There is nothing new in Italy except that our troops, who had been in the Kingdom of Naples with those of Lord Alessandro, Grand Constable, are now in Bolognese territory. His Holiness the Pope has sent his troops after them, as is said, in order to take Forlì, under the guise of defending it.[8]

We are sending you the enclosed letters with news about the Turks; however, we warn you not to mention anywhere Lord Agostino [de' Rossi] or Lord Gerardo.[9] It will be sufficient that you read those portions which seem suitable for His Majesty without naming anyone. Therefore, conduct the matter in such a way as not to lay blame either on Lord Agostino or on anyone else.

We have understood [what you wrote] about Antonello Scaglione,

Del facto de Ast te comendamo ti Iohannepetro de quanto hay dicto et questo medesmo, secundo etiam se contene in la instrutione[7] de ti Petro, havereti ad replicare alla prefata M.tà, sforzandove con bon modo operare ch'el S. Re stia fermo in proposto de farnello havere, et in questo non li mancati de cosa alcuna.

Le cose de qua passano bene et quiete, nè in Italia è altro de novo, salvo che le nostre gente erano nel Reame con quelle del S. Alexandro, Gran Comestabile, sono in Bolognese; et la S.tà de Nostro S. gli ha mandate le soe dreto, secundo se dice per tore Forlì, quale vene omnino ala scoperta de defenderlo.[8]

Del Turco ve ne mandamo incluse le novelle ne havimo. Ben dicimo che non nominati D. Augostino, né D. Girardo[9] in alcuno loco; basta legiati quelle parte sarano expediente, dove parerà alla M.tà del Re, senza nominare alcuno. Sichè governate queste cose in modo non dagate carico nè ad D. Augostino, nè ad alcuno altro.

De Antonello Scaglione havemo inteso, et non dicimo altro se non che stati attenti ad intendere quilli vano ad cerco de quilli del Duca Iohanne, et ne avisate.

De D. Antonio de Romagnano, dicimo non crediamo sia come è stato persuaso ad quello S. Re et al Baylì de Lione, perchè luy non se impazaria de fare cose moleste alla prefata M.tà, nè ad alcuno deli suoy, imo come quello che desydera aquistarse la gratia de Soa M.tà, sempre in ogni cosa se studiarà fare per quilli intendesse essere servitori de Soa M.tà tutto quello bene potesse; et anche perchè sa che compiaceria a nuy, quilli sa che siamo servitori del prefato S. Re, et non voria despiacere ala M.tà Soa et a nuy in uno tracto. Et cossì direti ad Soa M.tà de nostra parte, et anche al dicto Baylì, al quale ne offerirete quanto ve parerà conveniente.

Alla parte del Duca de Borbon, volimo rengraciati Soa Sig.a quanto ve parerà conveniente da nostra parte, de le soe bone demonstratione verso nuy, et ve sforzati tenerlo in questo bon proposito, et li direti che presto li mandaremo uno bono corsero con le barde.

and we say nothing else except that you should be alert in learning who are those seeking after Duke John's followers, and notify us.

We declare that we do not believe to be true what has been told to the King and to the Bailli of Lyons regarding Lord Antonio di Romagnano, because he would not seek to do harm to His Majesty nor to any other of his allies. On the contrary, being one who desires to acquire His Majesty's goodwill, he will always make every effort to do every conceivable good turn to whomever he understood to be His Majesty's servants. Moreover, he knows that it would please us, who are servants of the King, and thus he would not want to displease His Majesty and us at the same time—this is what you will say to His Majesty on our behalf and also to the aforementioned Bailli, to whom you will make whatever presentations seem convenient to you.

We want you to thank His Lordship, the Duke of Bourbon, on our behalf as much as seems suitable, for his good intentions toward us, and we want you to make every effort to keep him in this good disposition; you will tell him that soon we will send him a fine barded steed.

HISTORICAL NOTES

1. Docs. 38–43.

2. Pietro da Gallarate did not reach the royal court at Montargis until 6 July [Pietro to the Dukes, Montargis, 7 July 1466, *Francia*, cart. 532].

3. The Bishop of Cahors left Milan for Rome on 18 June [The Dukes to Agostino Rossi, Milan, 17 June 1466, *Roma*, cart. 59]. He entered Rome on 1 July [Rossi to the Dukes, Rome, 1 July 1466, ibid., cart. 60].

4. Having been alerted that the Pope already knew not only the object of the Bishop of Cahors's mission but also the fact that Milan had instigated this embassy, the Milanese rulers instructed their ambassador at the papal court to meet the Bishop outside Rome and prevail on him to deny any Milanese involvement but at the same time secure a papal bull promising the King that nothing would be attempted against Bologna or Milan. The Dukes feared that the Pope would give only vague assurances and then do as he pleased, once he had received the pledge of obedience from the King [The Dukes to Agostino Rossi, Milan, 19 June 1466, ibid., cart. 59]. In his audience

with the Pope, the Bishop duly stressed that the King had acted on his own initiative, and received assurances that a satisfactory agreement had been reached with Bologna [Rossi and Giovanni Giacomo Ricci to the Dukes, Rome, 5 July 1466, ibid., cart. 60].

5. See doc. 46, n. 12.

6. Colleoni had sent troops in the vicinity of Forlì. To counteract this move, the Milanese rulers notified the Pope that they had ordered their troops returning from the Kingdom of Naples to linger in the Bologna region, with the excuse that they did not have quarters for them in Lombardy [The Dukes to Agostino Rossi, Milan, 24 June 1466, *Roma*, cart. 59]. At the same time, the Pope himself, worried about Venetian intentions in Forlì, suggested that the Milanese troops remain in the area until the situation became clear [Rossi to the Dukes, Rome, 24 June 1466, ibid., cart. 59].

7. Since there is no mention of Asti in Pietro da Gallarate's instructions [doc. 36], or in the Memorandum [doc. 37], these instructions must have been given orally.

8. This paragraph is garbled. Cf. n. 6.

9. Gerardo de' Colli, Milanese ambassador in Venice.

The other day, after the King had dined, he called me into his chamber and said to me that in order to avoid any misunderstanding, I should advise Your Excellencies on behalf of His Majesty that (as I already knew) he had given full power to My Lord Filippo to conclude the match with Your Excellencies for the reasons he had explained to me at other times. He then [said] that Franceschino Nori, before his departure, had very zealously approached [the King] in order to have another proper power of attorney[1] drawn up, *which specified the sum of 150,000 ducats to which His Majesty would be obligated*; even though Franceschino had already obtained ample [powers], dating back to the time of the late Illustrious Lord, your husband and father.[2] Now, His Majesty has learned that during his travels Franceschino has been saying, especially to Gaston,[3] that nothing can be done without him since he has separate powers of his own. These words greatly displeased [the King], because he does not intend that Franceschino be more important than Filippo, or even be his equal, since one is a lord and the other a merchant; such expressions could be sufficient reason for generating disputes and anger between His Majesty and Filippo, or between Your Excel-

---

a. This word, written in the top left-hand corner, appears to be a Chancery's notation connecting this dispatch to another written by Panigarola on 1 July 1466 [Francia, cart, 532], to be published in the next volume. The second dispatch deals almost entirely with the Savoyard marriage, and it bears on the top left-hand corner the notation "secunda."

51·GIOVAN PIETRO PANIGAROLA *to the*

DUKE *and* DUCHESS OF MILAN

Francia, cart. 532. Orig.

L'altro giorno, disnato che ebbe questo S. Re, la M.tà Soa mi domandò in camera et mi disse che aciò che inconveniente non havesse a seguire, avisasse per parte di quella le V. Ex.tie che, como io sapeva, haveva dato possanza ad Filippo Monsignor di concludere el parentato cum quelle, per li rispecti et ragione che altre volte mi haveva dicto; et che poy Franceschino Nori, ananzi che partisse, studiosamente operò con quella che fusse facta una altra procura[1] in forma, *nominando ducati centocinquanta millia et de obligare la M.tà Soa.* Et già esso Franceschino ne ha una altra ampla, fino al tempo de lo Ill.mo quondam vostro consorte et patre;[2] et ha hora inteso la M.tà Soa che esso Franceschino ha dicto, maxime ad Gastoneto[3] in camino, che nulla si pò fare senza luy, et che ha una possanza a parte. Le quale parole grandemente li despiaceno, perchè non intende Franceschino sii più grande de Filippo prefato, nè anche li vadi di pari, essendo uno Signor, l'altro mercatante. Et tale parole ponno essere casone di metere differentia et disdegno fra la M.tà Soa et Filippo, o fra le V. Ex.tie et Filippo; el che, quando fusse, li doleria grandemente, perchè havendo Filippo quel payse di Savoya in mano, et essendo etiam ogni giorno per meglio haverlo, non voria alcunamente rimanesse male contento di quelle, aciò che quando acadesse bisogno, le potesse adiutare essendo vicino como hè, perchè el socorso di Franza non poria essere cha longo. Però voria che Filippo prelibato concludesse in

lencies and Filippo. If this were to come about, it would grieve him greatly, because Filippo has the country of Savoy in hand, and each day his control over it grows, so that he would not wish him in any way to be discontented with Your Lordships: in time of need he could help you, being nearby as he is, and help from France would take a long time. Therefore the King would want Filippo to conclude this matter with Your Highnesses. [The King] *suspects that Franceschino is delaying the conclusion of this matter and creating discord in a vain attempt to gain thirty or forty thousand ducats for Your Lordships, which would be nothing but paper promises, for, as he* [Franceschino] *and I well know, His Majesty at present is not in sound financial condition.* The King wants to *put the matter into effect* [without delay] *and wishes that My Lord Filippo have the honor of it; he has therefore revoked every previous power of attorney except that of My Lord Filippo,* writing to Franceschino that there is no need for him [to intervene] except with Filippo. He added many sinister words against Franceschino, showing himself very angry toward him. To these words I responded that Your Excellencies would not move in this matter, either for Franceschino or for others, except with the approval of His Majesty, with whom the matter had been negotiated and concluded, so that there was no reason to fear a misunderstanding. Moreover, Franceschino could not prevaricate in the matter, because Your Lordships were sure that His Majesty would persevere in the agreements originally arrived at, both with regard to the amount of the dowry and security for it, as well as for other considerations. [Your Lordships] also remained of the same mind, and for that reason you were sending the Magnificent Pietro da Gallarate to His Majesty—adding that I was certain his coming would render [the King] most content and satisfied. I also mentioned that Your Lordships, out of respect and reverence for His Majesty, had tried to maintain Filippo as a friend, and, *if any misunderstanding were to arise between you, you had prudently placed everything in this connection* [in the King's hands]. Moreover, I could not easily believe *that Franceschino would try to break or delay this match, because by the faith he bore* His Majesty, I

queste facende cum le V. Cel. *Et perchè dubita che Franceschino, per fare guadagnare trenta o quaranta millia ducati ad le S.rie Vostre in papero, che quando pure non fosse cha dare papero si potteria passare, che come lui et io potemo sapere, la M.tà Soa non hè al presente in dinari, vada differendo queste conclusione et li metta zizania, et* la prelibata Soa M.tà *voria che si venisse ad li efecti, volendo etiam che Filippo Mons. ne habii lo honore, ha facto revocare ogni procura facta de qui indrieto, salvo quela de Filippo Mons., et* scritto ad Franceschino che non li bisogni se non cum esso Filippo; dicendomi molte sinistre parole dil p.to Franceschino et monstrandosi sdignata fortemente contra di luy. Ad le qual parole, rispondendo io che per Franceschino nè altri le V. Ex.tie non si moveriano in questa materia, se non cum la M.tà Soa, con la quale era tractata et conclusa la materia, donde non haveva a dubitare de inconveniente; et più che Franceschino non poteva prevaricare la materia, perchè le V. S. erano certe che la M.tà Soa perseverava in li primi termini ragionati tanto de la somma de la dota et segureza di quella, como altramente, et loro etiam stavano in el medessimo proposito et per questo mandavano el Mag.co Piero da Gallarà da la p.ta Soa M.tà, per la venuta dil quale mi rendeva certo quela restaria contentissima et satisfacta; concludendoli etiam che le S. V. per rispecto et riverentia de la M.tà Soa si haverano cercato di conservare Filippo predicto amico, et *se diferentia fra loro fusse per venire, come prudentissime haverano remisso el tuto circha ziò ad quela.* Nè poteva io etiam ben credere *che Franceschino cercasse de rompere o dilatare questo parentato, perchè per la fede che* luy portava ad M.tà Soa, lo haveva visto sempre inclino et affectionatissimo al volere et piacere di quela; et che hora deviasse dal bon camino parevami difficile, allegando quele più conveniente parole che mi parse ad questo effecto, ma che nondimanco ne daria aviso ad le p.te V. Ex.tie incontinente. La M.tà Soa mi rispose che quelo diceva, diceva a bon fine et aciò che scandalo non havesse a seguire, et assay *fredamente mi disse che perseverava in el primo proposito per l'amore che porta ad le S.rie Vostre et* servitii receputi. Et a fine che meglio intendesse el tuto, et più a pieno sapesse notificare ad quelle el seguito, mi commisse ne parlasse a

had always seen him most inclined and most affectionate toward the will and pleasure of the King, and it seemed incredible to me that he would now deviate from the straight path—adding all those expressions which seemed proper to me in this regard. [I told him] that nevertheless I would notify Your Excellencies immediately. His Majesty answered me by insisting that all he had said was directed to a good end and in order to avoid a possible scandal, adding very *coldly that he would persevere in his decision because of the love that he bears Your Excellencies* and because of services received. In order that I better understand the whole matter, and more fully know how to inform Your Excellencies of the outcome, he ordered me to speak to Gaston, who was arriving from there fully informed, and would explain all to me.

My Lords, at Franceschino's departure, *because of certain signs that made us suspicious regarding the dowry, especially My Lord Filippo's power of attorney which was not properly drawn and stated that the amount of the dowry was to be negotiated, Franceschino and I sought to have another one made in proper form—one that expressly stated the sum of the dowry at 150,000 ducats and His Majesty's obligation to provide security for it according to the old agreements. This we did as our duty in order to understand what His Majesty's position was in this matter, especially since he was insisting that* Franceschino come there *with My Lord Filippo to conclude the matter and Franceschino did not want to come without any firm agreement.* From what I have always seen [Franceschino] has always acted correctly and in favor of Your Lordships' interests—[in this case] fearing that they were *not acting so willingly in this matter,* since up to that time nothing at all could be understood with certainty. Now, I understand that with all their energies *they are trying to diminish the dowry, and what is more with this strategy,* some are plaguing His Majesty and instigating him, *attempting if they can to break the match and not have it take place. Some would want that it already be broken, especially the Angevins. Also, My Lord Filippo seems to be saying that he does not wish that so*

Gastoneto, quale venendone di là informato mi explicaria el tuto. Signori mey, a la partita di Franceschino *per alcuni cigni che ne feceno dubitare circa la dota, maxime la procura de Filippo Mons. che diceva de acordare dela soma dela dota, et non essere in forma valida, cercassemo Franceschino et io che se ne facesse una altra in forma, nominando exprese ducati centocinquanta millia per la soma dela dota, et ulterius possanza ad obligare la M.tà Soa sicondo li vechii ragionamenti per secureza dela dota. Et questo fecemo per nostro debito, per intendere de che piede la M.tà Soa andava in questo facto, etiam instando quela che* Franceschino venisse di là *con Filippo Mons. ad concludere, non voleva* Franceschino *venire senza fondamento; el quale per quanto* sempre ho potuto vedere, hè andato drito et in favore de le V. S., dubitando che costoro *non li andasseno così liberamente.* Pure fino alhora non si poteva comprehendere cosa alchuna certa. Al presente intendo che totis viribus *cercano de sminuire la dota, et più con questa via* alchuni infestano essa M.tà et la instigano, *studiando si potesseno de rompere questo parentato et che non havesse loco, quali voriano che già fosse rotto, maxime Angiovini; etiam Filippo Mons. pare che dicha non volere che se dia tanta soma* ʻ*che hè oltra mesura, et che a meno assai et assai la toreti volentieri, quando la vogliano dare.*[4] *Le quale tute cose* significo ad le S.rie Vostre et così farò a la giornata di quanto intenderò. Quelle autem prudentissime fazano quelo pensiero che a loro parirà meglio, dandomi aviso di quanto haverò a fare et dire, et como mi haverò ad governare, perchè mi sforzarò seguire quanto le V. Ex.tie mi comandarano, a le quale in eternum me riccomando.

*large a sum be given, that it is extravagant, and that [Your Lordships]
would willingly take a lot less, when they decide to give it.*[4]

I notify Your Excellencies of all these things and will continue to
do so daily. You in your prudence will do whatever you think best,
notifying me of what I should do and say, and how I should conduct
myself, for I will make every effort to follow the commands of Your
Excellencies, to whom I eternally commend myself.

HISTORICAL NOTES

1. See docs. 34 and 38.

2. That is, in April 1464, when Nori was first sent by the King to Francesco Sforza to negotiate the marriage [Mandrot, *Dépêches*, 2:70–77].

3. Gaston du Lyon had recently returned from his mission to Milan and
Savoy. On his return trip, while he was in Lyon, he received letters from the
King instructing him to return to Savoy and then go to Monferrat to urge
these princes to extend their support to the new Milanese Dukes [See doc.
32, n. 2]. Having just received assurances on this score from both the Duchess
of Savoy and the Marquis of Monferrat, Gaston decided to continue his
journey to the royal court. It was at Lyon that he met Franceschino Nori
[Gaston to the Duke of Milan, Lyon, 9 June 1466, and Giovanni Bianchi to
the Duke, Lyon, 9 June 1466, *Francia, cart.* 532].

4. Panigarola's suspicions and fears were soon verified. Not only the
Savoyard rulers and Lord Philip wished to reduce the amount of the dowry
previously offered by the King, but were also opposed to the marriage altogether or to any alliance with Milan [Panigarola to the Dukes, Montargis,
1 July 1466, ibid., cart. 532].

From Lyons I wrote to Your Excellencies of my arrival and departure,[2] adding that I would not lose any time during the journey, as indeed I have not. This morning, having found here a courier who came from the Court, I decided to write the present letter to Your Lordships and notify you that tomorrow at dinner time I will be at Bourges where I expect some communication from Giovan Pietro Panigarola, or indeed he himself in person, because he thus wrote me by this same courier. Nevertheless, I will waste no time at all, because from Lyons I wrote him by special messenger that on Monday, that is tomorrow, I would be without fail at Bourges,[3] and that there I would await some letters from him. So, as I said, I believe that if I do not find him, at least I will find some letters from him, and according to the information received from him, I will regulate my conduct. Since this courier comes from the Court, it does not seem useful to me to write to Your Excellencies anything that has been going on in this country, for I am certain that Giovan Pietro, who is at the source and thus can be certain of everything, will advise Your Lordships of all that has been learned, more clearly than I would know or be able to write myself. However, as soon as I arrive at the Court, I will make every effort to execute Your Lordships' instructions with as much diligence and solicitude as possible, ac-

52·PIETRO DA GALLARATE *to the*

DUKE *and* DUCHESS OF MILAN

Francia, cart. 532. Orig.

Da Lione scripse ale S. V. del mio giungere et del mio partire,[2] e como non perdaria tempo al mio camino como non ho facto. E havendo ritrovato questa matina qui uno cavallaro che vene da la Corte, ho voluta scrivere la presente a V. S., per la quale le aviso como domane a disnare me ritrovarò a Borges, dovi aspectarò qualche littera da Iohanne-petro Panigarola, overo luy in persona, perché cussì me ha scripto per questo cavallaro. Ma però non perdarò tempo alcuno, perché fin da Lione li scripse per uno messo proprio como lunedì, che serà domane, me ritrovaria senza fallo ad Borges[3] e che lì aspectaria qualche sua littera. Siché como é dicto, credo che non o ritrovandolo luy, al manco ritrovarò qualche sua littera, e secondo lo aviso che haverò da luy, cussì me governarò. Venendo questo cavallaro da la Corte, non me pare extenderme a scrivere a le S. V. cosa alcuna che intenda per questo paese, perché son certo che da Iohannepetro, che sta ala fonte e che ha la certeza de ogni cosa, le S. V. seranno avisate de quanto se intende, più chiaramente che non saperia nì poteria scrivere mi. Ma como sia gionto ala Corte, me sforzarò exequire le commissione de V. S. con quella diligentia e sol-licitudine me serrà possibile, secondo che é mio debito, e di quanto ac-cadarà, continuamente ne avisarò le Ex.tie V., ala quale sempre me ricomando.

cording to my duty, and of all that occurs I will immediately advise Your Excellencies, to whom I always commend myself.

HISTORICAL NOTES

1. This locality may be La Châtre, which is not on the direct route from Lyon to Bourges, but lies 71 kilometers southwest of Bourges—a day's journey.

2. See doc. 48.

3. Pietro arrived punctually at Bourges on Monday, 30 June [Pietro to the Dukes, Gien, 5 July 1466, *Francia*, cart. 532].

APPENDICES

I · *The* DUCHESS OF MILAN *to*

the DUKE OF MILAN[1]

Milan [Mediolani], 11 March 1466
Francia, cart. 532. Minute

GALEAZO. Tu haveray più[a] nostre littere[2] et messi inteso el lacrimabile caso successo del Ill.mo quondam Signore tuo padre, et nostro
consorte, però non te ne replicaremo altro per questa nostra; ben a tuo
conforto te avisamo, che dapoy in qua non é seguito altro. Tutti questi
nostri populi stano con quella reverentia et obedientia et fede verso nuy
et Stato nostro, che erano alla bona memoria del prefato nostro consorte,
et ogni dì le cose passano meglio et più tranquilo, che non é may intervenuto alcuna minima novità de che maynera se sia et questo medesmo
dico de Zenovesi, quali ne hanno scripto per soe littere quanto vedray
per l'incluse copie quale te mando per tuo conforto. Nuy attendiamo ad
fare tutte quelle provisione ne pareno opportune per salveza deli subditi et Stato nostro, et già ne havemo facta bona parte, et dì et nocte non
cessamo provedere ad quanto ne pare de bisogno. Crediamo che prima
la ricevuta de questa,[3] te saray partito per venire in qua, et che prima te
sii posto in camino, haveray con prudentia examinato el tuto et facto
ogni provisione per venire securo, alla quale cosa vogli havere singular-
mente advertentia et mettere ogni tuo pensero et studio per venire securo
che non te incontra sinistro alcuno. Emanuel de Iacop[4] nel tuo partire
siamo certa l'haveray mandato dalla M.tà del Ser.mo S. Re per exequire
quanto haveva in commissione dal prefato quondam nostro consorte, et

---

a. Read: per.

per avisare Soa M.tà del caso et del tuo partire; el che quando non l'havessi facto, vogli subito havuta questa, mandarlo alla prefata M.tà consignandoli l'aligate per la qualle li scrivemo vadi subito da dicta M.tà et exequisca quanto dal prefato nostro consorte haveva in instructione, et etiam quanto se contene in una altra instructione li mandamo inclusa in la dicta soa littera alligata; de la quale instructione etiam mandamo inclusa la copia ad dì,[b] aciò che intendi el tutto, et streggello[c] ad andare tanto presto quanto al modo[d] sia possibile. Se ala recevuta de questa esso Emanuel fosse partito per andare alla prefata M.tà, volimo che subito sanza dimora alcuna li mandi dicta alligata littera, aciò possa exequire quanto li scrivemo.

b. Read: ti.
c. Read: strengello.
d. Read: mondo.

HISTORICAL NOTES

1. Galeazzo Maria. Although he did not receive the ducal insignia until he returned to Milan on 20 March [Appendix, doc. IV], the Duchess addressed him with that title.

2. The Duchess had written to Galeazzo Maria [Milan, 7 March 1466, BN, *Fonds Italien*, Cod. 1591, fol. 279] that since his father was gravely ill and in danger of death, he should return immediately to Milan with Count Gaspare da Vimercate and so notify the King, pledging to him that he would return to France should the Duke recover.

3. Galeazzo Maria left Beaurepaire for Milan on the day this letter was written [Appendix, doc. IV, n. 1].

4. For Emanuele de Iacopo's mission to the royal court, see doc. 2, n. 2.

II · *The* DUCHESS OF MILAN *to the*

KING OF FRANCE

Milan [Mediolani], 15 March 1466
BN, Fonds Italien, Cod. 1591, fol. 328. Copy; Francia, cart. 532. Minute

LA SERENITÀ VOSTRA per mie duplicate lettere, et da Galeazo mio figliolo, haverà inteso el doloroso caso de la morte del Ill.mo quondam mio Sig.re et consorte; et de esso, sono certo [*sic*] per soa innata humanità et carità paterna, ne haverà preso dispiacere et molestia grandissima. Per questa casone et per potere meglio provedere a la secureza del Stato mio, haveva scripto al dicto Galeazo subito venesse da mi, lassando le zente a la obedientia de la Sublimità Vostra. Pare che venendo luy, li homini da Susa dell Ill.mo S. Duca de Savoya gli habiano inhibito el passo, unde gli é stato necessario redurse ad una Abbatia de Sancto Petro lì vicina.[1] Io sono certa essere contra la voluntà de la M.tà Vostra et del prefato S.re Duca che al dicto Galeaz sia facto tale inhibitione in questo mio così arduo et importante caso, che concerne tutto el Stato mio, et che la M.tà Vostra l'haverà molestissimo; però la exhorto et supplico con quanta più instantia posso, se degni provedere con el prefato Ill.mo S. Duca de Savoya, che omnino dicto Galeaz sii lassato passare, et presto, per potersi subito retrovare qui, ove el é expectato con grandissimo desyderio. De la qual cosa essa Vostra M.tà me farà gratia singularissima. Le cose de questo mio Stato per divina clementia sono in bono termino[a]

---

a. Crossed out in the minute: é vero che Bartholomeo da Pergamo, soldato de la Ill.ma Signoria de Venesia, ha facto demonstratione de offendere el Stato mio, ma fin qui non ha facto altro, né credo el debia fare per l'avenire. [it is true that Bartolomeo da Bergamo, condottiere of the Most

et quiete, del che per mio debito m'é parso avisarne la M.tà Vostra, a la quale me ricommando.

Illustrious Signoria of Venice, has shown his intention to invade my territory, but up to now he has done nothing else nor do I believe that he will in the future].

HISTORICAL NOTE

1. See docs. 7, n. 2, and 8, n. 3.

III · *The* KING OF FRANCE *to*

COUNT GALEAZZO MARIA SFORZA

Orléans [Aureliani], 18 March 1466
Francia, cart. 532; Reg. Missive 77, fol. 49v. Copies[a]

Non sine maxima nostri animi turbatione litteras vestras hac hora nobis oblatas perlegimus. Dolemus equidem de casu vehementer, laudamusque prudentiam vestram, et placuit quod in hoc tanto et tali discrimine, mandatis Ill.me consanguinee nostre carissime Ducisse matris vestre ut decuit acquievistis. Pretera, si forte Ill.mus consanguineus noster carissimus Dux Mediolani, genitor vester, ab hoc seculo, quod Deus avertat, migraverit, contentamur et volumus ut armigeras gentes vestras, quas in Delphinatu reliquistis, ad vos illico pro Status et dominii vestri defensione repetatis, cum presentialiter nobis non multum necessarie videantur. Et ubi videbitis oportere, offerimus ex gentibus nostris tot quot volueritis, et illas sine mora ad vos mittemus, cum non minus preservationem Status vestri, quam Regni nostri caripendamus.[b] Verum si contingat prefatum Ducem, patrem vestrum, pristine sanitati restitui, ut toto corde peroptamus, hortamur ut quamcitius in Delphinatu revertamini, ut exinde ad nos iuxta ordinata venire possitis. Iam enim parati erant ad vos ire, quos elegimus pro societate vestra, velut cupidi vos videre. Agite demum prudenter et consulte omnia negotia vestra,

---

a. The original of this letter has not been found. There are three copies in cart. 532 and one in Reg. 77. All are identical except for the missing phrase noted below.
b. Cum . . . caripendamus: missing from two copies in cart. 532.

et ea omnia que videbitis per nos fieri posse ad vestri Status tuitionem et augumentum requirite confidenter, prout etiam latius Iohannipetro vestro diximus.

Loys

Toustain

IV · *The* DUKE *and* DUCHESS OF MILAN *to the*

KING OF FRANCE

Milan [Mediolani], 20 March 1466
*BN, Fonds Italien, Cod. 1595, fol. 417–17v. Copy; Fonds Italien, Cod. 1591,
fol. 301–1v. Minute*

CUM IN PROCINCTU atque expeditione in opido Belreparii essem
ego, Galeaz Maria, pro implendo non minus incredibili quodam desyderio meo quam paternis iussibus ut ad Serenitatis Vestre presentiam me
conferrem, acerbissimo nuncio veluti tonitruo quodam attonitus lachry-
mabilem nobis perpetuoque ingemiscendum casum Ill.mis quondam
Domini patrisque nostri accepi; iussuque Ex.me Venerandissimeque
Domine et matris mee in tam urgenti necessitate et Status huius nostri
discrimina evocatus coactusque, quam maximis potui itineribus, Alpium
interiacentium difficultatibus superatis, in hanc inclytam urbem dominii
nostri sedem et caput me recipere conabar, ubi rebus titubantibus ab
universis civibus et populis his nostris summis votis expectabar. Sed
hunc cursum meum biduo retardarunt oppidani Novalicii ibique cir-
cumstantes, qui agmine facto occurentes et me licet mutato habitu agnos-
centes, novo quodam tumultu repulerunt, et nisi me in quandam aedem
sacram beati Petri ibi vicinam, Deo, ut credo, inspirante recepissem, in
magno vite periculo versabar. Hac autem rei novitate a consularibus
viris magistratibusque Ill.mi Domini Ducis Sabaudie intellecta preter
quorum mentem et voluntatem hec omnia secuta esse facile, credo,
illico liberatus iter meum prosecutus sum et Mediolanum tandem attigi
incolumis; propinquanti autem, pro more institutoque patrie, emissa

mihi ducalia insignia atque ornamenta fuerunt. Eisque sumptis, urbem hanc ipsa die hora 18 ingressus, ab omnibus, tam sacri cleri quam civitatis ordinibus confertissimoque civium et populi cetu, atque occursu tanto gaudio tantaque letitia exceptus sum, ut maiorem dicere nequeam. Hunc etiam meum introytum satis decorarunt R.mus D. Apostolicus orator ac Illustres plerique domini et proceres oratoresque, qui mihi obvii simul cum Ill. D. fratribus meis in paternam sedem me perduxerunt; his omnibus ex ordine peractis, deposito ducali habitu et lugubri reasumpto, Ill.mam Ducem et matrem meam revisi, cuius virtute atque auctoritate res omnes Status huius nostri satis quietus paccatusque inveni. Hec sunt, Princeps Christianissime et Domine observandissime, quae post digressum ex Gallia mei Galeaz in hunc usque diem subsecuta sunt.[1] Quorum omnium debitam Ser.ti Vestre rationem reddendam putavimus. Que et si post funestum coniugis patrisque nostri obitum, divina indulgentia, satis fecunde foeliciter que nobis successerunt. Angit tamen me, Galeaz, plurimum quod officium meum erga Ser.tem Vestram in ea praesertim visenda et debita ei reverentia exhibenda implere nequiverim. Orantes illam suppliciter atque observantes ut in tanto discrimine et Status nostri titubatione, nos excusatos expurgatosque habere dignetur quenadmodum in summa sapientia vestra confidimus. Sibique persuadeat V. S. et pro indubitato teneat, nos semper omni quidem tempore et fortuna cum et hoc Statu nostro et filiis fratribusque nostris omnique denique facultate nostra, ad omnia eius placita iussaque fore promptissimos atque paratissimos. Et si quid ad eam fidei devotionis reverentieque affectum addi potest, que ipse Ill.mus quondam coniunx genitorque noster M. V. prosequebamur, qui certe sumus fuit ob incredibilia in nos collata beneficia in eo et superare contendimus; omnis enim nostra salus a Regia M.te V. dependet, sub cuius protectione vivimus, et in opportunitatibus nostris, si casus accideret, ad eius opem patrociniumque recureremus, in qua omnem spem nostram omneque presidium collocavimus. Eas vero copias gentesque quas mecum habebam in statione divisimus ad omnia M.tis Vestre iussa paratas; neque enim in tam ancipiti casu Sublimitatis Vestre exigentiam

aut honorem nostrum et debitum erga eam officium negligendum putavimus; de illis autem, sive retinendis sive ad nos pro Status huius nostri imo vestri tutela, quid M.tas V. statuerit expectamus, sicus eadem Ser. tas Vestra ex relatibus nobilis viri Francisci Norii et Iohannis Petri Panigarole latius intelliget. Reliquum est quod nos Statumque nostrum nostraque omnia, qualiacumque sint, M.ti V. commendamus et perpetuo dedicamus.

Christophorus   Ci[chus]

HISTORICAL NOTE

1. A more detailed chronology of Galeazzo Maria's return voyage to Milan is given in his letter to Pietro Francesco Visconti and Giovanni Pallavicino [Milan, 21 March 1466, BN, *Fonds Italien*, Cod. 1591, fols. 305–6]. He wrote as follows: "Come sapete, nuy ne partessemo el martedí, che fu a dì XI del presente, da Belrepparo, et dì et nocte seguitassemo el nostro camino per exequire li commandamenti de la Ill.ma Madonna, nostra matre. Et per camino havessemo la certeza de la morte de la felice memoria del Ill.mo Sig.re, nostro patre, pur per messi ad posta de la prefata Ill.ma Madona, nostra matre. Et havendo caminato quasi dì et nocte, el venerdì sequente arrivassemo a la Novelesa, loco de qua de li monti presso Susa, et lì fussemo per li homini de quello loco e li officiali retenuto, non senza nostro grande affanno et dispiacere, come possiti pensare, maxime in uno tanto caso. El sabbato circa le XX hore, mediante la divina gratia, con l'adiuto de li amici nostri et del Consiglio de Turino et de li gentilhomini da Romagnano, fussemo reducti in nostra libertà et se ne venessemo recto itinere, senza demorarne nel terreno del Ill.mo S.re Duca de Savoya, a l'Abbatia de San Nazaro in Novarese, che fessemo più de LX miglia, el dì de la dimenica, acompagnati da li prefati del Consiglio et Gentilhomini da Romagnano. El lunedì venessemo ad Novara, dove fussemo recevuti et dal chiericato et da tucti quelli nostri cittadini con tanto amore et con tanta affectione et carità che seria quasi una cosa incredibile ad dirla. El martedì, per commissione de la prefata Ill.ma Madonna nostra matre, venessemo ad Abbiate dove ne demorassemo el martedì. Hieri, con el nome de Dio, fessemo l'intrata de questa nostra inclyta città, circa le

XVIII hore . . . et tollessemo l'insignie del Ducato et Dominio, secondo el costume, con grande concurso et fervore de questo popolo milanese. . . ." See also Giuliano Gheilynes and Lancelotto Bossi to the Duchess, 15 March 1466, *Carteggio Interno-Pavia*, cart. 845; Galeazzo Maria to the Duchess, San Nazzaro, 16 March, and Novara, 17 March 1466, BN, *Fonds Italien*, Cod. 1591, fols. 287, 290].

V · *The* KING OF FRANCE *to the*

DUCHESS OF MILAN

Orléans [Orléans], 23 March [1466]
BN, Fonds Italien, Cod. 1591, fol. 309. Orig.

J'AY SCEU QU'IL A PLEU à Dieu faire son commandement de feu mon bel oncle le Duc de Millan, à qui Dieu par sa grace vueille pardonner. Je vous prie que de ce vous vueillez conforter. Et au regard de l'empeschement que en Savoye[1] l'on a donné à mon frere et cousin, vostre filz, en soy en alant devers vous, je vous certiffie que ce m'a esté le plus grant desplaisir que de chose qui jamais me soit advenue. Mais de ce ne vous vueillez troubler, car je suis deliberé de mectre ma personne et employer toute ma puissance, tant pour delivrer mon dit cousin, vostre filz, que pour maintenir et garder vostre Estat et Seigneurie, ainsi que je vouldroye faire pour mon propre fait. Et me escripvez souvent de voz nouvelles et comme voz faiz de par delà se porteront, et ce que vous vouldrez que je face pour le bien d'iceulx, et je le feray de trés bon cuer. Trés chiere et trés amée tante, Nostre Seigneur vous ayt en sa saincte garde.

Belle tante, tenez vous seure que je ne vous faudré de ryen. Ecryt de ma main.[a]

Loys

Leroux

---

a. The last sentence was written by the King's hand.

HISTORICAL NOTE
   1. See preceding doc. IV, n. 1.

VI · *The* KING OF FRANCE *to the*

DUKE OF MILAN

Orléans [Orleans], 24 March [1466]
BN, Fonds Italien, Cod. 1591, fol. 310. Orig.[a]

Nous avons sceu qu'il a pleu à Dieu faire son commandement de feu nostre trés chier et trés amé oncle le Duc de Millan, vostre pere, que Dieu absoille, et aussi l'empeschement qui a esté fait au pais de Savoye en vostre personne. Desquelz trespas et empeschement nous avons esté plus deplaisans que de chose qui jamais nous soit advenue; et desja avions fait toutes les provisions neccessaires, tant pour vostre delivrance que pour le passaige de voz gens d'armes, et aussi pour aidier à preserver et garder vostre Seigneurie et Duchié de Millan, comme plus à plain povez avoir sceu par voz serviteurs qui sont devers nous. Vray est que à ceste heure nous avons entendu par lectres et messaiges qu'estez relaxé et delivré,[1] et vous en allez par devers nostre trés chiere et trés amée tante, vostre mere; dont nous remercions Nostre Seigneur, car c'est la chose que avions plus à cueur et que desirions le plus. Et soiez certain que en tous voz affaires nous emploierons nostre personne et puissance pour aider à nostre dicte tante et à vous à entretenir et maintenir vostre dicte Seigneurie et Duchié, comme plus au long vous dira nostre amé et feal Conseiller et Chambellan, Gaston du Lion, lequel envoierons en brief par

---

a. Cod. 1591, fol. 311, contains contemporary Italian translations of this letter and of a similar one written by the King to the Duchess of Milan on the same date, of which the original has not been found.

devers vous. Trés chier et trés amé frere et cousin, Nostre Seigneur vous
ait en sa saincte garde.

Loys

Leroux

VII · *Instructions of the* KING OF FRANCE *to*

GASTON DU LYON *and*

GIOVANNI FILIPPO DA TRECATE

[Orléans], 27 March 1466
Reg. Ducale 39, p. 635; BN, Fonds Italien, Cod. 1591, fol. 315–15v. Copies[a]

PRIMO, presso a la presentatione di le littere,[1] faranno la salutatione costumata in tal caso et diranno che lo Re ha saputo la morte del quondam Duca di Milano suo barba. Deinde è stato et è si displicente che fare si può come dil suo bono barba et alligato, consyderando il bono et grande volere che gli ha monstrato per effecto a soccorrelo, servirlo et aiutarlo in ne le differentie che lo Re ha hauto nel suo Reame questo anno passato; et similemente di haver mandato suo primogenito in propria persona, compagnato di così bello et notabile exercito a sue spese, como ha facto. Del che li dicti ambassatori ringratiano ben caramente li dicti Duchessa et Duca de Milano suo figliolo.

Item diranno a li dicti Duchessa et Duca di Milano per parte dil Re che vogliansi confortare et haver bona patientia de la dicta morte, offerendoli per sua parte che in tutte le cose che al mondo possibile li saranno, è deliberato soccorrergli et defenderli a la conservatione de loro Signorie verso et contra tutti quelli vorranno alchuna cosa temptare

---

a. The unusual construction and orthography of this document are due to its being a translation of the original French text, which has not been found.

sopra loro, et intermettersi talmente che vorria fare per la guardia et defensione dil suo Reame et più se li fosse possibile.

Item diranno più oltra et dimonstraranno lo grande despiacere che lo Re ha hauto di lo impaciamento che è stato facto nel paese di Monsignore di Savoya a la persona del dicto Duca di Milano, dil quale impaciamento é stato più displicente che di cosa gli sia advenuta in sua vita; et che incontinenti che ha saputo dicto impacciamento, tutte cose ha lassiato. Appresso haver mandato il Sinescallo de Poytu et Uselino Duboys, Baylì di Montagna, soi ambassatori, verso lo Duca et Duchessa de Savoya per sua liberatione, mandoe con tutta diligentia il Conte di Runciglio,[2] che è maritato con la figlia di Re, et altri soi capitanei et capi di guerra con bono numero di gente d'arme, tanto per procedere de via de facto et de arme a la dicta liberatione, come per aiutarlo et donarli favore a guardare et defendere sua dicta Signoria di Milano.

Item diranno a li sopradicti Duchessa et Duca di Milano che le dicte provisione così facte et le dicte novelle sono venute al Re de la liberatione, deinde è stato più gioioso che de novelle che longo tempo gli siano state referte.

Et ulterius, dubitando lo Re che lo dicto Duca de Milano havesse a bisognare di la sua gente d'arme essendo in Delphinato, ha dato ordine et provisione al passaggio di loro per loro ritornare securamente al dicto paiese di Milano, così come li dicti ambassatori poranno dire et declarare più pienamente. Et con quello ha caricato il dicto Sinescallo di Santongia de dirli le offerte sopradicte, et de referirli el stato et dispositione de facti di là et le provisione che a loro parirà necessarie per provederli; et a bien lo Re ha voluto mandare per di là lo dicto Sinescallo perchè cognosce il paise, sperando che poterà più fare de servicio a li dicti Duchessa et Duca che altro non haveria facto, non cognoscendo li facti del dicto paese et così che li saria più grato.[3]

Item diranno dicti ambassatori che lo Re manda de presente per de là l'Arcivescho de Vienna et li S.ri di Gauart et di Rampot, a li quali done carico de dimorare a Milano tanto che piacerà a li dicti Duchessa et Duca

per darli conforto et aida et farli tutto servicio che porano, così come far porrano per le proprie facende di Re.[4]

Loys

Leroux

HISTORICAL NOTES

1. Identical letters of credence naming both ambassadors were issued by the King, addressed to the Dukes of Milan [Orléans, 27 March 1466, BN, *Fonds Italien*, Cod. 1591, fol. 314; Vaesen, *Lettres*, 3:42].

2. Louis, Bastard of Bourbon, Count of Roussillon in Dauphiné, married to Jeanne, natural daughter of Louis XI. On the measures taken by the King to secure Galeazzo Maria's release in Piedmont and in support of Milan, see docs. 7–10.

3. In 1459–1460 Gaston du Lyon had been sent on diplomatic missions to Francesco Sforza by the Dauphin Louis, and had been instrumental in the negotiation of the Treaty of Genappe (1460) [See vols. 1–2, passim].

4. See doc. 13. The Lord of Rampot [Roppolo] was Luigi di Valperga.

VIII · *The* DUKE OF MILAN *to the*

KING OF FRANCE

Milan [Mediolani], 13 April 1466
Francia, cart. 532. Minutes[a]

LA M.TÀ VOSTRA PER MIE LITTERE et per mei messi è stata
avisata della morte del Ill.mo quondam Sig.re mio patre, et successive
della presa mia alla Novarese, et poy della mia liberacione; deinde la
Ill.ma Madona mia matre et mi per littere della M.tà Vostra, et per
Mon.re de Logis, et ancora per littere de Iohannepetro Panigarola, siamo
certificati del affanno grandissimo et amaro dolore ha preso della morte
del prefato quondam Sig.re mio patre, et della presa mia et delle preparatione grande ordinate per la mia liberatione. Havimo ancora inteso
quanto piacere, allegreza, et contentamento ha recevuto che mi sia stato
liberato, como etiam non dubito haverà havuto non menore piacere della
assumptione mia ad questo Ducato, dela quale per littere duplicate commune della prefata Madona mia matre et de mi la M.tà Vostra sarà
remasta avisata. Per le quale tutte cose non me faticarò altramente ad
regratiare la M.tà Vostra, cognoscendome inhabile et impotente ad tale
cosa, ma pregarò Dio continuamente, per soa gratia, per mi ne renda
merito alla Vostra M.tà; quale per questa mia aviso, como questo nostro
et suo Stato, per gratia de Dio è in bono termine, et tutti li populi vivano
in quieto et pacifico, et con quella obedientia che vivevano essendoli el

---

a. There are two minutes of this letter, here designated as A and B. A is composed of three
paragraphs, while B has only two, which are identical to the first and third paragraphs of A
except for important variants registered below. The second paragraph of A is crossed out. B
appears to be the definitive text, which has been followed in this transcription.

prefato quondam S. mio patre. Et Zenoesi similiter perserverano in bona fede et disposicione verso la prefata Madona mia matre et mi; nè dubio gli è da canto alcuno, salvo de verso Venetia, per li movimenti et demonstratione ha facte, et continue fa Bartholomeo da Bergamo, como la M.tà Vostra da Emanuel de Jacopo et da Iohannepetro Panigarola, mei famegli, haverà inteso et intenderà. Del che però la prefata Madona mia matre et mi non dubitamo poterse defendere mediante li prudentissimi consigli, adiuti, et favori continue haveremo dalla M.tà Vostra et dalla M.tà del Ser.mo S. Re Ferrando,[b] in li quali è colocato et fundato ogni nostro conforto et speranza; et siamo certissimi quella haverà et pigliarà sempre de nuy, de l'altri Ill. mey fratelli, et de questo suo et nostro Stato, quello carico, speciale cura, et pensero che dele altre sue cose. Et perchè la prefata Madona mia matre et mi[c] manderemo alla M.tà Vostra uno delli nostri per lo facto del parentato,[1] et per più distinctamente et particularmente avisarla del tutto, quale partirà de subito, non me extenderò più oltra.[d]

---

b. A omits: et dalla M.tà del Ser.mo Re Ferrando.

c. Crossed out in A: mandamo [mandaremo substituted] . . . el spectabile mio parente, Petro da Galarà.

d. A's second paragraph, omitted in B, reads as follows: Quanto al parentato de Mon.re Chiaroloys, del quale Emanuel de Iacopo parlò ala M.tà Vostra et cossì Iohannepetro Panigarola, certifico essa Vostra M.tà che l'intentione della prefata Madona mia madre et mia é che ad quello in tutto se metta silentio, perché per cosa del mondo non facessemo cosa che non cognoscessemo essere ben grata et de bon contentamento dela M.tà Vostra, etiam se ne volesse dare el Stato suo et dominio, como in verità fo sempre la volontà del prefato S.re mio patre; né per modo alcuno metteressemo mai el pensero ad cosa che non cognoscessemo essere de bon contentamento de Vostra M.tà. De quello de Savoya, essa Madona mia madre et mi intendiamo de exequire et mandare ad effecto quello che sia de piacere et contentamento de Vostra Serenità, et fo de ordine, voluntà et desyderio del Ill.mo quondam S. mio patre et che fo tractato con la M.tà Vostra; alla quale cosa ed ad tutte l'altre siamo grati ad quella, siamo et saremo sempre volenterosi, bene edificati et dispositissimi. Né may partiremo da veruno suo consiglio, ricordo o parere, como da nostro Honorandissimo Sig.re et patre. Pur essendo cossì poco tempo ch'el prefato S.re nostro patre passò de questa vita, per nostro honore et debito non ne é parso de mandare alcuno alla Vostra M.tà per questa casone cossì presto, ma mandaremo Messe[r] Alberico per executione de quanto fo dicto et tractato in questa materia, como é dicto che fo intentione del Sig.re mio patre. Queste poche parole me é parso de scrivere de mia mano prima che si parta dicto Petro, acciò che se alla M.tà Vostra fosse dicto altramente, intenda l'animo et secreto del core et totale disposicione de Madona mia matre et de mi, che é apuncto quello che per questa mia scrivo, como ancora più largamente intenderà dal dicto Petro la Ser.ma Vostra M.tà; alla quale la prefata Madona mia madre et mi, quanto sapiamo et possiamo, recomandamo nuy et l'altri mey illustri fratelli, et questo suo et nostro Stato, del quale et delle persone sempre se porà valere como de quelle cose soe proprie, che sonno più al suo comando. [With regard to the marriage tie with the Count of Charolais, which Emanuele de Iacopo and Giovan Pietro Panigarola have discussed with Your Majesty, I

Demum aviso la M.tà Vostra, como lo Ill. S. Messer lo Marchese de Mantoa è conduto alli soldi et servicii dela M.tà del Re Ferrando et nostri;[2] el che se è facto per non poterse fare de manco per conservacione de questo Stato, et per non lassarlo accostare altrove che fosse stato periculoso, et non haverlo inimico, como più volte D. Alberico[3] scrisse al prefato S. mio patre, la M.tà Vostra consigliare che se facesse. Hogi giongerà qui la Ill. Madona Marchesana de Mantoa, quale vene solo per visitare la Ill.ma Madona mia matre, et condolerse del caso della morte del Ill.mo quondam S. mio patre, et non ad altro effecto; della quale cosa ho voluto avisare la M.tà Vostra, aciò che se alcuno de questo li dicesse più una cosa che un'altra, sia informata et sapia che respondere.[4] De quello che in l'altre cose nostre alla giornata succederà, ne darò continuo aviso alla M.tà Vostra,[e] all quale la prefata Madona mia matre et mi, quanto sapiamo et possiamo, insieme con l'altri mey Ill. fratelli, et questo suo et nostro Stato, strectamente se recomendamo.

---

assure Your Majesty that it is the intention of the Lady, my mother, and mine that it be completely laid to rest, for we would not do anything in the world that we knew to be but well pleasing and agreeable to Your Majesty, even if he [the Count of Charolais] wished to give us his state and dominion—as in truth it was always the will of the Lord, my father. Nor would we ever think of anything but what we knew to be agreeable to Your Majesty. With regard to the Savoyard marriage, the Lady, my mother, and I intend to execute and put into effect whatever is the pleasure and contentment of Your Serenity and was the command, will, and desire of the Illustrious late Lord, my father, as was negotiated with Your Majesty. So in this, as well as in all other matters, we are grateful to you, and we are, and always shall be, willing, well inclined, and most disposed. We shall never depart from your counsel, suggestion, or advice, as you are our most honored Lord and father. Nevertheless, since it has been such a short time from the death of the Lord, our father, we have thought fitting for our honor and obligation not to send anyone so soon to Your Majesty to pursue the matter. We shall, however, send Messer Alberico [Maletta] to execute what was discussed and negotiated in this matter, as was the intention of the Lord, my father. I have thought fitting to write these few words with my hand before the said Pietro's departure, so that if Your Majesty should hear otherwise, you will know my mind and my heart's secret, as well as the total disposition of the Lady, my mother, and mine, which is indeed as I write in this letter, as Your Most Serene Majesty will learn in more detail from the said Pietro. The Lady, my mother, and I commend, as much as we can and know how, ourselves, my illustrious brothers, and our state (which is equally yours), of all of which you can always avail yourself as you would of your own things that are at your more immediate disposal].

e. A has this ending: alla quale de novo con la prefata Madona mia matre, fratelli et Stato, humelmente me recomando, pregandola me perdoni se più presto non li ho scripto, che certo ne é stato casone le grandissime occupatione ho havute per provedere alle cose necessarie per conservatione de questo Stato. [to whom, together with the said Lady, my mother, brothers, and state, I again humbly commend myself, begging your pardon for not having written you sooner. Surely the delay was caused by the many preoccupations I have had in making all the necessary arrangements for the preservation of this state.]

HISTORICAL NOTES

1. Galeazzo Maria's projected marriage with Bona of Savoy.

2. On 1 April 1466, the Marquis Ludovico Gonzaga signed a contract to serve both Milan and Naples, thus ending the threat that he might serve Venice in opposition to Milan [E. W. Mahnke, "The Political Career of a Condottiere-Prince: Ludovico Gonzaga, 1444–1466" Ph.D. diss., Harvard University, 1974, pp. 361–62].

3. Alberico Maletta, Milanese ambassador in France, 1463–1465.

4. Marchioness Barbara Gonzaga's visit gave rise to hopes that Galeazzo Maria could be prevailed upon to marry the Marchioness's daughter, Dorotea. Their engagement in 1457 had been practically repudiated by Francesco Sforza in 1464, with the pretext that Dorotea was slightly hunchbacked, a deformity which afflicted the Gonzaga family and which had terminated a previous engagement between Galeazzo Maria and Susanna, Dorotea's sister [Mahnke, "The Political Career," chap. 5]. Actually Francesco had decided to accept Louis XI's offer of the Savoyard marriage, a more prestigious and advantageous one. In 1465 the Duke and Galeazzo Maria had issued full powers to Alberico Maletta to negotiate and conclude the marriage while the ambassador was still at the royal court [Milan, 4 March 1465, *Trattati*, cart. 1530], but the matter was postponed [Mandrot, *Dépêches*, 3:87]. Upon the Marchioness's arrival in Milan, however, Galeazzo Maria assured her and his mother, who ardently desired the Gonzaga marriage, that he would marry Dorotea.

Then, having held a session of the Secret Council in the presence of Louis XI's envoy, Josselin du Bois, he abruptly decided to pursue the Savoyard marriage. In drafting this reply to the King, the Duchess wanted to keep this matter open by simply informing him that soon an envoy would be sent to the royal court to announce her son's decision. "Et questo faceva la prefata Madonna [the Duchess] per poter in questo mezo trovar qualche scusa legitima per far remaner contento el Re, rendendosse certa ch'el prefato Ill.mo S.re havesse pur lo animo a la Dorothea." When the Duke inserted a paragraph committing himself to marry Bona of Savoy, the Duchess "cominciò a fulminare e a dire che questo non era quello che ge haveva promesso, et che per niente voleva che la pasasse in quella forma da parte de la Ex.tia Sua, perché l'era scripta in nome de tuti dui. S'el la voleva pur mandare, la facesse in nome de lui solo." This dramatic confrontation at the Milanese court, described in detail in a letter by Barbara Gonzaga to her husband [Milan, 23 April 1466, ASMA, *Lettere Originali dei Gonzaga*, B. 2099], explains the elimination of the second paragraph from this letter [see n.d], and the fact that the Duke wrote only in his own name and avoided making a firm commitment in reference to the Savoyard marriage. The uncertainty about this matter at the Milanese court is also underscored by the fact that this letter was not sent until 30 April [See doc. 24].

IX · *The* DUKE OF MILAN *to the*

KING OF FRANCE

[Milan?, 1 May 1466] [a]
Francia, cart. 532. Minute

L A ILL.MA MADONA MIA MADRE et mi subito mandaremo dala M.tà V. P[iero] de Galarà,[1] prima per fare la debita reverentia ala V. M.tà et regraciarla dele digne offerte etc., item notificarli le condicioni del Stato nostro in che termine se trovano etc., item per rechiederli consiglio et favore come in quella in chi persista tucta la nostra speranza etc.

Ultra de questo, perché forsia sariano de quelli che, havendo tanto tardato, dariano ad intendere ala V. M.tà che la prefata Ill. Madona mia madre et mi, circa lo parentado de Savoya, cognata de la M.tà V., non siamo de quella voluntà quale era la bona memoria del S. mio padre etc., de bona voluntà et licentia dela prefata Madona mia madre, prometto ad essa V. M.tà, como quello ad chi principalmente tocha questo parentado, essere contento de farlo et mandarlo ad execucione in quello modo et forma che havea ordinato el prelibato quondam S. mio padre.[2] E non se marvigli [*sic*] *la* M.tà V. se de presenti non mando Misser Alberico[3] per questa execucione, perché bisogna havere pur reguardo ala morte seguita de mio padre, ma quando parerà ala M.tà V. el tempo conveniente et honorevele al caso seguito, sarò apparichiato ad fare quanto sarà de soa voluntà.

---

a. The original of this letter has not been found and the minute lacks the city and date. In the instructions to Pietro da Gallarate [doc. 36, p. 240], Galeazzo Maria noted that he wrote it in his own hand on 1 May. Cf. also preceding doc. VIII, n.d, p. 408.

HISTORICAL NOTES

1. Actually Pietro da Gallarate did not receive his instructions until 1 June [doc. 36], and left for the royal court on 11 June [doc. 44].

2. It is evident that after the Marchioness of Mantua left Milan on 25 April, Galeazzo Maria prevailed on his mother to give her grudging consent to the Savoyard marriage. The Duchess herself wrote to the King [Milan, 30 April 1466, *Francia*, cart. 532], thanking him profusely for his many demonstrations of support, and announcing the impending departure of Pietro da Gallarate for the royal court, but refrained from mentioning the Savoyard marriage.

3. The postponement of Alberico Maletta's mission with this lame excuse, and the delay in the departure of Pietro da Gallarate, suggest that the question of the Savoyard marriage was still not definitely settled at the Milanese court. For additional evidence about Galeazzo Maria's indecision on this matter, see preceding doc. VIII and Introduction, p. xlviii.

X · *Reply of the* DUKE *and* DUCHESS OF MILAN *to* GASTON DU LYON *and* GIOVANNI FILIPPO DA TRECATE[1]

Milan [Mediolani], 10ª May 1466
Francia, cart. 532. Minute

BREVIS RESPONSIO ad ea que exposita sunt Ill. Dominis Blance Marie Ducisse et Galeaz Marie Duci Mediolani etc., per Magnificos Gastonum Duleon, Consiliarium et Senescalchum de Xantonge, et Iohannem Philippum de Trechate, Consiliarium et Presidentem Camere Computorum in Delphinatu, oratores Ser.mi ac Christianissimi Domini, Domini Lodovici, Dei gratia Regis Francorum etc.

Magnifici ambassatori. Inteso pienamente quanto bene et diligentemente et con sigulare prudentia et gravità et modestia le Mag.tie Vostre ne hano referto et explicato in nome et per parte dela Ser.ma M.tà del Christianissimo Re, se nuy volessimo extenderci in rispondere ad tutte le parte, et ringratiare Sua M.tà secundo che seria nostro debito et che rechiede una tanta et così degna materia, et li immortali beneficii recevuti da Sua Ser.tà per lo Ill.mo quondam Sig.re nostro consorte et patre honorandissimo, et per nuy, cognoscemo expressamente che ne mancariano le parole, et quanto più dicessimo, manco satisfaressimo ad nuy medesmi; ma confidandone nuy in la vostra grande prudentia et virtù, che havete meglio inteso l'animo et intrinseco del core nostro, che non havemo

---

a. Crossed out: VIIII.

saputo exprimere con le parole, et così per vostra humanità tutto referirete et farete bene intendere alla prefata M.tà, per questo ne passaremo più brevi, tocchando succinctamente le parte necessarie.

Primo, circa la condoglianza che fa con nuy tanto amorevolmente et affectuosamente el prelibato Re, del trappasso et morte del prefato Ill. quondam S.re nostro consorte et patre, nuy ringratiamo et così piaciavi ringratiare per nostra parte Sua Maiestà, con ogni humile reverentia et quanto più sapiamo et possiamo ad questo mondo, essendo più che certi che tale caso ad nuy sempre acerbissimo et amarissimo, sia stato molesto et rincresciuto ad Sua Ser.tà quanto vuy dicete, perchè essa M.tà pò dire col vero de havere perduto uno suo grandissimo et deditissimo servitore. Et non bisogni ch'essa M.tà ricorde in questa parte alcuno servitio ch'el habii recevuto in vita del prefato S.re nostro consorte et patre, perchè quelli son stati minimi, per rispecto alli grandissimi oblighi che luy et nuy havevamo verso Sua M.tà, per li grandissimi et immortali beneficii da essa recevuti, et per rispecto anchora alla grande voglia et acceso desyderio che luy haveva de servire et fare cosa che piacesse ad quella, per non parere ingrato de tanti beneficii et de tanta liberalità et amore et carità quanto essa M.tà gli ha monstrato. Et quanto alla parte del essere venuto in Franza de mi, Galeazo, con quelle gente d'arme, questo io me reputo spetiale obligo et gratia verso Sua M.tà, che me toccasse in sorte de venire in quelle parte con esse gente, perchè non essendo io più experto in questo mestero de l'arme come sia, me pariva non potere trovare megliore scola, come quella de Sua M.tà, dove potesse imparare et spechiarme in li grandi facti et magnanime imprese et virtute de Sua M.tà, donde ad mi era molto più honore et reputatione retrovarme lì alla obedientia d'uno tanto principe, che non era alcuno fructo che potesse recevere da mi essa M.tà. Et il maiore piacere et gratia che havesse potuto havere ad questo mondo, seria quando per tale caso dela morte del S.re mio patre non fosse turbato, et fosse potuto venire ad visitare et fare debita reverentia alla Ser.tà Sua, secundo el mio desyderio, et che era ordinato per esso S.re mio patre. Et per non havere potuto fare questo, ne ho recevuto grandissimo despiacere, certificando Sua M.tà che quan-

do Dio ne conceda gratia, como speramo, de assettare et bene quietare queste nostre cose del Stato et che le cose de Italia stiano in pace, io, Galeazo, intendo per ogni modo de fare mio debito in visitare Soa M.tà.

Alla parte, dove la prefata M.tà ne offere così largamente ogni suo favore et adiuto, per manutentione et defesa de questo nostro Stato, como dele cose sue proprie, similiter la ringratiamo immortalmente, et non dubitamo poncto che così sii sua bona voluntà et dispositione, et quando may da nuy non potesse havere altra remuneratione, quella debbe essere certa che facendo per nuy la fa per suoy veri et fidelissimi figlioli et servitori, et per si medesma, perchè essendo nuy in questo Stato, debbe essere certa haverli suoy servitori et disponere de nuy et cose nostre como de quelle che sono più sue.

Alla parte del despiacere havuto per Soa M.tà del arrestare de mi, Galeazo, in el dominio de Mon.re de Savoya, et dela subita provisione facta per Sua Ser.tà per la liberatione mia etc., similmente ringratiamo quella et siamo certissimi de quello ne havete dicto; et questa tale arrestatione credemo fusse facta senza saputa et contra voluntà del prefato Mon.re de Savoya,[2] et così ne apparse lo effecto quando liberamente io fui lassato venire. Et così siamo certi Sua M.tà havesse gran piacere de tale liberatione nostra, como ne havete dicto.

Alla parte, che Sua M.tà subito provedesse ad quelle nostre gente che erano in Delfinato et per de là de dinari, et ogni altra cosa expediente con che potesseno levarse et venire in Lombardia ad salvamento, como sono venuti et reducti qua tutti,[3] similiter rengriatiamo Sua Ser.tà, la quale ha facto molto più per nuy in questo caso che non haveressimo saputo domandare.

Et così in mandare qua vuy, Magnifici Ambassatori, et successiva deliberatione facta de mandare qua lo R.mo Mon.re Arcivescovo de Vienna et Mon.re de Gaucurt, alli nostri favori et per fare intendere ad tutta Italia la sua optima voluntà et dispositione verso nuy, non porressimo, como è dicto, rengratiare ad bastanza, nè dire quanto favore et reputatione et stabilimento seguano alle cose nostre per queste grande et larghe demonstratione, che ha facto et fa Sua M.tà verso nuy et questo nostro

Stato, in scrivere et mandare messi et ambassatori, dicendo alla prefata M.tà, como havimo scripto, non bisogna al presente la M.tà Soa dia questa fatica et disconzo ali dicti ambassatori. Ma in effecto, vuy rengratiareti Sua M.tà, como è dicto, et ne recommandarete in bona gratia de quella, offerendone con la persona et Stato et ogni nostra facultà, sempre et ad ogni tempo, ad ogni piacere et commandamento suo. Et in spetialiter, che nuy havemo cinque altri figlioli et fratelli,[4] quali sempre ad ogni suo piacere et commando venirano et anderano con le persone et gente et ogne facultà in ogni servitio et bisogno de Sua M.tà. Et circa questo, extendendovi largamente secundo che più ad pieno vi havemo dicto et replicato ad boca.

Et similiter referireti ad Sua M.tà como le cose nostre, per Dio gratia et per li grandi favori de Sua M.tà, sono al presente in bona conditione et tuttavia se vano adaptando, como più largamente havete inteso.

Item, como dal Signore Re Ferrando in questo nostro caso siamo stati adiutati et siamo denovo, de gente, denari, per mare et per terra, per conservatione de questo nostro Stato, como del suo Reame proprio, et così è soa intencione de servire et fare cosa che piaci ad Sua Ser.tà. Et questo posseti asserire largamente, et confortare Sua M.tà che ne facci bona stima et capitale, como etiandio Sua M.tà intese dal S.re nostro consorte et patre.

Circa el facto del parentato direte como io, Galeazo, ho scritto ad Sua M.tà[5] et per Petro da Gallarate mandaremo ad dire quanto bisognarà.

HISTORICAL NOTES

1. As it has been noted earlier [doc. 23, n. 2], the royal ambassadors arrived in Milan on 24 April and were given an audience by the Duke on the following day. They left shortly after this reply was given to them, for on 10 May the Dukes issued a letter of credence to them, addressed to the King [*Francia*, cart. 532]. Two days later they wrote to their ambassador at the papal court, Agostino Rossi, that the French envoys had already left [*Roma*, cart. 59]. For the matters treated in this reply, cf. doc. VII.

2. This, however, was not the view secretly held by Galeazzo Maria. A

month earlier he had written to his special emissary to the Council of Turin, demanding the restitution of funds taken from Pietro Beaqua, a Milanese merchant, during the Duke's detention. Unless this were done forthwith, he threatened "che significaremo punctalmente a la M.tà del Re de Franza tucto quello é stato facto verso la persona nostra, cossí come l'havemo taciuto fin qui per non irritarla" [The Duke to Bartolomeo de Chiozzi, Milan, 12 April 1466, *Francia*, cart. 532]. It is apparent that Galeazzo Maria had not revealed the whole story of his detention, and that by this time he probably had accepted Ziliolo Oldoini's view that the Duchess of Savoy had been responsible [Oldoini to the Duke, Chambéry, 21 March 1466, *Savoia*, cart. 482]. Finally, months later when opposition to his marriage with Bona increased at the Savoyard court, the Duke openly accused that court of connivance in his capture [The Dukes' instructions to Cristoforo da Bollate, bound for the French court, Milan, 30 October 1466, *Francia*, cart, 532, published by Cesare Violini, *Galeazzo Maria Sforza* (Turin: Sociétá Subalpina, 1943), pp. 207-9].

    3. The troops began their journey home on 16 April, escorted by Soffrey

Alleman, sent by the King for that purpose. Since the Duke of Savoy refused to grant them passage through the direct route of Mont Cenis, they had to cross the mountains further south at the Montgenèvre Pass, thus avoiding Savoy proper [Cristoforo da Bollate to the Duke, Chambéry, 10 April, *Francia*, cart. 532, and Grenoble, 11 and 18 April 1466, BN, *Fonds Italien*, Cod. 1593, fols. 244–46]. This action by the Duke of Savoy seems to have been prompted partly by the fear that the Milanese troops in passing through Savoy would be used to support the Marquis of Monferrat in his dispute with the Savoyard rulers [Barbara Gonzaga to Lodovico Gonzaga, Milan, 21 April 1466, ASMA, *Lettere Originali dei Gonzaga*, B. 2099]. By 8 May all the troops were back in Lombardy without incident [B. Giugni and L. Guicciardini to the Signoria of Florence, Milan, 8 May 1466, ASF, *Signori, X di Balia, VIII di Pratica, Legazioni e Commissarie, Missive e Responsive*, Reg. 63, fols. 90–91].

4. Namely, Filippo Maria b. 1449, Sforza Maria b. 1451, Lodovico Maria b. 1452, Ascanio Maria b. 1455, and Ottaviano Maria b. 1458.

5. See preceding doc. IX.

XI · *Instructions of the* KING OF FRANCE *to*

LUIGI DI VALPERGA

Meung-sur-Loire [Melin sopra Lera], 12 May 1466
Francia, cart. 532. Copy

INSTRUTIONE FATA PER IL Re ad Aluise de Valpaga, Signore de Ropoli, suo Consigliero e Camerlengo, de quanto ha a fare con il Ducha de Milano e Signoria de Venexia, unde el dito Re el manda al presente.[1]

Prima fate le salutatione usate, presentarà le littere ch'el Re li scrive.

Item li monstrerà como più dì fano, el dito S.re li ha scrito,[2] e pregati che la bona intelligentia e amore, quale li haviano con il Signore Ducha de Milano passato, che la voliano tegnire e perseverare con el Ducha presente; cussì facendo li farano grande piacere, il perchè el desidera l'augumento et fermeza de suo fratello e cusino, el Ducha de Milano, como el proprio.

Item, dirà a quelli, ch'el Re per el grande amore e afectione ch'el ha al dito Ducha, cussì a dita S.ria de Venexia, non voria per cossa del mondo che fra essi fusse diferentia, nè questione, per rispeti e rasone che se dechiarerano disoto; per quale cosse, et per fargele intendere, el ha voluto mandare Monsignore de Ropoli al presente da essi, et bene presto poso luy manderà una altra ambasiada più grande, per dite materie.

Item, li dirà e ricorderà la inteligentia, liga, e grande amore che continuo è stato com [*sic*] il S.re, che fu Ducha de Milano; e como el Ducha

presente de Milano, questo anno, è venuto in persona con grande compagnia, in sucorso e servitio del Re al suo bisogno. Per quale cosse, et anchora per la liga del matrimonio del dito Ducha e de Madamisela Bona de Savoya, sorela dela Regina, el dito Signore è deliberato de tegnire e conservare la dita intelligentia, liga, amore, e afectione con el dito presente Ducha. Cussì ha deliberato dito S.re de sostegnirlo, sucorerlo, e darli aiuto.

Item, le supradite cosse monstrerà al dito Duxe e S.ria, etiam como el è venuto a notitia al Re, como hano fato instantia ala S.tà del Papa che facesse guera a quelli de Bologna, che sono coligati e boni amici del dito Ducha de Milano. Quale cossa poteria essere e ritornaria a grande preiuditio e dano del Stado de dito Ducha de Milano, quale cossa molto despiaceria al Re, poteria anche esser casone de movere grande guere fra le lige d'Italia, unde poriano uscire de grandi inconvenienti.

Item, in quello caso, el Re, considerate le rasone e lige de diti S.ri, non voria disimulare a dare sucorso e aiuto al dito Ducha de Milano.

Per quale cosse, dirà al dito Duxe e S.ria de Vinexia per parte del Re, che vogliano fare cessare tale impresse e intertegnire quelli in bono amore con el Ducha de Milano, a quale el Re è tanto tenuto e obligato como è dito, e obviare a loro possanza che guera non sia fata a diti de Bologna, nè a quelli de Bentivoglio, quali hano el governo. Cussì facendo, el Re ge ne saperà bono grato e si riputarà grandemente obligato a loro.

Item, s'el dito Duxe e Sig.ria de Vinexia, disesseno a dito S.re de Ropolo, cha dando aiuto ala S.tà del Papa al ricoperare de Bologna, como terra de la Gesia, non si pretendeno fare guerra al Ducha de Milano, et ch'el Re non debe essere male contento, et che essi voriano aiutare conservare el Stato del Ducha de Milano, como già li hano scrito, il dito S.re de Ropolo li risponderà como el Re ha mandato dala S.tà del Papa, il Vescho de Chaors,[3] ch'el voglia lassare e conservare dita Bologna neli termeni e essere che l'era al tempo del Ducha de Milano passato; et el Re spera che a sua requisitione, la dita S.tà del Papa rimarà contento, e quando altramente fusse, el Re li prega che dal canto suo vogliano desistere, aciò ch'el habia casone de haverli continuo per soy boni amici.

Item, li dirà e farà intendere, como el Re è in termini de fare tregua con li Anglesi, e veduto ch'el Reame suo è in pace tale quale al [*sic*] fusse may, desidera e voria metere l'armata sua al incontro del Turcho, quale, como ha intexo, fa guerra ala Christianitade, e fra li altri a loro;[4] desideria dito Re, che la dita S.ria e dito Ducha de Milano e altre possanze d'Italia, se unisseno e giongesseno inseme con la S.tà del Papa per resistere a dito Turcho, in quale cosse el Re ha grande voglia de intrometerse, per el bene de la fede e de Christianitade, e dita Sig.ria.

Item, passerà dito S.re de Ropolo deverso il Ducha de Milano et con luy participarà de quanto ha a fare, et s'el Ducha de Milano li vole dare altro charicho per dire a dito Duxe e S.ria de Vinexia, il fatia e talmente como s'el ne havesse instructione signata de la man del Re.[5]

Signata: Le Prevost

HISTORICAL NOTES

1. Luigi di Valperga left the royal court four days after he received these instructions [doc. 32]. He passed through Lyon where he met Franceschino Nori, who was going on his mission to Savoy. On 10 June he left Lyon for Asti, intending to pass through the Dauphiné to meet the Bishop of Cahors, with whom he planned to cross the Alps [Giovanni Bianchi to the Duke, Lyon, 8 June 1466, *Francia*, cart. 532].

2. See Doge Cristoforo Moro's reply [3 May 1466, BN, *Fonds Italien*, Cod. 1591, fol. 340], in which the Doge acknowledged receiving the King's letter of 24 March, and pledged that Venice would continue to maintain good relations with Milan.

3. On the Bishop of Cahors's mission to the Holy See, see doc. 30 and n. 4.

4. Since 1463 Venice was waging war against the Turks, seeking to halt Mohammed II's northward march from the Morea [Franz Babinger, *Maometto il Conquistatore e il suo tempo* (Turin: Einaudi, 1957), pp. 336-80].

5. During the ambassador's stay in Milan, 15-18 July [The Duke to the Duchess, Vigevano, 15 July 1466, BN, *Fonds Italien*, Cod. 1591, fol. 357; the Dukes to Gerardo de' Colli, Milan, 18 July 1466, *Venezia*, cart. 353], the Milanese rulers made changes in these instructions to reflect current conditions in Italy. In particular, the references to Bologna were eliminated because the Pope had already assured the Bishop of Cahors that he had no intention of causing trouble in the city [The Dukes to Panigarola, Milan, 2 August, and Panigarola to the Dukes, Briare?, 26 August 1466, *Francia*, cart. 532].

423

Bibliography[1]

Manuscripts

Florence, Archivio di Stato [ASF]
  Signori, X di Balìa, VIII di Pratica, Legazioni e Commissarie, Missive
    e Responsive, Reg. 63.
  Signori, Carteggi, Missive. Legazioni e Commissarie, Elezioni e Istru-
    zioni a Oratori, Reg. 16.
Mantua, Archivio di Stato [ASMA]
  Carteggio-Milano, B. 1623
  Lettere Originali dei Gonzaga, B. 2099
Milan, Archivio di Stato[2]
  Potenze Estere
    Aragona e Spagna, cart. 652
    Borgogna e Fiandre [Borgogna], cartelle 515–19
    Firenze, cart. 272
    Francia, cartelle 528, 532–46, 555, 559, 561
    Genova, cartelle 425–26, 453–56, 996, 1514
    Napoli, cartelle 215, 1249
    Roma, cartelle 59–60

---

1. Includes only manuscripts and publications cited in the notes. Abbreviations used in the notes are placed within brackets.
2. Manuscripts cited in the notes without archival reference are located in the Archivio di Stato di Milano.

Romagna, cart. 165

Savoia, cartelle 481–83, 486, 490

Siena, cart. 264

Svizzera, cart. 596

Venezia, cartelle 353, 1314

Potenze Sovrane, cart. 1458

Carteggio Interno

Alessandria, cart. 775

Milano, cart. 878

Novara, cart. 828

Pavia, cart. 845

Registri delle Missive, Regs. 72, 74, 77, 111, 117

Registri delle Missive-Frammenti, cart. 7

Registri Panigarola, Reg. 10

Famiglie, cart. 136

Trattati, cart. 1530, 1542

Milan, Biblioteca della Società Storica Lombarda

Carte Morbio

Paris, Bibliothèque Nationale [BN]

Fonds Français, Cod. 20,420

Fonds Italien, Codices 1591, 1593

Fonds Latin, Cod. 10,133

Siena, Archivio di Stato [ASS]

Concistoro, Legazioni e Commissarie, Reg. 2608

Venice, Archivio di Stato [ASV]

Senato Secreta, Reg. 22

Printed Works

Ady, Cecilia M. *The Bentivoglio of Bologna. A Study in Despotism*. Oxford: Oxford University Press, 1937.

Babinger, Franz. *Maometto il Conquistatore e il suo tempo*. Translated by E. Polacco, Turin: Einaudi, 1957.

Barbieri, Gino. *Origini del capitalismo lombardo. Studi e documenti sull'economia milanese del periodo ducale.* Milan: Giuffré, 1961.

Belotti, Bortolo. *La vita di Bartolomeo Colleoni.* Bergamo: Instituto Italiano d'Arti Grafiche, 1923.

Calamari, Giuseppe. *Il confidente di Pio II. Card. Jacopo Ammannati-Piccolomini (1422–1479).* 2 vols. Rome–Milan: Augustea, 1932.

Calmette, Joseph, and Georges Périnelle. *Louis XI et l'Angleterre. (1461–1483).* Paris: Picard, 1930.

Calmette, Joseph. *Louis XI, Jean II et la révolution catalane (1461–1473).* Toulouse: Privat, 1903.

————. *La question des Pyrénées et la Marche d'Espagne au Moyen Âge.* Paris: Janin, 1947.

Cappellini, Antonio. *Dizionario biografico di Genovesi illustri e notabili.* 3d ed. Genoa: Tipografia Olcese, 1941.

Casanova, Enrico. *Dizionario feudale delle province componenti l'antico Stato di Milano all'epoca della cessazione del sistema feudale (1796).* 2d ed. Milan: Biblioteca Ambrosiana, 1930; repr. Bologna: Forni, 1970.

Catalano, Franco. *L'età sforzesca dal 1450 al 1500, Storia di Milano.* Vol. 7. Milan: Fondazione Treccani degli Alfieri, 1956.

Cerioni, Lydia. *La diplomazia sforzesca nella seconda metà del Quattrocento e i suoi cifrari segreti.* 2 vols. Rome: Centro di Ricerca, 1970.

Champion, Pierre. *Louis XI.* 2 vols. Paris: Champion, 1927.

Colombo, Elia. *Iolanda, Duchessa di Savoia (1465–1478). Studio storico corredato di documenti inediti, Miscellanea di storia italiana,* ser. 2, 16 (1894): 1–306.

Combet, Joseph. *Louis XI et le Saint-Siège (1461–1483).* Paris: Hachette, 1903.

Contamine, Phillipe. *Guerre, état et société à la fin du Moyen Âge. Études sur les armées des rois de France, 1337–1494.* Paris: Mouton, 1972.

Corio, Bernardino. *Storia di Milano.* Edited by E. de Magri. 3 vols. Milan, 1857; repr. Milan: Istituto Editoriale Cisalpino, 1975.

Courteault, Henri. *Gaston IV, Comte de Foix, Vicomte souverain de Béam, Prince de Navarre, 1423–1472.* Toulouse: Privat, 1895.

Croce, Benedetto. *Vite di avventure di fede e di passione.* Bari: Laterza„ 1936.

Cusin, Fabio. "L'Impero e la successione degli Sforza ai Visconti." *Archivio storico lombardo*, new ser., 1 (1936): 3–116.

————. "I rapporti tra la Lombardia e l'Impero dalla morte di Francesco Sforza all'avvento di Lodovico il Moro (1466–1480)." *Annali della R. Università degli Studi Economici e Commerciali di Trieste* 6 (1934): 213–322.

Damarco, Maria. "Guglielmo I Paleologo (Marchese di Monferrato, 1420–1483)." *Rivista di storia, arte e archeologia per le province di Alessandria e Asti* 42 (1933): 529–98.

Daviso di Charvensod, M. Clotilde. "Filippo Senza Terra: la sua ribellione nel 1462 e le sue relazioni con Francesco Sforza e Luigi XI." *Rivista storica italiana*, ser. 4, 6 (1935): 127–200.

————. *Filippo II, il Senza Terra*. Turin: Paravia, 1941.

Degert, Antoine. "Louis XI et ses ambassadeurs." *Revue historique* 154 (1927): 1–19.

De Roover, Raymond. *The Rise and Decline of the Medici Bank, 1397–1494*. Cambridge, Mass.: Harvard University Press, 1963; paperbound ed. New York: Norton, 1966.

Ernst, Fritz. "Über Gesandtschaftswesen und Diplomatie an der Wende vom Mittelalter zur Neuzeit." *Archiv für Kulturgeschichte* 33 (1951): 64–95.

Eubel, Conradum. *Hierarchia catholica Medii Aevi . . .*, vol. 2 (1431–1503). Münster: Typis Librariae Regensbergianae, 1914; repr. Padua: Il Messaggero di S. Antonio, 1960.

Ferorelli, Nicola. *Inventari e regesti del R. Archivio di Stato di Milano*. Vol. 3, *Registri dell'Ufficio del Governatore degli Statuti di Milano*. Milan: Archivio di Stato, 1920; repr. Milan: Cisalpino-Goliardica, 1971.

Fierville, Charles. *Le cardinal Jean Jouffroy et son temps (1412–1473)*. Coutances: Salettes, 1874.

Filippi, Giovanni. *Il matrimonio di Bona di Savoia con Galeazzo Maria Sforza*. Milan: 1890.

Forgeot, Henri. *Jean Balue, cardinal d'Angers (1421?–1491)*. Paris: Bouillon, 1895.

Gabotto, Ferdinando. *Lo Stato sabaudo da Amedeo VIII a Emanuele Filiberto, 1451–1504*. 3 vols. Turin and Rome: 1892–1895.

Ghinzoni, Pietro. "Spedizione sforzesca in Francia (1465–1466)." *Archivio storico lombardo*, ser. 2, 7 (1890): 314–45.

Gilbert, Creighton. "When Did a Man in the Renaissance Grow Old?" *Studies in the Renaissance* 14 (1967): 7–32.

Gingins-La-Sarra, Frederic de. ed. *Dépêches des ambassadeurs milanais sur les campagnes de Charles-Le-Hardi, duc de Bourgogne, de 1474 à 1477.* 2 vols. Paris, 1858.

Ilardi, Vincent. "The Italian League, Francesco Sforza, and Charles VII (1454–1461)." *Studies in the Renaissance* 6 (1959): 129–66.

Jaurgain, Jean de. "Deux Comtes de Comminges Béarnais au XVᵉ siècle." *Bulletin de la Société Archéologique du Gers* 14–19 (1913–1918).

Jones, P. J. *The Malatesta of Rimini and the Papal State. A Political History.* Cambridge: Cambridge University Press, 1974.

Kendall, Paul M. *Louis XI.* New York: Norton, 1971.

Lamansky, Vladimir I. *Secrets d'état de Venise* . . . St. Pétersbourg, 1884.

Lardy, Anne-Marie. "Gaston du Lyon, serviteur de Louis XI et de Charles VIII." École des Chartes, *Positions des thèses* (1936), pp. 87–93.

Lecestre, Léon. "Essai biographique sur Jean Batard d'Orléans, Comte de Dunois (1400–1468)." École des Chartes, *Positions des thèses* (1882), pp. 29–35.

Lecoy de la Marche, Albert. *Le roi René. Sa vie, son administration, ses travaux artistiques et littéraires* . . . 2 vols. Paris, 1875.

Lettenhove, Kervyn de. *Lettres et négociations de Philippe de Commynes.* 3 vols. Brussels, 1867–1874; repr. Geneva: Slatkine, 1972.

Lucius, Christian. *Pius II and Ludwig XI von Frankreich, 1461–1462.* Heidelberg: Winters, 1913.

Magistretti, Piero. "Galeazzo Maria Sforza prigione nella Novalesa." *Archivio storico lombardo*, ser. 2, 6 (1889): 777–807.

Mahnke, Elisabeth W. "The Political Career of a Condottiere-Prince: Ludovico Gonzaga, 1444–1466." Ph.D. dissertation, Harvard University, 1974.

Mandrot, Bernard de. ed., *Mémoires de Philippe de Commynes.* 2 vols. Paris: Picard, 1901–1903.

———. ed., *Dépêches des ambassadeurs milanais en France sous Louis XI et François Sforza.* 4 vols. Paris: Renouard, 1916–1923.

———. "Jacques d'Armagnac, duc de Nemours, 1433–1477." *Revue historique* 43 (1890): 274–316; 44 (1890): 241–312.

Marini, Lino. *Savoiardi e piemontesi nello Stato sabaudo (1418–1601).* Vol. 1, 1418–1536. Rome: Istituto Storico Italiano per l'Etá Moderna e Contemporanea, 1962.

Martinez Ferrando, Jésus E. *Pere de Portugal, rei dels Catalans.* Barcelona: La Renaixença, 1936.

———. *Tragedia del insigne Condestable Don Pedro de Portugal.* Madrid: Diana, Arte Gráficas, 1942.

Mattingly, Garrett. *Renaissance Diplomacy.* London: Jonathan Cape, 1955.

Natale, Alfio R., ed. *I diari di Cicco Simonetta.* Vol. 1. Milan: Giuffré, 1962.

———, ed., *Acta in Consilio Secreto in castello Portae Jovis Mediolani.* 3 vols. Milan: Giuffré; 1963–1969.

Pastor, Ludovico von. *Storia dei Papi dalla fine del Medio Evo.* New Italian translation by A. Mercati. Vol. 2. Rome: Desclée, 1961.

Pélicier, Paul. *Essai sur le gouvernement de la Dame de Beaujeu, 1483–1491.* Chartres, 1882; repr. Geneva: Slatkine, 1970.

Perret, Paul M. *Histoire des relations de la France avec Venise du XIIIᵉ siècle à l'avènement de Charles VIII.* 2 vols. Paris, 1896.

Pieri, Piero. *Il Rinascimento e la crisi militare italiana.* Turin: Einaudi, 1952.

Pius II, *The Commentaries of.* Translated by F. A. Gragg. Edited by L. C. Gabel. *Smith College Studies in History.* Book 3, 25 (1939–1940).

Queller, Donald E. *The Office of Ambassador in the Middle Ages.* Princeton: Princeton University Press, 1967.

Salvati, Catello. "I 'nomina sacra' nella normativa dell'edizione delle fonti documentarie." *Rassegna degli Archivi di Stato* 31 (1971): 104–12.

Samaran, Charles. *La maison d'Armagnac au XVᵉ siècle et les dernières luttes de la féodalité dans le Midi de la France.* Paris: Picard, 1907.

Santoro, Caterina. *Gli Uffici del Dominio sforzesco (1450–1500).* Milan: Fondazione Treccani degli Alfieri, 1948.

———. *Gli Sforza.* Milan: Dall'Oglio, 1968.

Schiappoli, Irma. *Napoli aragonese: traffici e attività marinare.* Naples: Giannini, 1972.

Soranzo, Giovanni. *Pio II e la politica italiana nella lotta contro i Malatesti, 1457–1463.* Padua: Fratelli Drucker, 1911.

Sorbelli, Albano. *Francesco Sforza a Genova (1458–1466). Saggio sulla politica italiana di Luigi XI.* Bologna: Zanichelli, 1901.

Stein, Henri. *Charles de France, frère de Louis XI.* Paris: Picard, 1921.

Terni de Gregorj, W. *Bianca Maria Visconti, Duchessa di Milano.* Bergamo: Istituto Italiano d'Arti Grafiche, 1940.

Thomas, Édith. "Cinq lettres inédites de Louis XI." Société de l'Histoire de France, *Annuaire-Bulletin* 77 (1941): 75–88.

Tranchedino, Francesco. *Codex Vindobonensis 2398 der österreichische Nationalbibliothek. Faksimileausgabe.* Edited by W. Höflechner. Graz: Akademische Druck- u. Verlagsanstalt, 1970.

Vaesen, Joseph, and E. Charavay, eds. *Lettres de Louis XI.* 11 vols. Paris: Renouard, 1883–1909.

Vaughan, Richard. *Philip the Good. The Apogee of Burgundy.* London: Longmans, Green, 1970.

———. *Charles the Bold. The Last Valois Duke of Burgundy.* New York: Harper and Row, 1974.

Vicens Vives, Jaime. *Juan II de Aragon (1398–1749). Monarquia y revolucion en la España del siglo XV.* Barcelona: Teide, 1953.

Violini, Cesare. *Galeazzo Maria Sforza.* 2d ed. Turin: Società Subalpina, 1943.

Walsh, Richard J. "Charles the Bold, Last Valois Duke of Burgundy 1467–1477, and Italy." Ph.D. dissertation, University of Hull, 1977.

Index

Abbeville, xxxviii n
Abbiate, xvii n, liii n
Abruzzo, 104, 106, 162, 164
Acciaioli, Angelo, xiv n
Aciani, Bartolomeo, xxvi n
Aiguebelle, 350n
Aiguilles, 256n
Albi, Cardinal of, *see* Jouffrey, Jean
Aleman, Hugonin, Lord of Arbent, xliii, 43n, 50n, 54
Alessandria, 174n, 344, 347n
Alfonso, Duke of Calabria, *see* Aragon, Alfonso of
Alfonso V, King of Aragon, Naples, and Sicily, *see* Naples, Alfonso V of
Allemand, Antoine, Bishop of Cahors, formerly Abbot of Ambronay, 184, 184n, 188, 190, 192n, 352, 354, 362, 366n–67n, 376n–77n, 421, 422n, 423n
Allemand, Soffrey, Lord of Châteauneuf, 8, 13n, 96, 98n, 306, 418n–19n
Alsace, xxxix
Amboise, 42
Ambronay, Abbot of, *see* Allemand, Antoine
Ambrosian Republic, lii, 334n
Amédée IX, Duke of Savoy, *see* Savoy, Amédée IX
Ammannati-Piccolomini, Iacopo, Cardinal of Pavia, 286, 370
biographical data, 288n–89n
Andreasi, Marsilio, 248n
Anglo-French truce, *see* Calais, treaty of

Anjou, Charles of, Count of Anjou and Provence, 97n
Anjou, Charles of, Count of Maine, Governor of Languedoc, 24, 338, 346n
biographical data, 28n, 346n
Anjou, Count of, *see* Anjou, Charles of
Anjou, Duke of, *see* Anjou, René of
Anjou, House of, xxxi, xxxv, xxxvii, xlv, xlix n, lii, liv, lv, 26, 34, 48, 92, 96n, 112, 114n, 174, 186, 190, 192, 212, 259, 260, 280, 282, 290, 292, 298, 302, 311n, 336, 342, 346n, 358, 362, 382
Anjou, John of, Duke of Lorraine, titular Duke of Calabria (son of King René), xliv, xlv, xlix n, 24, 26, 34, 70, 92, 94, 96n, 106, 112, 134, 172, 178, 186, 193n, 195n, 206, 208, 212, 216, 220, 234, 244, 256, 260, 290–96, 298n, 300–306, 336–42, 346n, 356–58, 364, 368, 376
biographical data, xxxvi, 24, 28n, 96n, 346n
Anjou, Marie of (mother of Louis XI), 28n
Anjou, René of, Duke of Anjou and King of Sicily, xiv n, xxxvi, liii, 8, 13n, 24, 112, 114n, 134, 176, 296
biographical data, 24, 28n, 112, 112n
Anjou, Yolande of (daughter of King René, wife of Ferry II of Lorraine), 112n
Anne, Madame de Beaujeu (daughter of Louis XI, wife of Pierre de Bourbon), xxvi n, xlv, 22, 27n, 64n, 86n, 148n, 272
Ann of Lusignan, *see* Lusignan, Ann of

Anne of Cyprus, *see* Lusignan, Ann of
Annone, Giorgio de, xxxix n
Appiano, Antonio de, xxii
Aragó, Jaume d', 11n
Aragon, Alfonso of (son of Ferrante), 164, 164n
Aragon, crown of, 335n
Aragon, John II of, King of Navarre and Aragon, xxn, xxxvi, xxxvii, liii, 11n, 198, 200n, 201n, 272–74, 277n, 310n, 330, 335n, 372
  biographical data, 335n
  his daughter (not named), 330, 335n
Aragon, King of, *see* Aragon, John II of; Naples, Alfonso V of
Arbent, Lord of, *see* Aleman, Hugonin
Archaselles, *see* Requesens, Galcerán de
Arcimboldi, Giovanni, xxix
Arezzo, Francesco de, 127n
Armagnac (county), 330
Armagnac, Annette d', 64n
Armagnac, Bastard of, *see* Lescun, Jean de
Armagnac, Count of, *see* Armagnac, Jean V
Armagnac, House of, xlv, 201n, 316
Armagnac, Jacques d', Duke of Nemours, 198, 201n, 268, 270, 320, 323n
  biographical data, 201n
Armagnac, Jean V, Count of Armagnac, 2, 4, 198, 268, 270, 308, 324, 372
  biographical data, 201n, 316–20, 322n
Ascoli, Bishop of, *see* Buccharelli, Giovanni Antonio
Ascoli, Cola da, 127n
Asti, Bailli of, *see* Dresnay, Regnault de
Asti, County of, xxxvii, 2, 4, 12n, 60, 142, 178, 180n–81n, 198, 262, 264, 288, 289n, 360, 374, 377n, 422n
Asti, Governor of, *see* Dresnay, Regnault de
Attendoli, Giovanni d', 91n
Aubert, Jean, 209n, 326, 334n
Auvergne, 4, 318
Auvergne, Bailli des Montagnes d', *see* Bois, Josselin du
Avellino, Count of, *see* Requesens, Galcerán de
Avignon, 92, 97n, 234, 288n

Bagé, Count of, *see* Savoy, Philip of
Balue, Jean, Bishop of Evreux, 27n, 328, 335n
Bar, Duke of, *see* Anjou, René of
Barbiano, Carlo de, Count of Belgioioso, xxvii n
Barbo, Pietro, Cardinal, *see* Paul II
Barcelona, 198, 200n, 272, 277n, 330, 335n
Bassignana, 170, 174n
Bayonne, Treaty of (1462), 11n
Beaqua, Pietro, 418n
Beaujeau, Lord of, *see* Bourbon, Pierre de
Beaujeau, Madam de, *see* Anne, Madame de Beaujeau
Beaumont, Louis de, Lord de la Forêt, 192
Beaurepaire, 42n, 98n, 240, 392n, 397
Belgioioso, Count of, *see* Barbiano, Carlo de
Benages, Joan, 11n
Bentivoglio, Giovanni, 127n, 168n–69n
Bentivoglio, House of, xl, 223n, 421
Bergamo, Bartolomeo da, *see* Colleoni, Bartolomeo
Bernard, Guy, Bishop of Langres, 112, 114n, 146, 270
Bernese, 82, 170
Berry, Duchy of, 330
Berry, Duke of, *see* France, Charles of
Bertini, Francesco, lv n
Besana, Antonio de, 28n
Betes, Garcia, 150, 210, 212, 234, 288n, 302, 304, 368, 370
Bethes, Garcia, *see* Betes, Garcia
Bettini, Sforza, xviii–xx, xxi n, xxix n, xxx, liii
  biographical data, xviii–xx
Bianchi, Giovanni, xxix, 38, 42n, 98n, 149n, 258n, 311n, 348, 360, 384n, 422n
Biandrà, Guglielmo da, 262, 372
Black Virgin, 76n
Blois, County of, 198, 201n
Boffa (courier), 38
Boido, Giovanni, 286, 289n
Bois, Josselin du, Bailli des Montagnes d'Auvergne and Quartermaster of Cavalry, 46, 50n, 51n, 54, 120, 126n, 226, 405, 411n
Bois, Lord of, *see* Bueil, Jacques de
Bollate, Cristoforo da, xx–xxii, xxix, xxx,

l, liii n, 63n, 154n, 276n, 418n, 419n
biographical data, xx–xxii
Bologna, xl, 68, 122, 127n, 166, 168n, 188, 190, 192n, 206, 218, 222n, 230, 294, 352, 354, 366n, 374, 376n–77n, 421, 423n
Bologna, Gandolfo de, 91n
Bologna, Tommaso Tebaldi da, lvi, 223n
Bona of Savoy, *see* Savoy, Bona of
Bordeaux, 58, 268
Bordeaux, Governor of, *see* Lescun, Jean de
Borghetto, 38
Borromei Bank of London, lii
Bossi, Giovanni Luigi de, xxix
Bossi, Lancelotto, 400n
Boulogne, Our Lady of, 196
Bourbon, Bastard of, *see* Bourbon, Louis de
Bourbon, Charles de, Duke of (father of Jean II, Duke of Bourbon, and Louis, Bastard of Bourbon), 43n
Bourbon, Duke of, *see* Bourbon, Charles; Bourbon, Jean II
Bourbon, Isabelle of, 27n
Bourbon, Jean II, Duke of Bourbon (son of Charles de Bourbon, husband of Jeanne of France), xxvi n, lv, 32, 40, 46, 56, 74, 88, 198, 200, 201n, 244, 262–64, 274, 286, 288n, 292, 294, 376
biographical data, 43n, 148n, 198, 262, 274, 354
Bourbon, Jeanne de (sister of Jean II, Duke of Bourbon), 318, 322n
Bourbon, Louis, Bastard of, Admiral of France, Count of Rousillon in Dauphiné (son of Charles de Bourbon and Jeanne de Bournan; husband of Jeanne, daughter of Louis XI), 32, 40, 43n, 56, 60, 66, 74, 88, 112, 114n, 146, 270, 405
biographical data, 43n–44n, 190, 194n, 406n
Bourbon, Louis de, Bishop of Liège, 11n, 196, 200n
Bourbon, Pierre de, Lord of Beaujeu, xxvi n, 142, 264
biographical data, 148n, 198, 201n, 262
Bourbonnais, xxxix, 60, 294, 320
Bourges, xxv n, 34, 348, 386, 388n
Bourges, Pragmatic Sanction of, 192n
Bournan, Jeanne de (mother of Louis de Bourbon), 43n

Boydo, Giovanni, *see* Boido, Giovanni
Brancas, Nicolas de, Bishop of Marseilles, 112
Brasca, Erasmo, xxvii n
Bresse, Count of, *see* Savoy, Philip of
Bresse, County of, 208n–9n
Briand, François de, Captain of Susa, 324, 326, 334n
biographical data, 334n
Briare, 222n, 423n
Brittany, 22, 48, 328
Brittany, Duke of, *see* Brittany, Francis II
Brittany, Francis, Count of Vertus and of Goello (son of Duke of Brittany), 28n
Brittany, Francis II, Duke of, xliv, 4, 22, 24, 28n, 50, 58, 74, 328
biographical data, 24, 28n
Buccharelli, Giovanni Antonio, Bishop of Ascoli, 249n
Bueil, Jacques de, Lord of Bois, xx n
Bueil, Jean de, Count of Sancerre and Admiral of France, 328
biographical data, 334n–35n
Burgundy, xiv, xxviii n, xlv, liv n, lv n, lvi, lvii, lviii n, lxii n, 2, 10n, 86n, 250n, 272, 274, 276n, 277n, 356, 364
Burgundy, Antoine, Bastard of Burgundy, 332
Burgundy, Charles the Bold, Count of Charolais and later Duke of Burgundy (son of Philip the Good), xix, xxviii, xliv, xlvii n, liii, liv n, 2, 4, 17n, 48, 58, 68, 74, 82–84, 120, 158, 174, 174n, 178, 190, 196, 198, 200n, 220, 242, 256, 262, 270, 274, 276n, 277n, 320, 330, 346n, 372
biographical data, xlv, 11n, 22, 26n, 27n, 174n, 198, 256, 272, 332, 340, 342, 356, 358, 408n–9n
Burgundy, Duke of, *see* Burgundy, Philip the Good
Burgundy, Marie of (daughter of Charles of Burgundy), 17n, 26n, 82, 86n
Burgundy, Order of, 274
Burgundy, Philip the Good, Duke of Burgundy (father of Charles, Count of Charolais), xxxvi, xxxvii, 190, 194n, 220, 242, 262, 356
biographical data, 11n, 242, 332

Cagnola, Giovanni Andrea, xxv–xxvi, xxix
Cahors, Bishop of, see Allemand, Antoine
Caimi, Benedetto, lviii n
Calabria, Duke of, see Anjou, John of
Calabria, Duke of, see Aragon, Alfonso of
Calais, 112, 114n, 200n, 270
Calais, treaty of (1466), 200n, 276n
Calco, Bartolomeo, xxvi n
Calixtus III (pope), 238
Camerino, Simone de, Friar, 161n
Camogli, Prospero di, xxxvi, lvi
Campofregoso, Paolo, Archbishop of Genoa (former Doge of Genoa), xl, 34, 37n, 102, 108n, 122, 280
    biographical data, 37n, 108n
Candale, Count of, see Foix, Jean de
Carafa, Fabrizio, 212
Cardino, xxix
Casale, 344
Casanova, Abbot of, see Lignana, Agostino di
Casate, Francesco da, xxvi n
Casate, Scipione de, 127n
Castano, fief of, lv
Castellazo, Janello de, 286, 289n
Castelnau, Antoine de, Lord of Lau and Seneschal of Guyenne, 192, 272
    biographical data, 195n
Castiglione, Arcimboldi de, xxix
Castiglione, Branda de, xxix
Castiglione, Cristoforo de, xxix
Castile, Henry IV, King of, 274
Castronovo, 150n
Catalonia, xx n, 11n
Catalonia, Governor of, see Requesens, Galcerán de
Cerdagne, County of, 11n
Chabannes, Antoine de, Count of Dammartin, 270
Chambéry, xliii n, xlvi n, 38, 43n, 51n, 52n, 54, 63n, 68, 76n, 126n, 149n, 350n, 418n, 419n
La Chambre, Count of, see Seyssel, Aymon de
Champagne, xlv
Charles, Archbishop of Lyon (brother of Duke of Bourbon), 354
Charles, Count of Anjou and Provence, see Anjou, Charles of

Charles, Count of Charolais, see Burgundy, Charles the Bold
Charles, Count of Maine, see Anjou, Charles of
Charles, Duke of Orléans, see Orléans, Charles of
Charles, Lord of Gaucourt and King's Chamberlain, see Gaucourt, Charles of
Charles VII, King of France, see France, Charles VII
Charles VIII, King of France, see France, Charles VIII
Charles, Prince of Piedmont, see Savoy-Piedmont, Charles
Charles of France, see France, Charles of (brother of Louis XI)
Charles the Bold, Count of Charolais, see Burgundy, Charles the Bold
Charotte, Queen of France, see France, Charlotte
Charolais, Count of, see Burgundy, Charles the Bold
Chartres, xvi n
Châteauneuf, Lord of, see Allemand, Soffrey
Chastel, Tanneguy du, Grand Master in Brittany, 24
Châtillon, de, Lord, see Laval, Louis de
Châtre, La, 388n
Chiozzi, Bartolomeo de, 418n
Cicinello, Antonio, lv n
Cigles, castle of, 252
Clermont-Lodève, Lord of, see Pons, Lord of Clermont-Lodève
Clèves, Marie de, Duchess of Orléans, 2, 10n, 142, 198, 262, 288, 289n
Colleoni, Bartolomeo, xli, 36, 37n, 104, 124, 127n, 140, 156, 160n, 169n, 232, 236, 249n, 282, 292, 296, 298n, 374, 377n, 408
Colletta, Alessandro, xxix
Colli, Gerardo de, xlvi n, l, 90n, 109n, 126n, 259n, 298n, 311n, 374, 377n, 423n
Colt, Thomas, 91n
Comminges, Count of, see Lescun, Jean de
Commynes, Philip de, xxii, xxiii n, xxv, xxvi n
Compari, Luigi di Piero de, 126n
Compiègne, xvii n, xviii n, xx n, lii n, liii n
Conflans, treaty of (1465), xxxix, 200n
Conte, Donato del, xxxix

Cario, Marco, xliii n, xlvi n, l, 149n

Cario, Zanone, xxix, xlix n, 17n, 38, 42n, 62n, 72

Corregio, Carlo de, 259n

Cossa, Giovanni, liii n

Cot, Claude, Treasurer of Dauphiné, 94-96, 146, 149n, 306

Council of Ten (Venice), xli, 36n

Cousinot, Guillaume, Governor of Montpelier, 210, 340

Craon, xix n

Craon, Lord of, see Trémoille, Georges de la

Cremona, l

Crescentino, 350n

Cristoforo (servant of G. P. Panigarola), 70, 110, 112n, 132

Crussol, Gerard de, Archbishop of Tours, and Deacon of Grenoble, 182, 184n

Crussol, Louis de, Seneschal of Poitou, 48, 56, 58, 68, 74, 76n, 182, 186, 226, 304, 340, 368, 405

Cyprus, Chancellor of, 146, 149n

Cyprus, King of, xlii

Dammartin, Count of, see Chabannes, Antoine de

Dauphiné, xxxix, xv, 8, 12n, 13n, 32, 42n, 48, 50n, 58, 60, 68, 90, 94, 98n, 102, 142, 149n, 226, 238, 252, 306, 330, 395, 405, 406n, 416, 422n

Dauphiné, Parlement and Chamber of Accounts of, 13n

Dauphiné, Treasurer of, see Cot, Claude

Delaven, Giovanni, 364

Dieppe, 276n

Dinant, 2, 10n

Deserto (courier), 166

Don Pedro of Portugal, see Portugal, Don Pedro

Dresnay, Regnault de, Governor and Bailli of Asti, 6, 288, 289n

Dunois, Count of, see Orléans, Jean d'

Edward IV, King of England, xxxvi, xlv, 91n, 220
    biographical data, 86n

Enghien, Mariette d', 12n

England, xiv, xxxvii, xlv, 58, 112, 114n, 146, 196, 270, 328, 374, 422

Este, Borso d', Duke of Modena, xli, 48, 104, 108n, 122, 170, 228, 256, 259n, 280
    biographical data, 106, 122, 228

Este, Ercole d' (brother of Duke of Modena), 106, 122, 228

Evreux, Bishop of, see Balue, Jean

Facino, Ugolotto de, 256, 259n

Ferrante, King of Naples, see Naples, Ferrante, King of

Ferrara, xxv, 68, 108n, 259n

Ferry II of Lorraine, see Lorraine, Ferry II of

Filippo, Lord, see Savoy, Philip of

Florence, xxv, xxxviii n, xl, l, 34, 48, 68, 104, 108n, 122, 136n, 154n, 162, 168, 223n, 230, 232, 248n, 249n, 284, 294, 374, 419n

Foix, Gaston IV de, Count of Foix, 274, 277n, 340, 372
    biographical data, 10n, 12n

Foix, Jean de, Count of Candale, Governor of Perpignan and Roussillon (son of Gaston de Foix), 4, 330
    biographical data, 12n

Foix, Marie de (daughter of Count Gaston IV of Foix), 10n, 347n

Folch, Juan Ramon II, Count of Prades, 330

Fontenay-le-Comte, xx n

Forêt, de la, Lord, see Beaumont, Louis de

Forez, 60

Forlì, 218, 366n, 374n, 377n

Forner, Pere, 274, 277n

Fou, Yvon du, Lord of the Ramenteresse and of Fou, Captain of Lusignan, 342, 347n

France, Admiral of, see Bourbon, Louis de; Bueil, Jean de; Montauban, Jean de

France, Charles of, Duke of Berry (brother of Louis XI), xliv, 22, 28n, 216, 328, 330, 335n, 340
    biographical data, xliv, 26n

France, Charles VII, King of (father of Louis XI), xiv n, 328
    biographical data, 28n

France, Charles VIII, King of (son of Louis XI), xxvi n

France, Charlotte, Queen of, 6, 58, 74, 86, 244

biographical data, 13n
France, Grand Chancellor of, *see* Ursins, Guillaume Jouvenel des
France, Grand Constable of, *see* Luxembourg, Louis de
France, Jeanne of (daughter of Charles VII of France, wife of Jean II, Duke of Bourbon), 274
France, Jeanne of (daughter of Louis XI, wife of Louis de Bourbon), 44n, 64n, 406n
France, Louis, Dauphin, later Louis XI, King of France, xlii, 194n, 209n, 406n
biographical data, xxxv
France, Marshal of, *see* Laval, Andre de; Lescun, Jean de; Rouault, Joachim
France, Queen of, *see* France, Charlotte, Queen of
Francis (sons of Louis XI), xlvi
Francis, Count of Vertus and of Goello, *see* Brittany, Francis, Count of Vertus and of Goello
Francis II, Duke of Brittany, *see* Brittany, Francis II
Franco-English truce, *see* Calais, treaty of
Frederick III, Emperor. *See* Holy Roman Empire, Frederick III
Frosano, 256

Galeota, Giacomo (Iacopo), 336, 346n
Gallarate, li
Gallarate, Pietro da, xxix, xxxviii n, lviii, 158, 178, 216, 220, 222, 248n, 284, 314, 350n, 362, 366n, 376n, 380, 413, 413n
Galliate, liii n
Gap, 8, 13n
Gascony, 58, 268
Gaston du Lyon, *see* Lyon, Gaston du
Gaston IV, Count of Foix, *see* Foix, Gaston IV
Gaucourt, Charles de, Lord of Gaucourt and King's Chamberlain, xvi, 60, 66, 88, 90n, 94, 134, 168, 176, 216, 290, 405, 416
biographical data, 64n
Genappe, Treaty of (1460), xv, xxxv, xxxvii, 406n
Geneva, lii, 326
Genoa, xx, xxii, xxxvi, xxxvii, xl, xli, li, lii, liii, liv, lv n, 18, 20n, 32, 66, 70n, 72, 78, 102, 122, 162, 192, 195n, 200n, 222, 230,

236, 238, 249n, 259n, 280, 310n, 358, 364, 367n, 391, 408
Germany, xiv, 360
Gheilynes, Giuliano, 400n
Giangiacomo, Marquis of Monferrat, 64n
Giano of Savoy, *see* Savoy, Giano of
Gien, 388n
Giovanni, Marquis of Monferrat, 347n
Giudice, Boffilo del, xxii, xxiii n
Giugni, Bernardo di Filippo, 109n, 154n, 223n, 248n–49n, 419n
biographical data, 109n
Goello, Count of, *see* Brittany, Francis
Gonzaga, Barbara, Marchioness of Mantua, xlviii n, 158, 161n, 234, 248n, 254, 257n, 286, 409, 410n–11n, 413n, 419n
Gonzaga, Doretea (daughter of Marquis Lodovico Gonzaga of Mantua), xlviii, 87n, 410n
Gonzaga, Lodovico, Marquis of Mantua, xlviii n, 48, 161n, 164, 232, 234, 254, 257n, 286, 409, 410n, 419n
biographical data, xlviii, 87n
Gonzaga, Susanna (daughter of Barbara and Lodovico Gonzaga), 410n
Govenzate, Sebastiano de, xxix
Grandson, battle of (1476), liv
Grenoble, 87n, 154n, 334n, 419n
Grenoble, Deacon of, *see* Crussol, Gerard de
Grenoble, President of, *see* Trecate, Giovanni Filippo da
Grenoble, President of Parlement of, *see* Gruel, Pierre
Grenoble, Pursuivant of Louis XI, 218, 222n
Gruel, Pierre, President of Parlement of Grenoble, 94
Guglielmo VII, Marquis of Monferrat, xiv n, 2, 36, 48, 68, 94, 104, 106, 109n, 122, 140, 142, 148n, 172, 174n, 178, 228, 252, 256n–57n, 262, 298, 344, 350n, 372, 384n, 419n
biographical data, 10n, 347n
Guicciardini, Luigi di Piero, 109n, 154n, 223n, 248n–49n, 419n
biographical data, 109n
Guyenne, 268, 270, 324, 330
Guyenne, Governor of, *see* Lescun, Jean de
Guyenne, Seneschal of, *see* Castelnau, Antoine de

Hastings, William, Lord, 91n
Hélène, see Luxembourg, Hélène
Henry IV, King of Castile, see Castile, Henry IV, King of
Holy Roman Empire, Frederick II, Emperor of, xlvii n
Holy See, xxx, l, 442n
Houaste, see Montespedon, Jean de

Iacopo, Emanuele de, xvi, xviii n, xix n, xxix, lviii, 18, 30, 166, 168n, 172, 240, 248n, 259n, 286, 391–92, 392n, 408, 408n
  biographical data, lvi
Isabel of Portugal (wife of Alfonso V), 335n
Isabella, Marchioness of Saluzzo (daughter of Marquis Giangiacomo of Monferrat), 64n
Isabelle of Bourbon, see Bourbon, Isabelle of
Italian League, xxxv, xxxvii, xl, xli, 108n, 230, 238, 246, 249n, 250n–51n, 421

Jargeau, 96, 98n, 149n
Jaurgain, Jean de, 335n
Jean, Bastard of Orléans, Count of Dunois, see Orléans, Jean d'
Jean II, Duke of Bourbon, see Bourbon, Jean II of
Jean V, Count of Armagnac, see Armagnac, Jean V
Jeanne of France, see France, Jeanne of
Jerusalem, 320, 323n
Joan of Arc, 12n, 76n
John of Anjou, see Anjou, John of
John II, King of Aragon, see Aragon, John II
Jouffrey, Jean, Cardinal, 356, 366n
Juan (son of Alfonso V and Isabel of Portugal), 335n

Kent, Thomas, 91n

Langres, Bishop of, see Bernard, Guy
Languedoc, 4, 346n
Languedoc, Governor of, see Anjou, Charles of
Lau, Lord of, see Castelnau, Antoine de
Laval, xix n

Laval, André de, Lord of Lohéac and Marshall of France, 74
Laval, Louis de, 195n
League of the Public Weal, 27n, 28n, 64n, 82, 122, 170, 195n, 201n, 346n
Leon (Spain), Bishop of, see Veneris, Antonio Giacomo de
Lescun, Arnaud-Guillaume de (father of Jean de Lescun), 64n
Lescun, Jean de, Bastard of Armagnac, Marshall of France, Count of Comminges, and Governor of Bordeaux and Guyenne, 48, 58, 204, 268, 330
  biographical data, 64n, 335n
Liège, 2, 10n, 196, 200n, 270, 332
Liège, Bishop of, see Bourbon, Louis de
Lignana, Agostino di, Abbot of Casanova, xliii, 38, 40, 43n, 50n, 54, 106, 109n, 140, 144, 148n
  biographical data, 43n
Limoges, xvi n, 1n
Loches, Castle of, 13n
Lodi, Peace of, xliii
Lodovico I, Marquis of Saluzzo, see Louis I, Marquis of Saluzzo
Lohéac, Lord of, see Laval, André de
Lombardy, xl, xli, xlvii n, li, 76n, 104, 122, 149n, 154n, 222, 236, 311n, 377n, 416, 419n
Lorraine, Duchy of, xxxix, 94, 97n
Lorraine, Duke of, see Anjou, John of
Lorraine, Ferry II of, Count of Vaudemont, 112
Louis, Bastard of Bourbon, see Bourbon, Louis de
Louis, Dauphin, see France, Louis Dauphin, later Louis XI, King of France
Louis, Duke of Orléans, see Orléans, Louis of
Louis I, Duke of Savoy, see Savoy, Louis I
Louis I, Marquis of Saluzzo, 60, 172, 174n
  biographical data, 64n, 335n
Louis of Luxembourg, see Luxembourg, Louis de
Louis XI, King of France, see France, Louis, Dauphin
Louis XII, King of France, see Orléans, Louis of
Lucca, 230

Ludovico I, Marquis of Saluzzo, *see* Louis I, Marquis of Saluzzo

Ludovico II (son of Ludovico I, Marquis of Saluzzo), 60, 66
biographical data, 64n

Lunigiana, 102, 122

Lusignan, Ann of, Duchess of Savoy (daughter of King of Cyprus, mother of Philip of Savoy), xlii, 12n, 334n

Lusignan, Captain of, *see* Fou, Yvon du

Luxembourg, Hélène (daughter of Louis de Luxembourg), 334n

Luxembourg, Louis de, Count of Saint Pol, Grand Constable of France, 198, 270, 326
biographical data, 217n, 276n–77n, 334n

Lyon, xxn, xxixn, xlixn, liiin, 17n, 30, 38, 42n, 43n, 54, 62n, 66, 80, 98n, 146, 149n, 190, 204, 209n, 216n, 311n, 324, 348, 350n, 384n, 386, 388n, 422n

Lyon, Archbishop of, *see* Charles, Archbishop of Lyon

Lyon, Bailli of, *see* Royer, François

Lyon, Gaston du, Seneschal of Saintonge and Chamberlain of France, lv, 8, 13n, 60, 66, 88, 90n, 94, 98n, 154n, 202, 206, 208n, 212, 226, 334n, 344, 364, 367n, 378, 382, 384n, 402, 406n

Lyonnais, xxxix, 60

Maestri delle Entrate, lviiin

Magalotti, Alberto, xvii, xviiin, xxiv, lii–liii

Maignelais, Antoinette de, 24, 28n

Maine, Count of, *see* Anjou, Charles of

Malatesta, Sigismondo Pondolfo, xl, 218
biographical data, 222n

Maletta, Alberico, xv, xvi, xx, xxxviin, xxxviii, l, li, lviin, lxin–lxiin, 16n, 86n, 232, 240, 286, 288n, 409, 409n, 410n, 413n

Manetti, Angelo, xxv

Mantua, 68

Mantua, Marchioness of, *see* Gonzaga, Barbara

Mantua, Marquis of, *see* Gonzaga, Lodovico

Margaret of York, *see* York, Margaret of

Margherita of Saluzzo (daughter of Marquis Louis I of Saluzzo), 335n

Mari, De (family), 367n

Mari, Luca De, 364

Maria of Savoy, *see* Savoy, Maria of

Marie of Anjou, *see* Anjou, Marie of

Marie of Burgundy, *see* Burgundy, Marie of

Marie of Orléans, *see* Orléans, Marie of

Marseilles, 296

Marseilles, Bishop of, *see* Brancas, Nicolas de

Medici Bank in Lyons, 43n, 98n, 136n, 149n

Medici Bank in Milan, 298n

Medici, Cosimo de, xxxviin–xxxviiin

Metz, 94, 97n

Meung-sur-Loire, 149n, 168n, 208n, 216n, 259n, 366n

Meurin, Baude, 202, 208n–9n, 212, 326, 334n, 348

Milan, Chancery of, xxviii, liv, lviiin, lxii, 367n

Milan, Council of, lii, liv, lviiin, 68, 71n, 154n, 248n, 367n, 411n

Milan, Duchess of, *see* Savoy, Bona of; Sforza, Bianca Maria

Milan, Duchess of, dowager, *see* Savoy, Maria of

Milan, Duchy of, 6, 60, 96n, 148n, 192n, 323n, 402

Milan, Duke of, *see* Sforza, Francesco; Sforza, Galeazzo Maria; Visconti, Gian Galeazzo

Miolans, Antelme de, 146, 149n, 170, 172, 222

Modena, xlv

Modena, Duke of, *see* Este, Borso d'

Mohammed II, 423n

Moirans, 84, 87n

Moncalieri, 149n

Moncalieri, Treaty of (1475), xxi, liii–liv

Monferrat, 350n, 384n

Monferrat, Marquis of, *see* Giangiacomo; Guglielmo VII

Montargis, 334n, 348, 366n, 367n, 376n, 384n

Montauban, Jean de, Admiral of France, 27n, 194n
biographical data, 190

Mont Cenis, 43n, 419n

Montefeltro, Federico III di, Count of Urbino, 104, 109n, 122, 164, 230, 280

Montespedon, Jean de (Houaste), Bailli of Rouen, 172, 174n
Montgenèvre Pass, 419n
Montgomery, Thomas, 91n
Montlhéry, Battle of (1465), xxxix, 64n, 276n, 320
Montpelier, Governor, see Cousinot, Guillaume
Monza, xvii n, xx n, xxi n
Morat, battle of (1476), liv
Morea, 222n, 423n
Moro, Cristoforo, Doge of Venice, xlvi n, li n, lvi n, 209n, 311n, 323n, 421, 422n
Morosini, Marco Antonio, li n, lvi

Nancy, lviii n
Naples, Alfonso V of, King of Aragon, Naples, and Sicily, 96n, 310n, 335n
Naples, Ferrante, King of (son of Alfonso V), xx n, xxv, xxxv, xxxviii, xl, xlv, xlvi n, xlix n, 17n, 34, 92, 102, 104, 109n, 122, 140, 144, 150, 162, 164n, 193n, 195n, 210, 212, 222, 230, 232, 234, 238, 242, 244, 249n, 250n, 280–86, 298n, 300–306, 310n, 336, 340–44, 354, 368, 370, 374, 408–9, 417
  biographical data, 96n
Naples, Grand Constable of, see Sforza, Alessandro
Naples, King of, see Naples, Alfonso V of; Naples, Ferrante of
Naples, Kingdom of, xxviii, xxxv, xxxvi, xxxvii, xlv, xlix n, l, lv n, 16n, 92, 94, 96n–97n, 109n, 112, 114n, 150n, 195n, 212, 238, 240, 244, 249n, 259n, 336, 338, 340, 346n, 354, 374, 377n, 410
Navarre, 274
Navarre, King of, see Aragon, John II
Nemours, Duke of, see Armagnac, Jacques d'
Neuss, li n, lvi n
Neville, Richard, Earl of Warwick, 58, 91n, 112, 196, 200n, 270
Nice, 304
Nori, Franceschino di Francesco, lv, 38, 43n, 132–34, 136n, 146, 152, 158, 166, 168, 188, 204, 212, 214–16, 216n, 260, 264, 292, 302, 304, 310n, 324–26, 348, 370, 378, 380, 382, 384n, 399, 422n

Normandy, 24
Notre-Dame des Miracles, Chapel of, 74, 76n
Notre-Dame of Boulogne, 196, 200n
Nouvion-en-Ponthieu, Treaty of (1463), xxxvii
Novalesa, xliii, 50n, 54, 118, 126n, 128, 257n, 350, 397
Novara, xviii n, xx n, 400n

Oldoini, Ziliolo, 52n, 63n, 76n, 126n, 144, 148n, 418n
Orléans, xlvi n, lvi n, lvii n, 13, 42n, 71n, 76n, 98n, 100, 112n, 148n, 276n, 302, 304, 324, 328, 340, 368, 406n
Orléans, Bastard of, see Orléans, Jean d'
Orléans, Charles of, Duke of Orléans (brother of Jean, Count of Dunois; father of Marie), 6, 88, 142, 148n, 180n
  biographical data, 6, 148n
Orléans, Duchess of, see Clèves, Marie de
Orléans, Duke of, see Orléans, Charles of; Orléans, Louis of
Orléans, House of, xxxi, xxxv, xxxvi, xxxvii, xlv, 12n, 92, 96n
Orléans, Jean d,' Bastard of, Count of Dunois (son of Louis of Orléans, brother of Charles of Orléans), 4, 6, 46, 56, 88, 92, 244–46
  biographical data, 12n, 96n
Orléans, Louis of, Duke of Orléans, later Louis XII, King of France, 12n, 200, 201n
Orléans, Madame de, see Clèves, Marie de
Orléans, Marie of (daughter of Charles of Orléans), xxxvi, 148n, 198–200, 201n, 262
Orsini, Napoleone, 218, 352, 366n
Our Lady of Boulogne, 196, 200n

Padua, 102
Padua, Bishopric of, 193n
Palearis (Paleari, Pagliari), Gabriele de, 364, 367n
Pallars, Count of, see Roger, Huc de
Pallavicino, Giovanni da Scipione, xxxix, 42n, 72, 76n, 98n, 306, 399n
Panigarola, Antonio, lii
Panigarola, Arrigo, lii
Panigarola, Cristoforo, lii

Panigarola, Giovanni Enrico (son of Giovan Pietro Panigarola), lv n

Panigarola, Giovanni Pietro, xx, xxiv n, xxviii, xxx, xxxvii n, xxxviii n, xlvi n, xlvii n, xlix n, lxi–lxii, 13n, 62n, 98n, 149n, 194n, 224, 230, 234, 254, 276n, 311n, 334n, 348, 367n, 386, 396, 399, 408, 408n–9n
biographical data, xv–xix, l–lviii

Panigarola, Luigi, lii

Paris, xviii n, xxi n, xxv n, liii n, 54, 64n, 144, 276n, 348

Paul II (pope), xvi, xl, xli, 17n, 48, 92, 102, 108n, 122, 146, 156, 162, 166, 168n–69n, 170, 178, 182, 188–90, 192n, 206, 218–20, 222, 222n–23n, 230, 232, 234, 246, 250n–51n, 284, 294, 352–56, 362, 366n, 370, 374, 376n–77n, 421, 423n
biographical data, xli, 108n, 193n, 222n

Pavia, Cardinal of, see Ammannati-Piccolomini, Iacopo

Pavia, County of, xix n, xxii n, xlvii n, liii n, lviii n, 148n

Pays de Vaud, xlii

Pazzi Conspiracy, xxv

Péronne, xvii n, xxv n, lii n

Perpignan, 330

Perpignan, Governor of, see Foix, Jean de

Philip, Count of Bresse, see Savoy, Philip of

Philip of Savoy, see Savoy, Philip of

Philip the Good, see Burgundy, Philip the Good

Philip II, Duke of Savoy, see Savoy, Philip of

Piccardy, 174, 272

Piccinino, Iacopo, Count, 238

Piedmont, xlii, lvii n, 64n, 66, 86, 170, 174n, 264, 324, 334n, 370, 406n

Piedmont, Prince of, see Savoy, Amédée IX; Savoy–Piedmont, Charles

Pierre, Lord of Beaujeau, see Bourbon, Pierre de

Pietrasanta, Antonio da, xxix

Pietrasanta, Francesco da, xxii, xxiv n, xxv n, xxx
biographical data, xxii, xxiv

Pietrasanta, Giovanni Pietro da, xxix

Pius II (pope), xxxvi, 188, 193n, 222n, 238, 288n
biographical data, 193n, 222n, 288n

Pizzighettone, 161n

Poisieu, Antoine de, Archbishop of Vienne, 88, 90n, 94, 134, 176, 405, 416

Poitiers, xvi n

Poitou, County of, 330

Poitou, Seneschal of, see Crussol, Louis de

Pons, Lord of Clermont-Lodève, 210

Portinari, Pigello, 292, 298n

Portugal, Don Pedro, Constable of, 2, 4, 198, 201n, 272, 274, 276n, 330, 372
biographical data, 11n, 270, 335n

Prades, Count of, see Folch, Juan Ramon II

Preuilly, Jeanne de, 64n

Preuilly, Raoul de, 64n

Provence, 92, 304, 364

Provence, Count of, see Anjou, Charles of; Anjou, René of

Provence, Joanna of, Countess, 97n

Pusterla, Pietro da, 124, 127n, 156, 282
biographical data, 127n

Quartermaster of Cavalry, see Bois, Josselin du

Ramenteresse, Lord of, see Fou, Yvon du

Rampot, Lord of, see Valperga, Lodovico di

Reims, Cathedral of, xxxv

René, Duke of Anjou and King of Sicily, see Anjou, René of

Requesens, Galcerán de (Archaselles), Count of Trivento, Avellino, and Ruvo; Governor of Catalonia; and Captain General of the Aragonese Fleet, 306, 310n

Reversmont, Count of, see Savoy, Philip of

Ricci, Giovanni Giacomo, 367n, 377n

Rieti, Tommaso Moroni da, lvi, 364, 367n
biographical data, 367n

Rimini, xli, 218, 222n, 366n

Rivière, Raes de, 200n

Roanne, xxii n

Rochelle, La, 192

Roger, Huc de, Count of Pallars, 198, 200n–201n

Romagna, xl, 220, 222n

Romagnano, Antonio di, xxix, xliii, xliv, 126n, 254, 257n–59n, 264–66, 334n, 376

Romagnano, House of, 126n, 258n

Rome, xln, xlin, xliin, ln, 68, 108n, 168, 184, 188, 246, 251n, 259n, 356, 358, 366n, 372, 376n–77n

Ropollo, Lord of, *see* Valperga, Lodovico di

Rosolino, *see* Bois, Josselin du

Rossi, Agostino, xv, xln, xlin, xliin, l, 108n, 222, 251n, 259n, 358, 367n, 372, 374, 376n–77n, 417n

Rouault, Joachim, Marshall of France, 74

Rouen, 364

Rouen, Baille of, *see* Montespedon, Jean de

Roussillon, Count of, *see* Bourbon, Louis de

Roussillon, County of, 4, 11n

Roussillon, Governor of, *see* Foix, Jean de

Royal Council, xxiv, xlv, lv, 2, 42, 48, 56, 62, 66, 70, 72, 112, 188, 254, 306, 308, 316, 338, 354

Royer, François, Bailli of Lyon, 4, 12n, 264, 266, 324, 332, 348, 350n, 376
   biographical data, 12n

Ruvo, Count of, *see* Requesens, Galcerán de

Saint Andrew, Benedictine monastery of, 286, 288n–89n

Saint Maur-des-Fossés, treaty of (1465), xxxix

Saintonge, Seneschal of, *see* Lyon, Gaston du

Saint Paul, Church of (Orléans), 74, 76n

Saint Peter, Abbey of, 50n, 393, 397

Saint Pol, Count of, *see* Luxembourg, Louis de

Saint Quentin, xxvn

Saint Trond, treaty of (1465), 10n, 200n

Salat, Pierre, 90n

Saluzzo, Marquis of, *see* Louis I

San Nazzaro, 400n

Sancerre, Count of, *see* Bueil, Jean de

Sanseverino, Leonetto, 249n

Sanserverino, Roberto da, Lord, 122, 127n, 142, 178, 230, 280
   biographical data, 127n, 249n

Sarathico, Leonardo de, 200–201n

Savona, xx, xxii, xxxvii, 66, 335n, 372

Savoy, xxii, xxxvii, xl, xli, xlii, xliii, xliv, xlv, xlvi, l, liii, 4, 43n, 48, 54, 58, 60, 82, 84, 109n, 144–46, 154n, 160n, 172, 174n, 182, 186, 202, 204, 209n, 226, 248n, 260, 284, 318, 324, 326, 334n, 350n, 360, 380, 384n, 401, 402, 413, 419n

Savoy, Amédée IX, Duke of, former Prince of Piedmont (son of Louis I), 4, 40, 46, 50, 76n, 106, 174n, 226, 254, 257n, 262, 264, 344, 393, 397, 405, 416, 419n
   biographical data, xliii, 44n, 208n

Savoy, Bona of, later Duchess and Regent of Milan (daughter of Louis I, Duke of Savoy; wife of Galeazzo Maria Sforza, Duke of Milan), xvi, xxiv–xxvi, xlviii, xlix, lvin, 240, 248n, 411n, 413n, 418n, 421
   biographical data, xvi, xxiv, xliv, xlixn, lviii, 16n, 86n–87n, 90n, 192n, 334n, 410n

Savoy, Chancellor of, *see* Valperga, Giacomo di

Savoy, Council of, 209n

Savoy, Duchess of, *see* Savoy, Yolande

Savoy, Duke of, *see* Savoy, Amédée IX; Savoy, Louis I

Savoy, Giano of (son of Louis I, Duke of Savoy and Anne of Cyprus), 334n

Savoy, House of, xlixn, 82, 120, 172

Savoy, Louis I, Duke of (father of Amédée IX, Bona, Maria, and Philip of Savoy), xlii, xliii, 12n, 86n, 208n, 334n

Savoy, Maria of (daughter of Louis I, Duke of Savoy), 86n, 216, 217n, 318, 322n

Savoy, Maria of, dowager Duchess of Milan (wife of Filippo Maria Visconti), xliv, 334n

Savoy, Philip of, Count of Bresse, later Duke of Savoy, Count of Bagé, Valbonne, and Reversmont (son of Louis I, Duke of Savoy), xxxvii, xlii–xliii, xliv, 6, 12n–13n, 58, 74, 82, 84–86, 144–46, 149n, 172, 178, 186, 190, 202–4, 214, 216n, 222, 254, 260, 266, 296, 304, 324–26, 334n, 350, 360–62, 378–82, 384n
   biographical data, xlii, 12n, 13n, 204, 208n–9n, 334n

Savoy, Yolande, Duchess of (sister of Louis XI), xxiin, xliii–xlv, liiin, 6, 38, 40, 46,

51n, 56–58, 74, 76n, 94, 136n, 144, 148n, 149n, 170–72, 178, 182, 202–4, 209n, 212, 222, 254, 258n–59n, 264, 266, 296, 324, 326, 334n, 360, 384n, 405, 419n
biographical data, xliii, 12n

Savoy-Piedmont, Charles, Prince of Piedmont (son of Amédée IX), 44n, 58

Scaglione, Antonello, 296, 298n, 374

Senlis, lii n, liii n

Serathico, Leonardo de, 310n

Sesto, Piero da (courier), 290

Seyssel, Aymon de, Count of La Chambre, 149n

Sfondrati, Battista, xxvi

Sforza, Alessandro, Lord of Pesaro in the Marches and Grand Constable of Naples (brother of Francesco Sforza), 104, 122, 162, 230, 280, 374
biographical data, 109n

Sforza, Ascanio Maria, 419n

Sforza, Bianca Maria, Duchess of Milan (wife of Francesco Sforza; mother of Galeazzo Maria Sforza), 17n, 136n, 392n, 395, 404, 407–9, 409n, 411n, 412, 413n
biographical data, xl, xlviii, l

Sforza, Elisa (sister of Francesco Sforza), 249n

Sforza, Filippo Maria, 419n

Sforza, Francesco, Duke of Milan, xv, xvi, xx, xxxv, xxxvii, xxxix, xli, xliii, xlvi–xlvii, xlix n, lii n, lvii n, lix, lxiv n, 12n, 17n, 28n, 36n, 37n, 42n, 108n, 114n, 136n, 160n, 169n, 180n, 248n–50n, 289n, 334n, 347n, 384n, 406n, 410n
biographical data, xl, xlviii, 10n, 127n, 249n

Sforza, Galeazzo Maria, Count, xxxix, xl, xlvii, 6, 8, 12n, 13n, 14, 16n–17n, 18, 20n, 26, 98n, 392n
biographical data, xxxvi, xl, xlvii n, xlix n, 16n–17n, 50n–51n, 76n, 86n–87n, 90n, 392n, 410n

Sforza, Gian Galeazzo, Duke of Milan (son of Galeazzo Maria), xxvi, lv

Sforza, Ippolita (daughter of Francesco Sforza; wife of Alfonso, son of Ferrante), xxxvi, 164n

Sforza, Leonardo, xxvi n

Sforza, Lodovico Maria, later Duke of Milan (brother of Galeazzo Maria Sforza), xxvi, lv n
biographical data, 419n

Sforza, Ottaviano Maria, 419n

Sforza, Sforza Maria, 419n

Sforza, Tristano, xxix

Sicily, King of, see Anjou, René of; Naples, Alfonso V

Sicily, Kingdom of, 97n

Siena, 108n, 122, 126n, 230, 294

Simonetta, Cicco, xvii n, l, lvi n, lviii n, lxiv

Simonetta, Giovanni, lxiv, 259n

Sixtus IV (pope), xxv

Spain, xiv

Spinola, Alessandro, xix n, xxix

Spinola, Battista, 259n

Spinola, Gerolamo, 259n

Sully, xxxviii n, 366n

Susa, xxii n, 43n, 50n, 66, 252, 256n, 324, 393

Susa, Captain of, see Briand, François de

Swiss, xliii, liv, lv, 26, 82, 170

Swiss League, 28n, 146, 360

Taster, Peter, 91n

Tebaldi, Tomasso, see Bologna, Tomasso Tebaldi da

Terzaghi, Luigi, lv n

Tizzoni, Giovanni Andrea, 38, 42n, 48, 50, 90, 120, 149n

Tortosa, 272, 277n

Tours, xxi n, xxii n, xxiii n, xxiv n, xxvi n, xxix n, 182, 190

Tours, Archbishop of, see Crussol, Gerard de

Toustain, Louis, 276, 372

Tranchedini, Nicodemo, xxxviii n, l, 136n

Trecate, Giovanni Filippo da, President of Grenoble, lv, 60, 68, 88, 90n, 94, 98n, 154n, 226, 334n, 344, 364

Trémoille, Georges de la, Lord of Craon, 22, 26n

Trezzo, Antonio da, l, 109n, 223n

Trivento, Count of, see Requesens, Galcerán de

Trofarello, co-Lord of, see Vagnone, Giovanni

Trotti, Marco, xix, xx n, xxiv, xxv, xxix, xxx

Turin, xlii, 149n, 259n, 350n, 418n

Turks, xxx, xlii, lvi, 108, 222, 246, 251n, 284, 294, 308, 358, 374, 422, 423n

Ufficio degli Statuti, li

Ufficio dei Panigarola, lii

Ugolini, Bartolomeo, xxvi n

Urbino, Count of, *see* Montefeltro, Federico III di

Ursins, Guillaume Jouvenel des, Grand Chancellor of France, 6, 32, 308, 328

Usie, Guiot d', Lord of Vaudrey, 272, 277n

Usson, castle of, 4

Vagnone, Giovanni, co-Lord of Trofarello, 144, 149n

Valbonne, Count of, *see* Savoy, Philip of

Valenza, 170, 174n

Valperga, Giacomo di, Chancellor of Savoy, xlii, xliii, 8, 204, 258n
  biographical data, xlii, 6, 12n, 64n

Valperga, Lodovico di, Lord of Roppolo (brother of Giacomo di Valperga), 6, 60, 209n, 405, 406n, 422n
  biographical data, 64n, 204

Varese, Gabriel de Paleariis da, *see* Palearis, Gabriele de

Vaudemont, Count of, *see* Lorraine, Ferry II of

Vaudrey, Lord of, *see* Usie, Guiot d'

Veneris, Antonio Giacomo de, Bishop of Leon (Spain), 108n, 230

Venice, xvi, xxv, xxviii, xxxviii, xl, xli, xlii, xliv, xlv, xlvi, l, lii, 32, 34, 36n, 37n, 48, 50, 68, 91n, 102, 104, 106, 109n, 112, 122, 124, 134, 140–42, 144, 148n, 156, 158, 160n, 162, 166, 168, 169n, 170, 172, 188, 190, 204, 206, 209n, 218, 222n–23n, 230, 232, 236, 246, 249n, 256, 259n, 280–84, 292–96, 298n, 306, 308, 311n, 312, 320, 322, 358, 370, 374, 377n, 408, 410n, 420, 422n, 423n. *See also* Council of Ten

Venice, Doge of, *see* Moro, Cristoforo

Vercelli, xlii, 334n, 350n

La Verpillière, 350n

Vertus, Count of, *see* Brittany, Francis

Vienne, 8

Vienne, Archbishop of, *see* Poisieu, Antoine de

Vigevano, xxii n, xlix n, lvii n, lxiv n, 423n

Villa Simigli, xix n, xx n

Village, Jean de, 66–68, 72, 122, 288, 358, 370
  biographical data, 66

Villanova, xxi n

Villequier, André de, Baron, 28n

Villequier, Madame de, *see* Maignelais, Antoinette de

Vimercate, Gaspare da, Count, xxxix, 50n, 54, 392n

Visconti, Azzone, xxix

Visconti, Alessandro, 347n

Visconti, Bianca Maria, *see* Sforza, Bianca Maria Visconti, Duchess of Milan

Visconti, Carlo, xxv–xxvi, xxix

Visconti, Filippo Maria, Duke of Milan, xli, xliv
  biographical data, xliv, 334n

Visconti, Gian Galeazzo, Duke of Milan, 12n

Visconti, Pietro Francesco, xxxix, 42n, 76n, 149n, 248n, 306, 399n

Visconti, Sagramoro, xxix

Visconti, Valentina (daughter of Gian Galeazzo Visconti), 12n

Vivarais, 60

War of the Public Weal (1645), xxxviii, 194n

Warwick, Earl of, *see* Neville, Richard

Wenlock, John, 91n

Whetehill, Richard, 91n

Yolande, Duchess of Savoy, *see* Savoy, Yolande of

Yolande of Anjou, *see* Anjou, Yolande of

York, Margaret of, Duchess of York (sister of Edward IV), xlv, 174, 198, 256, 270, 356, 372
  biographical data, 174n

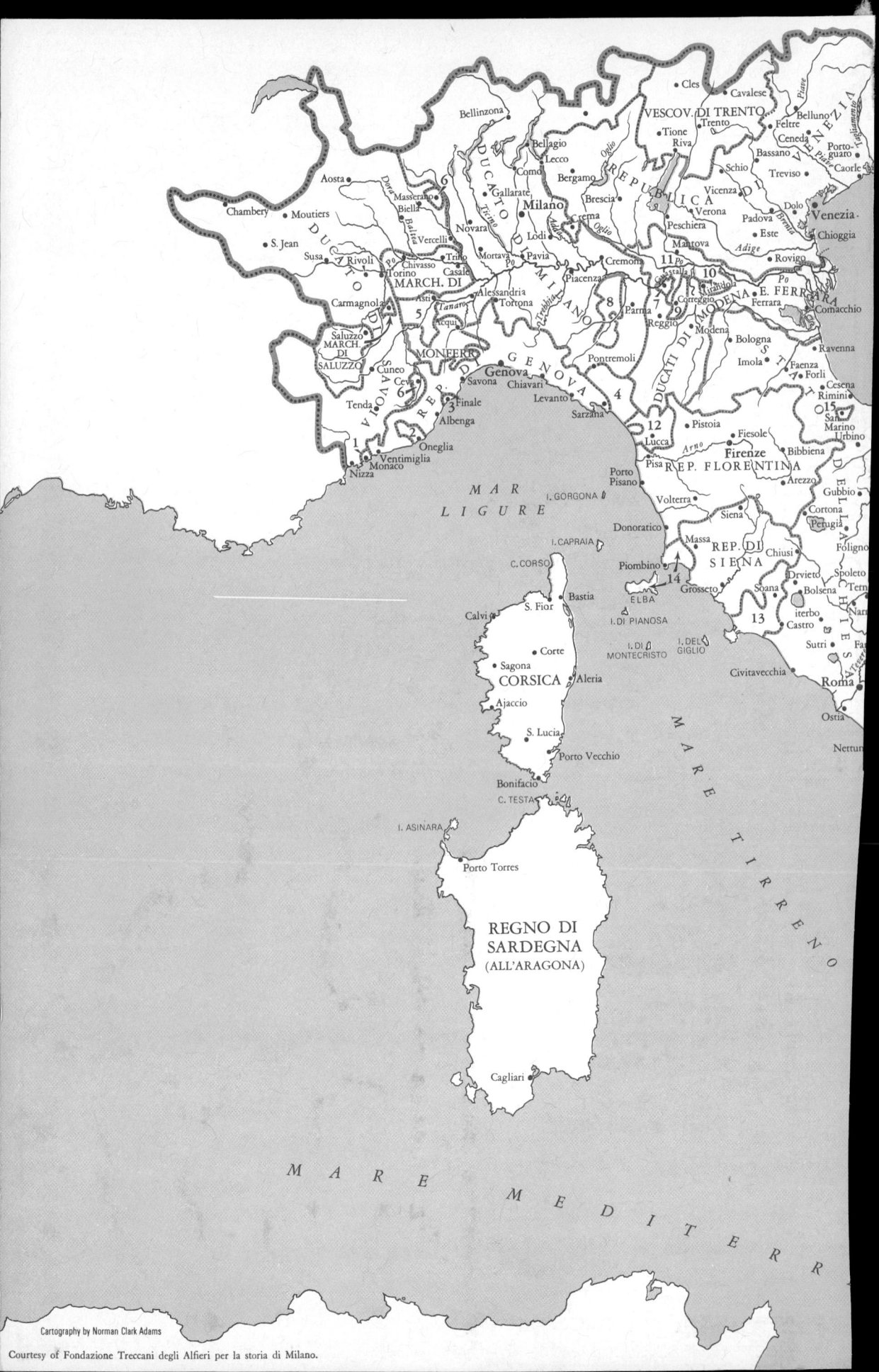

Bellinzona

Cles
Cavalese

VESCOV. DI TRENTO
Tione · Trento · Belluno
Riva · Feltre · Ceneda · Porto-guaro

Aosta
Masserano · Biella
Bellagio · Lecco
Como
Bergamo · Brescia
Schio · Bassano · Treviso

Chambery · Moutiers
Gallarate
Milano
Crema · Vicenza
Verona · Padova · Este

S. Jean
Novara · Lodi
Peschiera · Mantova · **Venezia**
Chioggia

Susa · Rivoli
Chivasso · Trino · Mortava · Pavia
Cremona · Adige · Rovigo

Torino · Casale
Piacenza · E. FERRARA

MARCH. DI
Asti · Alessandria · Tortona
Parma · Ferrara · Comacchio

Carmagnola
Reggio · Modena
Ravenna

Saluzzo
MARCH. DI
SALUZZO
MONFERR.
GENOVA
Bologna
Imola · Faenza · Forlì

Cuneo · Ceva
Savona · Chiavari
Pontremoli
Cesena · Rimini

Tenda · Finale
Levanto
Sarzana
San Marino · Urbino

Albenga
Lucca
Pistoia · Fiesole · Bibbiena

Oneglia
Pisa · REP. FLORENTINA
Arezzo · Gubbio

Ventimiglia · Monaco
Porto Pisano
Firenze
Cortona · Perugia

Nizza
Volterra
Siena · Chiusi · Foligno

MAR LIGURE

I. GORGONA
Donoratico
REP. DI SIENA
Orvieto · Spoleto · Terni

I. CAPRAIA
Piombino · Massa
Soana · Bolsena · iterbo · Nari

C. CORSO
Grosseto
Castro · Sutri · Fa

Bastia
ELBA
Civitavecchia
Roma

Calvi · S. Fior
I. DI PIANOSA
Ostia

Corte
I. DI MONTECRISTO · I. DEL GIGLIO
Nettun

Sagona · Aleria
MARE TIRRENO

CORSICA
Ajaccio

S. Lucia

Porto Vecchio

Bonifacio
C. TESTA

I. ASINARA

Porto Torres

REGNO DI SARDEGNA
(ALL'ARAGONA)

Cagliari

MARE MEDITERR

MARE